Navigating the Doctoral Journey

Navigating the Doctoral Journey

A Handbook of Strategies for Success

2nd Edition

Edited by

Amanda J. Rockinson, Lucinda S. Spaulding, and Jill Alexa Perry

BLOOMSBURY ACADEMIC

NEW YORK • LONDON • OXFORD • NEW DELHI • SYDNEY

BLOOMSBURY ACADEMIC
Bloomsbury Publishing Inc, 1359 Broadway, New York, NY 10018, USA
Bloomsbury Publishing Plc, 50 Bedford Square, London, WC1B 3DP, UK
Bloomsbury Publishing Ireland, 29 Earlsfort Terrace, Dublin 2, D02 AY28, Ireland

First published in the United States of America 2026

Library of Congress Cataloging-in-Publication Data is available

ISBN: HB: 978-1-5381-9750-9
PB: 978-1-5381-9751-6
ePDF: 979-8-7651-5495-3
eBook: 978-1-5381-9752-3

Typeset by Integra Software Services Pvt. Ltd.
Printed and bound in the United States of America

For product safety related questions contact productsafety@bloomsbury.com.

To find out more about our authors and books visit www.bloomsbury.com and sign up for our newsletters.

Contents

Foreword: Guides for the Forest Dark

Elizabeth C. Reilly

Midway upon the journey of our life
I found myself within a forest dark,
For the straightforward pathway had been lost.

Dante Alighieri *Inferno, Canto I*

I have often likened the doctoral journey to Dante's *The Divine Comedy*. You begin by winding your way through the labyrinthian nine circles of torment—the *Inferno*. You progress to *Purgatorio*, during which deep reflection guides transformation. At last, you reach *Paradiso,* where the stars align, the cosmos is in order, and the path is made clear.

When I entered my doctoral studies as an educational leader and single mother of a five-year-old, I had precious little guidance from anyone, and most assuredly, none from a book such as this. Electing to pursue a doctorate is not for the faint of heart. I have often said, "There is a reason why only 1% of the world holds a doctorate. It is and should be the most challenging intellectual exercise of your life. You will never be the same for the journey."

So, before you enter the forest dark, consider the help that awaits. Your Virgil, your Beatrice—your guides and muses—are three educators whose bona fides experiences provide you with the coaching and insight necessary to succeed at each step. Amanda J. Rockinson and Lucinda (Cindi) Spaulding, the original authors, have collectively spent decades supporting doctoral students. With this new edition, they have added Jill Alexa Perry, who serves as the Executive Director of the Carnegie Project on the Education Doctorate (CPED), an education forum and consortium comprising over 165 universities with professional doctoral programs. Between and among these three teachers, scholars, and leaders, you are in compassionate and skilled hands.

While the first edition of *Navigating the Doctoral Journey* has stood the test of time with its guidance, this second edition, a decade later, provides newly expanded and nuanced information around the five stages of the doctoral journey: the Entry Stage, the Knowledge and Skill Development Stage, the Consolidation Stage, the Inquiry Stage, and the Completion Stage.

In the Entry Stage, you will find a more detailed analysis of how to select the type of doctorate most suited for your professional goals. The purpose of the research doctorate (the PhD) is to understand the world, and the purpose of the professional doctorate (EdD, MD, JD, etc.) is to change it. It is one of the first and most essential steps that you face—determining the type of doctoral degree to pursue. Everything flows from that decision.

The Knowledge and Skill Development Stage invites you to consider both your personal resources and the other fundamentals necessary to engage deeply in theories, praxis, and methodologies foundational to your success. It is not atypical for you to face the loathed *imposter syndrome*, during which you question your ability to engage in so rigorous an endeavor. Your personal life and professional aspirations sometimes collide. Combining your growing mindfulness and skillfulness, the scholarly community you have forged with others will carry you through.

In the Consolidation Stage, you synthesize your first years of the doctoral journey. This phase typically includes a qualifying or comprehensive examination or portfolio assessment to certify your readiness for the final stage of doctoral work. It is also a good time to take stock of your assets and prepare for the next stage.

The Inquiry Stage places you front and center with your dissertation and its myriad components. Both research scientist and scholar practitioner often complete dissertations; thus, this section will explore the differences between the types of culminating projects that a future scientist and a scholarly practitioner would best benefit from.

None of these stages is fully linear. Consider all five as recursive. For example, just when you think you've got your research question settled on, which is salient in the Inquiry Stage, you need to reconsider personal priorities and support systems, which are presented at the Entry, and Knowledge and Skill Development Stages. So it is, then, that this handbook will serve you throughout your doctoral journey and beyond (e.g., the Completion Stage).

In the midst of doctoral studies, life happens. During my own journey, my divorce and the death of my mother bookended those years. Supporting my doctoral students for over two decades, I have seen it all: Births. Life-defining and defying health diagnoses. Promotions. Dismissals. Death. More than the prospect of wearing that four-foot velvet and satin doctoral hood kept me going. I had a dream, and I knew I must remain indefatigable in the face of any obstacles. ABD was not an option—the designation for those who complete coursework but remain forever branded "All but Dissertation." Remain persistent. Remain resilient. In brief, embrace grit.

You have selected this book because you possess grit. You know you are one of the few who should consider the doctoral journey. Amanda, Cindi, and Jill stand with you.

One day, when you look back on this journey, it is my hope that you celebrate your profound accomplishment, reflect on what it means to reach *Paradiso*, and declare to others, as Dante did, "Open your mind to what I shall disclose, and hold it fast within you; he who hears, but does not hold what he has heard, learns nothing." As a doctor, you now hold the imprimatur to serve as a guide and muse to others, as Amanda, Cindi, and Jill are serving for you.

Preface

The purpose of this second edition of *Navigating the Doctoral Journey* mirrors the first—to provide doctoral candidates across disciplines and programs with a resource we wish we had during our doctoral journeys—a comprehensive, yet practical resource to effectively guide individuals from initial program selection to final dissertation defense to beyond graduation.

In our collective roles as doctoral faculty and dissertation chairpersons, we recognize our postgraduate students face many of the same challenges, discouragements, and overwhelming emotions that we once encountered. Daily, we confer with and observe doctoral students who must make life-changing decisions and sacrifices to persist in their studies. We also see withdrawal each semester for a myriad of reasons—some internal, many external.

Our personal and professional interest in seeing our doctoral candidates persist to degree completion led us to search for resources as well as conduct research to understand the phenomena of doctoral preparation, persistence, and attrition (see Perry & Abruzzo, 2020; Perry et al., 2020; Rockinson-Szapkiw, 2019; Rockinson-Szapkiw et al., 2014a&b; Rockinson-Szapkiw et al., 2015; Rockinson-Szapkiw et al., 2016; Rockinson-Szapkiw et al., 2017; Rockinson-Szapkiw et al., 2019; Spaulding & Rockinson-Szapkiw, 2012).

In 2014, a small but growing number of researchers were examining doctoral persistence and attrition. A handful of books addressed the dissertation process specifically, but our search for a practical resource to assist our doctoral students from entry to completion fell short. We failed to uncover a practical, holistic, cross-disciplinary handbook for successfully navigating through the *multiple and varied stages* in the doctoral journey. We collaborated with esteemed colleagues and experts in higher education to develop the first edition of this handbook, guiding individuals from initial program selection to final dissertation defense.

In the decade since our 2014 publication of this handbook, we began to recognize the need to further differentiate and delineate strategies for students pursuing different program models (research or professional doctorate) and their different purposes, namely, to become research scientists or scholar-practitioners (e.g., experts in the field who use research to solve problems). Thus, in this new edition, we invited our esteemed colleague, Dr. Jill Alexa Perry, to join us as a coeditor given her expertise in and prolific scholarship on professional doctoral programs. Dr. Perry is also the executive director of the Carnegie Project on the Education Doctorate (CPED), a network of over 150 schools and colleges of education, with the aim to "transform the EdD to be more practical and applied by making it rigorous and directly relevant to real-world challenges, and by equipping graduates with the skills and knowledge to drive meaningful improvements in the field of education and beyond" (CPED, 2022).

Organization

Like the first edition, this book addresses the multiple and varied stages of the doctoral process, as well as the challenges encountered at each stage. It provides practical and applicable research-based strategies that lead to doctoral persistence. Drawing from research (e.g., Grover, 2007; Perry & Abruzzo, 2020; Perry et al., 2020; Rockinson-Szapkiw et al., 2014a&b; Rockinson-Szapkiw et al., 2015; Rockinson-Szapkiw et al., 2016; Rockinson-Szapkiw et al., 2017; Spaulding & Rockinson-Szapkiw, 2012) and our experience, the chapters and the strategies therein are organized into five primary stages of the doctoral journey:

Part 1: The Entry Stage
Part 2: The Knowledge and Skill Development Stage
Part 3: The Consolidation Stage
Part 4: The Inquiry Stage (formerly the Research and Scholarship Stage)
Part 5: The Completion Stage

Each stage is unique, yet the set of skills, knowledge, and strategies to successfully navigate each stage is not mutually exclusive to one stage; they build on each other and are needed across stages (Grover, 2007; Rockinson et al., 2014a&b; Rockinson et al., 2015; Rockinson et al., 2016; Rockinson et al., 2017; Spaulding & Rockinson, 2012).

Chapters are presented in a natural and organized easy-to-digest format, following a consistent structure:

- Introduction
- Personal Vignette or Case Study
- What the Research Says
- Strategies for Success
- Questions for Reflection
- Recommended Resources

The "Personal Vignette or Case Study" provides a relatable context for the problem or challenge addressed in the chapter, which is beneficial for global learners who appreciate seeing how the part fits within the whole. The "What the Research Says" section provides the empirical basis for the problem and the current research on the topic. This discussion of the literature is followed by a section on "Strategies for Success," which provides applications derived directly from the research. The "Questions for Reflection" provide a stimulus for self-reflection and consideration of practical ways to apply the recommendations provided. It is essential to note that this handbook offers an introduction to the various stages and the most effective strategies for navigating each stage. Hence, the "Recommended Resources" provides readers with a list of primary resources for more in-depth reading on the topics presented in each chapter.

Authorship

Each chapter of the coedited handbook is authored or coauthored by different authors who have each successfully navigated the doctoral journey, are experts and scholars in their field, and are currently serving in higher education institutions and professional organizations across various disciplines. Written by a variety of authors with diverse experiences and backgrounds from various disciplines and program models (e.g., professional and research doctorates), this book provides you with multiple and varied perspectives and strategies for successfully navigating your doctoral journey.

References

Carnegie Project on the Education Doctorate. (2022). *Carnegie Project on the Education Doctorate (CPED): A Knowledge Forum on the EdD.* https://www.cpedinitiative.org/

Grover, V. (2007). Successfully navigating the stages of doctoral study. *International Journal of Doctoral Studies, 2,* 9–21. http://www.ijds.org/Volume2/IJDSv2p009-021Grover21.pdf

Hudson, M. D. M., Spaulding, L. S., Ford, A. Y., & Jones, L. E. (2020). Growing grit to produce doctoral persistence. *International Journal of Doctoral Studies, 15,* 705–736. https://doi.org/10.28945/4671

Perry, J. A. & Abruzzo, E. (2020). Preparing the scholarly practitioner: The importance of socialization in CPED-influenced EdD programs. In J. C. Weidman & L. DeAngelo, *Socialization in higher education and the early career: Theory, research and application.* Springer.

Perry, J. A., Zambo, D. & Abruzzo, E. (2020). Faculty leader challenges and strategies in redesigning EdD programs. *Impacting Education: Journal for Transforming Professional Practice, 5*(1), 1–6.

Rockinson-Szapkiw, A. J. (2019). Toward understanding factors salient to doctoral students' persistence: The development and preliminary validation of the Academic-Family Integration Inventory. *International Journal of Doctoral Studies, 14,* 237–258. https://doi.org/10.28945/4248

Rockinson-Szapkiw, A. J., Holmes, J., & Stephens, J. (2019). Identifying significant personal and program factors that predict online EdD students' program integration. *Online Learning Journal, 23*(4), 313–335. https://doi.org/10.24059/olj.v23i4.1579

Rockinson-Szapkiw, A. J., Bray, O. R., & Spaulding, L. S. (2014). Examining the predictive validity of GRE scores on doctoral education students' success and methodology choices in the dissertation process. *Journal of College Student Retention: Research, Theory, & Practice, 14*(4), 203–218.

Rockinson-Szapkiw, A. J., Spaulding, L. S., & Bade, B. (2014). Completion of educational doctorates: How universities can foster persistence. *International Journal of Doctoral Studies, 9,* 293–308.

Rockinson-Szapkiw, A., Spaulding, L. S., & Heuvelman-Hutchinson, L. (2014). Connecting at a distance: The relationship between Facebook use and doctoral connectedness. *Journal of University Teaching & Learning Practice, 11*(3–4), 1–13.

Rockinson-Szapkiw, A., Spaulding, L. S., Swezey, J. A., & Wicks, C. (2014). Poverty and persistence: A model for understanding individuals' pursuit and persistence in a Doctor of Education program. *International Journal of Doctoral Studies, 9,* 181–190.

Rockinson-Szapkiw, A., Spaulding, L. S., & Knight, A. (2015). Protecting the concept: Marriage relationship during the doctoral journey—Strategies for students and partners based on the strong marital house concept. *Family Journal: Counseling and Therapy for Couples and Families*, *24*, 1–6.

Rockinson-Szapkiw, A. J., Spaulding, L. S., & Spaulding, M. T. (2016). Identifying significant integration and institutional factors that predict online doctoral persistence. *The Internet and Higher Education*, *31*, 101–112.

Rockinson-Szapkiw, A. J., Spaulding, L. S., & Lunde, R. M. (2017). Women in distance doctoral programs: How they negotiate their identities as mothers, professionals, and academics in order to persist. *International Journal of Doctoral Studies*, *12*, 49–71.

Rockinson-Szapkiw, A. J., Sosin, L., & Spaulding, L. S. (2018). Does family matter? A phenomenological inquiry exploring the lived experiences of women persisting in distance education, professional doctoral programs. *International Journal of Doctoral Studies*, *13*, 497–515.

Spaulding, L. S., & Rockinson-Szapkiw, A. J. (2012). Hearing their voices: Factors doctoral candidates attribute to their persistence. *International Journal of Doctoral Studies*, *7*, 199–219.

Part 1
The Entry Stage

Introduction

The Nature of the Doctoral Journey

Amanda J. Rockinson, EdD, PhD

Lucinda S. Spaulding, PhD

Jill Alexa Perry, PhD

The doctoral journey is unlike any other educational experience. Students have used words such as anxiety-provoking, stressful, competitive, distressful, and unsupportive to describe their experiences in doctoral programs (Bekkouche et al., 2022; Devos et al., 2017; Fernandez, 2019; Harnett & Katz, 1977; Lovitts, 2001; Zemirah, 2000). Throughout the literature, the doctoral journey has been characterized as primarily negative, an experience of a "different order," in which many students feel isolated and dissatisfied (Hawley, 2003). Even those who successfully finish the journey describe it as satisfying, yet demanding, grueling, and having a profound effect on them. These experiences are consistent across all doctoral programs, including both distance education and residential programs, as well as professional (e.g., EdD programs) and research (e.g., PhD programs) programs.

Some doctoral students, especially those pursuing research doctorates, uproot their lives to attend doctoral programs full-time, relying on fellowships, teaching assistant salaries, and stipends to support themselves. Other doctoral students, especially those in professional doctorates, remain in their professional occupation while completing their degrees. While this decision to remain in the field has professional and financial benefits, this often results in part-time rather than full-time enrollment. This factor contributes to longer time-to-degree completion rates (Wao & Onwuegbuzie, 2011). Even those who choose to attend full-time may require up to seven or more years to complete their degrees. While attrition and prolonged time-to-degree can be costly to universities, the personal, professional, and economic effects on doctoral students are tremendous (Lovitts, 2001; Terrell et al., 2009; Wao, 2010; Kaplan-Berkley et al., 2019).

In an environment doctoral students have described as competitive and non-supportive, feelings of isolation and loss of motivation often lead to attrition (Ali & Kohun, 2006; Lovitts, 2001; Willging & Johnson, 2004). Research over the past five decades has revealed that 40% to 60% of individuals who begin the doctoral journey never complete it (Bowen & Rudenstine, 1992; Smallwood, 2004; Council of Graduate Schools, 2018). Beginning a doctoral degree remains a "high-risk strategy" (Brailsford, 2010, p. 15). While approximately one in every two students who begin a doctoral degree fails to achieve their goal of completion, one out of every two students successfully persists to completion. In fact, in 2020, over 50,000 individuals in the United States completed a doctoral program (NSF, 2022). It is possible to succeed and overcome the challenges involved in this risky process (Brailsford, 2010; Rockinson-Szapkiw et al., 2016; Rockinson-Szapkiw et al., 2019). In fact, in many of our doctoral courses, we provide each student with a penny to illustrate the probability of degree completion. Coin flips influenced by physics demonstrate that the expected outcome of heads or tails is typically 50%, illustrating how many doctoral students are likely to see their degrees to fruition.

While often used as an example of pure probability, coin flips are influenced by physics and not entirely random, especially if the flipping technique is controlled. The expected outcome of heads or tails is typically around 50%, but factors such as initial position and the force applied can affect the result. Similarly, this book contains a wide repertoire of strategies, that when applied, significantly increases the likelihood of completion. The premise of this handbook is quite simply that doctoral persistence and degree completion can be better accomplished when risks and challenges are understood, skills are developed, and research-based strategies are directly applied.

This second edition of the handbook not only provides updated research, additional lessons learned over the past ten years, and new chapters, but it also includes an important focus on the differentiation between research doctorates (e.g., PhDs) and professional doctorates (e.g., EdDs). The first chapter in this new edition, "Choosing the Right Program Model: Research or Professional Doctorate," is written by our new coeditor, Dr. Jill Alexa Perry.

In addition to this foundational chapter explaining the differences between these two primary program models, chapters have been updated to include implications and recommendations for students earning professional doctorates, a focus that was not directly addressed in the first edition.

As doctoral faculty who have been teaching and mentoring doctoral candidates for more than fifty years combined, our collective motivation for this book remains the same—to see all doctoral students succeed. To support this aim, this handbook guides doctoral students, in both research and professional programs, through the five stages of the doctoral journey, from beginning to end, identifying challenges at each stage and providing strategies for meeting those challenges. By understanding the five stages and how to address the inherent challenges at each stage, doctoral students are better equipped to overcome the odds and complete their journies.

Part I: The Entry Stage

In the Entry Stage, selecting a program that aligns with your professional goals (researcher or scholar-practitioner) as well as personality, preferences, values, and lifestyle is vital to completion. You have the opportunity to select a distance, blended, or residential program. You can also decide between a professional (e.g., EdD, DNP, DBA) or research (e.g., PhD) doctorate. Carefully considering the advantages and disadvantages of these programs in terms of personal attributes and goals, as well as identifying a reputable program that meets your unique adult learning needs, is important.

Assessing familial and professional responsibilities, as well as personal and professional assets, is also essential, as failure to ensure a suitable fit between these aspects and a program or institution can result in attrition. You need to take the time to deliberately assess what is best for you personally and professionally, as well as what is best for your family, whether biological or chosen.

The role of proper diet, sleep, exercise, and meditation to maximize cognitive functioning and goal-directed behavior is also central to persisting. The Entry Stage of this book includes chapters on selecting the right program, preparing loved ones for the journey, managing and allocating resources, leveraging technology, and prioritizing personal wellness.

Part II: The Knowledge and Skill Development Stage

In the Knowledge and Skill Development Stage, you will complete coursework to develop and further hone your skills and knowledge. Coursework provides an opportunity to identify an appropriate topic for the dissertation or culminating project (also referred to as a cumulative and final project throughout the book and literature); course papers and presentations may serve as the impetus for selecting this topic. Interaction and dialogue with faculty and colleagues help refine research and analytical acumen, as well as identify topics for research. The development of a dissertation or project topic begins during your first course and is refined throughout the coursework.

Relationships with peers and faculty are also developed in this stage. Community with program peers can increase your connection and successful integration into the program (Darwin & Palmer, 2009; Rockinson-Szpakiw et al., 2019). While working on coursework and actively integrating into a doctoral program, you typically become acutely aware of the need to manage your stress effectively to avoid burnout. The Knowledge and Skill Development Stage of this book includes chapters on stress and burnout, community, and coursework, covering various research methods (quantitative, qualitative, and mixed-methods) and statistics.

Part III: The Consolidation Stage

Each course in your degree is a piece of a larger program designed to prepare you for a successful transformation from learner to expert in your chosen field. It is essential for this transition from being an autonomous learner to a self-directed learner to occur by the time your comprehensive exam is taken (if your program has one). Although there are many forms, the comprehensive exam serves as a benchmark to assess your understanding and ability to synthesize and apply the program's goals and objectives. In essence, it is designed to enable you to demonstrate readiness for your dissertation, cumulative project, or applied dissertation.

The Consolidation Stage of this book includes chapters that provide a myriad of strategies and approaches for successfully navigating this transformative phase in your doctoral journey, including topics such as transitioning from an autonomous to a self-directed learner and understanding the relationship between coursework, the comprehensive examination, and the dissertation or project.

Part IV: The Inquiry Stage

In the Consolidation Stage, you should transition from being an autonomous learner to a self-directed learner; however, in the Inquiry Stage, you transition from student to researcher or scholar-practitioner, depending on your program model. In this stage, you complete the final academic requirement for your doctoral degree and demonstrate the ability to independently design, conduct, analyze, interpret, and present your findings.

Successfully executing and orally defending your dissertation or cumulative project is evidence that you have successfully transitioned from student to researcher or scholar-practitioner. Final recommendation for conferment of the degree depends on the approval of your dissertation or project by your chair and committee members.

The Inquiry Stage of this book provides information-rich chapters that will help you navigate the process of identifying a dissertation topic that will contribute to the field or profession, selecting your chair and committee members, choosing the appropriate research method and design given the problem you are investigating, and navigating the Institutional Review Board (IRB) process.

Part V: The Completion Stage

The final part of the doctoral journey is your emergence as a doctor—an expert in your field of study with the capability to contribute new or practical knowledge to your chosen field. The Completion Stage of this book provides you with practical tips and strategies for publishing your findings, applying and interviewing for faculty positions, or developing and advancing as a scholar-practitioner, a leader in your profession. The book concludes with a discussion of the identity shift that occurs through the program, the challenges you might face upon completion, and strategies to prepare for successfully navigating the postdoctoral experience.

From this brief overview, it is evident that the doctoral journey likely bears little resemblance to your previous degree program experiences. The evolution from learner to doctor is unique to the doctoral journey. The attributes, skills, and therefore, the strategies needed to complete the degree successfully are unique (Gardner, 2008; Lovitts, 2008; Mantai, 2018; McCormick & Wilcox, 2020).

While understanding the challenges inherent in each stage and implementing effective strategies will increase your likelihood of completing a doctoral program, we would be remiss if we did not acknowledge the central role of motivation in completing a doctoral program. Motivation is perhaps the most significant factor associated with doctoral persistence (Durnen, 2019; Grover, 2007; Guillaume, 2019; Hoskins & Goldberg, 2005; Lehan et al., 2021; Skakni, 2018; Hudson et al., 2020). Our research on persistence demonstrates, first and foremost, that individuals beginning a doctoral degree need to be able to identify and articulate their intrinsic (e.g., personal) and extrinsic (e.g., professional) motivation for earning the degree (Spaulding & Rockinson-Szapkiw, 2012):

> *Professional incentives, such as the promise of a raise, the hope for a promotion, and the recognition that comes with a new title, may be compelling reasons to pursue a degree; however, on their own, they are unlikely to be sustainable. It is personal (intrinsic) motivations (e.g., feeling "called" to earn the degree, the love of learning, seeing the process as a personal challenge, gaining new skills and knowledge that translate into serving others) that will carry an individual through to a successful defense and to earning a doctoral degree. It is important to be able to identify reasons to persist when challenges come (Grover, 2007; Hoskins & Goldberg, 2005) and have clear and compelling reasons to continue.*
>
> *(p. 213)*

It is essential to understand that a reflective and proactive stance is necessary to navigate the journey successfully. You must understand the uniqueness of the journey and your personal and professional reasons for beginning and persisting when challenges arise.

Keep this handbook close and refer to it often. As you progress through your program and grow in your academic and professional identity, each chapter will take on a different meaning and have a new application. The journey is unlike any other, but we want to close by reiterating the premise of this text: you will significantly increase your likelihood of completion by understanding the challenges and applying research-based strategies for navigating each unique stage, from entry to completion.

References

Ali, A., & Kohun, F. (2006). Dealing with isolation feelings in IS doctoral programs. *International Journal of Doctoral Studies, 1*(1), 21–33.

Bekkouche, N. S., Schmid, R. F., & Carliner, S. (2022). "Simmering pressure": How systemic stress impacts graduate student mental health. *Performance Improvement Quarterly, 34*(4), 547–572.

Bowen, W., & Rudenstine, N. (1992). *In pursuit of the Ph.D.* Princeton University Press.

Brailsford, I. (2010). Motives and aspirations for doctoral study: Career, personal, and inter-personal factors in the decision to embark on a history Ph.D. *International Journal of Doctoral Studies, 5*, 15–27. http://ijds.org/Volume5/IJDSv5p015-027Brailsford283.pdf

Council of Graduate Schools. (2008). *Ph.D. completion and attrition: Analysis of Baseline Program Data from the Ph.D. Completion Project.*

Council of Graduate Schools. (2018). Taxonomy of fields of study, *DIMAC project.* Council of Graduate Schools. https://cgsnet.org/taxonomy-fields-study-dimac-projectP

Darwin, A., & Palmer, E. (2009). Mentoring circles in higher education. *Higher Education Research & Development, 29*, 125–36.

Devos, C., Boudrenghien, G., Van der Linden, N., Azzi, A., Frenay, M., Galand, B., & Klein, O. (2017). Doctoral students' experiences leading to completion or attrition: A matter of sense, progress, and distress. *European Journal of Psychology of Education, 32*, 61–77.

Durnen, A. K. (2019). Doctoral perseverance: An intrinsic desire. In Holmes, B. & Parker, D., *Doctoral Student Perspectives on Motivation and Persistence: Eye-Opening Insights Into the Ideas and Thoughts That Today's Doctoral Students Have About Finishing the Doctoral Degree*, 39. Open River.

Gardner, S. K. (2008). Fitting the mold of graduate school: A qualitative study of socialization in doctoral education. *Innovative Higher Education, 33*, 125–138.

Grover, V. (2007). Successfully navigating the stages of doctoral study. *International Journal of Doctoral Studies, 2*, 9–21. http://www.ijds.org/Volume2/IJDSv2p009-021Grover21.pdf

Guillaume, N. M. (2019). Persistence toward a doctoral degree: Motivation and dedication. In Holmes, B. & Parker, D.,. *Doctoral Student Perspectives on Motivation and Persistence: Eye-Opening Insights Into the Ideas and Thoughts That Today's Doctoral Students Have About Finishing the Doctoral Degree*, 47. Open River.

Fernandez, M., Sturts, J., Duffy, L. N., Larson, L. R., Gray, J., & Powell, G. M. (2019). Surviving and thriving in graduate school. *SCHOLE: A Journal of Leisure Studies and Recreation Education, 34*(1), 3–15.

Harnett, R. T., & Katz, J. (1977). The education of graduate students. *The Journal of Higher Education, 48*(6), 646–64.

Hawley, P. (2003). *Being bright is not enough: The unwritten rules of doctoral study*. C. C. Thomas.

Hitt, E. (2009). *Finding a partner for your Ph.D.* Science. http://sciencecareers.sciencemag.org/career_magazine/previous_issues/articles/2009_08_14/science.opms.r0900075

Hoskins, C. M., & Goldberg, A. D. (2005). Doctoral student persistence in counselor education programs: Student-program match. *Counselor Education and Supervision, 44*(3), 175–88.

Hudson, M. D. M., Spaulding, L. S., Ford, A. Y., & Jones, L. E. (2020). Growing grit to produce doctoral persistence. *International Journal of Doctoral Studies, 15*, 705–36. https://doi.org/10.28945/4671

Kaplan-Berkley, S., Strickland, C., & Dimartino, L. (2019). Post-dissertation: Surviving and thriving amidst doctoral transition. *Reflective Practice, 20*(6), 705–719.

Lehan, T., Hussey, H., & Hotz, T. (2021). Factors associated with online doctoral student persistence: A critical integrative review of the literature. *Current Issues in Education, 22*(2).

Lovitts, B. E. (2001). *Leaving the ivory tower: The causes and consequences of departure from doctoral study*. Rowman & Littlefield Publishers.

Lovitts, B. E. (2008). The transition to independent research: Who makes it, who does not, and why. *Journal of Higher Education, 79*(3), 296–325.

McCormick, K. & Willcox, L. 2020). Mind the gap: Transitioning from doctoral graduates to early career faculty. *International Journal of Doctoral Studies 14*, 543–566.

Mantai, L. (2018). "Feeling more academic now": Doctoral stories of becoming an academic. *Australian Educational Researcher. 46* 137–153. doi: 10.1007/s13384-018-0283-x

National Science Foundation (NSF). (2020). *Doctorate recipients from U.S. universities: 2020*. Chicago, IL: National Opinion Research Center.

Perry, J. A. & Abruzzo, E. (2020). *Preparing the scholarly practitioner: The importance of socialization in CPED-influenced EdD programs*. In Weidman, J. C. & DeAngelo, L. (2020). *Socialization in higher education and the early career: Theory, research and application*. Springer.

Perry, J. A., Zambo, D.& Abruzzo, E. (2020). Faculty leader challenges and strategies in redesigning EdD programs. *Impacting Education: Journal for Transforming Professional Practice, 5*(1), 1–6.

Rockinson-Szapkiw, A. J., Holmes, J. & Stephens, J. (2019). Identifying significant personal and program factors that predict online EdD students' program integration. *Online Learning Journal, 23*(4), 313–335. doi:10.24059/olj.v23i4.1579

Rockinson-Szapkiw, A. J., Spaulding, L. S., & Spaulding, M. T. (2016). Integration and institutional factors predicting online doctoral persistence. *Internet and Higher Education, 31*, 101–112. doi:10.1016/j.iheduc.2016.07.003

Skakni, I. (2018). Reasons, motives, and motivations for completing a PhD: A typology of doctoral studies as a quest. *Studies in Graduate and Postdoctoral Education, 9*(2), 197–212.

Smallwood, S. (2004). Doctor dropout. *Chronicle of Higher Education, 50*(2), 120–29.

Spaulding, L. S., & Rockinson-Szapkiw, A. J. (2012). Hearing their voices: Factors doctoral candidates attribute to their persistence. *International Journal of Doctoral Studies, 7*, 199–219.

Terrell, S. R., Snyder, M. M., & Dringus, L. P. (2009). The development, validation, and application of the Doctoral Student Connectedness Scale. *Internet and Higher Education, 12*(2), 112–16.

Tinto, V. (1993). *Leaving college: Rethinking the causes and cures of student attrition* (2nd ed.). University of Chicago Press.

Wao, H. O. (2010). Time to the doctorate: Multilevel discrete-time hazard analysis. *Educational Assessment, Evaluation and Accountability, 22*(3), 227–47.

Wao, H. O., & Onwuegbuzie, A. J. (2011). A mixed research investigation of factors related to time to the doctorate in education. *International Journal of Doctoral Studies, 6*, 115–34. http://ijds.org/Volume6/IJDSv6p115-134Wao320.pdf

Willging, P. A., & Johnson, S. D. (2004). Factors that influence students' decisions to drop out of online courses. *Journal of Asynchronous Learning Networks, 8*(4), 105–18. http://www.sloan-c.org/publications/jaln/v8n4/willging.asp

Zemirah, N. L. (2000). Burnout and clinical psychology graduate students: A qualitative study of students' experiences and perceptions. *Dissertation Abstracts International*, Section B: The Sciences and Engineering.

1 Choosing the Right Program Model: Research or Professional Doctorate

Jill Alexa Perry, PhD

Which program model is right for me, a *research doctorate* or *professional doctorate*? As an aspirant doctoral student, you need to consider this question before applying to a program. The degree you choose to pursue should prepare you with the skills, knowledge, and dispositions to advance in a particular career trajectory—academia, a research lab, or a professional field of practice. In this introductory chapter, you are introduced to doctoral education and two general doctoral program models, *research* and *professional* doctorates, to help you discern which is best for you and your goals. The characteristics of each degree model are discussed including student learning outcomes, dissertation designs, examinations and milestones, coursework, and admissions.

Case Study

Brenden, a dedicated registered nurse with 15 years of experience, is contemplating advancing his career through doctoral studies. With a Bachelor of Science in Nursing (BSN) already under his belt, he is now trying to determine his best path forward for his professional journey—a PhD in Nursing or a Professional Doctorate in Nursing Practice (DNP). Brenden sets out to investigate both.

First, Brenden reads about the PhD in Nursing at the flagship institution in his home state. Then, he jumps on a graduate school program search website to look for other programs. Through this investigation, Brenden learns much about becoming a PhD and finds himself very interested in this doctorate. He is intrigued by the academic rigor and emphasis on research skills inherent in PhD programs. He views the prospect of contributing to the scholarly discourse very exciting. Reflecting on his experience in the field, he thinks, "I have gathered questions over the years that I'd like to study, learn more about, and share that learning with other nurses." He can envision himself conducting independent research and making significant contributions to the scientific knowledge base in nursing. Brenden is also interested in potentially pursuing a career in higher education and thinks he might enjoy teaching people who are looking to enter the nursing field.

Next, Brenden looks up information about the Doctorate in Nursing Practice (DNP). While investigating this program, he comes across testimonials of DNP graduates. He learns that the DNP provides professional practitioners with leadership skills to effect change in clinical settings. One former student's testimonial talks about gathering data after implementing a change idea in a pediatric wing of a hospital to inform best practices. Another student describes an investigation they conducted with the hospital administration to address nursing concerns. Brenden has always thought of himself as a natural leader and has frequently stepped up, taking on additional work that required leadership to solve issues in his clinic. Having this kind of impact really appeals to him. He can envision himself leading teams of nurses in a hospital system, driving quality improvement initiatives, and directly impacting patient care standards.

After gathering information about program models, Brenden embarks on a thorough decision-making process, first reflecting on his career goals and aspirations. He considers whether his interests lie more in academic research or in hands-on practice and leadership. He thinks about what he has done with the research that he has read and how he once worked with a team of colleagues to implement their own study on infection rates in his clinic. Would he want to translate that work into a research article for the *American Nurse Journal*? Or would he want to lead these kinds of practical studies in clinical settings?

Next, Brenden reaches out to a few nurses with PhDs and a few with DNPs to conduct informational interviews, learning about their roles and experience in their doctoral studies. From this investigation, Brenden develops a comprehensive pro/con list, reflects on his extensive experience as a nurse, and speaks with his partner and family about his choice. Brenden recognizes he is more interested in impacting the practice of nursing through leadership and inquiry. He decides a DNP program can give him the skills he seeks as a seasoned practitioner. He sees this path as the perfect blend of scholarly pursuit and practical application, allowing him to leverage experience and skills to drive meaningful change in clinical settings. With his decision made, Brenden is ready to search and find a DNP program to embark on his doctoral journey.

What the Research Says

The Research Doctorate

Research doctorates, known as *Doctor of Philosophy (PhD)*, are traditionally what is thought about when you consider getting a doctorate. These doctorates are often referred to as *first generation doctoral programs* because they were the first doctorates awarded as early as the twelfth century in France. They were designed as a one-to-one tutoring style model where the faculty members would share knowledge with their mentees and guide them in learning about a particular knowledge base. Later in Germany, the PhD was redesigned to train students in the scientific model of investigation and prepare them to conduct empirical research. This German model is what most United States (US) land-grant universities adopted in the late 1800s and is the basis for a PhD today. The original purpose of this degree at US universities was to use research to advance agricultural technologies and scientific discovery for the improvement of states and the union. As such, for the students of PhD programs, their aim is to learn research skills for the expansion of scientific knowledge and to develop an identity as a research scientist or university academic.

Students in PhD programs can expect to acquire learning that is consistent with the role of *research scientists*. They gain broad and deep knowledge and skills, developing expertise in their discipline of study. This knowledge comes with the skills of critically applying theories, research methodologies, and extant literature to address and answer key questions in their discipline. These students are expected to use their knowledge and skills to promote inquiry and to generate new knowledge through independent research. They can gain oral and written communication skills that prepare them for presenting their work in scholarly forums, professional conferences, and publications in various peer-reviewed journals. Learning outcomes are assessed in the *dissertation*, which is an original, independent research study aimed at creating new knowledge, produced at the end of program coursework. Some PhD programs are designed for students to complete 90 credits, which includes a master's degree. Other programs require a master's degree as a prerequisite for entry and may be approximately 60 credits. PhD programs in the U.S. include a determined number of credits in core courses, in research courses, in specialization and elective courses, and in dissertation. Once course work is completed, students take qualifying or comprehensive exams before they move into *candidacy* and work on their dissertation in the *Inquiry Stage* of the degree. The dissertation process could take many years, though many institutions have been working to reduce the time. Generally, students have four to six years after the comprehensive exam to complete their dissertation.

The Dissertation

For PhD candidates, the dissertation is the culminating product that demonstrates their contribution to their specific discipline of study. Specifically, the dissertation is meant "to confer expertise by winnowing out the amateurs from the experts," which is done through the writing of an "elaborate thesis [or] rigorous test of intellectual mettle" (Loss, 2015, p. 3). The dissertation process begins with candidates reviewing the existing literature to find a "gap" in knowledge or a place where they might contribute to advance knowledge about their field. As such, candidates spend much time reading about theories and studies that have shaped their field. Boote and Beile (2005) explained,

> *a researcher needs to understand what has been done before, the strengths and weaknesses of existing studies, and what they might mean. A researcher cannot perform significant research without first understanding the literature in the field.*
>
> *(p. 3)*

The PhD candidate creates a literature review that both summarizes and synthesizes existing knowledge to formulate a question and the independent research conducted (Boote & Beile, 2005). The format of PhD dissertations is commonly known as the *traditional 5-chapter dissertation model* where each chapter serves a distinct purpose—Chapter 1: Introduction; Chapter 2: Literature Review; Chapter 3: Methods; Chapter 4: Findings; and Chapter 5: Discussion. Such works range between 200 and 300 pages but could be longer (See Chapter 18: Understanding the Different Types of Dissertations).

This culminating endeavor serves a few purposes. First, the traditional dissertation demonstrates the candidates have mastered the PhD program's learning outcomes and are ready to contribute to the discipline. Second, the research work is meant to serve as a foundation for the candidates' career path (e.g., tenure-track professor or research scientist) by giving them material to generate their first several publishable articles. Third, the suggestions for future research outline a path for continued knowledge generation in the field. However, more recently in some humanities fields, faculty have considered ways the traditional dissertation might be reshaped to be more practical and applied to service graduates who might not be able to find work as a traditional researcher. This effort has been made to better serve humanities graduates who are finding academic and research jobs in their discipline limited.

Mentoring and Advising

Another distinctive feature of PhD programs is the kind of mentoring and advising that takes place between faculty and PhD students. Because PhD studies focus on the development of research scientists, faculty advisors and dissertation chairs (not always the same person; see Chapter 17: Identifying and Developing a Relationship with a Dissertation Chair) spend one-on-one time with their students as they prepare them to assume a research role in their discipline. This time together might include the students working in a laboratory setting or in the field conducting research. Students might have teaching assistantships or fellowships where they support their faculty mentor in teaching undergraduates or master's students, grading, and advising. Research or teaching assistantships might come with full funding for tuition to enable the students to focus on their program and their preparation as research scientists. Their faculty mentors might coauthor articles with the students, again to give them experience and skills in academic publishing. They might present at professional conferences together. Faculty mentors view their role as experts, exposing mentees to experiences and specialized knowledge.

Exams

Prior to the dissertation, before PhD students advance to candidacy (moving from coursework to the dissertation phase), they must complete qualifying or comprehensive examinations. While Chapter 16: Navigating the

Comprehensive Exam includes a more in-depth discussion of the purpose and range of comprehensive exam formats, it is important to communicate here that these examinations assess the students' core knowledge of discipline and prerequisite skills for the Inquiry Stage of the doctoral journey. These exams have many different formats. Some exams are oral, where students present their knowledge and answer questions from a committee. Other exams are written, where students sit in three-hour writing sessions to answer questions related to core program knowledge. Some include both a written and oral exam. Still others may require students to generate a literature review or the first three chapters of their dissertation. The design of the qualifying or comprehensive exam depends on the faculty, the discipline of study, and the higher education institution. Because many exams are focused on the core knowledge of the discipline, PhD programs may have a set of required core courses that introduce the student to the foundational knowledge of their discipline. In addition to these courses, students complete a set of required research courses. From there, the course choices are open to support the students in designing their own program of study that suits their interests. Course selections are usually made with PhD advisors, who supports the students in selecting courses that will enhance their discipline's core knowledge, provide additional skills beyond basic research courses, and lead the students toward designing a dissertation study.

Admissions

To be admitted to a PhD program, aspirant students need a solid academic background, express a strong interest in the discipline, and demonstrate an aptitude in qualitative and quantitative logic and writing. The academic background requires a completed master's degree in a related discipline (this may be a part of some PhD programs), a high grade point average in their prior studies, and academic references many require standardized test scores. Through the production of a written essay, and perhaps writing samples, the aspirants will outline their research interests or questions that drive their desire to pursue doctoral study. In their application, aspiring students might identify the members of a particular program's faculty who share similar interests and with whom they would like to work. The admissions process may include an interview with several faculty members. Potential students should note PhD programs are typically full-time and require students to be available for classes during the day. Many potential students receive graduate assistantships that not only help to fund their studies but also provide them with opportunities to conduct research and/or teach alongside a faculty mentor. Few students are accepted into these programs as funding is limited and faculty members have limited capacity to mentor students in their discipline. The Council of Graduate Schools in the United States defined the PhD as "the highest academic degree granted by North American Universities, awarded by faculty stewards of the discipline to those who have demonstrated the highest level of mastery of intellectual principles of their chosen field" (CGS, 2007, p. 1). Thus, the selection of students is intentional as faculty wish to develop future stewards of their discipline (Walker et al., 2007).

PhD programs are designed to prepare students for research careers. Depending on the discipline, aspiring doctoral students might go straight from undergraduate study into a PhD program. Alternatively, they may go back to study in a PhD program after several years working in a field because they have questions about the field that they wish to investigate deeply. Either way, students of PhD programs aspire to make research an integral part of their career trajectory.

The Professional Doctorate

Known as *second generation doctoral programs*, professional doctorates (also called professional practice doctorates) place an emphasis on research and inquiry as tools for improving practice. Students in these programs develop professional identities in their field and become *scholarly practitioners*. According to the Council of Graduate Schools Taskforce on the Professional Doctorate (2007), professional doctorates fall into two categories: those with a dissertation and those without. The degrees that have a dissertation have "no direct relationship to licensure and have a significant relationship to clinical, translational, or engaged research" (p. 12). That is, doctorates such as Medical Doctor (MD), Juris Doctor (JD), Doctor of Dental Medicine (DMD), or Doctor of Veterinary Medicine (DVD) have licensing boards that require candidates to pass a national-level examination before they can fully practice in their field. Other professional doctorates such as the Education Doctorate (EdD), Doctor of Nurse Practitioner (DNP), Doctor of Engineering (DEng), or the Doctor of Psychology (PsyD) require a culminating project that applies research and inquiry to a problem found in practice to demonstrate competency in the field. The Council of Graduate Schools Taskforce (2007) sought to distinguish a professional doctorate by stating these doctorates "are designed for professional training or focus on applied research related to professional practice" (p. 3). Therefore, those who seek professional doctorates are looking to advance their professional careers by acquiring the appropriate and specific skills needed to address the daily concerns in the professional field.

The Council of Graduate Schools Taskforce (2017) also recognized the confusion surrounding the distinction between professional degrees and Doctor of Philosophy degrees, particularly those professional degrees that focused on applied research. Therefore, they clearly stated, a "Professional degree should represent preparation for the potential transformation of that field of professional practice just as the PhD represents preparation for the potential transformation of the basic knowledge of a discipline" (p. 7). This statement applies to professional degrees that require licensure as much as those that do not. In this chapter, the focus is on professional doctorates that aim to teach applied research and require some form of a dissertation or culminating project rather than those with licensure requirements, which are more specialized.

Students in professional doctorate programs learn competencies needed as a *scholar-practitioner*. Piantanida et al. (2019) explained that the term *scholar-practitioner* infers a "way of being, [or] the embodiment of a mindset that one brings to one's professional work" (p. 3). This mindset is learned through the professional doctoral program where students gain knowledge in inquiry and research and their professional practice. This marriage between scholarship and practice (Perry, 2023) marks the distinction of a professional doctorate from a research doctorate. Students are taught academic theories and research skills but with an added skill—*the ability to apply this knowledge and skills to improve the practice setting or field.* Consider what Brenden learned about the distinction between a PhD in Nursing and a Doctor of Nursing Practice (DNP). The PhD in Nursing is meant to prepare a highly qualified and seasoned nurse for a career in scientific study of nursing. Graduates of the PhD program typically work in research laboratories or higher education, whereas the DNP is for nurses who seek leadership positions in clinical settings and who desire skills to improve the quality of nursing care.

Students in professional doctorates connect their doctoral program learning to their daily professional practice. As such, many professional doctorates (that do not require licensure) are part-time programs where students continue to work in practice while pursuing their doctorate. Their duration is usually three to six years. These programs often employ a *cohort model*, a group of students who learn collaboratively; that is starting, progressing, and completing core and research coursework together. Generally, professional programs contain a heavy emphasis on leadership; thus, the curriculum includes courses focused on applied research skills and leadership development. This course work is very hands-on and often brings the professional setting into course assignments and dissertation work.

The Dissertation

The dissertation experience varies from program to program, including culminating research experiences such as capstone projects, theses, or a dissertations in practice (DiP). These works all require candidates to conduct research in practice settings that support the improvement of practice and demonstrate their ability to apply research skills. To be clear, the culminating research experience required for this degree model is not a "less than" activity when compared to the PhD dissertation. Rather, it serves different purposes. That is, students in professional doctorates learn research and inquiry to be used in practice. Their dissertation experience represents an opportunity to practice research and inquiry for a practical purpose. Archbald (2008) suggested the dissertation, what he calls the problem-based thesis, should persuade the reader a problem exists rather than prove its existence. The problem should be investigated both through extant literature (both research and professional) and within its local context. Research or inquiry questions might be numerous, and studies might focus on trying out interventions using applied methods like improvement science, action research, and evaluation (see Chapter 18: Understanding the Different Types of Dissertations). The Carnegie Project on the Education Doctorate (CPED), for example, defined the dissertation in practice experience for the education doctorate as a "scholarly endeavor that impacts a complex problem of practice" (CPED, 2010, para 10). This definition highlights the distinction of the work that candidates will do in a professional doctorate as both scholarly and practical. Finally, the culminating product or write up of the study might take more practical forms (e.g., white papers, executive reports, formal presentations) so learning may be applied immediately in the practice setting.

Mentoring and Advising

The students in professional doctoral programs are typically older than in a PhD program as many are returning to doctoral studies later in their careers seeking to lead and improve their field. At times, the faculty members who advise or chair these students' studies may not have worked in the specific field for many decades. Therefore, in many ways, the students are the experts on the issues or problems plaguing their practice. This practitioner knowledge is very important in mentoring and advising relationships. The students bring the expertise from the field, while the faculty mentor brings the experience and expertise in research and theoretical knowledge and skill. Together, the faculty mentors and students form a partnership that supports student learning (Perry, 2023); therefore, mentorship feels more like a collaboration than a traditional top-down mentoring relationship. Additionally, because students in professional doctorates have limited time, advising meetings might take place outside of the traditional workday—in the evenings or on weekends, often virtual. These sessions might also be done in groups where the faculty member brings all their advisees to share and learn together, creating a support group.

Exams

Comprehensive exams are less common in professional doctoral programs. When they do exist, they serve as a way for students to demonstrate their professional expertise and take many formats. For example, some programs require *portfolios*, where students compile artifacts that demonstrate they have mastered the set of student learning outcomes outlined by the program. Such artifacts might be developed in coursework (e.g., written papers, projects) or they might be a specific experience (e.g., clinical experience videos, a written review of scholarly and practical knowledge, or written response to prompts). In short, the comprehensive exam in a professional doctorate is meant to assess the student's mastery of the core knowledge of their field and their ability to critically synthesize and apply inquiry and research knowledge and skills to improve practice.

Admissions

To be admitted into a professional doctorate, students generally must have a certain number of years of professional experience in the field of study. They are often asked to submit professional references over academic references because aspiring students may not have been in a university setting in many years. Likewise, standardized tests such as the graduate record exams (GRE) are often not required as students demonstrate more potential through their established professional practice. Aspiring students may be asked to write an essay outlining their professional goals, what the program will do to support them in achieving those goals, and what they, as practitioners, bring to the program to enhance their learning and the learning of others. Essay prompts might also ask students to reflect upon a specific problem they have encountered in practice or a current issue in their field. These essays help faculty members understand the students' interests and aims, assess their writing, and their current knowledge of their field. Interviews, either alone or in groups, may also be required as part of the admissions process. Group interviews are common with cohort programs because they help the faculty to see how aspiring students interact with others.

Professional doctorates are designed to enhance students' field specific skills, knowledge, and research and inquiry competencies as tools for transforming practice. The programs aim to develop students as leaders. Consider Brenden, who had many years of practice as a nurse, but sought to do more. Gaining a DNP, he concluded, would give him the inquiry and leadership skills needed to advance in his career and improve his practice. As such, these students have been on a career trajectory and return to gain additional skills. Generally, graduates of these programs stay in practice and advance in their career until retirement.

Strategies for Success

Table 1.1 demonstrates the fine distinction of program elements between the two doctorate models, namely using a PhD in Education and a Doctor of Education (EdD). In the field of education, the distinction between a PhD in Education and a Doctor of Education (EdD) has been confused for a variety of reasons since the inception of the EdD in 1920. Meant to be a professional practice degree at birth, the elements of the EdD were not originally clearly defined as distinct from the PhD. As a result, academics and organizations like the University Council of Education Administrators and the Carnegie Project on the Education Doctorate have worked to develop clear distinctions and

Table 1.1 *Side-by-Side Comparison of PhD and EdD (adapted from Young, 2013)*

Program Component	PhD in Education	Education Doctorate (EdD)
Career Goals	Research Scientist—research, teaching at university, college, institute, or educational agency.	Leadership roles in educational or related organizations.
Degree Objectives	Prepare researchers and scholars through the development of competence in conducting research that generates new knowledge.	Prepare professional leaders who are competent in identifying and solving complex problems of practice through the development of reflective practice.
Knowledge Base	Fosters theoretical and conceptual knowledge with an emphasis on understanding the relationships to leadership practice and policy.	Research knowledge themes and theory are integrated with practice with emphasis on application of knowledge base.
Internship/Laboratory of Practice	Practical experiences in conducting research (gathering and analyzing data) and teaching.	Field experience in applying research to practice.
Comprehensive or Qualifying Exams	Written and oral assessments that evaluate a student's understanding of the theoretical and conceptual knowledge in the field.	Knowledge and practice portfolios provide evidence of ability to improve practice based on theory and research as well as demonstration of competencies.
Research Preparation	Courses develop an understanding of inquiry and of qualitative and quantitative research. Developing competencies in research design, analysis, synthesis, and writing.	Develops skills in critically consuming research, provides an overview and understanding of research skills for application such as action research, improvement science program measurement, and program evaluation.
Dissertation/ Culminating Project	Original research demonstrating a mastery of theories in the discipline and contribution to advancing those theories.	An applied-research project that addresses a complex problem of practice through the application of theory and applied research skills.
Dissertation/ Culminating Project Committee	Composed primarily of active researchers who are experts in the discipline.	Composed of faculty and at least one practicing professional with a terminal degree.

direct potential students into the most appropriate path for their doctoral journey and their future career goals.

Other degrees that have suffered similar confusion include the Doctor of Psychology (PsyD) and PhD in Psychology. Spelling out such distinctions of program components can help aspiring students understand the type of work that will be completed in the program and the career opportunities available following completion.

The following recommendations are provided to assist you in the process of differentiating whether a research or professional doctorate is best for you:

- Select the program that prepares you for the career trajectory you seek. Having a clear understanding of research scientist and scholar-practitioner preparation is a start to that process.
- When investigating programs for your doctoral degree, explore program websites and ask questions. Often descriptions about coursework and program requirements can be found on program websites. However, do not hesitate to ask admissions and program faculty, via phone, chat, or email, for more information about the program.
- No matter what doctoral program model you choose, recognize that a doctorate requires a lot of effort and an openness to push yourself to learn new skills, knowledge, and dispositions.
- A doctorate is not simply a credential; rather it represents training for transforming you, your skills and knowledge, and the discipline or field you enter. Doctoral programs stretch your thinking, your abilities, your energy, and your self-confidence.

Questions for Reflection

1. What is my goal for getting a doctorate? Do I see myself teaching, doing research, or publishing in journals? Do I envision myself leading change in my professional practice with research and inquiry?
2. Who are the exemplars that I look to—those with doctorates in my field who I want to emulate?
3. Who can I speak with about their jobs and doctoral journies?

4 What is my timeline for pursuing a doctoral degree?—Can I quit my job to be a full-time student? Do I need to work fulltime?

Recommended Resources

Grad Schools Search https://www.gradschools.com/

Jones, M. (2018). Contemporary trends in professional doctorates. *Studies in Higher Education*, *43*(5), 814–825.

Perry, J. A. (Ed.) (2016). *The EdD and scholarly practitioners: The CPED path*. Information Age Publishing.

Young, S. N., VanWye, W. R., Schafer, M. A., Robertson, T. A., & Poore, A. V. (2019). Factors affecting PhD student success. *International Journal of Exercise Science, 12*(1), 34.

References

Archbald, D. (2008). Research versus problem solving for the education leadership doctoral thesis: Implications for form and function. *Educational Administration Quarterly*, *44*(5), 704–739.

Boote, D. N., & Beile, P. (2005). Scholars before researchers: On the centrality of the dissertation literature review in research preparation. *Educational Researcher, 34*(6), 3–15. https://doi.org/10.3102/0013189X034006003

Carnegie Project on the Education Doctorate (CPED). (2010). *Definitions of CPED Design-Concepts*.

Council of Graduate Schools (2007). *CGS taskforce report on the professional doctorate.* Council of Graduate Schools.

Loss, C. (2015). Future of the dissertation: A brief history of doctoral discourse. Proceedings from the Council of Graduate Schools, What Is a Doctorate? Online Proceedings of the 2016 Global Summit.

Perry, J. A. (2023). *Reclaiming the education doctorate: A guidebook for (re)designing EdD programs*. Myers Education Press.

Piantanida, M., McMahon, P. L., & Llewellyn, M. (2019). *On being a scholar-practitioner: Practical wisdom in action*. Learning Moments Press.

Walker, G. E., Golde, C. M., Jones, L., Conklin Bueschel, A., & Hutchings, P. (2007). *The formation of scholars: Rethinking doctoral education for the twenty-first century*. Jossey-Bass.

2 Choosing the Right Program Modality: Distance Education or Residential Doctorate

Jason D. Baker, PhD

Introduction

It wasn't that long ago when doctoral study was a full-time endeavor. Students were required to move to a residential campus, or at least be within driving distance, to pursue doctoral studies. Today, however, a doctoral degree can be earned from almost anywhere and often without quitting a job. Further, researchers suggest that *distance education (DE) learning* can be as effective as *on-campus learning* (also called residential, face-to-face, and traditional learning), particularly when courses are effectively designed for the online environment. However, there exists significant variability in effectiveness of distance education doctoral programs based on instructional design and student populations. Because the doctoral journey *can* be pursued via distance education (e.g., online, virtual) does not mean that it should be pursued in this modality.

There are significant differences associated with on-campus and distance education doctoral programs—they offer different learning experiences, require different skills to succeed, and may open up different career opportunities after graduation. Drawing from professional experiences and the literature, this chapter discusses the differences between distance education, namely online, and on-campus learning experiences; offers guidance about selecting the right *program modality* to promote academic and professional success; and concludes with questions to consider as part of the Entry Stage in the doctoral journey.

Case Study

Becoming a history professor has been one of Tina's professional goals since she was an undergraduate student. She completed her master's degree in her early twenties and took a few doctoral courses. However, she became pregnant, so she stopped her doctoral journey. Once her firstborn became a teenager, Tina's thoughts turned back to her uncompleted doctoral journey. Listening to a favorite podcast while driving to work, she heard a commercial for a university that offered distance education doctoral degrees. The program was part-time and fully online, so it could be pursued from anywhere. Tina was elated to discover that they offered a PhD in history. She began her application the next day.

One year later, Tina was wrapping up her third semester of online courses and giving serious thought to quitting the program. It wasn't that the program was too hard—she found the courses to be challenging but also interesting—rather it was increasingly difficult to juggle her coursework, job, and family responsibilities. Furthermore, she started inquiring about faculty positions and was told by more than one professor that her online doctorate, while accredited, probably wouldn't land her a full-time faculty position. One professor noted, "We get hundreds of applications for a single position, so we can be choosy about who we hire." Additionally, she felt increasingly disconnected from her professors and classmates and wondered whether they'd even notice if she dropped out.

What the Research Says

The COVID-19 pandemic offered many students an introduction to online learning. Although universities had been offering *online*, *hybrid* (or blended), and *pre-online* distance education courses for decades, the pandemic forced institutions to suddenly switch to remote learning for everyone. Shankar et al. (2023) noted that enrollment in online learning had increased over time due to 2006 changes in the Higher Education Act and emergence of Massive

Open Online Courses (MOOCs). However, the pandemic-induced shutdown of universities' residential offerings moved everyone into online classrooms.

Arguably, this event could be seen as heralding the sixth generation of distance education, succeeding the previous five generations identified by Taylor (2001). The first generation was correspondence using print media, which was then succeeded by the *multimedia second generation* using audio and videotapes along with some *computer-based learning*. The third generation was *telelearning* that used audio teleconferencing and video conferencing, as well as broadcast television and radio. The fourth generation was the *flexible learning model* that used interactive multimedia, online resources, and computer-mediated communication. The fifth generation was labeled the *intelligent flexible learning model* that continued the Internet-centric approach of the fourth generation but added automated response systems and online portals to manage the distance learning experience.

Although not identified by Taylor (2001), the sixth generation can be understood as online learning within the context of ubiquitous connectivity; in other words, education delivered online to a society of pervasively connected students. According to the Pew Research Center, a majority of adults in surveyed countries worldwide use the internet, with usage exceeding 90% in most countries including 92% in Brazil, 94% in Singapore, 95% in the United States, and 99% in South Korea (Poushter et al., 2024). In such a context where numerous daily activities are conducted via smartphone, online learning is no longer a novel concept. Additionally, a combination of online and on-campus is referred to as blended or hybrid learning, which has the benefits and challenges of both types of learning discussed in this chapter. Some research even suggests that a blended educational experience might provide a richer experience than purely online or on-campus education (Marcus, 2022).

It's probably not too surprising that the first question many prospective students ask when considering an online modality is: "Is online learning as effective as face-to-face education?" It seems this question is asked every time an educational modality differs from the dominant practice. It was asked about every previous generation of distance education (e.g., correspondence, telelearning) and now is regularly asked about online learning, even after the pandemic experience.

The answer according to the research literature (e.g., Russell, 1999; Bernard et al., 2004; Castro & Tumibay, 2021) is a resounding "yes, but." This "but" caveat highlights the importance of being clear about what's being asked. Can a well-designed online doctoral program be as effective as a well-designed on-campus program? Yes. Are all online programs as effective as their on-campus counterparts? No. Are on-campus doctoral experiences always better than online ones? No. Do employers view online and on-campus credentials as identical? Not necessarily. Is an online degree program the ideal modality for *all* doctoral students? Of course not.

What the research reveals is that alternative educational experiences, such as online learning, have the potential of producing outcomes comparable to face-to-face instruction, but there are numerous factors that determine effectiveness. In other words, the modality is not the sole determining factor in educational effectiveness.

An examination of effectiveness literature early in the emergence of online learning summarized this under the label of the *no significant difference phenomenon* (Russell, 1999). Russell (1999) compiled the results of 355 research reports, summaries, and papers from the 1920s to the 1990s and found that distance education (regardless of delivery medium) is just as effective as traditional instruction. Although it was an annotated bibliography rather than a meta-analysis, it served to highlight numerous studies that found distance education (DE) to be as effective as campus-based instruction.

A follow-up meta-analysis published five years later by Bernard et al. (2004) examined 232 comparative studies and reaffirmed that there was no average difference in student achievement between distance and residential courses; however, the authors noted that the achievement results demonstrated wide variability. In other words, "a substantial number of DE applications provide better achievement results, are viewed more positively, and have higher retention rates than their classroom counterparts. On the other hand, a substantial number of DE applications are far worse than classroom instruction" (p. 406).

Similarly, a 2010 report by the US Department of Education, Office of Planning, Evaluation, and Policy Development examined over a thousand online learning studies published between 1996 and 2008 and demonstrated that students in online learning programs performed slightly better than their on-campus counterparts. Interestingly, this meta-analysis found that "the difference between student outcomes for online and face-to-face classes was larger in those studies contrasting conditions that blended elements of online and face-to-face instruction with conditions taught entirely face-to-face" (p. ix).

Findings from the large-scale transition to online learning prompted by the pandemic highlighted that instructional design and pedagogical practices, rather than the online medium itself, is at the center of effective online learning (Castro & Tumibay, 2021; Marcus, 2022). If an online program includes methods and technologies appropriate to the instructional tasks, student interaction, and timely instructor feedback, doctoral students can expect to receive a quality education.

For example, Kedia and Mishra (2023) found that instructor-student interaction, use of social media, family support, and technical support positively affected students' learning performance in online courses. Shanker et al. (2023) observed that interaction opportunities afforded by online learning made large enrollment classes more engaging than their on-campus counterparts, while smaller seminar-style courses could be more challenging than their in-person alternatives. Accordingly, if there's some degree of blended instruction such as the use of residency sessions or modular campus courses within online programs, students may benefit from a best of both experience.

The second question that doctoral students often ask when considering an online modality is whether a degree earned online will be accepted when applying for a job. The answer to this is less straightforward than the effectiveness question, particularly for those seeking university faculty positions. This is something that Tina learned in the case study.

Overall, there appears to be a trend toward increasing acceptance of online degrees by employers. A 2010 poll by the Society for Human Resource Management found that only 34% of hiring managers held a favorable view of online degrees (SHRM, 2010). However, by 2018 approximately 61% of human resource leaders viewed online degrees as having the same or higher quality as in-person degrees, with 71% of human resource leaders having personally hired someone who earned a degree or credential online (Gallagher, 2018).

Increased experience with online learning due to COVID-19 seems to have further enhanced the reputation of online degrees. According to a 2023 nationally representative survey by Champlain College Online, 84% of adults think that employers are more accepting of online degrees than before the pandemic. Additionally, 90% believe that online learning is effective at equipping students with the knowledge and skills to succeed in their careers.

Within industry hiring, the learning modality itself doesn't appear to be the sole determinant of perceived academic quality. According to Zupek (2010), "employers said such factors as the accreditation of the college or university, the quality of its graduates and the name of the institution awarding the degree were among other things they considered to make an online degree more credible" (para. 7). Despite this increased acceptance, employers appear to hold online degrees in higher standing than university faculty, with online doctoral degrees being potentially problematic for prospective faculty hires.

Allen and Seaman (2013) reported the results of ten years of surveying chief academic officers at higher education institutions throughout the United States and looked at their perceptions of learning effectiveness but also their beliefs of how their own faculty viewed online degrees. In response to the former, they noted, "in the first report of this series in 2003, 57.2 percent of academic leaders rated the learning outcomes in online education as the same or superior to those in face-to-face. That number is now 77.0 percent" (p. 4). On the other hand, "only 30.2 percent of chief academic officers believe their faculty accept the value and legitimacy of online education. This rate is lower than the rate recorded in 2004" (p. 5).

Such skepticism is even greater in faculty hiring, with Slagle et al. (2021) observing "Students graduating with doctoral degrees from online institutions may face bias from those at other institutions of higher education regarding how well-prepared these graduates are to be faculty" (p. 24). Karl and Peluchette (2013) surveyed management department faculty at universities accredited by the Association to Advance Collegiate Schools of Business (AACSB), with 90% responding that they would not hire an online degree graduate for a tenure-track faculty position. More recently, a 2021 study examined graduates from online doctoral programs in public affairs, finding they were significantly less likely to be hired than comparable graduates from traditional campus programs. Summarizing their findings, Slagle et al. (2021) cautioned online learners, "If the desired outcome for their doctoral studies is to enter academia, students should be aware that they face a great disadvantage when they seek employment" (p. 36).

The third question is often whether an online doctoral program is right for a particular student. The answer to that is that "it depends." While the "Strategies for Success" section later in this chapter addresses this in greater detail, there are two key findings from the research that should be considered. First, potential doctoral students should be aware that the overall doctoral completion rate in the United States is less than 50% within seven years of enrollment and less than 65% within ten years (Council of Graduate Schools, 2008). Second, although there has been little study specifically examining completion rates within online doctoral programs, online programs tend to have lower completion rates than their campus counterparts. According to Leeds et al. (2013), students dropped out of online courses at rates up to 20% higher than on-campus courses, and retention strategies did little to change this dynamic. Similarly, Fiore et al. (2019) noted that online doctoral programs had attrition rates 10–20% higher than residential doctoral programs.

Higher attrition rates have been attributed to inherent limitations of the online environment particularly in sustaining deep academic relationships. The occurrence of poor technology skills, reduction in nonverbal communication cues, the difficulty in communicating emotions, and the lack of interaction and community are a few of the challenges. These factors are especially important in a doctoral program as the relationship between the faculty and student is central to persistence (Terrell et al., 2009) (See Chapter 9: Creating a Scholarly Community and Chapter 17: Identifying and Developing a Relationship with a Dissertation Chair). Burrington (2020) found feedback that was timely, thorough, and relevant—ideally one-on-one through whatever mode(s) of communication that the doctoral student found most helpful—was important to promote student success.

The online environment can pose unique relational communication challenges as students and their mentors lose opportunities to interact in person and instead exchange information via email, text, telephone, or other channels that may lack immediacy (see Mehrabian, 1967); *immediacy* can be defined as "those communication behaviors that reduce perceived distance between people" (Thweatt & McCroskey, 1996, p. 198) or nonverbal cues. Confounding this is the potential for lost messages and delayed document exchange resulting in feelings of dissatisfaction and isolation (Doherty, 2006; Meyer, 2003). This is particularly relevant for online doctoral programs where the faculty mentoring relationship is central. In a systematic review of two decades of online doctoral research, Melián et al. (2023) found that the supervisory relationship determined the quality of the student experience.

Students who recognize the challenges of online communication and have strong technology skills are more likely to perform better in online programs. Additionally, Puzziferro (2008) found that time management, self-regulation of the study environment, and effort regulation were significant predictors of students' success and satisfaction in their online courses. Given that online education often moves the teacher from being a "sage on the stage" to a "guide on the side," while also increasing the role of peer interaction in the learning process, successful students are those who are more proactive and self-directed in their learning. Similarly, Melián et al. (2023) found that motivation, personality, and skills modulate fit with online doctoral programs and a strong sense of community can contribute to student success.

While online programs are more attractive to busy students such as Tina, doctoral students may find the experience to be isolating, particularly if they have poor faculty mentoring. Work/life balance may be difficult to maintain (Melián et al., 2023). Accordingly, prospective doctoral students should consider strategies to maximize their likelihood of success.

Strategies for Success

As a doctoral student considering the pursuit of a doctoral degree, how do you know whether to choose a distance education or residential modality? In weighing the options, you should consider issues of (a) alignment, (b) availability, (c) program design, (d) technological literacy, and (e) personal connection.

Strategy 1: Consider Alignment

Perhaps the most foundational consideration is alignment—does the doctoral program align with your personal and professional goals? Perhaps the most common reason to pursue a doctoral degree is a desire to pursue research, often in the context of becoming a university professor (Sarrico, 2022). However, the supply of doctoral graduates has outpaced the market demand for full-time faculty, leaving many graduates without academic positions (OECD, 2021). As Sarrico (2022) observed, "Many doctorate holders find themselves in a long period of postdoctoral work on temporary, and often short-term or undesired part-time contracts in academia" (p. 8). Enrollment and hiring trends suggest that this gap will increase over time, as a greater percentage pursue doctoral study while universities simultaneously reduce full-time positions and replace them with part-time and adjunct faculty.

Accordingly, it's important to consider whether an investment in doctoral study will realistically position you for the type of job you seek. Non-academic jobs have significantly different dynamics than university faculty positions, and even within academia there can be differences by discipline. As a rule, it's easier to find full-time faculty positions within fields that are in high demand outside of academia since doctoral holders have many employment sectors to pursue. If universities are the dominant source for full-time positions that align with a particular field, then it's likely that the supply of doctoral degree holders will exceed the supply of jobs.

Additionally, the previously mentioned bias, while abating, about online degrees within academic hiring still exists and should be seriously considered. If you know that the competition for a faculty position is going to be fierce, and you believe that an online doctoral program will be negatively evaluated, then perhaps an online modality is not an ideal option. It's not that one modality guarantees a better learning experience or even a better hiring experience, but pursuing a doctoral degree is a significant investment of time and resources. So, before beginning a program, you should ensure a strong alignment between the opportunities afforded by your preferred program and the professional outcomes that you seek.

One practical step is to investigate where graduates of your preferred program have been hired. If you don't see the program represented in the sectors you seek employment, that may be a sign that the program modality or institutional reputation isn't highly valued in that corner of the market. Tina would have benefited from such information prior to enrolling in her doctoral program, particularly given her faculty interest.

Strategy 2: Consider Availability

The next area to consider is availability. Not every university offers doctoral programs, and those that do differ on the available disciplines, both distance education and residential. Depending on the desired subject of study at the doctoral level, you will find only a select number of accredited higher education institutions that offer doctoral degrees in that discipline and some disciplines may not even be available in a DE format. This may reflect the marketplace's acceptance of an online degree within a given discipline, or it may simply reflect student demand.

For example, DE doctoral degrees in education, the social sciences, and the humanities are more prevalent than those in the natural sciences. It's easier to find a variety of delivery choices when looking for a doctoral degree in education, for example, than in engineering. It may be that the only option is to pursue a residential program, which eliminates the decision altogether. Here it is important to note that not all programs are accredited, so it is important to research accreditation when examining program options, while also considering institutional quality and reputation factors.

In Tina's case, she found an online doctoral program in her discipline, although she applied to the first program that caught her ear while listening to a popular podcast. Given the investment of time required for successful doctoral study, Tina might have discovered additional opportunities had she examined local universities to see whether they had any part-time doctoral programs. Additionally, comparing multiple online doctoral programs in her field before enrollment might have provided her with additional options.

Strategy 3: Consider Program Design

Program design is another area to examine when choosing between doctoral studies on campus or via DE format. How is the program organized? How long is the academic term? How many classes do students take simultaneously? Do courses have assignments that can connect to professional life? Many DE doctoral programs, many of which are professional doctorate programs, assume students have significant professional experience and may even connect courses and assignments to work environments. On the other hand, many residential programs are designed for full-time doctoral students. Either approach can be effective, but the design needs to fit your needs.

Similarly, how is the program experience designed? This is particularly important to evaluate when comparing DE doctoral degrees. Are courses designed as *synchronous* (live, real-time) DE sessions or are they *asynchronous* in which students engage online at various times throughout a week? Can students move at their own pace through a course or are assignments on a prescribed schedule? Is the dissertation designed as an individual research project or is it more collaborative? While dissertations have historically been solo ventures, group dissertations have grown in popularity (Smith, 2022). One model isn't necessarily superior to the other, but different students may perform better in one type of program or another.

Additionally, what types of campus residency requirements, if any, are involved with the program? A residential program generally requires the doctoral student to relocate on or around a university campus. DE doctoral programs may also have in-person requirements such as completing some coursework on campus, attending on-campus limited residency sessions scattered throughout the program, or modular or blended courses that combine on-campus classroom time with online work. Residency requirements are designed to foster personal and academic relationships between faculty and students (and among the students themselves) and can be valuable components; however, they also need to fit into the doctoral students' schedule and budget. Therefore, it's important to consider the relationship between the program design and your personal and professional situations.

Juggling doctoral study, work, and life proved particularly challenging for Tina. In her zeal to pursue doctoral study, she may have selected a program that wasn't as well-designed for part-time study as other options.

Strategy 4: Consider Technological Literacy

Another consideration when choosing between a DE or residential program is your technological literacy. In other words, how comfortable are you with a computer and other DE technology? If you regularly use social networking to maintain relationships and feel comfortable spending a significant amount of time online, then a DE doctoral program may be a wise consideration. Do you regularly use a laptop, tablet, or smartphone? Do you have experience with DE course management systems (e.g., Canvas, Blackboard, Coursera), collaborative productivity tools (e.g., Slack, Teams, Discord), or video conferencing systems (e.g., Zoom, Webex)? How fluent are you with productivity tools like email, texting, Microsoft Office, or Google Docs? Do you use apps for daily tasks such as reminders or calendaring? Can you find quality academic resources online using tools? While you don't need to be a technology guru to pursue a DE doctoral program, you will need to have skills to interact in a virtual classroom environment. If you are not comfortable with technology and interacting virtually, going to a physical campus may be a wiser option for you.

Prior to applying for and entering a doctoral program, read about effective DE instructional design (e.g., Simonson & Zvacek, 2024) and ask relevant questions. Are there opportunities for students to regularly connect with faculty and students online? What technologies are used for academic and social interaction to promote connection with others as real people? Is there evidence of organization, instructor facilitation of discourse, and direct faculty instruction through various mediums? How is the DE experience similar to the on-campus experience and how is it different? How do programs ensure that DE doctoral students receive the same level of engagement and support as their on-campus counterparts?

Comfort in an online environment wasn't a problem for Tina. She was fluent enough in technology to succeed in the online doctoral courses she had taken and found the experience to be robust. However, had that not been the case, the technological barriers could have hindered her ability to master the doctoral course content and thus thwarted her desire to succeed as an online learner.

Strategy 5: Consider Connection, Community, and Self-Directedness

Finally, you should consider personal and academic connections that may affect your success in a doctoral program, whether it be DE or residential. Meet or speak with program faculty before applying for a program. Doctoral study typically requires extensive one-on-one work with a faculty advisor or chair, and you want to evaluate your connection and capacity to develop healthy, productive relationships with program faculty as you are making a multiyear relationship commitment with the faculty and institution when enrolling in a doctoral program. Both the quality and nature of your connection with faculty, both academic interactions (e.g., instruction, receiving timely feedback) and nonacademic interactions (e.g., social, empathy, care), is highly associated with your persistence (Holmes & Rockinson-Szapkiw, 2020; Rockinson-Szapkiw et al., 2019).

Relatedly, you also want to understand the modalities and technologies, whether online or on campus, used for communication with faculty and with peers. Then, consider your level of comfort with the primary communication used. Connection and community with faculty as well as peers is critical for your persistence (see Chapter 9: Creating a Scholarly Community).

Alternatively, you need to evaluate personal characteristics and skills, such as self-directedness and time management, in relation to the doctoral program modality you are selecting. While all doctoral programs require good time management and self-direction, Means et al. (2009) meta-analysis of online learning literature suggested that self-regulation and self-directed learning were advantageous for online learner success. This finding continues to be supported throughout the research; studies have revealed the importance of self-regulation, which require students to employ a combination of cognitive, metacognitive, and time management skills, to persist in online courses and programs (Broadbent, 2017, Lee et al., 2013; You, 2016) (see Chapter 14: Transitioning from Autonomous to Self-Directed Learning).

Tina didn't examine the faculty prior to enrollment and was instead moved to action by the podcast advertisement. Although she did not experience any conflicts with the program faculty, she wondered whether they'd even notice if she withdrew from the program. The negative feedback when she inquired about faculty positions was a surprise and made her feel a bit misled. Had she sought out interaction with program faculty during the admissions process, she might have gotten a better sense of the level of personal interaction to expect with the professors and how they viewed their program within the academic ecosystem.

Questions for Reflection

The options for pursuing a doctorate are arguably greater than ever before. Previously, students had to relocate to university campuses to pursue a doctoral degree, but now there are a variety of modalities available. As part of the Entry Stage, a prospective doctoral student should consider the following questions as part of the decision-making process:

- What types of accredited distance education and residential programs are available in my chosen discipline?

- What is the reputation of the institution I am considering? Do I see examples of doctoral graduates in jobs that interest me?
- Is the design of the doctoral program consistent with my skills, preferences, and professional goals? What are the residency requirements? What will I gain or lose with the residency requirements of one program versus another?
- Does the course and program design exhibit characteristics of effective education? If applicable, is the distance education program designed to support the part-time, remote learner?
- How comfortable am I with technology as a primary means of communication?
- What has been my experience connecting with the doctoral faculty in the program I am considering? Can I picture myself working well with the faculty over a number of years? Am I comfortable with the technology and tools used for communication?
- What personal characteristics and skills do I have that will enable me to be a successful residential or distance education doctoral student?

Recommended Resources

Gallagher, S. R. (2017). *The future of university credentials: New developments at the intersection of higher education and hiring*. Harvard University Press.

Sheldon, J. & Sheppard, V. (Eds.). (2022). *Online communities for doctoral researchers and their supervisors: Building engagement with social media*. Routledge.

Stephen, J. S. (2024). *Academic success in online programs: A resource for college students*. Springer.

References

Allen, I. E., & Seaman, J. (2013). *Changing course: Ten years of tracking online education in the United States*. Babson Survey Research Group and Quahog Research Group, LLC.

Bernard, R. M., Abrami, P. C., Lou, Y., Borokhovski, E., Wade, A., Wozney, L., Wallet, P. A., Fiset, M., & Huang, B. (2004). How does distance education compare to classroom instruction? A meta-analysis of the empirical literature. *Review of Educational Research*, *74*(3), 379–439.

Broadbent, J. (2017). Comparing online and blended learner's self-regulated learning strategies and academic performance. *The Internet and Higher Education, 33,* 24–32.

Burrington, D., Madison, R. D., & Schmitt, A. (2020) Dissertation committee chairs' current practices to support doctoral students in an online doctoral program. *Online Journal of Distance Learning Administration*, *23*(3), 1–11.

Castro, M. D. B., Tumibay, G. M. (2021). A literature review: Efficacy of online learning courses for higher education institution using meta-analysis. *Education and Information Technologies*, *26*, 1367–1385. https://doi.org/10.1007/s10639-019-10027-z

Champlain College Online. (2023, November 9). Data reveals new insights on online higher education post-pandemic. https://online.champlain.edu/blog/data-reveals-new-insights-online-higher-education-post-pandemic

Council of Graduate Schools. (2008). *Ph.D. completion and attrition: Analysis of baseline program data from the Ph.D. completion project*. Council of Graduate Schools.

Doherty, W. (2006). An analysis of multiple factors affecting retention in web based community college courses. *The Internet and Higher Education*, *9*(4), 245–255.

Fiore, T. D., Heitner, K. L., &Shaw, M. (2019). Academic advising and online doctoral student persistence from coursework to independent research. *Online Journal of Distance Learning Administration*, *23*(3). https://www.westga.edu/~distance/ojdla/fall223/fiore_heitner_shaw223.html

Gallagher, S.R. (2018). *Education credentials come of age: A survey on the use and value of educational credentials in hiring*. Northeastern University Center for the Future of Higher Education and Talent Strategy.

Holmes, J. L. & Rockinson-Szapkiw, A. (2020). The development and validation of the distance doctoral program integration scale. *Online Learning*, *24*(4), 182–203. https://doi.org/10.24059/olj.v24i4.1951

Karl, K., & Peluchette, J. (2013). Management faculty perceptions of candidates with online doctorates: Why the stigma? *American Journal of Distance Education*, *27*(2), 89–99. https://doi.org/10.1080/08923647.2013.773221

Kedia, P., & Mishra, L. (2023). Exploring the factors influencing the effectiveness of online learning: A study on college students. *Social Sciences & Humanities Open*, *8*(1). https://doi.org/10.1016/j.ssaho.2023.100559

Lee, Y., Choi, J., & Kim, T. (2013). Discriminating factors between completers of and dropouts from online learning courses. *British Journal of Educational Technology*, *44*(2), 328–337.

Leeds, E. M., Campbell, S., Baker, H., Ali, R., Brawley, D., & Crisp, J. (2013). The impact of student retention strategies: An empirical study. *International Journal of Management in Education*, *7*(1), 22–43.

Marcus, J. (2022, October 6). With online learning, "Let's take a breath and see what worked and didn't work." *The New York Times*. https://www.nytimes.com/2022/10/06/education/learning/online-learning-higher-education.html

Means, B., Toyama, Y., Murphy, R., Bakia, M., & Jones, K. (2009). Evaluation of evidence-based practices in online learning: A meta-analysis and review of online learning studies. U.S. Department of Education. https://www2.ed.gov/about/offices/list/opepd/ppss/reports.html

Mehrabian, A. (1967). Orientation behaviors and nonverbal attitude communication. *Journal of Communication, 17*, 324–332.

Melián, E., Reyes, J. I., & Meneses, J. (2023). The online PhD experience: A qualitative systematic review. *The International Review of Research in Open and Distributed Learning, 24*(1), 137–158. https://doi.org/10.19173/irrodl.v24i1.6780

Meyer, K. A. (2003). Face-to-face versus threaded discussions: The role of time and higher-order thinking. *Journal of Asynchronous Learning Networks, 7*(3), 55–65.

Organisation for Economic Co-operation and Development. (2021, May). Reducing the precarity of academic research careers. *OECD Science, Technology and Industry Policy Papers, 113*. https://doi.org/10.1787/0f8bd468-en.

Poushter, J., Gubbala, S., & Austin, S. (2024, February 5). *8 charts on technology use around the world*. Pew Research Center. https://www.pewresearch.org/short-reads/2024/02/05/8-charts-on-technology-use-around-the-world/

Puzziferro, M. (2008). Online technologies self-efficacy and self-regulated learning as predictors of final grade and satisfaction in college-level online courses. *American Journal of Distance Education, 22*(2), 72–89.

Rockinson-Szapkiw, A. J., Holmes, J. & Stephens, J. (2019). Identifying significant personal and program factors that predict online EdD student's program integration. *Online Learning Journal, 23*(4). 313–335. doi:10.24059/olj.v23i4.1579

Russell, T. L. (1999). *The no significant difference phenomenon: A comparative research annotated bibliography on technology for distance education*. Office of Instructional Telecommunications, North Carolina State University.

Sarrico, C. S. (2022). The expansion of doctoral education and the changing nature and purpose of the doctorate. *Higher Education, 84*, 1299–1315.

Shankar, K., Arora, P., & Binz-Scharf, M. C. (2023). Evidence on online higher education: The promise of COVID-19 pandemic data. *Management and Labour Studies, 48*(2), 242–249. https://doi.org/10.1177/0258042X211064783

Simonson, M., & Zvacek, S. (2024). *Teaching and learning at a distance: Foundations of distance education* (8th ed.). Information Age Publishing.

Slagle, D. R., Blankenberger, B., & Williams, A. M. (2021). Are online doctoral program graduates viewed as hireable for academic positions? The case of public affairs programs. *The Journal of Continuing Higher Education, 70*(1), 21–41. https://doi.org/10.1080/07377363.2020.1859349

Smith, B. (2022). Group dissertations as leadership learning. *Journal of Research on Leadership Education*, *17*(1), 3–23. https://doi.org/10.1177/1942775120933932

Society for Human Resource Management (2010, August 19). Hiring Practices and Attitudes: Traditional vs. Online Degree Credentials SHRM Poll. https://www.shrm.org/hr-today/trends-and-forecasting/research-andsurveys/pages/hiringpracticesandattitudes.aspx.

Taylor, J. C. (2001). Fifth generation distance education. *e-Journal of Instructional Science and Technology*, *4*(1), 1–14. Retrieved from http://www.ascilite.org.au/ajet/e-jist/docs/vol4no1/Taylor.pdf

Terrell, S. R., Snyder, M. M., & Dringus, L. P. (2009). The developmental, validation, and application of the doctoral student connectedness scale. *The Internet and Higher Education*, *12*(2), 112–16.

Thweatt, K. S., & McCroskey, J. C. (1996). Teacher nonimmediacy and misbehavior: Unintentional negative communication. *Communication Research Reports*, *13*, 198–204.

U.S. Department of Education, Office of Planning, Evaluation, and Policy Development. (2010). *Evaluation of evidence-based practices in online learning: A meta-analysis and review of online learning studies*. U.S. Department of Education.

You, J. W. (2016). Identifying significant indicators using LMS data to predict course achievement in online learning. *The Internet and Higher Education*, *29*, 23–30.

Zupek, R. (2010, March 29). Employers on online education. *CNN*. Retrieved from http://www.cnn.com/2010/LIVING/worklife/03/29/cb.employers.online.education/index.html

3 Assessing University Assets

Jacqueline S. Stephen, EdD
Chelsie M. Dubay, EdD
Jessica Herring Watson, EdD

Introduction

The pursuit of a doctoral degree, in combination with employment and family obligations, requires an assessment of personal assets (see Chapter 4: Assessing Personal Assets) as well as program and university assets. Doctoral students' awareness of personal strengths and weaknesses and how the program and university can support them can inform selecting a doctoral program.

The doctoral journey necessitates an assessment of personal assets, namely, time allocation, physical learning space, technology, and cognitive and emotional schemas from past experiences. Self-reflection may be instrumental in helping to unearth not only negative thoughts and feelings from past learning experiences that are likely to conflict with new learning experiences, but also in identifying personal growth needs and anticipated challenges. Forethought and planning are essential to identifying and assessing personal assets and then determining if the program and university can provide the support needed. This chapter examines course, program, and university assets that can be accessed to promote doctoral success across research and professional doctoral programs, both residential and distance education.

Case Study

Miriam is a 42-year-old woman enrolled in an online doctoral program. She completed her master's degree in Teaching and Learning when she was 28 years old, and she decided, at 40 years old, to pursue a doctorate in Educational Leadership. Miriam believes that a terminal degree will help her to advance her career and remain abreast of trends in the profession. She is employed full-time as an educator and has two children. Given her familial and vocational responsibilities, as well as goals for pursuing the degree, she selects an online, professional doctorate (EdD) program.

After being accepted, Miriam feels anxious about her first semester, which requires her to take her very first statistics course. Miriam has historically struggled with mathematics, and statistics was not required for her undergraduate or master's degree programs. She feels anxious about her ability to learn statistics through an online, asynchronous course delivery format. Miriam considers delaying enrollment in the statistics course until a future semester, but she learns the course is a prerequisite to other courses. She is overwhelmed with feelings of anxiety. Miriam asks some of her friends about their experience with statistics, and she receives mixed feedback regarding the difficulty of the course. She also worries that she may not be able to handle her family, work, and academic responsibilities well. She wonders if the university has supports in place to help her flourish in her program.

What the Research Says

The National Center for Education Statistics (NCES) reports that student demand for doctoral degrees continues to grow, prompting many universities to expand their distance education as well as professional doctorate program offerings to accommodate nontraditional students (Irwin et al., 2023). The United States Department of Education and the Association of Nontraditional Students in Higher Education (ANTSHE) defines nontraditional graduate students as adult learners who pursue a doctoral degree after a prolonged gap due to life events or enroll in a doctoral program on a full-time or part-time basis alongside other obligations, such as employment or family responsibilities. The flexibility of distance education doctoral programs, namely online, makes them attractive to nontraditional students, who can assume the role of student while maintaining other life responsibilities. This increased accessibility opens opportunities for nontraditional students to achieve their academic goals and boost their career prospects. The professional doctorate supports career advancement for individuals who do not plan to pursue an academic career.

However, this particular population of students, no matter what program model and modality chosen, requires unique university resources and support systems to persist as they assume the doctoral student role in addition to other personal and professional aspects of their lives (Rockinson-Szapkiw & Herring Watson, 2020). The National Center for Science and Engineering Statistics (2023) highlights that this population is made up of an increasing number of women as the number of women doctoral students has increased over the years. These women are often over the age of 40 with children. While these women are more likely to pursue doctoral degrees, they, unfortunately, are less likely to finish doctoral programs (Rockinson-Szapkiw et al., 2018). Consequently, this segment of the nontraditional student population demands additional support to overcome unique challenges.

Miriam reflects this doctoral student profile; she is a woman in her 40s with two children. Assuming the role of a student can be a major life transition, especially for a nontraditional student returning to academic life after many years (Bellare et al., 2023). Miriam has not been a student in 14 years. At the age of 42, she is completing her first year of an online doctoral program. Higher education has evolved over the past 14 years, including a shift to online learning and the differentiation between a professional and research doctorate (see Chapter 1: Choosing the Right Program Model: Research or Professional Doctorate). Like many other students, Miriam is pursuing a doctorate to advance her career, works full-time, and has family responsibilities (Bellare et al., 2023; Strukel et al., 2023), so she is apprehensive about integrating all her responsibilities.

Each student is unique in their needs. In Miriam's case, learning statistics in an online asynchronous course delivery format is the source of her anxiety. Her feelings of anxiety are amplified by her past negative learning experiences in math courses (see Chapter 10: Overcoming Statistics Anxiety). However, another student's source of anxiety may stem from decreased levels of self-confidence and self-efficacy in their ability to effectively manage their time or seek help through program and university assets. Knowing what course, program, and university assets are available is critical to meeting every need and overcoming every challenge in doctoral programs.

Nontraditional student access to assets is fundamental to their persistence and overall success (Kebritchi et al., 2023; Stephen, 2023). Residential and distance education students across research and professional doctoral programs may need to access various academic (e.g., course, program, and university) and professional assets throughout the stages of their doctoral journey. Aspiring distance education doctoral students must ensure their university and program provide access to the same assets accessible to residential students. Program and university assets can be categorized based on their intended purpose. Some assets focus specifically on the academic experience of the student, while other assets emphasize professional experience and personal challenges. Ultimately, all assets serve a common purpose: to promote academic success and, ultimately, degree completion.

Academic Assets

Academic assets at the program or university level encompass a variety of services and resources to help students enhance their skills and competencies to address gaps in learning. At the university level, academic assets may include resources that provide students with access to technology, orientation programs, tutorial services, research and statistics assistance, developmental workshops, and accommodation tools and services. Access to technology is especially critical for students enrolled in distance education programs (Lahiya & Mokodenseho, 2023). Online courses rely on the use of a wide range of media and tools, and students need to know how to access these and use them to facilitate their learning. Remote access often involves a multi-step process of authentication and installation. While some students may feel confident in their ability to accomplish this, others may experience technological anxiety and require guidance and support (Lee et al., 2024). Miriam, for example, may need remote access to statistical software provided by the university. She may need assistance accessing, downloading, and using the software on her computer. Ongoing access to technology support (i.e., IT help desk) can help students overcome technological barriers and anxiety associated with technology use (Martin & Bolliger, 2022). Online doctoral students, like Miriam, may feel less anxious and more confident knowing they will receive support and guidance as they attempt to access and navigate the use of remote media and tools. Residential doctoral students may need similar on-campus support to access and download the required software to their computers.

All doctoral students may have additional needs that can be addressed through orientation programs aimed at helping them navigate the university and program culture, learning management systems, expectations and policies, and other assets beyond technology. Orientation programs can exist at the university or program level. Programs typically focus on navigating the learning management system used for courses, accessing and reviewing the student handbook, installing and testing software and applications, communicating policies and procedures, and recommending best practices for academic success (Stephen, 2023; Trespalacios et al., 2023). A program-level orientation may also include specific information related to program requirements (i.e., coursework, registration, portfolio), the dissertation process, comprehensive exams, expectations, policies, and procedures. Participating in an orientation at the university or program level can help students, like Miriam, discover how to access and utilize academic assets.

Many universities provide tutorial services and research assistance for both residential and distance education students (Shepherd & Bolliger, 2023). Research assistance, librarian services, developmental workshops, and tutorial services (i.e., statistics, writing) may be available through online asynchronous and synchronous formats. For all doctoral students, having access to these services outside of normal business hours may also be important. Since Miriam works and has children, she may need to interact synchronously online with librarians and tutors during the evenings or weekends. She also needs to consider whether she can participate in online synchronous workshops and webinars or access the recordings related to tutoring services. Although Miriam's source of anxiety is statistics, she needs to recognize that statistics is integrated into other aspects of her coursework. Hence, she may also require assistance from a librarian with locating relevant resources and receiving feedback from a statistical lab tutor on her written analysis of a statistical test. Miriam may also need to use these assets to ensure the effective application of the appropriate style guide to her written work. Consequently, Miriam may need to access and use a combination of assets to successfully complete coursework.

Students returning to academic life after many years may encounter gaps in their knowledge and skills (Bellare et al., 2023; Stephen, 2023). Miriam embarked on an online doctoral journey after a 12-year hiatus from academia. She will need to address gaps in her knowledge and skills to effectively approach coursework. Miriam may need to seek additional learning opportunities beyond the academic course setting. Such opportunities may exist in the form of developmental workshops, webinars, writing and statistical consulting services, and non-credit self-paced courses and certificate programs.

Miriam may discover she is unable to overcome difficulties with learning statistics even after seeking opportunities to improve her knowledge and skills. As such, she may need access to resources to help her determine if an undiagnosed learning difference is presenting barriers to her learning (O'Shea & Thurman, 2017). Universities have a dedicated unit to support students in need of accessible learning environments and coordinate their efforts with course instructors to provide adjustments for various types of instruction and assessment. Doctoral students have learning, physical, mental health, chronic illness, or other disabilities. These disabilities may be visible or invisible. Therefore, it is important when doctoral students consider a program, that they understand the assets and services that the university offers, and also be familiar with the Americans with Disabilities Act (ADA), which ensures equal access to education for students with disabilities.

Additional academic assets are also available to students at the program and course levels. Course instructors, peers, and academic advisors serve as sources of support and can help to promote student use of additional assets based on individual needs (Stephen, 2024). Academic advisors work with students to develop a plan for their degree and select relevant courses. A student should expect to maintain regular contact with their academic advisor (see Chapter 17: Identifying and Developing a Relationship with a Dissertation Chair). Academic advisors are sometimes also program coordinators and course instructors. Course instructors can help to clarify course-level student expectations, assumptions, or misunderstandings (Stephen et al., 2020). Peers can also be a fundamental asset to students because they help to promote interaction and engagement through shared experiences (Leland et al., 2020). Some programs even offer cohort models, in which a small group of students enter a program together and work through the same or similar coursework until finished. Being a member of a cohort can provide opportunity for collaboration. They provide a structured support system, professional network, and sense of community. The many benefits of cohorts are well documented, and being in a cohort during a doctoral program is associated with persistence (Bista, 2014). As in Miriam's case, she can leverage her access to these assets to learn more about the statistics course. She can connect with her academic advisor and the course instructor to learn more about how other students successfully navigated the course. Miriam, if part of a cohort, may also want to connect with members of her cohort to form a study group for peer support and encouragement. She may also find it helpful to join a graduate association on campus related to her profession or interest. Finally, she may join the graduate school student council to meet other doctoral students like herself across campus.

Professional Assets

Similarly, doctoral students should consider the professional assets available through their university and program. Professional assets are often external pathways that help students develop research acumen, gain practical experience, and grow their professional network. These assets are vital for doctoral students to advance their careers or transition into a new field.

One key professional asset is the opportunity to research with faculty members. Many doctoral programs encourage or require students to collaborate with faculty on research projects. This experience can provide valuable hands-on experience in conducting research, analyzing data, and writing for publication. Working closely with faculty can also help students build relationships with mentors who can provide guidance and support throughout their doctoral journey and beyond (Keefer, 2015). Here, mentorship is a "process of mutual learning and scholastic engagement" (Mullen et al., 2010, p. 170). Collaborating with faculty on projects and seeking out mentors can act as a catalyst for engagement and connection within a particular field. It is important to recognize that you may often need to initiate this collaboration.

Additionally, demonstrating competence, dependability, and commitment to the project or endeavor is essential. Failing to do so may negatively impact future opportunities. In line with the literature on doctoral persistence, establishing research competence through experiential learning opportunities and publication or presentation collaborations can build your "doctorateness," which is a foundational cornerstone of doctoral success (Sanganyado et al., 2023; Yazdani & Shokooh, 2018). Doctoral programs may also support and provide funding for you to attend and present at professional conferences (Fakunle et al., 2019). Attending conferences can help doctoral students stay up-to-date on the latest research and trends in your field and network with other professionals (Campbell et al., 2021; Subramanian, 2020). Presenting at conferences can allow doctoral students to share your research, gain peers' feedback, and establish themselves as an emerging scholar (Henderson & Burford, 2020).

Professional organizations are another valuable, although sometimes cost-prohibitive, asset for doctoral students (Blackford, 2018). Many fields have professional organizations at the national and international levels that offer resources, networking opportunities, and professional development for their members. Some organizations may have reduced student membership rates or provide scholarships and awards, which work to incentivize membership and participation (Holm et al., 2020). Joining a professional organization can help students feel connected to their field and provide opportunities to get involved through committees, special interest groups (SIGs), or leadership roles (Markova et al., 2013).

Finally, universities and programs may offer resources to support career development and job search. These assets could include workshops on résumé writing, interviewing skills, and networking. Some programs may partner with employers or organizations that can provide internships, contract work, or job opportunities (Riforgiate, 2022). Career services offices can supplement program-level mentorship by assisting in preparing students for their post-graduation careers.

In Miriam's case, she may want to explore what professional assets are available through her doctoral program in Educational Leadership. Even though Miriam feels uncertain about her statistics course, she could build confidence and competence in her research skills by following up on an opportunity to collaborate on a research project with a faculty member in her program. Miriam could contact faculty members to show interest and initiative and express her willingness to join the writing team. This hands-on experience would allow her to gain practical skills in running statistical tests, performing data analysis, and articulating the results, all while receiving guidance and feedback from her faculty mentor. Engaging in this research project can help Miriam build her research skills and boost her confidence in applying statistical concepts to real-world problems. Reflecting on this experience, Miriam recognizes that this participation, while voluntary and self-directed, is instrumental to her doctoral success. By taking advantage of these professional assets, Miriam can enhance her doctoral experience and set herself up for success as she explores her postgraduation trajectory.

Personal Assets

In addition to evaluating academic and professional assets within a doctoral program, it is vital to reflect on one's own personal and familial needs. As in Miriam's case, many doctoral students are employed full-time and must negotiate a new balance between professional, academic, and family life (see Chapter 5: Navigating Family, Academic and Work Integration). Finding this new balance can lead to higher levels of perceived stress that can negatively impact doctoral persistence (Feizi et al., 2024), making it important to acknowledge the change in one's responsibilities that occurs upon entering a doctoral program and seek out supports to ensure well-being and success.

Research has demonstrated that academic-family integration differs based on enrollment in a residential or online doctoral program. People in residential doctoral programs tend to segment their life responsibilities more firmly, whereas those enrolled in online doctoral programs, especially women, are more likely to be integrators whose varied roles (academic, family, professional) often extend into one another (Rockinson-Szapkiw et al., 2018; Rockinson-Szapkiw & Herring Watson, 2020). Women are more likely than men in online doctoral programs to struggle with placing firm boundaries around their engagement in doctoral studies (Rockinson-Szapkiw & Herring Watson, 2020). Engaging in intentional conversation with one's family about a place and time throughout the week to set aside for coursework can help set clear expectations around when and how you plan to read, study, and engage with other university and program assets to support academic success (Rockinson-Szapkiw & Herring Watson, 2020; Rockinson-Szapkiw et al., 2017). However, it is important to evaluate not only personal assets within the home relative to a dedicated workspace, time to study, finances, and family support for pursuing a doctoral degree (see Chapter 4: Assessing Personal Assets) but also university supports related to these factors.

Being aware of family friendly policies, initiatives designed to support doctoral students with family responsibilities, is essential to the success of many doctoral students, especially those with children or aging parents (Bodkin & Fleming, 2019). Family friendly policies may include childcare assistance, on-campus daycare and schools, flexible work arrangements and parental leave for graduate assistantships, access to lactation rooms for nursing mothers, and any other accommodations that allow doctoral students to successfully integrate their academic pursuits with familial responsibilities.

Engaging in thoughtful and intentional planning regarding financial assets available to pursue doctoral studies can also support doctoral persistence. Doctoral students with greater access to financial support, whether through federally funded student loans, grants, research assistantships, or departmental support, experience a greater sense of well-being and persistence within their programs, whether they are in residential or distance education program (Sverdlik et al., 2018). Some universities and programs offer financial support and subsidies specific to doctoral students with children (Yale Graduate Financial Aid, n.d.). Given the potentially significant financial impact of pursuing a doctoral degree, it is valuable to explore all avenues of financial support available through the university, department, and program. This may include small research grants available through or external to the university as well as travel grants for conferences, often available at the program, college, and university levels.

Finally, pursuing a doctoral degree is rewarding but brings with it challenges and stressors. In Miriam's case, she is excited to keep learning academically and growing professionally through her doctoral program, but she is experiencing significant anxiety about taking her first statistics course. Additionally, as a first-year doctoral student, she is still learning to negotiate her work-life-academic balance. While she is comfortable reaching out to friends and family for support, she might also benefit from accessing counseling services provided by her university as she makes this significant life transition. University students who engage with counseling services report lower levels of stress and higher academic achievement (Biasi et al., 2017). Meeting with a counselor may help Miriam discuss her anxiety about statistics in a neutral, supportive environment and develop a proactive plan for addressing her areas of concern when it comes to a course she feels uncertain about. If Miriam's university does not offer virtual counseling sessions to students in online programs, she could also check to see if her employer participates in an Employee Assistance Program (EAP) that offers access to low- or no-cost counseling services. Determining whether these assets are available to support mental and emotional well-being is a valuable strategy for supporting doctoral program persistence and degree completion.

Strategies for Success

- Make a list of university assets—academic, professional, and personal—you may need.
- Prior to entering the doctoral program, assess the university's resources.

Academic Assets

- Explore library resources and meet with a graduate-focused librarian.
- Participate in any orientation programs provided by your university and program.
- Explore the Information Technology (or similar) office to familiarize yourself with what technology-related access is provided through your enrollment.
- Access tutoring services (e.g., writing centers and statistical labs) to improve competencies throughout coursework and in the dissertation process.
- Participate in workshops or webinars to learn about university processes and skills and knowledge needed to be successful. For example, attend webinars about completing the paperwork for Institutional Review Board (IRB) approval at your institution.
- Determine your institutional access to tools like Qualtrics survey software, statistical analysis software like SPSS (Statistical Software for the Social Sciences), and NVivo software for qualitative research. Seek assistance in accessing, downloading, and using software from the university technology offices.
- Access student success and disability services as needed.

Professional Assets

- Participate in professional organizations. Attend conferences.
- Seek out internship and research opportunities. Determine if your program supports industry partnerships, contract work, and discipline-specific networking. Join a faculty-led research project or team. If pursuing a research doctorate and desiring a university faculty position, it is essential to have numerous publications before graduating.
- Identify opportunities to engage in service learning as part of your coursework that would further build your professional skills and résumé.
- Identify opportunities for portfolio development of deliverables as part of your program coursework.
- Use career services for career development.

Personal Assets

- Prior to entering a doctoral program, identify what family friendly services are needed. Assess what the university offers.
- Seek financial aid opportunities, including tuition assistance, graduate assistantships, research and dissertation grants, and conference grants.
- Use counseling services available as you transition and take on the role of doctoral student.

Questions for Reflection

- What university assets (i.e., academic, professional, and personal) are the highest priority for me when choosing a doctoral program?
- Are the university and program assets I would most like to access easily accessible to me, whether learning in a residential or distance education program or professional or research doctorate?
- Is a program with a cohort model important? Do the programs I am considering have cohorts?

- Are there opportunities to interact and engage with university and program assets during the evenings and weekends?
- What media, technology tools, applications, and software are available to me? What support will I be provided in accessing and using them?
- What resources are available to me if I suspect that I may have a learning difficulty or mental health issue?
- What opportunities exist outside of the course environment for engagement and interaction with program faculty, students, alumni, practitioners, and experts?
- What financial supports exist for me as a student related to tuition, research, and professional development?
- What do I need to consider regarding family needs? What resources does the university offer in supporting my role as a mother or father, partner, son or daughter, etcetera?

Recommended Resources

Stephen, J. S. (2024). *Academic success in online programs: A resource for college students*. Springer. https://link.springer.com/book/9783031544385

Tremblay-Wragg, É., Vincent, C., Mathieu-C, S., Lison, C., Ponsin, A., & Déri, C. (2022). Writing retreats responding to the needs of doctoral candidates through engagement with academic writing. *Qualitative Research in Education, 11*(1), 29–57. https://doi.org/10.17583/qre.9195

References

Bellare, Y., Smith, A., Cochran, K., & Lopez, S. G. (2023). Motivations and barriers for adult learner achievement: Recommendations for institutions of higher education. *Adult Learning, 34*(1), 30–39. https://doi.org/10.1177/10451595211059574

Biasi, V., Patrizi, N., Mosca, M., & De Vincenzo, C. (2017). The effectiveness of university counselling for improving academic outcomes and well-being. *British Journal of Guidance & Counselling, 45*(3), 248–257. http://dx.doi.org/10.1080/03069885.2016.1263826

Bista, K. (2014). Cohort-based doctoral programs: What we have learned over the last 18 years. *International Journal of Doctoral Studies, 9*, 1–20. https://doi.org/10.28945/1941.

Blackford, S. (2018). Harnessing the power of communities: Career networking strategies for bioscience PhD students and postdoctoral researchers. *FEMS Microbiology Letters*, *365*(8). https://doi.org/10.1093/femsle/fny033

Bodkin, C. P., & Fleming, C. J. (2019). Supporting women scholars' paths to academia: An examination of family-friendly policies of public affairs doctoral programs. *Journal of Public Affairs Education*, *27*(3), 301–325. https://doi.org/10.1080/15236803.2019.1694385

Campbell, A., Wick, D., Marcus, A., Doll, J., & Yunuba Hammack, A. (2021). "I felt like I was not just a student:" Examining graduate student learning at academic and professional conferences. *Studies in Graduate and Postdoctoral Education*, *12*(3), 321–337. https://doi.org/10.1108/SGPE-08-2020-0061

Fakunle, O., Dollinger, M., Alla-Mensah, J., & Izard, B. (2019). Academic conferences as learning sites: A multinational comparison of doctoral students' perspectives and institutional policy. *International Journal of Doctoral Studies*, *14*, 479–497. https://doi.org/10.28945/4383

Feizi, S., Knäuper, B., & Elgar, F. (2024). Perceived stress and well-being in doctoral students: effects on program satisfaction and intention to quit. *Higher Education Research & Development*. 1–18. https://doi.org/10.1080/07294360.2024.2317276

Friedman, J. & Claybourn, C. (2023, January 24). Accreditation of online college degree programs: What to know. *U.S. News*. https://www.usnews.com/education/best-colleges/articles/accreditation-of-online-college-degree-programs-what-to-know

Henderson, E. F., & Burford, J. (2020). Thoughtful gatherings: Gendering conferences as spaces of learning, knowledge production and community. *Gender and Education*, *32*(1), 1–10. https://doi.org/10.1080/09540253.2019.1691718

Holm, S. E., Stutz-Tanenbaum, P., & Greene, D. (2020). What drives engagement in professional associations? A national survey of occupational therapy students. *Journal of Occupational Therapy Education*, *4*(3), 1. https://doi.org/10.26681/jote.2020.040301

Irwin, V., Wang, K., Tezil, T., Zhang, J., Filbey, A., Jung, J., Bullock Mann, F., Dilig, R., and Parker, S. (2023). Report on the Condition of Education 2023 (NCES 2023-144rev). U.S. Department of Education. Washington, DC: National Center for Education Statistics. https://nces.ed.gov/pubsearch/pubsinfo.asp?pubid=2023144rev

Kebritchi, M., Rominger, R., & McCaslin, M. (2023). Contributing factors for success of nontraditional students at online doctoral programs. *Journal of College Student Retention: Research, Theory & Practice*, *27*(1). https://doi.org/10.1177/15210251231155488

Keefer, J. M. (2015). Experiencing doctoral liminality as a conceptual threshold and how supervisors can use it. *Innovations in Education and Teaching International*, *52*(1), 17–28. https://doi.org/10.1080/14703297.2014.981839

Lahiya, A., & Mokodenseho, S. (2023). Examining the relationship between technological infrastructure and the quality of online education programs. *West Science Interdisciplinary Studies*, *1*(02), 74–83. https://doi.org/10.58812/wsis.v1i2.90

Lee, K., Zawacki-Richter, O., & Cefa Sari, B. (2024). A systematic literature review on technology in online doctoral education. *Studies in Continuing Education*, *46*(1), 38–64. https://doi.org/10.1080/0158037X.2022.2135499

Leland, A. S., Firestone, W. A., Perry, J. A., & McKeon, R. T. (2020). Examining cohort models in the education doctorate. *Studies in Graduate and Postdoctoral Education*, *11*(3), 249–262. https://doi.org/10.1108/SGPE-01-2020-0004

Markova, G., Ford, R. C., Dickson, D. R., & Bohn, T. M. (2013). Professional associations and members' benefits: What's in it for me? *Nonprofit Management and Leadership*, *23*(4), 491–510. https://doi.org/10.1002/nml.21076

Martin, F., & Bolliger, D. W. (2022). Designing online learning in higher education. In O. Zawacki-Richter & I. Jung (Eds.), *Handbook of open, distance and digital education* (pp. 1–20). Springer. https://doi.org/10.1007/978-981-19-0351-9_72-1

Mullen, C. A., Fish, V. L., & Hutinger, J. L. (2010). Mentoring doctoral students through scholastic engagement: Adult learning principles in action. *Journal of Further and Higher Education*, *34*(2), 179–197. https://doi.org/10.1080/03098771003695452.

National Center for Science and Engineering Statistics (NCSES). 2023. Diversity and STEM: Women, Minorities, and Persons with Disabilities 2023. Special Report NSF 23-315. National Science Foundation. Available at https://ncses.nsf.gov/wmpd.

O'Shea, A., & Thurman, S. K. (2017). Perceptions of how doctoral students with learning disabilities and ADHD use disability services. *Advances in Neurodevelopmental Disorders*, *1*, 149–157. https://doi.org/10.1007/s41252-017-0023-7

Riforgiate, S. E. (2022). Graduate student socialization: Getting somewhere. *Communication Education*, *71*(1), 71–74. https://doi.org/10.1080/03634523.2021.1995765

Rockinson-Szapkiw, A., & Herring Watson, J. (2020). Academic-family integration: How do men and women in distance education and residential doctoral programs integrate their degree and family? *Online Learning Journal*, *24*(4), 112–130. https://doi.org/10.24059/olj.v24i4.2318

Rockinson-Szapkiw, A., Sosin, L., & S. Spaulding, L. (2018). Does family matter? A phenomenological inquiry exploring the lived experiences of women persisting in distance education, professional doctoral programs. *International Journal of Doctoral Studies*, *13*, 497–515. https://doi.org/10.28945/4157

Rockinson-Szapkiw, A., Spaulding, L. S., & Lunde, R. (2017). Women in distance doctoral programs: How they negotiate their identities as mothers, professionals, and academics in order to persist. *International Journal of Doctoral Studies*, *12*, 49–72. https://doi.org/10.28945/3671

Sanganyado, E., Nunu, W. N., & Sanganyado, S. (2023). Towards a framework for embedding doctorateness in research proposals. *Innovations in Education and Teaching International*, *60*(6), 930–940. https://doi.org/10.1080/14703297.2022.2124186

Shepherd, C. E., & Bolliger, D. U. (2023). Institutional, program, and professional community: A framework for online higher education. *Educational Technology Research and Development*, *71*(3), 1233–1252. https://doi.org/10.1007/s11423-023-10214-3

Stephen, J. S. (2023). Persistence of nontraditional undergraduate online students: Towards a contemporary conceptual framework. *Journal of Adult and Continuing Education*, *29*(2), 438–463. https://doi.org/10.1177/14779714221142908

Stephen, J. S. (2024). *Academic success in online programs: A resource for college students*. Springer. https://link.springer.com/book/9783031544385

Stephen, J. S., Rockinson-Szapkiw, A. J., & Dubay, C. (2020). Persistence model of non-traditional online learners: Self-efficacy, self-regulation, and self-direction. *American Journal of Distance Education*, *34*(4), 306–321. https://doi.org/10.1080/08923647.2020.1745619

Strukel, D., White, L., & Alhabash, S. (2023). The good, the bad, the ugly: Predictors of positive and negative experiences of traditional and nontraditional graduate students. *Journal of Adult and Continuing Education*, *29*(2). https://doi.org/10.1177/14779714231151836

Subramanian, S. (2020). The importance of conferences and networking in PhD and postdoctoral training. *Current Protocols Essential Laboratory Techniques*, *21*(1), e44. https://doi.org/10.1002/cpet.44

Sverdlik, A., Hall, N. C., McAlpine, L., & Hubbard, K. (2018). The PhD experience: A review of the factors influencing doctoral students' completion, achievement, and well-being. *International Journal of Doctoral Studies*, *13*, 361–388. https://doi.org/10.28945/4113

Trespalacios, J., Uribe-Flórez, L., Lowenthal, P. R., Lowe, S., & Jensen, S. (2023). Students' perceptions of institutional services and online learning self-efficacy. *American Journal of Distance Education*, *37*(1), 38–52. https://doi.org/10.1080/08923647.2021.1956836

Yale Graduate Financial Aid (n.d.) Family support subsidy for parenting PhD students. *Yale University*. https://gsas.yale.edu/resources/graduate-financial-aid/family-support-subsidy-parenting-phd-students

Yazdani, S., & Shokooh, F. (2018). Defining doctorateness: A concept analysis. *International Journal of Doctoral Studies*, *13*, 31. https://doi.org/10.28945/3939

4 Assessing Personal Assets

Jessica Herring Watson, EdD
Jaclyn Gish-Lieberman, EdD

Introduction

Pursuing a doctoral degree while also navigating the demands of personal and professional life can be challenging and requires an honest assessment of one's personal assets, both internal and environmental. All doctoral programs are a significant undertaking that require time, energy, and resources. It is a life change; thus, critically reflecting on self-directed learning dispositions, leveraging self-regulated learning strategies, and evaluating social support systems can help contribute to a happier and healthier doctoral journey.

Whether doctoral students are earning a research or professional doctorate degree, at a distance or in residency, the doctoral journey is filled with potential challenges. It is why attrition rates in doctoral programs can be as high as 50% (Kebritchi et al., 2023; Lehan et al., 2021). However, there are many research-based strategies to support doctoral persistence. This chapter provides practical strategies, emphasizing critical self-reflection and identification of personal assets to ensure success in the doctoral journey.

Case Study

Thomas is an elementary school counselor who was recently accepted in an online PsyD in clinical psychology. He is excited to begin his doctoral journey, but his excitement is tempered by anxieties about balancing his personal and professional commitments. He is an engaged parent; he and his partner do their best to equally share parenting duties for their three young children. He also has two aging parents that regularly depend upon him to run errands. As a school counselor, he invests significant time in activities outside the regular school day. He is also an active volunteer in his community's Boys and Girls club. While he chose an online doctoral program for its flexibility and a professional doctorate that will likely involve integration of school and his practice, he worries about how he will negotiate this new responsibility. He wonders if it will impact his well-being, time he can commit to his responsibilities, and relationships. Thomas's partner is supportive of his return to graduate school. Thomas knows he and his partner can financially fund his schooling, but he wonders how the program will impact his engagement as partner and parent. Thomas also recognizes his personal limits, knowing he can easily become overwhelmed, which paralyzes his ability to get things done. He worries that this particular characteristic will not serve him well in his new online program. He's spoken to colleagues who are currently enrolled in similar programs about his concerns, and they have assured him he can do it. However, he wants to be sure he is setting himself up for success.

What the Research Says

Reflecting on Self-Directed Learning Dispositions

Intrinsic motivation and self-efficacy are foundational self-directed learning dispositions that help to ensure a successful doctoral journey. According to Ryan and Deci (2000; 2020), people are inherently inclined toward curiosity, learning, growth, and connection; thus, all have the capacity for intrinsic motivation to learn. Thomas, for example, feels excited about continuing his learning journey as he begins his doctoral program, and his personal motivation to engage in the learning process will likely serve him well as he navigates the challenges of transitioning into the role of doctoral student. Intrinsic motivation, defined as the motivation to engage in an activity out of inherent interest and enjoyment rather than out of a desire to earn external rewards, is associated with higher levels of academic achievement, engagement, and persistence in formal education (Ryan & Deci, 2020). However, not all academic programs are designed to bolster learners' intrinsic motivation, and it is important to understand one's own sense of motivation and develop strategies to maintain intrinsic motivation, even when confronted with challenges in the learning process.

Intrinsic motivation is often fueled by a strong sense of self-efficacy, a person's belief in their skills and abilities to successfully engage in a behavior or achieve a goal (Bandura, 1977; Hartnett, 2019). Self-efficacy beliefs differ from a person's sense of self-esteem, in that they are informed by one's perception of their individual abilities, rather than their perceptions of their innate qualities. Thus, self-efficacy is malleable, and learners should regularly reflect on their sense of self-efficacy as they work toward their goals. Self-efficacy is positively associated with higher performance in doctoral education, including increased engagement, critical thinking, and willingness to set higher goals for achievement (Hartnett, 2019). According to Bandura (1977, 2006), there are four sources of self-efficacy:

- Performance Accomplishment: Personal experiences of success
- Vicarious experiences: Observations of others' success
- Social persuasion: Encouragement from others that the doctoral student can be successful
- Emotional arousal: Emotions that inform one's sense of personal competence

As Thomas begins his doctoral journey, it will be important for him to reflect on the factors informing his sense of self-efficacy. For example, he was successful in his previous graduate-level coursework to earn his counseling degree and licensure (e.g., performance accomplishment). He can use that prior success to fuel his motivation for doctoral-level coursework. Thomas has also already spoken to colleagues currently enrolled in online doctoral programs and has observed their ongoing success. He is using those observations to inform his ideas of whether or not he can be successful in his online doctoral program (e.g., vicarious experience). Thomas has a supportive circle of family and friends who want him to pursue his doctorate (e.g., social persuasion), which is a significant factor in supporting doctoral persistence (Rockinson-Szapkiw & Herring Watson, 2020; Rockinson-Szapkiw et al., 2014). However, even with all of these positive factors influencing his self-efficacy, Thomas has expressed mixed emotions—stress, anxiety, and excitement—related to beginning his doctoral journey (e.g., emotional arousal). To further bolster his self-efficacy and maintain his intrinsic motivation, Thomas can engage in practical, research-based self-regulation strategies, such as goal setting, reflection, and self-evaluation (Zimmerman, 2000).

Leveraging Self-Regulated Learning Strategies

Even with high intrinsic motivation and a strong, positive sense of self-efficacy, there will inevitably be obstacles along the path toward completing a doctoral degree. Doctoral programs, especially distance education programs, are rife with attrition and delayed completion (Kebritchi et al., 2023; Lehan et al., 2021). Therefore, it is important for doctoral students to leverage self-regulated learning strategies to overcome challenges that might otherwise impede progress toward the degree.

Goal Setting

One such strategy is intentional goal setting. Satterfield et al. (2022) emphasized the crucial role of explicit goal-setting strategies in supporting doctoral students' motivation, career planning, and persistence. Frameworks like Universal Design for Learning (UDL) can provide helpful guidance for goal-setting strategies. While the UDL guidelines are primarily associated with course design, the UDL strategies for multiple means of engagement can be repurposed by doctoral students as a personal reflective framework. This adaptation can guide goal-setting processes and enhance reflection and self-assessment practices. A prime example is UDL Consideration 8.1, "Clarify the meaning and purpose of goals," which outlines specific research-based strategies for establishing and maintaining focus on learning objectives. These include directly formulating goals, displaying them in various ways within the learning environment, and supporting goal attainment through the creation of objectives or checkpoints along the path to achieving long-term goals (CAST, 2024).

Implementing these goal-setting strategies could significantly benefit Thomas as he embarks on his doctoral journey, potentially alleviating stress and anxiety. By articulating and visually displaying his personal and professional goals in his work and home spaces, Thomas could maintain a clear sense of purpose and improve focus when faced with competing responsibilities. Moreover, initiating each semester by setting overarching goals and developing weekly objectives could enable Thomas to efficiently break down larger course projects into manageable tasks, preventing feelings of being overwhelmed. This approach not only aids in task management but also cultivates a sense of progress toward achieving goals. Notably, doctoral students who perceive such progress are more likely to persist in their coursework (Devos et al., 2017). Thus, by adopting these goal-oriented strategies, Thomas can potentially enhance his motivation, focus, and overall success in his doctoral program.

Reflection

UDL Consideration 9.3 "Promoting individual and collective reflection" offers research-based practical strategies for reflection and self-evaluation, including adopting protocols for reflection and using progress monitoring tools to aid in deeper and more accurate reflection on progress (CAST, 2024). To leverage these strategies, Thomas might consider keeping a journal to reflect on his progress, celebrate the completion of short-term and long-term goals, and document adjustments to goals as his professional and academic interests evolve. The effectiveness of reflective practices in supporting the learning process has been documented throughout the literature (Hokanson et al., 2019; Thao & Thuy, 2024).

Time Management

Distance education and professional doctoral programs draw nontraditional students in with a promise of flexibility and integration of course work into professional practice (Akojie et al., 2019; Kebritchi et al., 2023; Melián et al., 2023). For example, in distance education, anytime, anywhere access to course materials is attractive to students juggling professional careers and families. However, research into online doctoral students' experiences and perceptions repeatedly identifies time management and academic/life balance as top concerns (Kebritchi et al., 2023; Melián et al., 2023). Working from home, students struggle with the blurred lines between school, work, and the rest of their lives and dealing with the stress of time scarcity (Akojie et al., 2019; Melián et al., 2023). Students who successfully overcame these challenges reported developing time management skills (Amida et al., 2021; Kebritchi et al., 2023). Time management is emphasized in the literature because it is a key predictor of success in doctoral programs and because it can be developed (Miertschin et al., 2012).

As Thomas considers the time management skills he will need for school, he should start by consulting his course syllabi. Instructors often provide time estimates they believe students will need for reading and completing assignments. Peers who have taken the course may be a useful source of information regarding the time needed to complete the course. In general, a three-credit-hour doctoral-level course typically requires the allotment of three hours a week for class time and an additional three to six hours for studying over a 14- to 16-week course. Thomas can use these as a baseline and add time if he finds academic reading and writing more challenging (Petersen, 2021). He should also keep in mind that the asynchronous format of online courses means that it may take longer to ask questions and receive answers about assignments than it would in an in-person course. Frequently logging into the learning management system (LMS), whether it be an online, blended, or residential course, has been linked with greater student success (Petersen, 2021). For example, Thomas may find that someone else has asked his question on a discussion board and already received an answer. Leveraging course technology, like the LMS and discussion boards, in addition to his own tools (i.e., calendar alerts) will also help Thomas stay on track and manage his time effectively.

Once Thomas has a realistic idea of how much time he will need to spend on courses each week, he should also take steps to make effective use of that time. It is a common mistake to focus only on due dates since most doctoral school assignments are large and complex and require a paced approach for successful completion. He should prioritize tasks (Amida et al., 2021) and divide those tasks into smaller, more manageable sub-tasks. Thomas may want to research and trial project management strategies like the Pomodoro technique, which prescribes working on sub-tasks in 20-minute chunks with breaks in between to refocus (Petersen, 2021). Thomas can also proactively reduce distractions by curating a learning environment conducive to studying. This may include designating a quiet space in his home where he will not be bothered (e.g., not the kitchen table or couch, but personal office or space separated by a room divider) and putting his phone on Do Not Disturb. Investing in a study space with an ergonomic chair, mouse, external monitors, and noise-canceling headphones or even earplugs can help create a clearer boundary between school and life.

Evaluating Social Support Systems

Finally, social support systems play a pivotal role in navigating the doctoral journey. Previous research has established the importance of a social support network in cultivating and maintaining doctoral persistence (Rockinson-Szapkiw et al., 2014; Rockinson-Szapkiw et al., 2017). However, finding balance among academic, family, and work domains can be complex, and there are several factors that Thomas should consider as he begins his doctoral program. Just as working adults must endeavor to establish a reasonable work-life balance, doctoral students benefit from intentionally working to establish some level of academic-family-professional balance. Rockinson-Szapkiw and Herring Watson (2020) found that men and women have different experiences of academic-family integration, with women reporting a greater perceived need to segment their academic and personal lives, creating firmer boundaries between these two domains. Men tend to report more academic-family integration. Furthermore, doctoral students in online programs report lower levels of academic-family balance than their peers in residential programs (Rockinson-Szapkiw & Herring Watson, 2020). This finding highlights the importance of reflectively and collaboratively setting boundaries and norms within the household around when and how time will be set aside to dedicate to doctoral coursework. For Thomas, having a conversation with his partner about how household routines and tasks will be adjusted could serve them both well in setting clear, flexible, shared expectations regarding how Thomas's doctoral journey will impact their family life.

In addition to leaning into support from his family as he begins the doctoral journey, Thomas should explore how, if at all, he can connect with other students in his program for social support. Research has established the value of the cohort model in supporting doctoral persistence in online programs like the one Thomas has chosen for his doctoral studies (Lehan et al., 2021; Lee et al., 2020; Melián et al., 2023). Doctoral students in a cohort model begin their program and move through all of their coursework together, often developing a strong sense of social support for one another along the way. As Thomas begins his program, he can talk to his program coordinator or advisor to determine the level of cohort-based interaction he can expect from his program.

Strategies for Success

- Set long-term goals and link them to short-term objectives.
- Share your goals with a network of family and co-learners to invite support and encouragement during the doctoral journey.

- Reflect on your personal preferences for segmenting or integrating each aspect of your life (academic/family/work/social) and create appropriate supports to dedicate time to your studies.
- Seek out workshops, webinars, and other avenues of learning that align with your research interests and spark intrinsic motivation.
- As you develop your research interests, start a journal of research project ideas to support goal-setting and goal attainment as you move through your studies.
- Actively engage in academic discussions with peers to build a community that supports your persistence.
- Link academic goals to long-term professional goals.
- Discuss time allocation for work/academic balance with colleagues.

Questions for Reflection

- What are my current levels of intrinsic motivation and self-efficacy as they relate to my doctoral studies?
- What strategies can I employ to maintain positive self-directed learning dispositions?
- How can I create a learning environment that invites focus, organization, and success?
- What kind of boundaries am I willing to set within my family and social life to create space for the doctoral journey?

Recommended Resources

CAST (2024). Universal Design for Learning Guidelines version 3.0. https://udlguidelines.cast.org

Clear, J. (2018). *Atomic habits: An easy & proven way to build good habits & break bad ones*. Avery.

Crawford, K. F., & Windsor, L. C. (2021). *The PhD parenthood trap*. Georgetown University Press.

Duhigg, C. (2014). *The power of habit: Why we do what we do*. Random House.

References

Akojie, P., Entrekin, F., Bacon, D., & Kanai, T. (2019). Qualitative meta-data analysis: Perceptions and experiences of online doctoral students. *American Journal of Qualitative Research*, *3*(1), 117–135. https://doi.org/10.29333/ajqr/5814

Amida, A., Algarni, S., & Stupnisky, R. (2021). Testing the relationships of motivation, time management and career aspirations on graduate students' academic success. *Journal of Applied Research in Higher Education*, *13*(5), 1305–1322. https://doi.org/10.1108/JARHE-04-2020-0106

Bandura, A. (1977). Self-efficacy: Toward a unifying theory of behavioral change. *Psychological Review*, *84*(2), 191–215.

Bandura, A. (2006). Toward a psychology of human agency. *Perspectives on Psychological Science*, *1*, 164–180.

CAST (2024). Universal Design for Learning Guidelines version 3.0. https://udlguidelines.cast.org

Devos, C., Boudrenghien, G., Van der Linden, N., Azzi, A., Frenay, M., Galand, B., & Klein, O. (2017). Doctoral students' experiences leading to completion or attrition: A matter of sense, progress and distress. *European Journal of Psychology of Education*, *32*, 61–77. https://doi.org/10.1007/s10212-016-0290-0

Hartnett, M. (2019). Motivation in distance education. In M. G. Moore & W. C. Diehl (Eds.), *Handbook of distance education* (4th ed., pp. 145–153). Routledge.

Hokanson, S. C., Grannan, S., Greenler, R. et al. (2019). A study of synchronous, online professional development workshops for graduate students and postdocs reveals the value of reflection and community building. *Innovative High Education*, *44*, 385–398. https://doi.org/10.1007/s10755-019-9470-6

Kebritchi, M., Rominger, R., & McCaslin, M. (2023). Contributing factors for success of nontraditional students at online doctoral programs. *Journal of College Student Retention: Research, Theory & Practice*, *27*(1). https://doi.org/10.1177/15210251231155488

Lee, H., Chang, H. & Bryan, L. (2020). Doctoral students' learning success in online-based leadership programs: Intersection with technological and relational factors. *International Review of Research in Open and Distributed Learning*, *21*(1), 61–81. https://doi.org/10.19173/irrodl.v20i5.4462

Lehan, T. J., Hussey, H. D., & Hotz, T. (2021). Factors associated with online doctoral student persistence: A critical integrative review of the literature. *Current Issues in Education*, *22*(2). http://cie.asu.edu/ojs/index.php/cieatasu/article/view/1961

Melián, E., Reyes, J. & Meneses, J. (2023). The online PhD experience: A qualitative systematic review. *International Review of Research in Open and Distributed Learning*, *24*(1), 137–158. https://doi.org/10.19173/irrodl.v24i1.6780

Miertschin, S., Goodson, C., & Stewart, B. (2012). Managing time in online courses: Student perceptions. *2012 ASEE Annual Conference & Exposition Proceedings*, 25.911.1-25.911.14. https://doi.org/10.18260/1-2–21668

Petersen, N. J. (2021). Strategies for efficient, meaningful, and inclusive online learning environments: It's about time. In I. R. Management Association (Ed.), *Research anthology on developing effective online learning courses* (pp. 434–473). IGI Global. https://doi.org/10.4018/978-1-7998-8047-9.ch024

Rockinson-Szapkiw, A., & Herring Watson, J. (2020). Academic-family integration: How do men and women in distance education and residential doctoral programs integrate their degree and family? *Online Learning Journal*, *24*(4), 112–130. https://doi.org/10.24059/olj.v24i4.2318

Rockinson-Szapkiw, A. J., Spaulding, L. S., & Bade, B. (2014). Completion of educational doctorates: How universities can foster persistence. *International Journal of Doctoral Studies*, *9*, 293–308.

Rockinson-Szapkiw, A. J., Spaulding, L. S., & Lunde, R. M. (2017). Women in distance doctoral programs: How they negotiate their identities as mothers, professionals, and academics in order to persist. *International Journal of Doctoral Studies*, *12*, 49–71. https://doi.org/10.28945/3671

Ryan, R. M., & Deci, E. L. (2000). Self-determination theory and the facilitation of intrinsic motivation, social development, and well-being. *American Psychologist*, *55*(1), 68–78. https://psycnet.apa.org/doi/10.1037/0003-066X.55.1.68

Ryan, R. M., & Deci, E. L. (2020). Intrinsic and extrinsic motivation from a self-determination theory perspective: Definitions, theory, practices, and future directions. *Contemporary Educational Psychology*, *61*, 101860. https://doi.org/10.1016/j.cedpsych.2020.101860

Satterfield, D. J., Parker, M. C., Bahnson, M., Perkins, H. L., Tsugawa, M., Scarlaro, K., Cass, C., & Kirn, A. (2022, June 26–29). *Unpacking engineering doctoral students' career goal setting and future time perspectives* [Conference presentation]. American Society for Engineering Education Annual Conference.

Thao, L. T. & Thuy, P. T. (2024). Enhancing the doctoral experience: Factors influencing academic success and well-being of Ph.D. students in a cultural context. *Cogent Arts & Humanities*, *11*(1), 2391645. https://doi.org/10.1080/23311983.2024.2391645

Zimmerman, B. J. (2000). Self-efficacy: An essential motive to learn. *Contemporary Educational Psychology*, *25*, 82–91. https://doi.org/10.1006/ceps.1999.1016

5 Navigating Family, Academic, and Work Integration

Amanda J. Rockinson, EdD, PhD
Lucinda C. West, PhD

Introduction

Familial support is central to doctoral persistence (McCallum, 2016). Researchers have acknowledged marital satisfaction and familial support as contributors to the doctoral students' overall mental stability, stress management, and degree completion (Hyun, 2009; Rockinson-Szapkiw et al., 2014; Spaulding & Rockinson-Szapkiw, 2012). On the other hand, poor familial relationships are often attributed to attrition from a doctoral program (Lovitts, 2001). The stress of family responsibilities experienced during the doctoral program is related to poor well-being (Schmidt & Umans, 2014); and the unsuccessful integration of the degree and family can result in dissatisfaction, psychological, and health issues, leading doctoral students to depart (Rockinson-Szapkiw et al., 2017). Family relationships may be strained, leading to ruptures related to the increased stress that occurs when a family member engages in doctoral studies (Rockinson-Szapkiw et al., 2018; Rockinson-Szapkiw et al., 2017). Thomas (2014) and others concluded that married students often experience marital discord when trying to manage academic and personal expectations (Allen & Dory, 2001; Brannock et al., 2000; Hudson & O'Regan, 1994; Raddon, 2002; Thomas, 2014). Doctoral work can be disruptive to marriages, with some studies reporting that approximately 50% of doctoral students choose to divorce (Culpepper et al., 2020; Wedemeyer-Strombel, 2018). This chapter outlines strategies for doctoral students to prepare their family members for the doctoral journey. It offers ideas for integrating family and academic life in a manner that supports persistence and fosters positive relationships.

Case Study

Sydney is a working mother of two children (ages ten and fifteen). She is married to her husband of twenty-one years and is enrolled in a distance education EdD program. She is the only person in her family of origin to attempt a doctoral degree. She waited to start her doctorate until her children were older, as she felt they would be less demanding of her time. She chose a distance education program to have the flexibility of working on her degree while maintaining her full-time job. Sydney also did not want to uproot her family. If she had chosen a residential program, she or her entire family would have had to move.

Within the first few months of her program, Sydney quickly realizes that papers and assignments consume most of the time she had previously available for her family. Sydney's preadolescent child is becoming increasingly needy. Her teenage son started withdrawing from the family and was caught vaping at school. Her husband complains that Sydney spends too much time with her computer and not enough time with him. Dinner is often late or overlooked, and Sydney finds it easier to delve into schoolwork at a local café than to stay home to deal with familial tension.

Sydney's family feels neglected, and she feels unsupported. When she tries to talk to her parents, she comes away from the conversation feeling worse. They reprimand her for taking on too much, with her mother pointing out Sydney's neglect of her. By the end of her first year, Sydney's internal conflict is intense. She wonders if she made the right decision in pursuing her dream of earning a terminal degree, and she contemplates dropping out of her program so things at home can return to "normal."

What the Research Says

The demographics of doctoral students are changing. Programs offered via distance education make it possible for individuals who once had limited access to enter doctoral programs more easily. While the most common type of doctorate awarded remains the Doctor of Philosophy (PhD) (National Center for Science and Engineering Statistics, National Science Foundation, 2021), the emergence of professional doctorate programs has motivated individuals who desire further expertise in their fields to pursue doctoral degrees. With professional and distance programs enabling students, who were not traditionally able to pursue degrees, to enter doctoral programs. For example, many women could not pursue a doctoral degree because they could not move to the location of the university due to familiar responsibilities.

In the past decade, women have achieved parity with men in graduating from most doctoral programs across all ethnic groups. They outnumber men in some fields (OECD, 2021; Sarrico, 2022). Many of these women are married and have children, with ample research documenting that the family has both beneficial and adverse effects on women's likelihood to persist. Stimpson and Filer (2011) noted that academic and family integration "is a complicated issue for female [students]... they face more difficulty balancing family commitments, academics, work, and personal lives, as well as have less satisfaction in their ability to balance work and life" (p. 69).

Qualitative research demonstrates that women, like Sydney, experience internal conflict and stress as their familial roles, including wife, daughter, and mother, compete with their roles as students (Oswalt & Riddock, 2007; Rockinson-Szapkiw et al., 2017). Conflict between these roles can lead to poor well-being, dissatisfaction, and ultimately attrition (Schmidt & Umans, 2014). Alternatively, women often attribute persistence to family support (McCallum, 2016; Rockinson-Szapkiw et al., 2014). In the discussion of gender, it is noteworthy to mention that few statistics and research reports include nonbinary genders, and most national reports use "sex" and "gender" interchangeably. Therefore, this chapter primarily presents what is documented in the research related to men and women.

The profile of doctoral students is shifting. No longer is the traditional doctoral student a young white man, a full-time student, and single. Over the past twenty years, a significant increase in doctorates has been awarded to Black, Indigenous, and People of Color (BIPOC) compared to previous generations (National Center for Science and Engineering Statistics, National Science Foundation, 2021). Doctoral students are diverse, and individuals are choosing to reenter their academic careers at older ages (Offerman, 2011), often with partners and children in tow. Studies of doctoral students report that the majority of students are married or living in a domestic partnership. In a study of over 5,000 students, more than one-fourth of the participants reported dependent children living in the household (Pearson et al., 2011). In a study of Australian doctoral candidates, 94% (n = 5,395) of students reported spending at least twenty hours per week on domestic responsibilities (Pearson et al., 2011), with women reporting spending even more time. Doctoral students, therefore, face familial challenges, including childbearing, raising children, caring for aging parents, and being the primary breadwinner, while attempting to complete their degree. A focus on family is thus warranted as family is vital to persistence, not only for women but for all genders (Lovitts, 2001).

The Challenges of Integrating Familial and Academic Responsibilities

In studying doctoral students in the United States, West et al. (2011) found that honoring family and academic commitments was a source of stress. In another qualitative study, West et al. (2011) concluded that "Among the challenges experienced by the students, those most commonly reported were time management issues, including balancing work and life commitments" (p. 8). Similarly, Gardner (2009) noted that PhD students who are married and have children often struggle to balance their family and academic responsibilities. Like Sydney, many students enter a doctoral program without fully grasping the nature of the doctoral process and the time commitment required for success. Feelings of disrespect and loneliness can ensue when family members do not understand the doctoral process or belittle the doctoral endeavor (Patton, 2012).

Sydney faces challenges as she balances family responsibilities with her enrollment in a doctoral degree program. While many doctoral students face challenges, numerous examples exist of doctoral students who successfully manage multiple roles and earn their advanced degrees while also being parents, partners, and caregivers to aging parents (Kulp, 2016; Ward & Wolf-Wendel, 2012). However, to be successful, the doctoral student and their family members need to understand the unique nature of the doctoral process. Family members need to be informed about the challenges the doctoral student faces and how they can offer emotional, cognitive, and physical support. Helping the family understand the doctoral process and what is required increases the doctoral student's likelihood of persistence (Spaulding & Rockinson-Szapkiw, 2012; Hyun, 2009).

Identity Transformation

The student and their family must acknowledge that identity transformation occurs during the doctoral process (McAlpine et al., 2009). This identity transformation can place stress on intimate relationships. Bowen's (2004) family systems theory denotes a need for individuals within a family to *differentiate*. That is, the individual's need to develop a set of independent thoughts and the ability to control oneself, rather than being controlled and told what to think by those within the family. Differentiation represents an important progression in the doctoral process as the student transitions toward becoming an independent researcher (Lovitts, 2008).

Differentiating oneself from the family of origin (i.e., from parents) or within the current family system (i.e., from the spouse or partner) produces tension as family members may try to regain a sense of control over the individual when experiencing the disequilibrium that often ensues upon graduation from doctoral studies. The family may unconsciously pull the doctoral student family member back into the system to reestablish equilibrium. When the independent identity of the doctoral student begins to form, family members may act in a way that produces guilt, often in an unconscious attempt to return the family to its prior state (Bowen, 2004). Merging back into the set family pattern, regardless of its dysfunction, decreases anxiety in the individual.

For example, in response to Sydney spending time away from the family to complete academic projects, Sydney's parents and husband instill guilt as a means of trying to control her behavior to something more suitable for them (e.g., spend more time with the family and spend more time taking care of household responsibilities). Sydney considers dropping out of her program to reduce tension in the household. However, this would not eliminate her desire to complete her degree. Decreasing tension and fulfilling the doctoral goal involves understanding self and development, while simultaneously managing change within the family.

Related to the discussion of differentiation are personal and familial beliefs, which can often be obstacles to the successful completion of a doctoral program (e.g., the belief that a doctoral program can be accommodated within an already busy schedule needs to be recognized and evaluated). Gardner (2009) suggested that before embarking on a doctoral journey, the prospective student's evaluation of personal values and beliefs, as well as the family's belief system, is essential to success. This is especially the case, as cognitive dissonance often occurs when a belief and behavior are incongruent (Cohen, 2011).

When a doctoral student believes, "I should not take time away from my family," but has to take time away from the family to work on the degree, cognitive dissonance is experienced. The doctoral student must learn to reconcile dissonance. For example, as Sydney progresses in her doctoral program, a disruption occurs in her family system. Her parents are accustomed to being her advisors, yet now she turns to colleagues and faculty for consultation about her future goals and ask tough questions. Her parents are left feeling unwanted and unneeded. They are uncertain of how they fit into her new life. Her husband is used to finding dinner on the table when he comes home from work, and Sydney believes, "A good wife cooks dinner." This belief and her behavior incongruence result in Sydney feeling guilty and her husband feeling frustrated.

Further, as Sydney's independence increases, she is spending less time with her husband and more time engaging in collegial relationships (Cohen, 2011). Less time together has resulted in not only physical but also emotional distancing and less marital satisfaction (Gold, 2006; Gottman & Silver, 1999). Sydney's new behaviors and focus on school challenge the status quo. Her children also notice changes. They are used to their mom being a chauffeur and doing anything they ask. Until entering the doctoral process, Sydney's identity was closely tied to pleasing her family. Sydney's identity is evolving to encompass who she is as a student, professional, and family member.

According to Bowen (2004), Sydney began the process of self-differentiation from her family members during her first year of doctoral studies. Their actions (e.g., neediness, complaining) may be viewed as an unconscious effort to decrease anxiety and reestablish harmony or equilibrium within the family. In essence, Sydney's family members want things to return to the way they were. They want their mom, wife, and daughter to remain the same. They attempt to pull her back into her old patterns of responding to their every request by acting out (i.e., her teenager), clinging to her (i.e., her younger child), or making her feel guilty (i.e., her parents and her husband). Her children are also growing up, with their own need to differentiate from their family of origin (Bowen, 2004) and look to Sydney's example to effectuate this process.

Projecting changes in herself, as well as her family, is critical in the first phase of Sydney's doctoral development. Preparing her family for the changes that will occur is a high priority. Sydney must maintain open communication with her family members, monitoring their feelings and needs, while setting clear boundaries and expectations throughout the process.

Relational Conflict

In light of the differentiation process, which involves navigating and reformulating personal and familial beliefs, as well as demands on time, energy, and attention, it is not uncommon for partner or marital conflict to arise within doctoral students' relationships. While married students generally persist at higher rates than single students (Lott et al., 2009; Price, 2006), married students reported lower adaptability to the doctoral process than nonmarried students in a comparison study (Gold, 2006). Negotiating the relationships while transitioning from student to scholar is a challenge. Hargrave and Pfitzer (2003) discussed the power of give and take within a marriage relationship. Throughout a marriage, each partner gives and takes based on merit or obligation, and this "spousal ledger" (p. 32) will shift over time as the needs of each partner change.

Two important components in stabilizing this give-and-take relationship are (a) love and (b) trust. When partners love one another compassionately, they altruistically give to the other and do not expect the ledger to always balance exactly. As Sydney completes her doctoral program, she will require more from her husband. As he gives within the relationship altruistically, he trusts that Sydney will reciprocate when the time is needed.

Strategies for Success

The following strategies involve the family at all stages of the doctoral process, including the elements discussed above. The goal is for family members to share the value of a successful education completion. Strategies for increasing relational satisfaction and decreasing conflict are also important. The strategies for this chapter are discussed in the context of the case study, rather than in a list format, as they are best understood in a practical context.

Strategy 1: Help Family Understand the Doctoral Journey

At the beginning of the program, invite family members who have a vested interest to attend orientation meetings or meetings prior to enrollment may establish a deeper understanding of the expectations and as a result, a more substantial commitment to your success at the familial level as well as the university level (Gold, 2006).

In the case of Sydney, she brings her husband, children, and parents to an online video conference orientation meeting to establish a greater connection with her university. During this conference, they see the learning management system that she will use to complete coursework and discuss the program requirements with faculty. This experience provides the family with a greater interest in her doctoral success as they can witness where she attends classes and meet her professors. The family also gains a greater understanding of what will be expected from their wife, mother, and daughter, and recognizes that they need to help with household responsibilities to support her and maximize her potential to succeed. If she were a residential student, she might bring her family members to campus for a visit.

Strategy 2: Engage in Open Communication

Engaging in open communication with all family members is central to your success. Before enrolling in a doctoral program, Sydney must open communication with her husband and children. Without their support, she is less likely to succeed. They talk about their relationship and evaluate their past, current, and future relationship with questions such as: how much are they willing to sacrifice for Sydney to complete her degree? What roles and responsibilities will need to shift? They discuss the pros and cons of her pursuing a degree, as well as, how it might impact the family on a day-to-day basis.

Furthermore, open communication and understanding family values, beliefs, and societal and cultural norms help strengthen resilience when a crisis hits (Walsh, 2006). Incorporating shared family beliefs, such as "education is valuable" or "we never give up," can provide motivation for your family to rally behind you when you think about quitting. Values like "family sticks together" encourage you to make time for family members while working on your doctorate, and rather than withdrawing in a time of conflict, brings them on the journey.

Understanding underlying beliefs within the family like "men should be the primary breadwinner" and "women are the caretakers" can help you and your families unravel the emotional threads that may underscore the family's support at any point during the journey.

Moreover, understanding the normative social and cultural expectations that may be put on you or family members can help identify undue pressure that outside sources may place on the family. Researchers often describe a "double bind" for doctoral students, especially women like Sydney, with both family and academic responsibilities (Estes, 2011). Sydney may be part of a community where "good mothers" must intensively invest themselves in their children's well-being (Lynch, 2008) and "good daughters" must be "present." Failure to do so results in her being labeled a "bad mother" (Estes, 2011, p. 199). Alternatively, being a "good student," as Brus (2006) explained, is an "unstated but closely held expectation that students who are truly committed to their fields of study will make themselves available to their professors and advisors at any time of day or night, on short notice, and without complaint" (p. 36). This is an extension of Hochschild's (1995) concept of the *ideal worker norm*, which characterizes academics as being dedicated to their work above all other outside pursuits. Being fully committed to academia is clearly more problematic for students, like Sydney, who have other roles (e.g., full-time workers, family members).

Identifying beliefs held by Sydney's family is critical since belief systems are socially constructed (Walsh, 2006). Sydney must incorporate her family to engage them in supporting her. Through open dialogue the family must identify their beliefs and values so that successful completion of the doctorate may be impeded. Assessing each family member's time commitment, personal values, and strengths can start a doctoral student down a successful path.

Depending on where you are in the family life cycle when embarking on the journey, communication with family may vary. In addition, you progress through the various phases of the doctoral process, different discussions may also be necessary. In Sydney's case, her children could be included in the conversation, as they are old enough to discuss the implications of the time Sydney's academic work will take away from the family and negotiate roles and expectations.

For the single student, an honest disclosure of financial plans with parents may be necessary. For young couples without children, negotiating when to have children and how this will impact their lives is an important consideration. Families with young children need to discuss alternative childcare options and renegotiate household chores to support the doctoral student, as well as consider when to include grandparents in the picture. Older children can also accept additional tasks at home to support a parent in completing the degree, while the parent maintains boundaries and a hierarchy.

The critical point is that you and your family need to openly communicate with one another and support each other throughout the doctoral program, acknowledging the sacrifices that will be made and recognizing that this is a family task where *all* can feel a sense of accomplishment when the degree is conferred.

Strategy 3: Practice Loyalty and Trustworthiness

Trustworthiness and loyalty are powerful resources in family relationships (Hargrave & Pfitzer, 2003). At each stage of the journey, your family members must know they can trust one another. *Balance* and *justice* mean the equity of give and take in the relationship shifts from one person to the next as the need dictates. When children are small, they are needier and take more than they give. As they mature, they can begin to contribute to the running of the household in tangible ways like making simple meals, cleaning, doing their laundry, etc.

During a doctoral program, the balance shifts as well. During the school year, the family may give more to the household than you have time to give. While this may get balanced out in the offseason with you giving back to the family. The family must understand it is not a "tit-for-tat" relationship. Family members support one another when they embark on an adventure, face a crisis, or prepare for a new career. Family members willingly sacrifice for one another. Keeping promises and maintaining schedules is a way to maintain a sense of loyalty to your personal and family values held dearest, which will enable you to complete this journey successfully.

When Sydney promises to attend her daughter's soccer game and does so despite her busy schedule, she communicates that she respects her daughter and is trustworthy. When Sydney has a paper due at midnight the day of one of her daughter's games, she communicates to her daughter her need to fulfill the academic responsibility and miss a game. Despite her daughter's disappointment, she tells Sydney, "Mom, I am disappointed, but you have made an effort to attend many of my games this season. I understand if you need to miss this one."

Strategy 4: Seek Resources to Maintain Good Quality Relationships

Understanding how to maintain relational satisfaction, quality, and ultimately, stability, throughout the doctoral journey is essential to doctoral persistence. To achieve this, you may require additional skills and may need to utilize support services. It may be helpful to reach out to your advisor (if in the Knowledge and Skill Development Stage) or dissertation chair (if in the Inquiry Stage) to learn about the support services the university offers, so they can utilize these services when needed.

In Sydney's case, she and her husband decide to attend counseling as a couple and with their family to learn coping skills for handling the stressful times ahead. They recognize they would have been prudent to do this *before* Sydney entered the doctoral program as Sydney learned through Gardner's (2009) study that what is done in stage one of the doctoral process "greatly affects the rest of [the] program… even influences [the] decision to persist in doctoral education altogether" (p. 9).

Sydney and her husband also discovered books by Drs. John and Julie Gottman and Ester Perel. They begin reading them and start implementing suggested strategies for building a "sound marital house" (see the resource list for recommended reading; Rockinson-Szapkiw et al., 2015), as well as discussing their needs related to safety and excitement in their relationship (Perel, 2006).

Strategy 5: Decide How to Integrate Academics and Family

The concepts within the work-family literature are salient in understanding strategies doctoral students use to effectively integrate academics and family within their doctoral programs and in postdoctoral experiences (Rockinson-Szapkiw, 2019). A doctoral student's satisfaction with their academic-family integration is dependent upon the success they feel in the division of time and attention to each domain (Clark, 2002; Friedman & Greenhaus, 2000) and "the 'fit' between the degree and family values" (Rockinson-Szapkiw et al., 2014, p. 196).

In border theory (Clark, 2000) and boundary theory (Ashforth et al., 2000; Nippert-Eng, 1996), theorists note that how doctoral students construct, negotiate, and hold boundaries (e.g., level of flexibility and permeability) with time, space, and people profoundly effects "satisfaction and good functioning at home and [school], with a minimum role conflict" (Clark, 2000, p. 751). Successful integration is achieved by setting different levels of flexibility and permeability between school and family to satisfy the doctoral students' need for a "sense of connectedness with family members is met while pursuing the doctorate" (Rockinson-Szapkiw et al., 2014, p. 196). You may find allowing little flexibility and permeability helpful (e.g., segmenters and compartmentalizers), or you may prefer high flexibility and permeability between work and family (e.g., integrators).

In Sydney's case, she finds that compartmentalizing work, academic, and home activities is most effective. For example, she keeps separate calendars for family appointments, academic responsibilities, and work obligations. She works on her schoolwork after her children go to bed and takes her computer to the local coffee shop to work on the weekends. One way of holding boundaries is no better than another. The extent of segmentation or integration that you choose is based upon personal choice and other factors such as socio-cultural factors at home and work (Clark, 2000; Rockinson-Szapkiw, 2019). The important thing is that you decide what is best for you and discusses it with your family.

Questions for Reflection

You are encouraged to answer these questions as a family unit. This is both a self-appraisal and a family assessment. While it is best to conduct this assessment before starting the journey, these questions can be helpful at any point in the process as a check-in.

The key is to establish open communication with each family member and share. Prepare a nice dinner or go to a restaurant to discuss the struggles and successes each family member may face during the doctoral journey. Allow each family member an opportunity to speak. Take notes, especially on your thoughts through this conversation. Remember, this is an individual journey, but a family commitment.

- What messages did my parents give me about higher education? What are my current family's beliefs about education?
- What messages did my parents give me about being a child, parent, and partner? What shared beliefs do I currently have about the roles and responsibilities of a parent or partner? What normative social and cultural expectations related to family roles and responsibilities may put undue pressure and stress on me?
- What are my thoughts about my (self, mother, father, etc.) going back to school? In what ways, if any, can this degree improve my family?
- On a scale of 1–10, 1 being extremely unimportant and 10 being extremely important, how important is it to *me* for my (self, mother, father, sister, brother, etc.) to earn this degree? After everyone shares their number, discuss the chosen number.
- How do I think this doctoral journey will change each family member? (Each family member should consider how it could change each family member, including him or herself or themselves.)
- What concerns do I have about changes that will occur in family roles and rituals when (I, mom, dad, etc.) go back to school?
- Achieving a doctorate takes several years and it involves a significant time commitment. What challenges might we face as a family while embarking on this doctoral journey together? Talk about various milestones the family will go through over the next several years and how the doctoral program will fit into those various milestones.
- How might each person help the doctoral student to complete the program successfully? Discuss family roles and responsibilities, as well as the responsibilities that family members can take on for the doctoral student. Each family member should first consider how they can assist and then provide suggestions for others in the family as well.
- What is one strategy, ritual, or support service that can be implemented through the doctoral journey to ensure quality marital/relationship and family time is not neglected (e.g., dinner time, monthly getaways, etc.)?
- Do I prefer compartmentalizing, like Sydney, work, academic, and home activities? Or, do I prefer to integrate home, academic, and work activities (e.g., keeping one shared calendar, inviting a peer over for a cookout, or talking about family during class)?

Recommended Resources

Gottman, J. M., & Silver, N. (1999). *The seven principles for making marriage work.* Crown Publishing.

Gottman Institute. (n.d.). Gottman Card Deck. Application for iPhone, iPod, and iPad. https://www.gottman.com/product/52-questions-marriage-moving-card-deck/

Perel, E. (2006). *Mating in captivity: Unlocking erotic intelligence.* Harper Perennial.

Perel, E. (n.d.) *Where Should We Begin—A Game of Stories.* Card Game. https://game.estherperel.com/products/where-should-we-begin-a-game-of-stories-2nd-edition?

Rockinson-Szapkiw, A. J., Spaulding, L. S., & Knight, A. (2015). Protecting the marriage relationship during the doctoral journey: Strategies for students and partners based on the strong marital house concept. *The Family Journal, 23*, 1–6, doi: 10.1177/1066480714565106.

Talicor. The Ungame (This is a noncompetitive card game designed to enhance communication among family members. There are different versions for couples, families with children, teens, and more.

Ester Perel's website and The Gottman Institute offer courses, articles, and other resources.)

References

Ashforth, B. E., Kreiner, G. E., Clark, M. A., & Fugate, M. (2007). Normalizing dirty work: Managerial tactics for countering occupational taint. *Academy of Management Journal, 50*, 149–174.

Bowen, M. (2004). *Family therapy in clinical practice.* Rowman & Littlefield.

Brus, C. (2006). Seeking balance in graduate school: A realistic expectation or a dangerous dilemma? *New Directions for Student Services. 2006*(115), 31–45. doi: 10.1002/ss.214

Clark, S. C. (2000). Work/family border theory: A new theory of work/family balance. *Human Relations, 53*, 747–770. doi: 101177/0018726700536001.

Clark, S. C. (2002). Communicating across the work/home border. *Community Work Family, 5*, 23–48.

Cohen, S. M. (2011). Doctoral persistence and doctoral program completion among nurses. *Nursing Forum, 46*(2), 64–70.

Culpepper, D., Goodman, M. & Norris, L. (2020). Linked lives: The experiences of higher education and student affairs doctoral students and their partners. *Journal for the Study of Postsecondary and Tertiary Education, 5*, 105–123. doi: 10.28945/4554.

Di Pierro, M. (2012). Strategies for doctoral student retention: Taking the roads less traveled. *The Journal for Quality and Participation, 35*(3), 29–32.

Espinoza, R. (2010). The good daughter dilemma: Latinas managing family and school demands. *Journal of Hispanic Higher Education, 9*(4), 317–330. doi: 10.1177/1538192710380919

Estes, D. K. (2011). Managing the student-parent dilemma: Mothers and fathers in higher education. *Symbolic Interaction, 34*(2), 198–219. doi: 10.1525/si.2011.34.2.198

Friedman, S. D., & Greenhaus, J. H. (2000). *Work and family—Allies or enemies? What happens when business professionals confront life choices.* Oxford University Press.

Gardner, S. K. (2009). Understanding doctoral education. *ASHE Higher Education Report, 34*(6), 29–40.

Gold, J. M. (2006). Profiling marital satisfaction among graduate students: An analysis of the perceptions of master's and doctoral students. *Contemporary Family Therapy, 28,* 485–95.

Gottman, J. M., & Silver, N. (1999). *The seven principles for making marriage work.* Crown Publishing.

Hargrave, T. D., & Pfitzer, F. (2003). *The new contextual therapy: Guiding the power of give and take.* Brunner-Routledge.

Hochschild, A. R. (1995). The culture of politics: Traditional, postmodern, cold-modern, and warm-modern ideals of care. *Social Politics, 2,* 331–346.

Hyun, J. H. (2009). An exploration of the coping strategies in female counseling doctoral students' marriages. *Dissertations.* Paper 37. Retrieved from http://digitalar-chive.gsu.edu/cps_diss/37.

Kulp, A. M. (2016). The effects of parenthood during graduate school on PhD recipients' paths to the professoriate: A focus on motherhood. *New Directions for Higher Education, 176,* 81–95. https://doi.org/10.1002/he.20211

Kurtz-Costes, B., Helmke, L. A., & Ülkü-Steiner, B. (2006). Gender and doctoral studies: The perceptions of Ph.D. students in an American university. *Gender and Education, 18*(2), 137–55.

Lott, J., Gardner, S. K., & Powers, D. A. (2009). Doctoral student attrition in the STEM fields: An exploration of event history analysis. *Journal of College Student Retention: Research, Theory & Practice, 11*(2), 247–266. https://doi.org/10.2190/CS.11.2.e

Lovitts, B. E. (2001). *Leaving the ivory tower: The causes and consequences of departure from doctoral study.* Rowman & Littlefield.

Lovitts, B. E. (2008). The transition to independent research: Who makes it, who doesn't, and why. *The Journal of Higher Education, 79*(3), 296–325.

Lynch, K. D. (2008). Gender roles and the American academe: A case study of graduate student mothers. *Gender and Education, 20,* 585–605.

Mason, M. A., Goulden, M., & Frasch, K. (2016). Why graduate students reject the fast track: A study of thousands of doctoral students shows that they want balanced lives. *AAUP Journal of Academic Freedom, 7*, 1–24. https://www.aaup.org/article/why-graduate-students-reject-fast-track

McAlpine, L., Jazvac-Martek, M., & Hopwood, N. (2009). Doctoral student experience in education: Activities and difficulties influencing identity development. *International Journal for Researcher Development, 1*(1), 97–109.

McCallum, C. M. (2016). Mom made me do it: The role of family in African Americans' decisions to enroll in doctoral education. *Journal of Diversity in Higher Education, 9*(1), 50–63. https://doi.org/10.1037/a0039158

Miller, J. K., & Lambert-Shute, J. (2009). Career aspirations and perceived level of preparedness among marriage and family therapy doctoral students. *Journal of Marital and Family Therapy, 35*(4), 466–80. doi: 10.1111/j.1752-0606.2009.00150.x

National Center for Science and Engineering Statistics, National Science Foundation. (2021). *Doctorate Recipients from U.S. Universities: 2020.* NSF 22-300. Alexandria, VA. https://ncses.nsf.gov/pubs/nsf22300/.

Nippert-Eng, C. (1996). *Home and work.* University of Chicago Press.

OECD (2021). Reducing the precarity of academic research careers. *OECD science, technology and industry policy papers, No. 113*, OECD Publishing. https://doi.org/10.1787/0f8bd468-en

Offerman, M. (2011). Profile of the nontraditional doctoral degree student. *New Directions for Adult and Continuing Education*, Wiley Periodicals, Inc. Published online in Wiley Online Library (wileyonlinelibrary.com) doi: 10.1002/ace.397.

Oswalt, S. B., & Riddock, C. C. (2007). What to do about being overwhelmed: Graduate students, stress and university services. *College Student Affairs Journal, 27*(1), 24–44. https://files.eric.ed.gov/fulltext/EJ899402.pdf

Patton, S. (2012). Here's smarty-pants, home for the holidays. *Chronicle of Higher Education, 59*(15).

Pearson, M., Cumming, J., Evans, T., Macauley, P., & Ryland, K. (2011). How shall we know them?: Capturing the diversity in Australian doctoral candidates and their experiences. *Studies in Higher Education, 36*(5), 527–42.

Price, J. (2006). *Does a spouse slow you down? Marriage and graduate student outcomes.* Unpublished manuscript.

Rockinson-Szapkiw, A. J. (2019). Toward understanding factors salient to doctoral students' persistence: The development and preliminary validation of the Academic-Family Integration Inventory. *International Journal of Doctoral Studies, 14*, 237–258. https://doi.org/10.28945/4248

Rockinson-Szapkiw, A. J., Sosin, L. S., & Spaulding, L. (2018). Does family matter? A phenomenological inquiry exploring the lived experiences of women persisting in distance education, professional doctoral programs. *International Journal of Doctoral Studies, 13,* 497–515. https://doi.org/10.28945/4157

Rockinson-Szapkiw, A. J., Spaulding, L. S., & Knight, A. (2015). Protecting the marriage relationship during the doctoral journey: Strategies for students and partners based on the strong marital house concept. *The Family Journal, 23,* 1–6. doi: 10.1177/1066480714565106.

Rockinson-Szapkiw, A. J., Spaulding, L. S., & Lunde, R. M. (2017). Women in distance doctoral programs: How they negotiate their identities as mothers, professionals, and academics in order to persist. *International Journal of Doctoral Studies, 12,* 49–71. Retrieved from http://www.informingscience.org/Publications/3671

Rockinson-Szapkiw, A. J., Spaulding, L. S., Swezey, J. A., & Wicks, C. (2014). Poverty and persistence: A model for understanding individuals' pursuit and persistence in a Doctor of Education program. *International Journal of Doctoral Studies, 9,* 181–190. Retrieved from http://ijds.org/Volume9/IJDSv9p181-203Rockinson0606.pdf

Sarrico, C. S. (2022). The expansion of doctoral education and the changing nature and purpose of the doctorate. *Higher Education, 84*(6), 1299–1315. https://doi.org/10.1007/s10734-022-00946-1

Schmidt, M., & Umans, T. (2014). Experiences of well-being among female doctoral students in Sweden. *International Journal of Qualitative Studies on Health and Well-Being, 9.* doi:10.3402/qhw.v9.23059

Spaulding, L., & Rockinson-Szapkiw, A. J. (2012). Hearing their voices: Factors doctoral candidates attribute to their persistence. *International Journal of Doctoral Studies, 7,* 199–219.

Stimpson, R. L., & Filer, K. L. (2011). Female graduate students' work–life balance and the student affairs professional. In P. A. Pasque & S. E. Nicholson (Eds.), *Empowering women in higher education and student affairs: Theory, research, narratives, and practice from feminist perspectives* (1st ed., pp. 107–122). Routledge. https://doi.org/10.4324/9781003444442

Thomas, T. (2014) *Daddy, can we play Beatles Rock Band? The lived experiences of a married student with children in a cohort-based education doctoral program.* (Unpublished Dissertation) Indiana State University.

Walsh, F. (2006). *Strengthening family resilience.* The Guilford Press.

Ward, K., & Wolf-Wendel, L. E. (2012). *Academic motherhood: Managing work and family.* Rutgers University Press.

Wedemeyer-Strombel, K. R. (2018). Why does graduate school kill so many marriages? *The Chronicles of Higher Education* (October 17).

West, I. J. Y., Gokalp, G., Peña, E. V., Fischer, L., & Gupton, J. (2011). Exploring effective support practices for doctoral students' degree completion. *College Student Journal, 45*(2), 310–323.

6 Becoming a Digital Scholar: Technology for Learning and Research

Victoria Lowell, PhD

Introduction

Technology is one of doctoral students' greatest allies. Whether searching for scholarly literature, managing research data, writing a dissertation, or collaborating with peers and advisors, the right technological tools can enhance efficiency, organization, and productivity. This chapter explores the most relevant technologies available, offering guidance on selecting, utilizing, and optimizing these resources to support the doctoral journey.

Case Study

Maria entered a PhD program in sociology. During previous graduate work, she relied on familiar technologies such as Microsoft Word and email. But she quickly discovered that these technologies were not sufficient in a doctoral-level program. She had to read dozens of dense academic articles each week, organizing her notes and the articles. Although she was not in an online program, her courses required her to use a learning management system (LMS) and engage in online discussion forums. She was overwhelmed by the flood of course announcements in the LMS and found it difficult to manage multiple submission deadlines, weekly readings, and collaborative projects. Moreover, many of her assignments required multimedia components. Early in her first semester, Maria struggled to stay organized and use unfamiliar technologies.

Maria decided to attend a university workshop on technologies for doctoral students. In this workshop, she learned about a suite of tools that could enhance her research, learning, and coursework management. The workshop provided her with knowledge about the available tools and how to use them effectively.

She adopted a web-based productivity and note-taking tool (e.g., Notion) as a flexible digital workspace to manage her course notes, discussion assignments, and reading reflections. She began using a virtual personal research assistant (e.g., Zotero) for reference management and reading annotations. With the additional web-based note-taking software (e.g., Microsoft OneNote), she created a centralized place for lecture notes and synced them across her devices. She learned that she could also use her tablet, stylus, and OneNote to create handwritten diagrams and annotations during class.

Maria also began reading PDFs on a tablet using PDF Expert, which allowed her to highlight and annotate articles efficiently and do so while she completed other tasks such as working out or waiting in a doctor's office. She used an AI-powered summarization tool (e.g., Scholarcy) to quickly generate article overviews that helped her prioritize what to read in depth. For collaborative assignments, Maria began using a collaborative real-time word processing product (e.g., Google Docs) and a cloud-based communication platform (e.g., Slack) to collaboratively complete assignments, discuss assignment details, and share materials with peers. These tools made group projects easier and helped her stay connected to her classmates outside class.

Maria also started using her LMS (e.g., Canvas) more effectively by syncing it with her web-based Calendar, allowing her to visualize upcoming coursework deadlines. She installed browser extensions that provided calendar reminders and streamlined access to assignment rubrics and submission portals. For oral presentations, she learned how to create and edit short videos using a screen recording and editing software (e.g., Camtasia). Moreover, she began making visually appealing and interactive presentations using graphic design tools such as Canva. Although Maria had initial anxiety and was skeptical about learning new technologies, she was glad that she overcame her anxiety and learned about how to use new tools. By accepting and adopting technologies to support her learning and research, Maria noticed that her stress decreased. She became more organized and efficient.

What the Research Says

Technology has become a central component of higher education, shaping how doctoral students learn and engage with research. Various tools, ranging from learning management systems (LMSs) to data analytics software, to cloud platforms, have evolved to support the increasing demands of doctoral education. The need for doctoral students' adoption of technology has been driven by factors such as increased blended and distance programs, internet access, and students' desire for flexibility in learning (Allen & Seaman, 2023; Bonk, 2021). Moreover, technology can improve doctoral students' productivity, communication, and opportunities for collaboration (Joo et al., 2021).

Collaboration technologies, like Slack, Zoom, and Google Docs, have reshaped how students engage in group work and scholarly communication, enabling more effective collaboration across national and international locations (Joo et al., 2021). Technology tools also continually enhance doctoral students' productivity and scholarship (Garrison & Kanuka, 2020), with artificial intelligence (AI) and data analytics tools more recently being the most influential. These technologies are increasingly seen as essential for improving the efficiency and quality of research. AI-powered tools, such as automated data analysis, predictive models, and writing assistants, are becoming widely used to manage data, streamline literature reviews, and assist with writing and editing (Garrison & Kanuka, 2020).

In addition to AI and data analytics, other emerging technology trends are influencing doctoral education. For instance, the increased adoption of mobile devices has given rise to mobile-first learning, where students frequently access course content and research materials via smartphones or tablets, rather than on computers. Gamification and microlearning strategies—such as using game elements in study apps or providing bite-sized lessons—are being introduced to boost engagement and knowledge retention. Extended reality (XR) technologies (encompassing virtual, augmented, and mixed reality) are also improving learning. For example, VR simulations allow students in fields like engineering or health care to practice skills in immersive environments without having to enter practicum or internship experiences.

While technological advancements offer numerous benefits for doctoral students, technology may also cause stress and anxiety, especially when students have limited technological proficiency like Maria. Despite owning personal devices such as laptops and smartphones, many students lack familiarity with more advanced academic technologies (Walker, 2014). Walker (2014) noted that students often possess limited proficiency with formal learning applications and research tools critical for doctoral program success. Other studies have shown that *computer anxiety*, stemming from fear of using unfamiliar technologies (Celik & Yesilyurt, 2013; Venkatesh et al., 2003) and perception about *ease of use* and usefulness (Davis, 1989) are significant barriers to doctoral students' technology use. For example, Maria at first, did not perceive technology as easy to use or useful. However, she did not let this become a barrier to learning about how to use new tools as she chose to attend a university hosted workshop. And, many scholars have proposed models to encourage faculty to integrate technology in their courses (e.g., TPACK, SAMR) to help students develop the necessary skills for technologies used in the course. For example, Stelma (2011) suggested an ecological model that encourages structured interactions with faculty, peers, and institutional resources to help students build proficiency with academic technologies. Such models promote active involvement with discipline-specific tools and emphasize the importance of using technology to enhance research productivity and quality (Garrison & Kanuka, 2020).

Ethical concerns, especially with AI and data analytics tools, may also be a barrier to technology use. As AI and data analytics tools become more embedded in the research process, data privacy, security, and the responsible use of AI in research are areas that writers and researchers say need to be discussed (Harnisch, 2023). Researchers have called for developing comprehensive guidelines to ensure the ethical use of emerging technologies, particularly when handling sensitive or proprietary data (Harnisch, 2023).

Strategies for Success

Strategy 1: Recognize Potential Technology Challenges

As you adopt technology within your doctoral journey, you may experience some frequently documented challenges. Being aware of them and being able to identify them may assist you in overcoming them.

- **Tool Overload and Choice Paralysis**: With countless apps and platforms available for tasks like notetaking, data analysis, and project management, you may struggle to decide which tools to adopt. This overload can lead to indecision or inefficiently fully mastering any tool. Choose a few tools and learn them well.
- **Steep Learning Curves**: Many advanced research tools (e.g., statistical software, programming languages, reference management systems) require significant time and effort to learn. It can be daunting to become proficient in a new tool, while also keeping up with coursework and research deadlines. If possible, seek formal training like was provided to Maria at her university.
- **Technical Issues and Compatibility**: Software bugs, hardware failures, or operating system incompatibilities can disrupt your work. For example, a qualitative analysis program like NVivo may have certain features on Windows that are absent or limited on the Mac, potentially complicating data analysis for Mac users. Such issues often require technical support or workarounds, which many university IT help desks can assist.
- **Cost and Access Limitations**: Some cutting-edge software and hardware come with high price tags. Licenses for software like SPSS and MATLAB or buying a high-performance computer can be financially challenging. However, universities may offer free services and software, so always ask about this.
- **Time Management and Distraction**: Like the case of Maria demonstrated, adopting new technologies demands an upfront investment of time to learn and integrate them into workflows. Exploring a new tool can encroach on research and writing time without planning. Moreover, technology can introduce distractions (e.g., social media, notifications, and the lure of constantly checking email), which can pull focus away from deep academic work if not appropriately managed.
- **Technology Anxiety or Lack of Confidence**: Like Maria, you may feel anxious about using unfamiliar technology or worry you will "break something" by doing it wrong. This lack of confidence can lead to avoidance of potentially helpful tools and a reliance on less efficient manual methods. Overcoming the fear of technology failure is itself a challenge.

Recognizing these challenges early and seeking support or strategies to address them is important. Often, universities provide IT help desks, library support for research software, and peer support groups that can assist with troubleshooting and skill development so that students are not left to tackle these issues alone.

Strategy 2: Overcome Barriers to Technology Adoption and Use

If you struggle with adopting new technologies, you are not alone. Many students experience barriers related to cost, steep learning curves, or lack of institutional support. However, research suggests that you can overcome these challenges through intentional strategies (Ng, 2019), including choosing technologies that benefit your academic and scholarly needs. Students who actively engage with technology for research, writing, and collaboration often experience increased confidence and efficiency (Henderson et al., 2021). Here are some ways to overcome common challenges and barriers:

- **Be Selective and Intentional:** To avoid becoming overwhelmed by the vast number of technologies, it is important to be selective about which technologies to test and adopt. Explore and test different tools to see which ones meet your needs, prioritizing tools that align with your academic needs and goals.
- **Leverage Institutional Support:** Many universities provide IT assistance, free software licenses, and training workshops. Like Maria, take advantage of these resources to build your skills.
- **Discounts and Free:** Many high-quality tools offer free options or significant student discounts. Look for student or education discounts. Look for free trials or contact companies for student options.
- **Engage in Peer Learning and Mentorship:** Collaborating with more experienced colleagues can help you learn specific tools more efficiently. Faculty mentorship can also guide you toward the most useful technologies in your field.
- **Seek Affordable or Free Alternatives:** If a particular software is too expensive, look for open-source alternatives (e.g., R instead of SPSS, Overleaf instead of LaTeX editors) or student discounts that reduce financial burdens.

- **Set Aside Learning Time:** Every new tool has a learning curve. Investing time to learn a tool early on will save you significant time in the long run. Consider scheduling dedicated time to explore and practice new technologies. Create a technology group with your peers where each of you present and instruct others on how to use different technologies.
- **Integrate AI Tools for Efficiency:** AI-powered applications like ChatGPT, Grammarly, and Scholarcy can assist with writing, summarizing research, and improving workflow automation.
- **Consider Regional Availability:** Some tools and platforms may not be accessible in certain countries due to licensing restrictions, government policies, or technological infrastructure limitations. If a tool is unavailable in your region, explore alternative options or use a virtual private network (VPN) when appropriate and allowed by institutional policies.

Strategy 3: Be Strategic in Your Use of Technologies

Beyond simply acquiring hardware and software, how you use technology can make a big difference in your productivity. Being strategic and organized, like Maria, in your approach to technology will help you get the most benefit. Here are some practices for using technology more insightfully in your academic journey:

- **Organize Your Digital Workspace**: Develop a clear system for organizing files and notes. For example, create dedicated folders for each course, research project, or dissertation chapter, and use consistent file naming conventions (e.g., "2025_LitReview_Draft1.docx"). This makes it much easier to find materials when you need them. Utilizing cloud storage (e.g., Google Drive, OneDrive, or Dropbox) to mirror your folder structure can ensure your documents are accessible and backed up across devices and on the cloud.
- **Use Digital Note-Taking Tools**: Consider using a note-taking app like Maria, (e.g., Microsoft OneNote, Evernote, or Notion) to centralize your notes and ideas. These tools allow you to create separate notebooks or pages for coursework, literature notes, meeting minutes, and brainstorming. For instance, you might keep a OneNote section for each class, where you integrate lecture notes, reading summaries,

and questions. Many of these apps support tagging and searching, so you can quickly retrieve information. If you prefer handwriting notes or annotating PDFs, like Maria, a tablet with a stylus (or a digital pen tablet device) can combine the benefits of handwritten notes with digital organization.

- **Leverage Calendar and Task Apps**: Use digital calendars and task management tools to stay on top of deadlines and responsibilities. Input all important due dates related to assignment deadlines, conference submissions, grant applications into a calendar such as Outlook or Google Calendar. Set reminders for yourself. You can also schedule regular blocks of time for writing or data analysis to ensure consistent progress on your dissertation. For daily task management, apps like Trello or Asana can help break projects into tasks and track your progress. Even simple to-do list apps or the built-in reminders on your phone can be effective if used consistently to prioritize and check off tasks.
- **Optimize Reading and Literature Management**: Instead of printing dozens of articles, use technology to read and annotate effectively. PDF readers and reference managers (e.g., Adobe Acrobat, Foxit Reader, or the built-in PDF reader in Zotero or Mendeley) allow you to highlight text and add searchable notes. Some students use tablets or e-readers to read journal articles, which can be easier on the eyes and allow freehand annotation with a stylus. Whichever method you choose, organize your collected papers in a reference management tool with folders and tags for each theme or chapter of your research. Maria used Zotero, but others include Mendeley or EndNote. This way, when writing, you can quickly locate the citation or quote you remember reading.
- **Automate and Integrate Your Workflows**: Take advantage of tool integrations to save time. Many software ecosystems allow apps to connect to Microsoft Word or LaTeX that will let you insert citations and build your bibliography automatically as you write. You can sync your to-do list with your calendar or have meeting scheduling apps (e.g., Calendly or Doodle) automatically add events to your calendar. Email rules or filters can automatically sort or label incoming messages (e.g., moving all academic alerts or listserv emails to a separate folder to read later). These small automations reduce manual effort to ensure nothing important falls through the cracks.

- **Maintain Cross-Platform Compatibility**: Be conscious of using tools that work on the devices and operating systems you prefer. If you use a Windows PC in the lab and a Mac laptop at home, or if you like to access notes from your iPad, favor software that is cross-platform or cloud-based, so your work stays in sync. For example, OneNote and Evernote work on almost all platforms, and cloud-based tools like Google Docs or Overleaf can be accessed from any device with a browser. Keep in mind the operating system requirements of key software in your discipline. If your program uses an analysis tool that only runs on Windows and you have a Mac, plan for solutions (e.g., running a Windows virtual machine or finding a Mac-compatible alternative). Ensuring compatibility upfront will save you from headaches mid-semester.

By thoughtfully organizing your digital life and making intentional choices about how you use technology day to day, you will reduce stress and save time. Strategic use of technology reduces lost files, missed deadlines, and duplicated efforts, allowing you to focus more on the substance of your academic work.

Strategy 4: Identify Helpful Technologies for Your Doctoral Journey

Throughout your doctoral program, you will engage with various types of technology to support different aspects of your research and coursework. Below are key hardware and software tool categories that can significantly enhance your academic experience. Each table includes technology examples, and the purpose each serves.

Hardware

Hardware refers to the physical devices and equipment that support your work, including computers, mobile devices, and peripherals. Choosing appropriate hardware ensures you have the necessary performance and reliability for data analysis, writing, and communication tasks. Keep in mind that hardware needs can vary by discipline and personal workflow. It is always developing and evolving. For example, certain apps may work differently or have limitations on one operating system versus another (e.g., some features of NVivo are available on Windows but not on macOS). Additionally, graphic design or engineering students might need a high-end graphics card or a specialized input device. In contrast, a student in education might prioritize a lightweight laptop and a good webcam for online teaching. Table 6.1 summarizes essential hardware categories and their purposes.

Table 6.1 *Essential Hardware for Doctoral Students (Recommended Specs and Purpose)*

Hardware Category	Purpose
Desktop/ Laptop	Primary computing device for coursework, writing, data analysis, and everyday research tasks. A fast processor and ample RAM ensure smooth multitasking (e.g., running statistical software alongside writing).
Tablet	Great supplemental tools for notetaking, annotation, lightweight productivity, or mobile data collection.
Headset with Microphone	Essential for clear, professional communication during virtual meetings, online classes, interviews, and collaborative research. It reduces background noise, improves audio quality for both speaking and listening, and helps maintain focus in shared or noisy environments.
Web Camera	For professional presentations, virtual conferencing, and potential teaching assistant duties. Note, most laptops and tablets will include a web camera.
Microphone	For professional presentations, virtual conferencing, and potential teaching assistant duties. (Note, most laptops and tablets will include a microphone.)
External Monitor	Using an external monitor with a laptop or tablet can improve productivity and ergonomics for writing, coding, and data analysis.
Reliable Backup Solution	A backup solution protects against data loss due to hardware failure, accidental deletion, or system crashes by safely storing research, writing, and sensitive files in multiple locations. It also supports ethical research practices and enables version recovery.
Digital Pen Tablets	Ideal for annotating PDFs, sketching concepts, note-taking, or creating learning assets.
Document Scanner	For digitizing research materials or annotating handwritten notes.
XR Devices (Needed for some disciplines)	For immersive tech needed for research (e.g., testing instructional scenarios or simulations in XR environments).

Software

Software (e.g., applications and platforms) comprises the other side of the technology equation. In the context of doctoral work, software includes everything from writing and analysis programs to communication and project management tools. Choosing the right software can streamline workflows, facilitate collaboration, and even open new research methods (e.g., using an AI tool to analyze literature). It is wise to familiarize yourself with the software commonly used in your field and note which tools your university provides. Also, consider the licensing and cost. Many software tools have free versions or offer student licenses at reduced cost, whereas others might require budgeting or finding an alternative. Always check compatibility with your operating system (for instance, a program might be Windows-only or require a recent OS version). Table 6.2 outlines key software categories, examples of tools in each category, and their primary use or description.

Strategy 5: Cybersecurity: Safeguarding Your Research and Digital Identity

As you deepen your engagement with digital tools for research and scholarship, cybersecurity becomes an essential and ongoing part of your academic life. Throughout your academic journey, you will likely work with sensitive information, including unpublished manuscripts, grant proposals, proprietary research data, and personal details collected from study participants. These types of data are valuable not only to you and your institution but also to cybercriminals. Individuals need to be more vigilant than ever to protect themselves against cybercrime, as students, colleges, and universities have increasingly become targets of cyber threats. According to the *EDUCAUSE Horizon Report, Cybersecurity and Privacy Edition*, cybersecurity remains one of the most urgent IT challenges in higher education, with rising incidents of phishing scams, ransomware attacks, and unauthorized access to research databases (EDUCAUSE, 2024).

Developing strong cybersecurity habits as part of your everyday academic routine is important to guard against these risks and uphold the ethical standards of scholarly work. Use strong, unique passwords for all accounts, and enable multifactor authentication wherever possible. Secure any sensitive files, especially those containing data from human subjects, by storing them in encrypted, institution-approved systems. You should regularly update

Table 6.2 *Essential Software Tools for Doctoral Students (Categories, Examples, and Uses)*

Category	Technology	Description/ Use
Learning Management Systems	Canvas & Brightspace	Widely used for course management and collaboration
	Blackboard Learn	Content organization and discussion forums
	Moodle	Open-source LMS, customizable features
Cloud Storage & File Management	Google Drive	Secure cloud storage with easy collaboration
	Dropbox	File storage and sharing platform
	OneDrive	Integrated with Office 365
	Nordlocker	Secure storage with encryption
Video Conferencing & Communication	Zoom	Virtual meetings lectures, collaboration
	Microsoft Teams	Integrated team collaboration and chat
	Google Meet	Google-based conferencing
Time Management	Microsoft Calendars on Teams or Google Calendars	Time management
	When2meet, Doodle, Calendly	Scheduling software
Time Management & Productivity	Trello & Asana	Project management, task tracking
	Notion	Flexible workspace, notes, planning
	Forest	Focus and productivity through gamification
	Slack	Team productivity and collaboration
Video Editing	Adobe Premiere Pro	Professional-grade editor (subscription-based)
	Camtasia	Screen recording, popular for instructional videos
Literature & Reference Management	Google Scholar	Access scholarly articles
	PubMed	Health and life sciences database

Category	Technology	Description/ Use
	Scopus & Web of Science	Comprehensive citation tracking
	Zotero, Mendeley, EndNote	Reference management tools
	Elicit	AI literature analysis
Writing & Collaboration	Microsoft Word	Standard document processor
	LaTeX & Overleaf	Complex document formatting
	Grammarly	Grammar and clarity enhancement.
	Google Docs	Real-time collaboration
	ChatGPT, CoPilot, Claude	AI assistants for writing support
AI-Powered Research Tools	Scite	Citation credibility analysis
	Scholarcy	AI-driven summarization
	ResearchRabbit	Citation mapping tool
Data Collection	Survey Monkey, Qualtrics	Surveys and questionnaires
	Zoom, Microsoft Teams, Otter.ai	Recording and transcription
Data Analysis & Visualization	SPSS & SAS	Statistical analysis
	R & Python	Data analysis and visualization
	NVivo	Qualitative analysis
	Tableau & Power BI	Data visualization and reporting
Extended Reality (XR)	Virtual Reality (VR)	Immersive simulations
	Augmented Reality (AR)	Interactive data overlays
	Mixed Reality (MR)	Hybrid research environments
Ethical & Security Tools	Turnitin	Plagiarism detection
	Nordpass, Bitwarden	Secure password management
	VPN	Secure remote access

Note: Many tools listed offer free options or significant student discounts.

your devices and software to address known vulnerabilities, and ensure you back up your research frequently to protected locations. These actions align with the *NIST Cybersecurity Framework* (NIST, 2018), a widely adopted guide designed to help individuals and organizations reduce digital security risks.

If your research involves people, your responsibility extends beyond protecting your data; it includes protecting the privacy and rights of your participants. Depending on your field and research methods, you may need to comply with regulations such as the Family Educational Rights and Privacy Act (FERPA) or the Health Insurance Portability and Accountability Act (HIPAA). These laws establish strict standards for the ethical collection, handling, and storage of sensitive data. Fortunately, most institutions offer cybersecurity training, IT support, and policy guidance to help you navigate these responsibilities. By incorporating cybersecurity into your daily research practices, you are protecting your academic work and contributing to a culture of digital responsibility and establishing habits that will support your success throughout your doctoral journey

Questions for Reflection

The following questions will assist you when considering potential technology requirements and needs while completing a doctoral program.

- What technologies are recommended and required by my university, college, and program?
- What potential challenges will I encounter in accessing and learning to use the required technologies?
- What are my resources for accessing and learning to use technologies that will be recommended or required?
- How can I best prepare myself to engage with technologies that will be important for my success in my program and engagement in professional communities of practice?
- Are there ethical or security considerations unique to my research that technology could address or complicate?
- How can I ensure ongoing skill and knowledge development as technologies evolve during my doctoral journey?
- When does my quest to learn about new technologies interfere with my time and energy for my doctoral studies?

Recommended Resources

Online Learning Platforms and Tutorials

- **Coursera** (https://www.coursera.org/) offers free and paid courses on technology skills, including data analysis, AI, and more.
- **LinkedIn Learning** (https://www.linkedin.com/learning/) provides tutorials on research tools, software, and productivity strategies for academics.

Tech-Specific Communities and Forums

- **ResearchGate** (https://www.researchgate.net/) is a professional network where students can access research publications, engage with peers, and join discussions on technology use in research.
- **Academia.edu** (https://www.academia.edu/) can help you connect with researchers, share papers, and explore technological resources for academic research.

Professional Development and Software Training

- **LinkedIn Learning** (https://www.linkedin.com/learning/) focuses on professional development and skill-building, offering leadership, communication, and software development courses. In addition, LinkedIn offers free tech courses and certifications through various initiatives.
- **Lynda.com** (https://www.lynda.com/) provides in-depth training on various research tools, including qualitative data analysis, reference management, and collaboration tools.
- **Tableau Training** (https://www.tableau.com/learn/training) offers free tutorials on mastering data visualization, a valuable skill for dissertation work and research analysis.
- **edX.com** (https://www.edx.org) provides courses from top universities, covering a broad spectrum of topics, including computer science, programming, and software engineering. In addition, some of edX.com courses can be audited for free.

- **Udemy** (https://www.udemy.com) offers a wide selection of courses, including those in professional development and software skills, with many free options.

Ethical and Legal Resources for Technology in Research

Below are some sources for guidelines and recommendations for responsible AI practices in academia.

- **Ethical AI for Teaching and Learning**—https://teaching.cornell.edu/generative-artificial-intelligence/ethical-ai-teaching-and-learning
- **Ethical Use of Artificial Intelligence for Scientific Writing: Current Trends**—https://journals.sagepub.com/doi/10.1177/08903344241235160
- **Guide for Doctoral Students: Ethical Use of Generative AI Tools in Dissertation Research and Writing**—https://www.linkedin.com/pulse/guide-doctoral-students-ethical-use-generative-ai-tools-russo-phd-btouc/
- **Data Protection and Privacy Resources Data Protection and Privacy Resources—Chapter References**—Consult your university's research data management policies and ethical guidelines, and work with your university's Institutional Review Board (IRB) to ensure your research is ethical and compliant with regulations.

References

Allen, I. E., & Seaman, J. (2023). Grade change: Tracking online education in the United States. Babson Survey Research Group. https://www.bayviewanalytics.com/reports/gradechange.pdf

Bonk, C. J. (2021). *The world is open: How web technology is revolutionizing education*. Jossey-Bass.

Celik, V., & Yesilyurt, E. (2013). Attitudes to technology, perceived computer self-efficacy and computer anxiety as predictors of computer supported education. *Computers & Education*, *60*(1), 148–158. https://doi.org/10.1016/j.compedu.2012.06.008

Davis, F. D. (1989). Perceived usefulness, perceived ease of use, and user acceptance of information technology. *MIS Quarterly*, *13*(3), 319–339.

DelCampo, R. G., Haggerty, L. A., Haney, M. J., & Knippel, L. A. (2011). *Managing the multi-generational workforce*. Gower Publishing.

EDUCAUSE. (2024). *2024 EDUCAUSE Horizon Report: Information Security Edition*. https://library.educause.edu/-/media/files/library/2024/9/2024hrcybersecurityprivacy.pdf

Ferriter, W. M. (2010). *Building a professional learning community at work: A guide to the first year*. Solution Tree Press.

Garrison, D. R., & Kanuka, H. (2020). Blended learning: Uncovering its transformative potential in higher education. *The Internet and Higher Education*, *45*, 10–20. https://doi.org/10.1016/j.iheduc.2004.02.001

Harnisch, D. L. (2023). *Collaboration and open science in research education: The role of technology in shaping doctoral studies*. Springer.

Henderson, M., Selwyn, N., & Aston, R. (2021). What works and why? Student perceptions of "useful" digital technology in university teaching and learning. *Studies in Higher Education*, *46*(7), 1321–1332. https://doi.org/10.1080/03075079.2015.1007946

Howe, N., & Strauss, W. (2007). The next 20 years: How customer and workforce attitudes will evolve. *Harvard Business Review*, *85*(7–8), 41–52.

Huffman, J. B., & Huffman, R. J. (2011). The use of technology in higher education: A review of current trends and practices. *Journal of Higher Education Research*, *20*(1), 1–13.

Joo, Y. J., Lim, K. Y., & Kim, D. H. (2021). A study on the collaborative role of social media in graduate student learning. *Computers & Education*, *89*, 16–29. https://doi.org/10.1016/j.compedu.2015.09.009

Lowell, V. L., & Morris J. (2019). Multigenerational college classrooms: Equity and learning with technology. *The International Journal of Information and Learning Technologies*, *36*(2), 78–93. https://doi.org/10.1108/IJILT-06-2018-0068

National Institute of Standards and Technology. (2018). *Framework for Improving Critical Infrastructure Cybersecurity, Version 1.1*. https://nvlpubs.nist.gov/nistpubs/CSWP/NIST.CSWP.04162018.pdf

Ng, W. (2019). Conceptualizing digital literacy: Toward a unified framework. *Computers & Education*, *136*, 61–74. https://doi.org/10.1016/j.compedu.2019.03.011

Stelma, J. (2011). An ecological model of developing researcher competence: The case of software technology in doctoral research. *Instructional Science*, *39*, 367–385. https://doi.org/10.1007/s11251-010-9132-7

U.S. Department of Education. (2021). *FERPA General Guidance for Students*. https://studentprivacy.ed.gov

U.S. Department of Health and Human Services. (n.d.). *The HIPPA Privacy Rule*. https://www.hhs.gov/hipaa/for-professionals/privacy/index.html

Venkatesh, V., Morris, M. G., Davis, G. B., & Davis, F. D. (2003). User acceptance of information technology: Toward a unified view. *MIS Quarterly*, *27*(3), 425–478. https://doi.org/10.2307/30036540

Walker, V. L. (2014). Leveraging technology for scholarship. In A. Rockinson-Szapkiw & L. Spaulding (Eds.), *Navigating the doctoral journey: A handbook of strategies for success* (pp. 77–84). Rowman & Littlefield Publishing.

7 Creating a Personal Wellness Plan

Amanda J. Rockinson, EdD, PhD
Charles R. Cadle, EdD

Introduction

Well-being is a complex phenomenon that has been defined in numerous ways throughout the literature. Researchers state that well-being encompasses physical, mental, emotional, and social factors. Medin and Alexanderson (2001) describe well-being as "the individual's experience of his or her health" (p. 75), and well-being is strongly linked to satisfaction with self, purpose, relationships, and quality of life. Strategies developed to maintain well-being throughout academic careers are shaped during doctoral studies (Agevall et al., 2016). Unfortunately, academics are often identified as having the most unstable well-being compared to other professionals (Schmidt & Hansson, 2018; Taris et al., 2001), leading to adverse effects on professional and personal life.

With demanding workloads, constant deadlines, financial difficulties, pressures to publish, uncertainty about future employment, poor advisor relationships, and often conflicting roles and responsibilities (Charles et al., 2022; Hish et al., 2019; Madera & Smith 2006; Liu et al., 2019; Schmidt & Umans, 2014), doctoral students also often struggle with poor well-being and never develop strategies to mitigate this (Evans et al., 2018). Doctoral students are more than six times as likely to have poor well-being, specifically reporting depression and anxiety, when compared to the general population (Barreira et al., 2020; Flaherty, 2018). Poor well-being is associated with doctoral students' poor cognitive functioning, cognitive processing, and learning (Meera et al., 2025; Pyykkonen, 2021).

Without strategies to optimize physical, mental, emotional, and social functioning, learning, brain functioning, personal life, and persistence suffer throughout the doctoral journey (Duckworth et al., 2007; van Gelderen, 2012). Therefore, it is vital to understand the factors that contribute to well-being and develop strategies to maintain and enhance it through the doctoral journey (Woolston, 2019).

Case Study

Sawyer is preparing to embark on his doctoral journey. He has an above-average IQ and intends to complete his degree within three to four years. While in his doctoral orientation, he meets peers who are of similar intellectual caliber and share the same intentions he does—to complete their degree in a timely and successful manner. So, he is surprised to hear, during the dean's opening speech, that statistics indicate more than half of the doctoral students in the room will drop out of the program and never have their degree conferred.

The dean goes on to explain:

> *Obtaining a doctoral degree is a mental marathon requiring significant discipline and focus to persevere through coursework and the inquiry phase of dissertation writing. It may be easy for individuals to become easily distracted from this prolonged effort. A loss of progress toward a goal due to adversity, setbacks, difficulties, or obstacles, often encountered during the doctoral journey, can lead to a reassessment of outcome expectancies, resulting in a sense of doubt or avoidance tendencies. If individuals are not intentionally fostering their well-being to optimize functioning, they may become one of the statistics and not finish.*

Sawyer wonders what the dean means by "fostering your well-being to optimize functioning," and decides he needs to learn more if he intends to complete the program.

What the Research Says

Optimizing well-being begins with self-imposed interventions, such as a healthy diet, rest, physical activity, and self-regulation, which are essential for doctoral students' persistence. Alternatively, substance abuse and avoidance coping mechanisms (e.g., overeating, restricting, or bingeing) can become unhealthy "crutches" that disrupt well-being. While every doctoral student needs to determine what works best for their well-being, and even consult their primary care physician, this chapter outlines research on these topics.

Nutritious Eating

Nutrition affects well-being and cognitive functioning. Doctoral students who do not consume the appropriate amounts of nutrients may experience inhibited functioning (D'Anci et al., 2009; Wurtman et al., 2010). For example, glucose is essential for ensuring efficient cognitive processing, allowing the brain to operate at its peak level (Gailliot, 2008; Turner, 2011). Thus, diets too low in carbohydrates have been shown to impair cognitive performance negatively (D'Anci et al., 2009). Brain health and cognitive performance are also influenced by a diet rich in antioxidants, omega-3 fatty acids, and brain-supporting nutrients such as vitamin B12 and folate, all of which positively impact cognitive processing and learning (Puri et al., 2023). Alternatively, high fat diets, especially those high in saturated fats and refined sugars, cause cognitive and mood (e.g., stress, anxiety, depression) disruptions (Bolton & Bilbo, 2014; Beilharz et al., 2016; Deng et al., 2022). If doctoral students ignore the benefits of healthy nutrition and do not balance *macronutrients* (i.e., nutrients the body needs in large amounts, including carbohydrates, proteins, and fats) and *micronutrients* (i.e., nutrients the body needs in smaller amounts, including vitamins and minerals), their mental alertness begins to slow, resulting in poorer academic performance and less than desirable well-being (Carlson et al., 2007; D'Anci et al., 2009; González Olmo et al., 2021).

To maximize well-being and cognitive functioning, doctoral students need to develop nutritional plans to optimize peak performance (Gailliot, 2008; Igase et al., 2010; Turner, 2011). Specific dietary choices can support optimal functioning. For example, leafy greens such as kale, spinach, collards, and broccoli are rich in brain-healthy nutrients, including vitamin K, lutein, folate, and beta-carotene. Berries, such as blueberries and strawberries, contain flavonoids that improve memory. The caffeine in a morning cup of coffee or tea might offer more than just a short-term concentration boost. Researchers suggest caffeine might also help solidify new memories. Walnuts are excellent sources of protein and healthy fats associated with improved learning (Arab & Ang, 2015).

Sawyer, from the case study, conducted research on introducing enriching food into his diet to enhance brain health and well-being. He began eating the following: (a) blueberries, known as the brain's super food as they are high in antioxidants and phytochemicals, which can slow memory decline and protect a person from free radical damage; (b) avocados, known to be a good source of monounsaturated fats and are rich in Vitamin E; (c) hummus, known to provide enhanced energy as a source for complex carbohydrates, protein, and fats; and (d) an ounce of almonds, known to maintain sugar levels (glucose) and to provide a food that is high in good fat, protein, and nutritious minerals.

Sawyer also noted that the stress of a doctoral program and increased sitting were having a significant effect on his eating habits. He unconsciously snacked throughout the day and often overate at meals. So, he decided to prepare portioned snacks. He also decided that he needed to be more mindful in his eating and adopted the *intuitive eating* (IE) approach (i.e., *mindful eating*; learning to eat when hungry and stopping eating when full while also being aware of specific causes of hunger; Camilleri et al., 2017; Warren et al., 2017; Van Dyke & Drinkwater, 2014), as he found a study demonstrating that it takes twenty minutes for his stomach to communicate to his brain that he is full (Berthoud et al., 2017; Stevenson et al., 2017).

Physical Activity

Physical activity improves mental and physical health, including body composition, glucose regulation, insulin sensitivity, and cardiac function, having a positive overall effect on well-being (Chekroud et al., 2018; Ghrouz et al., 2019; Graves et al., 2022; Herbert et al., 2020). Regular physical activity can mitigate depression and anxiety, as physical activity regulates levels of neurotransmitters associated with anxiety and depression (e.g., serotonin, norepinephrine, and dopamine) (Rethorst et al., 2009). Moreover, physical activity improves executive control processes (i.e., scheduling, planning, working memory, multitasking, and dealing with ambiguity) and provides doctoral students quality time to reflect on their current situations, imagine solutions, and visualize success (Hillman et al., 2008). Evidence also suggests that running and other aerobic physical activities have a positive impact on cognitive capacities, improve overall health, and enhance brain functioning (Colcombe & Kramer, 2004; Winter et al., 2006). For example, physical activity increases blood flow and glucose delivery to the brain, improving information processing speed and memory (Vaynman & Gomez-Pinilla, 2006).

The social environment is an important consideration for doctoral students' physical activity. Research demonstrates doctoral students are more likely and prefer to engage in physical activity when it is a shared experience, a mutual agreement, and accountability is present (Kahn et al., 2002; Wills & Shinar, 2000).

Sawyer recognized the importance of physical activity after listening to a podcast about researchers at Columbia University who examined 20,000 participants who took regular movement breaks. Sawyer noted that walking five minutes after every thirty minutes of sitting counteracted the harmful effects of a sedentary life (e.g., fatigue was reduced by 25%; positive emotions increased, negative emotions decreased), which is common for him as a doctoral student given the number of hours he has to sit in front of a screen. Sawyer committed to setting a 30-minute timer when studying to remind himself to take walking breaks. He also adopted a goal of exercising between 150 and 300 minutes per week (20-40 minutes daily) after reading that this was optimal (Piercy & Troiano, 2018).

In addition to aerobic exercise, mobility and stability exercises are essential in releasing stress and tension in the body (Tomes & Lewis, 2019; Vancini et al., 2017). Mobility (i.e., the ability of joints to freely move and have a full range of motion) and stability (i.e., the ability to control movement and maintain proper alignment) can help reduce tension and stress held in the body that are byproducts of sitting in front of a computer and the stress of the doctoral journey. Regular exercise, including mobility exercises and stretching, can help relax muscles and release endorphins that naturally boost mood. Specifically, pilates and yoga have been shown to relax muscles and promote mental clarity, reduce stress, and improve the ability to cope (Mental Health, 2019).

Rest

Take a moment to think about the biology of the human body. Bodies were made to stay awake for sixteen hours and then sleep for seven to nine hours.

If individuals live to be 75 years old and sleep eight hours a day, they will spend approximately 25 years of their lives sleeping. Bodies were made for and need rest. To be productive, doctoral students need a plan to get a sufficient amount of sleep, as it rejuvenates both the body and the mind.

Sleep may be the single most important behavior associated with doctoral students' persistence, as healthy sleep patterns are critical for self-regulation, the executive function of the brain that helps doctoral students initiate and persist in behaviors (Barber et al., 2010). Without adequate sleep, the brain is less equipped to control behaviors and direct them toward goals. Sleep contributes to neural plasticity (i.e., reorganization of neural pathways in the brain based on experiences) and; thus, memory consolidation and learning (Huber et al., 2004; Maquet, 2001).

Sleep also affects the mental health, mood, energy levels, and physical health of doctoral students (Billman, 2020; Saruhanjan et al., 2021). Sleep is a state during which the body restores itself and the brain subconsciously seeks clarity and connectedness in problem-solving (Beijamini et al., 2021; van den Berg et al., 2023). Doctoral students who do not get enough sleep are vulnerable to stress, health issues, and poor academic performance (Allen et al., 2021; Yang & Smallfield, 2020). With limited time, doctoral students are often tempted to forgo sleep. For example, Sawyer's busy schedule tempted him to shorten the hours he was sleeping; however, he decided to prioritize sleep once he found an article stating that adults need at least seven to nine hours of sleep for optimal functioning—physical, emotional, and cognitive (Ou et al., 2025; Watson et al., 2015).

However, sleep is only one type of rest needed to be successful in a doctoral program. Sleep and rest are not the same thing (Dalton-Smith, 2017). Simply sleeping may not address being chronically tired or burned out, as seven types of rest need to be practiced (Dalton-Smith, 2017). Sleeping and napping are types of passive physical rest. However, there is also active physical rest that restores the body, including its circulation and flexibility—for example, yoga, stretching, massages, foam rolling, and using an acupuncture mat. In addition to physical rest, there are also mental, sensory, creative, emotional, social, and spiritual aspects to consider.

Sawyer began to recognize that he needed rest in all these areas. He often found himself feeling forgetful and struggling to concentrate. When he tried to sleep, he struggled to "turn off" his brain, as all the course content he had been studying filled his thoughts. Even when he did sleep, he woke feeling exhausted. Given the cognitive demands of his doctoral program, he was mentally exhausted. Thus, Sawyer found two strategies to help him mentally rest. Every 30 minutes throughout his studying, he scheduled short brain breaks and took a 10-minute walk around his house. He also kept a journal near his bed to jot down ideas and thoughts that kept him awake at night.

Exposure to fluorescent lights at school and work, as well as the computer screen and constant interaction on Zoom calls, led Sawyer to feel overwhelmed and experience sensory overload. Thus, Sawyer needed sensory rest, which he found by intentionally unplugging from all electronics for five hours a week. He also signed up for a monthly massage membership and plans to try a sensory deprivation float to take a break from all the overstimulation.

Sawyer sometimes felt his passion for earning his doctorate wane, and at other times, he struggled to generate creative ideas for research, writing, and course assignments. When experiencing this, he knew he needed creative rest. To address this need, he took hikes to appreciate nature, took pictures, and framed inspiring photographs for his home office, where he frequently worked on doctoral work.

Social and emotional rest were also important to Sawyer, as the doctoral program was emotionally draining and often left him feeling isolated. As such, he made space and time to express his feelings by journaling freely and to intentionally spend time with friends who were positive and supportive, avoiding those who felt draining. He recognized that all individuals have mirror neurons (Acharya & Shukla, 2012) that result in mirroring the individuals one spends time with. So, he chose to surround himself with friends and family who were positive.

Finally, Sawyer realized he needed spiritual rest, or a deep sense of belonging, love, acceptance, and purpose. So, he integrated meditation and prayer into his daily routine.

Self-Regulation

One's emotional state impacts cognitive processes, including the ability to pay attention, make decisions, choose to act, and solve problems (Cole et al., 2004). Emotions, such as happiness and excitement, may enhance motivation to learn and drive doctoral students toward long-term goals. Fear and stress can negatively affect cognitive processes and motivation.

While some stress may motivate doctoral students to meet the challenges presented in the doctoral journey, stress beyond a certain threshold (i.e., distress) can have the opposite consequence, as it can affect the decision to remain in the doctoral program (LeDoux, 2002) (see Chapter: 8: Overcoming Stress and Burnout). For example, Sawyer has six hours to complete a paper, study for a test, and finalize a project for his boss at work. Additionally, his wife expects him to attend their son's baseball game. Faced with this stressful situation of meeting the expectations of his professors, boss, and wife, Sawyer's body has a stress response. Hormones such as epinephrine and norepinephrine, and later cortisol, are secreted, resulting in heightened blood pressure, heart rate, and alertness.

This response, particularly the hormones that modulate Sawyer's cognitive functioning, influences his ability to process information and retain knowledge. While some stress motivates Sawyer to meet the challenges currently presented in the doctoral journey, excessive stress can have the opposite consequence, as it can affect Sawyer's mental functioning and eventually his decision to stay in his doctoral program (LeDoux, 2002).

While emotional states are felt, they can also be regulated. In Sawyer's case, when he feels a heightened level of stress, he needs to be able to self-regulate so that it does not inhibit his learning and intentions to reach his goal of finishing his program. *Self-regulation*, including emotional regulation, has been identified as one of the most crucial skills necessary for effective learning, achieving goals, and navigating social contexts, such as educational settings.

Self-regulation, and specifically, *emotional regulation*, is defined in numerous ways; no universal definition exists. Gros (2003) referred to emotional self-regulation as any process which an individual uses to influence their emotions; and Thompson (1994) referred to it as the internal and external processes of monitoring, analyzing, and modifying emotions to meet personal goals. For doctoral students, this goal includes optimal cognitive functioning and finishing the program.

Controlling impulses to delay gratification is an aspect of emotional regulation. Regulation strategies, such as repetitive self-talk, strengthen neural pathways (Cooper, 2005) and influence goal-directed behavior and self-beliefs (Cronin-Golomb & Bauer, 2023). Positive self-talk, self-monitoring, and the process of writing down goals can mitigate the negative influence of faulty emotions on decision-making, especially in social situations (Akyol & Garrison, 2011; Amen, 2005). The Mayo website offers a list of evidence-based techniques for emotional regulation:

- *Guided meditation*, meditating or visualizing images (i.e., recalling smells, sounds, and sights) that are relaxing;
- *Mantra meditation*, calmly and slowly repeating words and sayings to avoid damaging, distracting thoughts and ideas; and
- *Mindfulness meditation*, increasing awareness and acceptance of the present moment, such as observing, describing, acting-with-awareness, and accepting thoughts and feelings without judgment.

Emotional intelligence (EI) is also related to emotional regulation and encompasses self-awareness, emotional management, self-motivation, affective awareness, and social competence (Bar-On et al., 2003). Having high EI is related to both well-being and cognitive competency for evaluating and overriding initial emotional responses in social situations, especially in stressful situations that doctoral students often encounter (Bar-On et al., 2003; Mayer et al., 2000). Although many techniques can help build EI, journaling for self-awareness, training to develop empathy and active listening skills, engaging in meditation and deep breathing, and role-playing real-life social situations are some practical ways to build EI.

Strategies for Success

As reflected in the strategies below, cognitive functioning and motivation to persist are optimized through self-imposed interventions, including a healthy diet, rest, physical activity, and self-regulation.

Strategy 1: Practice a Healthy Lifestyle

Well-being can be optimized through a healthy lifestyle, specifically by consuming the proper nutrients, ensuring adequate sleep and all other types of rest, and regular physical activity. Avoidance of any unhealthy "crutches" should be a high priority. For example, the use of alcohol initially increases dopamine in the brain; however, excessive use causes the brain to reduce natural dopamine production, which results in dependency and poor functioning. You need to have a nutritional strategy that considers both *macronutrients* (i.e., nutrients the body needs in large amounts, including carbohydrates, proteins, and fats) and *micronutrients* (i.e., nutrients the body needs in smaller amounts, including vitamins and minerals to maximize functioning) (Gailliot, 2008; Igase et al., 2010; Turner, 2011).

Prioritize sleep. Develop a good sleep routine and good sleep hygiene by establishing a consistent sleep schedule, creating a bedtime routine, and practicing the following habits that promote sleep:

- Go to bed and wake up at the same time every day to regulate your body's circadian rhythm.
- Sleep for seven to nine hours, which is the recommended amount for most adults.
- Develop a relaxing bedtime routine to signal to your body that it is time to sleep, which may include taking a warm bath with Epsom salts, listening to relaxation music, or practicing yoga or meditation.
- Optimize your sleep environment by making your bedroom dark (e.g., blackout curtains), quiet, and cool (65–68°F or 18–20°C). Only use your bed for sleep and use essential oils associated with relaxation (e.g., lavender).
- Avoid stimulants before bed, including caffeine, alcohol, heavy meals, blue light from screens (e.g., phones, tablets, computers). If you have to use a screen, use blue light blocking glasses, especially at least 60 minutes before bed.
- Plan strategies for all seven types of rest (i.e., physical, mental, sensory, creative, emotional, social, and spiritual).

Finally, as physical activity can enhance well-being, develop a good strategy for incorporating weekly physical activity, such as taking a brisk 15- to 30-minute walk daily, riding a bike, or attending weekly gym classes that involve aerobic activity. Moreover, social support, which supports increased physical activity, should be considered when developing plans for physical activity. You may be more successful if you plan physical activities (e.g., hikes, basketball at a local gym, running groups, yoga classes, competing on walking apps for the most number of steps) with peers. Do not forget to include mobility and stability in the plan.

Strategy 2: Practice Meditation

Meditation is another method you may use to influence your well-being. Stress (anxiety and depression) may be expressed as physical, mental, or emotional responses to doctoral program demands and life changes. Stress produces the hormone cortisol, which, in low levels, can be a driver of creativity and resourceful actions; however, higher levels of cortisol can be harmful.

Although several techniques can help regulate emotions, meditation is a particularly effective strategy for managing emotions during stressful times (Tanner et al., 2009). Meditation is a structured practice that helps you cultivate mindfulness, a sustained reflective processing of experiences (Zelazo & Lyons, 2011), and focus. Mindfulness training may be considered. For example, an evidence-based approach such as Jon Kabat-Zinn's Mindfulness-Based Stress Reduction (MBSR) program is a structured eight-week training designed to help manage stress, anxiety, and pain by utilizing mindfulness practices.

Strategy 3: Practice Self-Regulation

Strategies such as preparing written goals that you review daily; internal self-talk, such as "my doctoral work is vital to me"; writing reminder notes about how delays or starting over are not strategies for success; and making to-do lists to heighten awareness of task timelines and enable celebration of completed tasks are all helpful.

Self-regulatory strategies can be enhanced through practice, which in turn increases resilience in the medium and long term (van Gelderen, 2012). A good example of this is the use of positive *self-talk*, which involves verbalizations or statements addressed to oneself (Hardy, 2006). Self-talk aligns with Bandura's (1977) self-efficacy theory, in which you can visualize success in a situation to achieve efficacious beliefs.

In addition to positive attribution, two other self-regulatory strategies are introjection and integration (Deci et al., 1994; Dreisbach & Goschke, 2004). *Introjection*, a form of forced self-regulation, may sometimes be necessary to forge through complex or new material or experiences; however, *self-integration* is the ability to sustain behaviors that are congruent with a person's goal and can influence coping skills (i.e., conscious volitional efforts to regulate emotion, cognition, behavior, physiology, and the environment in response to stressful events or circumstances) (Sullivan, 2010).

Bandura (1977) referred to introjection as a form of verbal persuasion that contributes to corrective performance, and further suggested that social persuasion, a benefit of connectedness, can facilitate sustained effort. One successful method of working through introjection involves performing a self-analytic evaluation to determine feelings about the difficulty (Schlesinger & Wolitzky, 2002).

There are many instruments, such as surveys and questionnaires (e.g., the Positive and Negative Affect Schedule, the Academic Coping Strategies Scale, and various EI tests), that may assist you in identifying tendencies of disengagement. These assessments can lead to an understanding of stressors and the creation of adaptive coping skills, enabling the doctoral student to maintain cognitive control.

Questions for Reflection

Upon entering a doctoral program, it is essential to develop self-imposed strategies to sustain and direct goal-oriented actions, as well as maintain high-level cognitive function. To do this, it is important to assess what habits you have in place and what habits you need to develop by reflecting on the following questions:

- What are my diet, physical activity, and rest habits? Do they need to change to optimize functioning and overall well-being?
- What skills do I have for regulating my emotions?
- What skills or practices do I need to develop further to maximize cognitive processing, goal attainment, and social functioning?
- What messages do I tell myself? How can I better regulate my thinking to reach my goal of completing my doctoral journey?

Recommended Resources

Amen, D. G. (2005). *Making a good brain great.* Three Rivers Press. The Dana Foundation.

Ayres, Z. J. (2022). *Managing your mental health during your PhD: A survival guide.* Springer.

Chambers, L., McCrickerd, K., & Yeomans, M. R. (2015). Optimising foods for satiety. *Trends in Food Science & Technology, 41*(2), 149–160.
Dalton-Smith, S. (2017). *Sacred rest: Recover your life, renew your energy, restore your sanity.* Faithwork.
Harvard T. H. Chan School of Public Health (2023). Intuitive Eating Article (https://nutritionsource.hsph.harvard.edu/intuitive-eating/)
Kabat-Zinn, J. (2002). *Guided mindfulness meditation.* Sounds True. *Note:* There are Series 1, 2, and 3
Office of Disease Prevention and Health Promotion's Physical Activity Guidelines for Americans (https://health.gov/our-work/nutrition-physical-activity/physical-activity-guidelines/current-guidelines)
Wansink, B., & Sobal, J. (2007). Mindless eating: The 200 daily food decisions we overlook. *Environment and Behavior, 39*(1), 106–123.

References

Acharya, S., & Shukla, S. (2012). Mirror neurons: Enigma of the metaphysical modular brain. *J Nat Sci Biol Med, 3*(2), 118–124. doi: 10.4103/0976 9668.101878. PMID: 23225972; PMCID: PMC3510904.
Adams, C. (2019). Physical and mental health benefits of yoga, barre, Pilates & spinning. RIPPED.ME. https://ripped.me/physical-and-mental-health-benefits-of-yoga-barre-pilates-spinning/
Akyol, Z., & Garrison, D. R. (2011). Understanding cognitive presence in an online and blended community of inquiry: Assessing outcomes and processes for deep approaches to learning. *British Journal of Educational Technology, 42*(2), 233–250. https://doi.org/10.1111/j.1467-8535.2009.01029.x
Allen, H. K., Barrall, A. L., Vincent, K. B., & Arria, A. M. (2021). Stress and burnout among graduate students: Moderation by sleep duration and quality. *International Journal of Behavioral Medicine, 28*(1), 21–28. https://doi.org/10.1007/s12529-020-09867-8
Allen, H. K., Barrall, A. L., Vincent, K. B., & Arria, A. M. (2021). Stress and burnout among graduate students: Moderation by sleep duration and quality. *International Journal of Behavioral Medicine, 28*(1), 21–28. https://doi.org/10.1007/s12529-020-09867-8
Amen, D. G. (2005). *Making a good brain great.* Three Rivers Press.
Arab, L., & Ang, A. (2015). A cross sectional study of the association between walnut consumption and cognitive function among adult US populations represented in NHANES. *J Nutr Health Aging.* 2015 *19*(3), 284–290. doi: 10.1007/s12603-014-0569-2. PMID: 25732213..

Bandura, A. (1977). Self-efficacy: Toward a unifying theory of behavioral change. *Psychological Review*, *84*(2), 191–215.

Bar-on, R., Tranel, D., Denburg, N. L., & Bechara, A. (2003). Exploring the neurological substrate of emotional and social intelligence. *Brain*, *126*, 1790–1800.

Barber, L. K., Munz, D. C., Bagsby, P. G. and Powell, E. D. (2010). Sleep consistency and sufficiency are both necessary for reduced psychological strain. *Stress and Health*, *26*, 186–193. https://doi.org/10.1002/smi.1292

Barreira, P., Basilico, M., & Bolotnyy, V. (2020). *Graduate student mental health: Lessons from American economics departments*. Working Paper. Harvard University. https://scholar.harvard.edu/bolotnyy/publications/graduate-student-mental-health-lessons-american-economics-departments

Beijamini, F., Valentin, A., Jäger R., Born, J., & Diekelmann, S. 2021. Sleep Facilitates Problem Solving with No Additional Gain Through Targeted Memory Reactivation. *Front Behav Neurosci*. *15*:645110. doi: 10.3389/fnbeh.2021.645110. PMID: 33746720; PMCID: PMC7965947.

Beilharz, J. E., Maniam, J. & Morris, M. J. (2016). Short-term exposure to a diet high in fat and sugar, or liquid sugar, selectively impairs hippocampal-dependent memory, with differential impacts on inflammation. *Behavioural Brain Research*. *306*, 1–7.

Berthoud, H. R., Münzberg, H., & Morrison, C. D. (2017). Blaming the brain for obesity: Integration of hedonic and homeostatic mechanisms. *Gastroenterology*, *152*(7), 1728–1738.

Billman, G. (2020). Homeostasis: The underappreciated and far too often ignored central organizing principle of physiology. *Frontiers in Physiology*, *11*. doi: 10.3389/fphys.2020.00200.

Bolton, J. L. & Bilbo, S. D. (2014). Developmental programming of the brain and behavior by perinatal diet: Focus on inflammatory mechanisms. *Dialogues Clinical Neuroscience*, *16*, 307–320

Camilleri, G. M., Méjean, C., Bellisle, F., Andreeva, V. A., Kesse-Guyot, E., Hercberg, S., & Péneau, S. (2017). Intuitive eating dimensions were differently associated with food intake in the general population–based NutriNet-Santé study. *The Journal of Nutrition*, *147*(1), 61–69.

Carlson, O., Martin, B., Stote, K. S., Golden, E., Maudsley, S., Najjar, S. S., & Mattson, M. P. (2007). Impact of reduced meal frequency without caloric restriction on glucose regulation in healthy, normal-weight middle-aged men and women. *Metabolism Clinical and Experimental*, *56*, 1729–34.

Charles, S. T., Karnaze, M. M., & Leslie, F. M. (2022). Positive factors related to graduate student mental health. *Journal of American College Health*, *706*, 1858-1866. doi: 10.1080/07448481.2020.1841207

Chekroud, S. R., Gueorguieva, R., Zheutlin, A. B., Paulus, M., Krumholz, H. M., Krystal, J. H., & Chekroud, A. M. (2018). Association between physical exercise and mental health in 1.2 million individuals in the USA between 2011 and 2015: A cross-sectional study. *Lancet Psychiatry, 5*(9), 739–746. doi: 10.1016/S2215-0366(18)30227-X

Colcombe, S. J., Kramer, A. F., Erickson, K. I., Scalf, P., McAuley, E., Cohen, N. J., & Elavsky, S. (2004). Cardiovascular fitness, cortical plasticity, and aging. *PNAS, 101*(9), 3316–21.

Cole, P. M., Martin, S. E., & Dennis, T. A. (2004). Emotion regulation as a scientific construct: Methodological challenges and directions for child development research. *Child Development, 75*, 317–33.

Cooper, S. J. (2005). Donald O. Hebb's synapse and learning rule: A history and commentary. *Neuroscience and Biobehavioral Reviews, 28*, 851–74.

Cronin-Golomb, L., & Bauer, P. (2023). Self-motivated and directed learning across the lifespan. *Acta Psychologica, 232*, 103816. doi: 10.1016/j.actpsy.2022.103816

Dalton-Smith, S. (2017). *Sacred rest: Recover your life, renew your energy, restore your sanity.* Faithwork.

D'Anci, K. E., Watts, K. L., Kanarek, R. B., & Taylor, H. A. (2009). Low-carbohydrate weight-loss diets: Effects on cognition and mood. *Appetite, 52*, 96–103.

Deci, E. L., Eghrari, H., Patrick, B. C., & Leone, D. R. (1994). Facilitating internalization: The self-determination theory perspective. *Journal of Personality, 62*(1), 119–42.

Deng Y, Rong S, & Cheng G, et al. (2022). Association between adherence to three healthy dietary patterns and risk of cognitive disorders: Meta-analysis. *Wei Sheng Yan Jiu. 51*(5),725–732. doi:10.19813/j.cnki.weishengyanjiu.2022.05.009

Dreisbach, G., & Goschke, T. (2004). How positive affect modulates cognitive control: reduced perseveration at the cost of increased distractibility. *Journal of Experimental Psychology, 30*(2), 343–53.

Duckworth, A. L., Peterson, C., Matthews, M. D., & Kelly, D. R. (2007). Grit: Perseverance and passion for long-term goals. *Journal of Personality and Social Psychology, 92*(6), 1087.

Evans, T. M., Bira, L., Gastelum, J. B., Weiss, L. T., & Vanderford, N. L. (2018). Evidence for a mental health crisis in graduate education. *Nature Biotechnology, 36*(3), 282–284. doi: https://doi.org/10.1038/nbt.4089

Flaherty, C. (2018). New study says graduate students' mental health is a "crisis." *Inside Higher Ed.* www.insidehighered.com/news/2018/03/06/new-study-says-graduate-students-mental-health-crisis

Gailliot, M. T. (2008). Unlocking the energy dynamics of executive functioning: Linking executive functioning to brain glycogen. *Association for Psychological Science, 3*(4), 245–63.

Ghrouz, A. K., Noohu, M. M., Dilshad Manzar, M., Warren Spence, D., BaHammam, A. S., & Pandi-Perumal, S. R. (2019). Physical activity, sleep quality, and mental health among college students *Sleep Breath, 23*(2), 627–34. doi: 10.1007/s11325-019-01780-z.

González Olmo B. M., Butler M. J., & Barrientos R. M. (2021). Evolution of the human diet and its impact on gut microbiota, immune responses, and brain health. *Nutrients, 13*(1), 196. doi:10.3390/nu13010196

Graves, R. J, Williams, S. G, Hauff, C., Fruh, S. M., Sims, B., Hudson, G. M., McDermott, R. C., Sittig, S., Shaw, T., Campbell, M., Barinas, J. L., & Hall, H. R. (2022). Undergraduate versus graduate nursing students: Differences in nutrition, physical activity, and self-reported body mass index. *J Am Coll Health, 70*(7), 1941–1946. doi: 10.1080/07448481.2020.1842421

Gros, B. (2003). The impact of digital games in education. *First Monday, a peer-reviewed journal on the Internet.* https://mackenty.org/images/uploads/impact_of_games_in_education.pdf.

Hardy, J. (2006). Speaking clearly: A critical review of the self-talk literature. *Psychology of Sport and Physical Activity, 7,* 81–97.

Herbert, C., Meixner, F., Wiebking, C., & Gilg, V. (2020). Regular physical activity, short-term exercise, mental health, and well-being among university students: The results of an online and a laboratory study. *Frontier Psychology, 11,* 509. doi: 10.3389/fpsyg.2020.00509

Hillman, C. H., Erickson, K. L., & Kramer, A. F. (2008). Be smart, exercise your heart: Exercise effects on brain and cognition. *Nature Reviews/Neuroscience, 9*(1), 58–65.

Hish, A. J., Nagy, G. A., Fang, C. M., Kelley, L., Nicchitta, C. V., Dzirasa, K., & Rosenthal, M. Z. (2019). Applying the stress process model to stress–burnout and stress–depression relationships in biomedical doctoral students: A cross-sectional pilot study. *CBE—Life Sciences Education, 18*(4), ar51.

Huber, R., Ghilardi, M. F., Massimini, M., & Tononi, G. (2004). Local sleep and learning. *Nature, 430,* (6995), 78–81.

Igase, M., Mizoguchi, T., Ogushi, Y., Miki, T., & Ueki, A. (2010). Brain aging and nutrition. *Anti-aging Medicine, 7*(14), 167–73.

Jenkins, A. C., & Mitchell, J. P. (2011). How has cognitive neuroscience contributed to social psychological theory? In A. Todorov, S. T. Fiske, & D. A. Prentice (Eds.), *Social Neuroscience: Toward understanding the underpinnings of the social mind* (pp. 3–13). Oxford University Press.

Kahn, E. B., Ramsey, L. T., Brownson, R. C., Heath, G. W., Howze, E. H., Powell, K. E., Stone, E. J., Rajab, M. W., & Corso, P. (2002). The effectiveness of interventions to increase physical activity. A systematic review. *American Journal of Preventive Medicine, 22(4 Suppl)*: 73–107. doi: 10.1016/s0749-3797(02)00434-8

Jones-White, D. R., Soria, K. M., Tower, E. K., Horner, O. G. (2020). Factors associated with anxiety and depression among US doctoral students: Evidence from the gradSERU survey. *Journal of American College Health, 70*(8), 1–12.

LeDoux, J. (2002). *Synaptic self: How our brains become who we are.* Penguin Books.

Liu, C., Wang, L., Qi, R., Wang, W., Jia, S., Shang, D.,… & Yan, S. (2019). Prevalence and associated factors of depression and anxiety among doctoral students:

The mediating effect of mentoring relationships on the association between research self-efficacy and depression/anxiety. *Psychology Research and Behavior Management*, *12*, 195.

Madera, J., & Smith, B. (2009). The effects of leader negative emotions on evaluations of leadership in a crisis situation: The role of anger and sadness. *Leadership Quarterly*, *20*, 103–114. doi: 10.1016/j.leaqua.2009.01.007

Maquet, P. (2001). The role of sleep in learning and memory. *Science*, *294*(5544), 1048–52.

Mayer, J. D., Caruso, D. R., & Salovey, P. (2000). Emotional intelligence meets traditional standards for an intelligence. *Intelligence*, *27*(4), 267–98.

Mayo Clinic Staff. (2013). Meditation is a simple and effective way to reduce stress. Retrieved from http://www.mayoclinic.com/health/meditation/HQ01070

Medin, J., & Alexanderson, K. (2001). Health and health promotion—A literature study . Lund, Swedish: Studentlitteratur.

Meera D., Wright, S. T. & Beck Dallaghan, G. L. (2025). Exploring the role of cognitive capacity and adaptive learning in professional education: A scoping review. *Medical Science Educator*, *35*(2), 1123–36.

Mental Health. (2019). Pilates, a total mind and body workout. Retrieved from http://www.mentalhealthy.co.uk/home/about-us.

Nursing Assistant Central. (2008). 100 fascinating facts you never knew about the human brain. Retrieved from: http://www.nursingassistantcentral.com/blog/2008/100-fascinating-facts-you-never-knew-about-the-human-brain/

Ou, C., Lou, N. M., Maheshka, C., Shi, M., Takemura, K., Cheung, B. & Heine, S. J. (2025). Healthy sleep durations appear to vary across cultures. *Proceedings of the National Academy of Sciences of the United States of America*,*122*(19), e2419269122, https://doi.org/10.1073/pnas.2419269122

Piercy, K. L., & Troiano, R. P. (2018). Physical activity guidelines for Americans from the US Department of Health and Human Services: Cardiovascular benefits and recommendations, *Circulation: Cardiovascular Quality and Outcomes*, *11*, e005263. https://doi.org/10.1161/CIRCOUTCOMES.118.005263

Puri, S., Shaheen, M., & Grover, B. (2023). Nutrition and cognitive health: A life course approach. *Front Public Health*,*11*, 1023907. doi: 10.3389/fpubh.2023.1023907. PMID: 37050953; PMCID: PMC10083484.

Pyykkonen, B. A. (2021). Cognitive processes and the impact of stress upon doctoral students: Practical applications for doctoral programs. *Christian Higher Education*, *20*(1–2), 28–37. https://doi.org/10.1080/15363759.2020.1852134

Rethorst, C. D., Wipfli, B. M., & Landers, D. M. (2009). The antidepressive effects of physical activity: A meta-analysis of randomized trials. *Sports Medicine*, *39*(6), 491–511.

Saruhanjan, K., Zarski, A. C., Bauer, T., Baumeister, H., Cuijpers, P., Spiegelhalder, K., Auerbach, R. P., Kessler, R. C., Bruffaerts, R., Karyotaki, E., Berking, M., & Ebert, D. D.

(2021). Psychological interventions to improve sleep in college students: A meta-analysis of randomized controlled trials. *Journal of Sleep Research*, *30*(1):e13097. doi: 10.1111/jsr.13097. Epub 2020 Jul 16. PMID: 32672865.

Schlesinger, G., & Wolitzky, D. L. (2002). The effects of a self-analytic physical activity on clinical judgment. *Psychoanalytic Psychology*, *19*(4), 651–85.

Schmidt, M. & Umans, T. (2014). Experiences of well-being among female doctoral students in Sweden. *Int J Qual Stud Health Well-Being*; *9*:23059. doi: 10.3402/qhw.v9.23059. PMID: 24746246; PMCID: PMC3991832.

Society for Neuroscience. (2012). *Brain facts: A primer on the brain and nervous system* (7th ed.). Society for Neuroscience.

Stevenson, R. J., Francis, H. M., Attuquayefio, T., & Ockert, C. (2017). Explicit wanting and liking for palatable snacks are differentially affected by changes in physiological state and are differentially related to salivation and hunger. *Physiology & Behavior*, *182*, 101–6.

Sullivan, J. R. (2010). Preliminary psychometric data for the academic coping strategies scale. *Assessment for Effective Intervention*, *35*(2), 114–27.

Tanner, M. A., Travis, F., Gaylord-King, C., Haaga, D. A. F., Grosswald, S., & Schneider, R. H. (2009). The effects of the transcendental meditation program on mindfulness. *Journal of Clinical Psychology*, *65*(6), 574–89.

Taris, T. W., Schreurs, P. J. G., & Van Iersel-Van Silfhout, I. J. (2001). Job stress, job strain, and psychological withdrawal among Dutch university staff: Towards a dual process model for the effects of occupational stress. *Work & Stress*, *15*(4), 283–296. https://doi.org/10.1080/02678370110084049

Tester, N. J. & Jackson Fosse, J. (2018). Sleep as an occupational need. *American Journal of Occupational Therapy*, *72*(1), 7201347010p1–7201347010p4. https://doi.org/10.5014/ajot.2018.020651

Thompson, R. A. (1994). Emotional regulation: A theme in search of a definition (pp. 25–52), in N. A. Fox (Ed.), *The development of emotion regulation: Biological and behavioural considerations. Monographs of the Society for Research in Child Development*, Serial No. 240, Vol. 59, No. 2–3. University of Chicago Press.

Tomes, C. D. & Lewis, M. D. (2019). Effects of personal body armor on functional movement capability. *International Journal of Exercise Science*, *12*, 536–546. doi: 10.70252/PJNG8109

Tran, D. M. & Westbrook, R. F. (2017). A high-fat, high-sugar diet-induced impairment in place-recognition memory is reversible and training-dependent. *Appetite, 110*, 61–71.

Turner, J. (2011). Your brain on food: A nutrient-rich diet can protect cognitive health. *Journal of the American Society on Aging*, *35*(2), 99–106.

Vancini, R. L., Rayes, A. B. R., Lira, C. A. B., Sarro, K. J., & Andrade, M. S. (2017). Pilates and aerobic training improve levels of depression, anxiety, and quality of life in overweight and obese individuals. *Archives of Neuropsychiatry*, *75*, 850–857. doi: 10.1590/0004-282X20170149 van den Berg, N.H., Smith, D., Fang, Z., Pozzobon, A., Toor, B., Al-Kuwatli, J., Ray, L., & Fogel, S. M. (2023). Sleep strengthens resting-state functional communication between brain areas involved in the consolidation of problem-solving skills. *Learn Mem*, *30*(1), 25–35. doi: 10.1101/lm.053638.122. PMID: 36669853; PMCID: PMC9872190.

Van Dyke, N., & Drinkwater, E. J. (2014). Review article relationships between intuitive eating and health indicators: Literature review. *Public Health Nutrition, 17(8)*, 1757–66.

van Gelderen, M. (2012). Perseverance strategies of enterprising individuals. *International Journal of Entrepreneurial Behaviour & Research*, *18*(6), 630–48.

Vaynman, S., & Gomez-Pinilla, F. (2006). Revenge of the "sit": How lifestyle impacts neuronal and cognitive health through molecular systems that interface energy metabolism with neuronal plasticity. *Journal of Neuroscience Research*, *84*, 699–715.

Warren, J. M., Smith, N., & Ashwell, M. (2017). A structured literature review on the role of mindfulness, mindful eating, and intuitive eating in changing eating behaviours: Effectiveness and associated potential mechanisms. *Nutrition Research Reviews*, *30*(2), 272–83.

Watson, N. F., Badr, M. S., Belenky, G., Bliwise, D. L., Buxton, O. M., Buysse, D., Dinges, D. F., Gangwisch, J., Grandner, M. A., Kushida, C., Malhotra, R. K., Martin, J. L., Patel, S. R., Quan, S. F., & Tasali, E. (2015). Recommended amount of sleep for a healthy adult: A joint consensus statement of the American Academy of Sleep Medicine and Sleep Research Society. *Sleep*, *38*(6), 843–44. doi: 10.5665/sleep.4716. PMID: 26039963; PMCID: PMC4434546.

Wills, T. A., & Shinar, O. (2000). Measuring perceived and received social support. In: S., Cohen, L. G., Underwood, B. H., Gottlieb (Eds.). *Social support measurement and intervention: a guide for health and social scientists*. Oxford University Press.

Winter, B., Breitenstein, C., Mooren, F. C., Voelker, K., Fobker, M., Lechtermann, A., Krueger, K., Fromme, A., Korsukewitz, C., Floel, A., & Knecht, S. (2006). High-impact running improves learning. *Neurobiology of Learning and Memory*, *87*, 597–609.

Woolston, C. (2019, August 30). A better future for graduate-student mental health. *Nature*. https://doi.org/10.1038/d41586-019-02584-7

Wurtman, R. J., Cansev, M., Sakamoto, T., & Ulus, I. (2010). Nutritional modifiers of aging brain function: Use of uridine and other phosphatide precursors to increase formation of brain synapses. *Nutrition Reviews*, *68*(2), 88–101.

Yang, K. M., & Smallfield, S. (2020). Exploring sleep health among occupational therapy students. *Journal of Occupational Therapy Education*, *4*(1). https://doi.org/10.26681/jote.2020.040108

Zelazo, P. D., & Lyons, K. E. (2011). Mindfulness training in childhood. *Human Development*, *54*, 61–65.

Part 2
The Knowledge and Skill Development Stage

8 Overcoming Stress and Burnout

John J. S. Harrichand, PhD
Christine Mayorga, MA

Introduction

A doctoral degree is one of the highest academic degrees (Cornwall et al., 2019). However, the stress that doctoral students face is substantial (Powers & Swick, 2012), and there is growing recognition that students' mental health issues are a concern globally (Byrom et al., 2022). While stress can result in positive outcomes throughout the doctoral experience, it can also have negative effects. Positive stress, or *eustress* (Lazarus, 1974), refers to stress that facilitates productivity and achievement. Eustress can be a motivator to produce, complete tasks, and seek excellence. Stress can compel doctoral students to progress in their program and, ultimately, finish their degrees.

Alternatively, *distress*, when doctoral students are overwhelmed by stress and pressures to perform exceed their capacity, or perceived capacity, to produce, is detrimental in the doctoral journey (Kofoworola & Alayode, 2012). The human body is not made to function under constant distress that is often inherent in the doctoral journey due to the relentless demands of course work and the dissertation. For doctoral students, distress, especially when chronic, can have negative consequences on biologically, psychologically, and social functioning, resulting in medical, mental health, and social problems (American Psychological Association [APA], 2022; Clay, 2011; Shrand, 2012). Stress can also result in high attrition across doctoral programs (Cornwall et al., 2019; Powers & Swick, 2012).

Thus, this chapter discusses stress, and its consequences, with the aim of providing doctoral students with strategies to manage the stress to mitigate mental, physical, and social problems that threaten a successful doctoral journey.

The Case of Xochitl

Xochitl is a first-generation Mexican American student who relocated with her partner to pursue a PhD. Initially, she felt confident in her ability to succeed, having graduated with honors in her master's program while balancing an internship, classes, a full-time job, and newlywed life. However, this confidence diminished as a doctoral student. Xochitl began to experience imposter syndrome, feeling that she didn't belong in the program and questioning her skill and intellect. She began to engage in negative self-talk and seeking perfection. Her inability to meet her unrealistic expectations caused her to procrastinate on assignments. She began to experience burnout, headaches, dizziness, and stomach aches. Xochitl's mental and physical health declined. She did not seek support and remained unaware of the support resources available at the university. She began distancing herself from her peers, professors, and even her partner. Although she made it through her first semester, Xochitl started questioning whether she could continue in the program, realizing that if she continued this path, she wouldn't make it through the second year of the program. She even began feeling indifferent toward her doctoral work.

What the Research Says

Positive stress, *eustress*, can be a motivating force that enhances productivity and results in a successful doctoral journey. For example, eustress can result in motivation to work on a manuscript for journal submission. Distress, however, inhibits success in the doctoral journey (Kofoworola & Alayode, 2012).

The body's stress response originally evolved for the purpose of survival. When a treat is perceived, the body initiates a physiological reaction. This stress response begins with increased breathing and a release of fat and glucose into the bloodstream. Heart rate rapidly increases, causing rises in blood pressure, and the blood races to the brain away from other parts of the body. The body prepares to move into action preparing for fight, flight, or freeze (Shrand, 2012).

The stress response is activated, usually, in emergency situations. For example, this stress response is activated if an individual is being chased by a wild animal or hears a fire alarm. It can also be activated due to challenges like academic pressures and financial strain (APA, 2022). Once the danger is mitigated, normal physiological processes are automatically resumed. When the threat does not recede, the stress response is chronically activated (Shrand, 2012). Unfortunately, the academic pressures within a doctoral program coupled with other responsibilities, like those Xochitl faced (e.g., family, job) often result in ongoing stress across the time spent in the program.

The human body is not made to function under constant distress, and chronic stress. This type of stress affects cognitive functions like memory, attention, and decision-making, ultimately impairing performance and well-being (Pyykkonen, 2021). Chronic stress can lead to various health and mental health problems, including heart disease, anxiety, and depression (APA, 2022).

Stress is an intrinsic aspect of doctoral education across all fields and all program types (Pyykkonen, 2021) as doctoral training is inherently demanding and significantly drains personal resources such as time, finances, and relationships. Doctoral students are often overwhelmed by these demands in a manner that exceeds the capacity, or perceived capacity, to produce and perform (Kofoworola & Alayode, 2012). The stress can become chronic and accumulated (APA, 2022).

Doctoral students balance a multitude of personal, professional, societal, and academic roles and responsibilities, each demanding a significant amount of attention, time, and commitment (Spaulding & Rockinson-Szapkiw, 2012).

Doctoral students often poise themselves between the dynamic and commanding responsibilities of marriage, parenting, life-cycle transitions (e.g., caring for aging parents), employment, health, relationships, financial responsibilities, and other commitments (Harrichand et al., 2020). Upon entering the doctoral program, doctoral students add required academic roles, assignments, research, requisite skills, tasks, deadlines, and professional relationships. While each role and responsibility in and of itself requires a reasonable amount of demand, the composite mass can result in chronic and cumulative stress.

The reality, however, is that a large majority of doctoral students report stress and mental health concerns such as depression, during their journeys, with 10% reporting thoughts of suicide (Fogg, 2009). The situation is further compounded by doctoral students' lack of sharing of concerns with those around them for fear of being seen as inadequate and incapable of holding up under the pressure (Fogg, 2009). Doctoral students are also unaware of resources to assist with their stress and related concerns.

Burnout

Stress unattended or accumulated over time has the potential to result in burnout (Fogg, 2009). Researchers such as Nagy et al. (2019) have discovered that doctoral students often experience burnout and consequentially develop mental health challenges. Burnout is attributed to the high academic pressure, isolation, and lack of mentorship of doctoral students. McAlpine et al. (2020) noted poor balance across personal, work, and academic life can result in increased susceptibility of burnout among PhD students.

Burnout was originally defined as a state of fatigue or frustration resulting from dedication to a cause, way of life, or relationship that failed to produce the desired outcome. Burnout is a psychological syndrome characterized by "emotional exhaustion, depersonalization, and reduced personal accomplishment" (Maslach et al., 1996, p. 4). Warning signs of burnout are inclusive of medical problems, low immunity, anxiety (e.g., feeling tense, irritable, agitated, fearful, tired), depression (e.g., feeling hopeless, guilty, ashamed, disinterested, sleep and weight changes, and thoughts of suicide), interpersonal problems, and decreased overall functioning (Clay, 2011). The consequences of doctoral students' burnout may also include reduced job performance, diminished productivity, and lower work quality. In severe cases, this may lead students to leave their programs or withdraw from academic pursuits altogether (Galdino et al., 2016; Maslach & Leiter, 2016). Watching for these signs throughout the course of the doctoral journey is vitally important. Moreover, it is important that doctoral students develop a plan to mitigate stress and burnout, especially during doctoral stages that are demanding.

Although the doctoral journey is demanding in general, there are phases when doctoral students incur increased stress. These times coincide with habitually intensified dropout rates and include the period following the first year, before finishing coursework, and during the dissertation phase (Gardner, 2009). Moreover, experiences of work overload, lack of control, insufficient reward, and value conflict during the doctoral journey increase the likelihood of burnout (Maslach & Leiter, 2016).

- *Work Overload.* Doctoral students often face intense pressure to balance research, coursework, internships, and other academic obligations, coupled with community, vocational, and family responsibility, leading to exhaustion and stress.
- *Lack of Control.* Many doctoral students experience limited control over their academic progress, feeling constrained by rigid deadlines, high expectations, and a lack of autonomy in their research.
- *Insufficient Reward.* Many doctoral students perceive that their mentors and chairs fail to recognize their efforts—with accomplishments going unnoticed or undervalued—which can diminish both motivation and overall satisfaction.
- *Value Conflict.* Studies on the doctoral experience demonstrate that a perceived fit or misfit influences doctoral students' experience and program completion (Golde, 2005). Golde (2005) found that a misfit between doctoral students' goals and the practices within their scholarly community affected their persistence. A perceived misfit between doctoral students' goals and the program goals may also contribute to student attrition (Golde, 1998). This is one reason why it is important for doctoral students to understand the difference between the research doctorate and professional doctorate and choose a program model that is consistent with their professional goals (see Chapter 1: Choosing the Right Program Model: Research or Professional Doctorate).

Strategies for Success

Experts recommend that doctoral students have multiple sources and tools to mitigate the negative effects of stress and burnout (Marinšuo & Turkulainen, 2011). Developing wellness and *academic resilience*, the ability to succeed in an educational setting despite exposure to risk factors (Morales, 2008), and building relevant competencies (Gibson et al., 2021) are evidence-based tools that you can employ. According to Myers et al. (2000), *wellness* is defined as "a way of life oriented toward optimal health and well-being in which body, mind, and spirit are integrated by the individual to live more fully within the human and natural community" (p. 252). Wellness is an active, positive process in which the doctoral student intentionally chooses to cultivate optimal functioning across multiple dimensions (Perera & Moe, 2020). The following are strategies for success for doctoral students drawn from the wellness and resilience research (Brien et al., 2021; Gibson et al., 2021).

Strategy 1: Set Realistic Expectations

Set realistic expectations, for failing to do so can result in negative consequences. Xochitl expected too much from herself in a short period of time without accounting for her varied roles and responsibilities. This resulted in her diminished self-confidence and procrastination. If Xochitl had set realistic expectations by acknowledging her limits, she may have avoided burnout.

Strategy 2: Set Boundaries

You can define what you need to feel healthy and secure when you need it and communicate and create tools to ensure these needs are met (Ennenbach, 2014). Accepting that she is most productive when she can work on doctoral assignments when given a large amount of time (e.g., insight and self-awareness), Xochitl may set times and days for when she prefers to rest and prefer to work on assignments. However, she also recognizes that her partner has needs related to spending time together, resting, and working, so Xochitl may communicate with her partner her needs as well as discuss boundaries around time that works for both of them (Davila et al., 2017; Ennenbach, 2014). Xochitl may also set boundaries with her peers, communicating when she wants them to contact her (e.g., no phone calls after 10 p.m.).

Strategy 3: Control Your Time

Take control of your schedule. Prioritize important things and manage time effectively. Time must be scheduled to complete academic responsibilities, spend time with family and friends, and practice care of self. Powers and Swick (2012) advised compiling important dates and setting deadlines that optimize stress rather than promote excessive stress or distress. Xochitl may minimize stress if she creates a planner where she schedules academic assignments, family responsibilities, and even time for herself.

Strategy 4: Foster Community

A supportive community provides a safe space where you can share your experiences and feel understood, reducing feelings of isolation, like Xochitl experienced. Xochitl may have developed relationships with her peers in the program, meeting regularly for coffee or in a virtual environment, to remind her that her peers had struggles similar to hers (see Chapter 9: Creating a Scholarly Community). Xochitl can also prioritize spending time with her partner, friends, and family to maintain strong connections in her personal life and reduce stress.

Strategy 5: Set and Remember Goals

It is normal to experience complacency and indifference, as did Xochitl. The first year of the journey eroded Xochitl's purpose, so she no longer cared about finishing her degree. This apathy trap can be sidestepped, at least in part, by writing down the reason for pursuing a doctorate and placing it in a visible location.

Strategy 6: Develop a Wellness Plan

You need to plan for and engage in stress management strategies including but not limited to practicing mindfulness, getting sleep, and engaging in physical activity (see Chapter 7: Creating a Personal Wellness Plan). Xochitl designates time for walking, swimming, listening to a mediation app, and engaging in her favorite hobbies to decrease her stress. She practices her spirituality through daily prayer, which helps her stay grounded. She also finds hope in her belief in a higher power, which guides her through life's obstacles.

Strategy 7: Use University Resources and Seek Professional Help

Whether an online or residential student, most universities help doctoral students navigate their transition into doctoral life including professional counseling, tutoring, statistics labs, and a variety of student organizations.

Xochitl may have avoided burnout if she had familiarized herself with university resources within year one of her program and began seeing a counselor to assist her with her transition into a doctoral program.

Questions for Reflection

- What is my reason for pursuing a doctoral degree?
- What are the one or two things I want to prioritize in my personal life and my academic life?
- What tools can I employ to organize my time (e.g., planner, online calendar) to decrease stress and mitigate burnout, while prioritizing the things I value and need?
- What do I need to feel healthy and secure, when do I need it, and what strategies do I need to employ to ensure my needs are met?
- What are my specific needs (e.g., alone time, regular meals, weekly book club) that if not met leave me feeling depleted?
- What boundaries do I need to set concerning my needs and values? To whom do I need to communicate these?
- What may be "red flags" mentally, emotionally, and socially that I am stressed or experiencing burnout? Do I have psychosomatic issues, such as Xochitl experienced, including headaches, body tension, and insomnia? Do I feel exhausted no matter how much sleep I get? Do I lack motivation to attend classes or start assignments? Do I lash out at others? Do I lack inspiration and creativity for projects and class discussions? Do I lack confidence in academic abilities? Do I engage in bad habits such as overeating, staying up too late, nail biting? Am I having trouble concentrating on schoolwork or lectures?
- What tools can I use to cope with stress and burnout?
- What strategies can I use in creating a wellness plan for my doctoral journey?
- What type of support do I need from my family and friends?
- What professional and university resources can I access to prevent stress and burnout?

Recommended Resources

Books

Doyle, R., & Robertson, F. (2023). *The PhD handbook: How to take care of yourself, your research project and your future*. Open University Press.

Smith, A. (2001). *The wellness manual*. Ebook-case.com

Articles

Martínez-García, I., De Witte, H., García-Martínez, J., & Cano-García, F. J. (2024). A systematic review and a comprehensive approach to PhD students' well-being. *Applied Psychology: Health and Well-Being, 16*(4), 1–19. https://doi.org/10.1111/aphw.12541

Mercer, J., & Thomas, J. (2024). How understanding doctoral researchers' coping strategies can inform higher education institutions' response to their stress. *Research in Post-Compulsory Education, 29*(1), 117–137. https://doi.org/10.1080/13596748.2023.2285632

Ripp, J. A., Privitera, M. R., West, C. P., Leiter, R., Logio, L., Shapiro, J., & Bazari, H. (2017). Well-being in graduate medical education: A call for action. *Academic Medicine: Journal of the Association of American Medical Colleges, 92*(7), 914–917. https://doi.org/10.1097/ACM.0000000000001735

Online Resources

Barna, G. (1989). *Grad resources*. https://gradresources.org

Community LLC. (2018). *PhD balance*. https://www.phdbalance.com/pdb-community-only

Chi Sigma Iota. (n.d.). *Wellness in counseling*. https://www.csi-net.org/group/wellness

Miller, A. (2000). *The dissertation coach*. https://www.thedissertationcoach.com

Myers, J. E., & Sweeney, T. J. (2005). *Personal wellness plan*. https://cdn.ymaws.com/www.csi-net.org/resource/dynamic/blogs/20170305_191138_25050.pdf

Wheel of life. (2024). Retrieved from https://goal-life.com/en/

Apps

Acton, M. & Tew, A. (2012). *Calm*. (Version 6.54) [Mobile app]

Lee, M. & Lee, A. (2005). *MyFitnessPal*. (Version 24.39.0) [Mobile app]

Puddicombe, A. & Pierson, R. (2010). *Headspace*. (Version 3.339.0) [Mobile app]

References

American Psychological Association. (2022, October 21). *How stress affects your health*. https://www.apa.org/topics/stress/health#:~:text=This%20can%20put%20you%20at,and%20memory%20and%20concentration%20impairment

Brien, D. L., Batty, C., Ellison, E., & Owens, A. (Eds.). (2021). *The doctoral experience: Student stories from the creative arts and humanities*. Palgrave Macmillan.

Byrom, N. C., Dinu, L., Kirkman, A., & Hughes, G. (2022). Predicting stress and mental wellbeing among doctoral researchers. *Journal of Mental Health*, *31*(6), 783–791. https://doi.org/10.1080/09638237.2020.1818196

Clay, R. A. (2011). Is stress getting to you? *Monitor on Psychology*, *42*(1), 58. Retrieved from http://www.apa.org/monitor/2011/01/stress.aspx

Cornwall, J., Mayland, E. C., van der Meer, J., Spronken-Smith, R. A., Tustin, C., & Blyth, P. (2019). Stressors in early-stage doctoral students. *Studies in Continuing Education*, *41*(3), 363–380. https://doi.org/10.1080/0158037X.2018.1534821

Davila, J., Mattanah, J., Bhatia, V., Latack, J. A., Feinstein, B. A., Eaton, N. R., Daks, J. S., Kumar, S. A., Lomash, E. F., McCormick, M., & Zhou, J. (2017). Romantic competence, healthy relationship functioning, and well-being in emerging adults. *Personal Relationships*, *24*(1), 162–184. https://doi.org/10.1111/pere.12175

Ennenbach, M. (2014). *Buddhist psychotherapy: A guideline for positive changes*. Lotus Press.

Fogg, P. (2009). Grad-school blues. *Chronicle of Higher Education*, *55*(24), B12–B16. https://research.ebsco.com/linkprocessor/plink?id=e0e04c18-2b13-3f46-b0d0-981f363645af

Galdino, M. J. Q., Martins, J. T., Haddad, M. D. C. F. L., Robazzi, M. L. D. C. C., & Birolim, M. M. (2016). Burnout syndrome among master's and doctoral students in nursing. *Acta Paulista de Enfermagem*, *29*(1), 100–106. https://doi.org/10.1590/1982-0194201600014

Gardner, S. K. (2009). Conceptualizing success in doctoral education: Perspectives of faculty in seven disciplines. *Review of Higher Education: Journal of the Association for the Study of Higher Education*, *32*(3), 383–406. https://doi.org/10.1353/rhe.0.0075

Gibson, D. M., Pence, C., Kennedy, S. D., Gerlach, J., Degges-White, S., & Watson, J. (2021). Development of the counselor wellness competencies. *Journal of Counselor Leadership and Advocacy*, *8*(2), 130–145. https://doi.org/10.1080/2326716X.2021.1925997

Golde, C. M. (1998). Beginning graduate school: Explaining first-year doctoral attrition. In M. S. Anderson (Ed.), *The experience of being in graduate school: An exploration* (pp. 55–64). Jossey Bass.

Golde, C. M. (2005). The role of the department and discipline in doctoral student attrition: Lessons from four departments. *Journal of Higher Education, 76*(6), 669–700. https://doi.org/10.1080/00221546.2005.11772304

Harrichand, J. J. S., Kirk, K. E., & Mwendwa, J. M. (2020). Deepa's discovery: An examination of intersectionality when multiple identities collide – Managing family roles, doctoral work, and clashing Eurocentric worldviews. In B. King, & T. Stewart (Eds.), *Cases on cross-cultural counseling strategies* (pp. 192–218). IGI Global. https://doi.org/10.4018/978-1-7998-0022-4.ch010

Hunter, K. H., & Devine, K. (2016). Doctoral students' emotional exhaustion and intentions to leave academia. *International Journal of Doctoral Studies, 11*, 35–61. http://ijds.org/Volume11/IJDSv11p035061Hunter2198.pdf

Hyatt-Burkhart, D. (2020). Counselor self-care and personal development. In L. L. Levers & D. Hyatt-Burkhart (Eds.), *Clinical mental health counseling: Practicing in integrated systems of care* (pp. 281–305). Springer.

Katerndahl, D. A., & Parchman, M. (2002). The ability of the stress process model to explain mental health outcomes. *Comprehensive Psychiatry, 43*(5), 351–360. https://doi.org/10.1053/comp.2002.34626

Kofoworola, O., & Alayode, A. (2012). Strategies for managing stress for optimal job performance. *International Journal of Psychological Studies, 4*(2), 162–68. https://doi.org/10.5539/ijps.v4n2p162

Lazarus, R. S. (1974). Psychological stress and coping in adaptation and illness. *International Journal of Psychiatry in Medicine, 5*, 321–33. https://doi.org/10.2190/t43t-84p3-qdur-7rtp

Marinšuo, M., & Turkulainen, V. (2011). Personal commitment, support, and progress in doctoral studies. *Studies in Higher Education, 36*(1), 103–120. https://doi.org/10.1080/03075070903469598

Maslach, C., Jackson, S. E., & Leiter, M. P. (1996). *Maslach Burnout Inventory manual.* Mountain View.

Maslach, C., & Leiter, M. P. (2016). Burnout. In G. Fink (Ed.), *Stress: Concepts, cognition, emotion, and behavior* (pp. 351–357). Academic Press. https://doi.org/10.1016/B978-0-12-800951-2.00044-3

McAlpine, L., Skakni, I., & Pyhältö, K. (2020). PhD experience (and progress) is more than work: Life-work relations and reducing exhaustion (and cynicism). *Studies in Higher Education, 47*(2), 352–366. https://doi.org/10.1080/03075079.2020.1744128

Morales, E. E. (2008). Academic resilience in retrospect: Following up a decade later. *Journal of Hispanic Higher Education, 7*(3), 228–248. https://doi.org/10.1177/1538192708317119

Myers, J. E., Luecht, R. M., & Sweeney, T. J. (2004). The factor structure of wellness: Reexamining theoretical and empirical models underlying the Wellness Evaluation of Lifestyle (WEL) and the five-factor Wel. *Measurement and Evaluation*

in Counseling and Development, 36(4), 194–208. https://doi.org/10.1080/07481756.2004.11909742
Myers, J., Sweeney, T., & Witmer, J. (2000). The wheel of wellness counseling for wellness: A holistic model for treatment planning. *Journal of Counseling & Development, 78*(3), 251–266. https://doi.org/10.1002/j.1556-6676.2000.tb01906.x
Nagy, G. A., Fang, C. M., Hish, A. J., Kelly, L., Nicchitta, C. V., Dzirasa, K., & Rosenthal, M. Z. (2019). Burnout and mental health problems in biomedical doctoral students. *CBE life sciences education, 18*(2), 1–14. https://doi.org/10.1187/cbe.18-09-0198
Perera, D. M., & Moe, J. (2020). The wellness treatment plan. In W. W. Ishak (Ed.), *The handbook of wellness medicine* (pp. 45–56). Cambridge University Press.
Powers, J., & Swick, D. (2012). Straight talk from recent grads: Tips for successfully surviving your doctoral program. *Journal of Social Work Education, 48*(2), 389–394. https://doi.org/10.5175/JSWE.2012.201000073
Pyykkonen, B. A. (2021). Cognitive processes and the impact of stress upon doctoral students: Practical applications for doctoral programs. *Christian Higher Education, 20*(1–2), 28–37. https://doi.org/10.1080/15363759.2020.1852134
Rico, Y., & Bunge, E. L. (2020). Stress and burnout in psychology doctoral students. *Psychology, Health & Medicine, 26*(2), 177–183. https://doi.org/10.1080/13548506.2020.1842471
Shrand, J. (2012). *Managing your stress*. St. Martin's Press.
Spaulding, L. S., & Rockinson-Szapkiw, A. J. (2012). Hearing their voices: Factors doctoral candidates attribute to their persistence. *International Journal of Doctoral Studies, 7*, 199–219. https://www.ijds.org/Volume7/IJDSv7p199-219Spaulding334.pdf
Waight, E., & Giordano, A. (2018). Doctoral students' access to non-academic support for mental health. *Journal of Higher Education Policy and Management, 40*(4), 390–412. https://doi.org/10.1080/1360080X.2018.1478613

9 Creating a Scholarly Community

Alfred P. Rovai, PhD

Amanda J. Rockinson, EdD, PhD

Introduction

Becoming an independent scholar is an essential part of the doctoral process and its successful completion. Independence and self-direction can be challenging for many students who have become accustomed to the structure and support provided by their previous educational experiences. Solitude and independence can feel lonely and isolating. As such, building community and integrating into an academic community becomes vital. As the rigorous demands of independent research and uncertainties of academia can take an emotional toll on most doctoral students, a strong and supportive community of faculty and peers who understand the doctoral journey can serve as a lifeline, encouraging a sense of belonging, and providing knowledge needed to persist and overcome obstacles. Community is fundamental to the development of a doctoral scholar and the social and psychological support necessary for successful doctoral completion (Corcelles-Seuba et al., 2023; Owens et al., 2020).

Gardner (2008) described the ultimate paradox in doctoral education, as expressed by a student, "If someone holds your hand too much, you will never learn to think for yourself, and if someone does not hold your hand enough, you will fall flat on your face" (p. 327). Success in the doctoral journey is rooted not only in learning to become a self-directed learner but also in integrating into and building a strong community. Building community begins during the Knowledge and Skill Stage, carrying doctoral students through to the completion of the Inquiry Stage.

Research highlights the importance of community and integration in academic programs and communities (e.g., Holmes & Rockinson-Szapkiw, 2020; Rovai, 2002; Rockinson-Szapkiw et al., 2019). Both are related to academic program satisfaction, learning, and persistence (Rovai, 2002; Davidson & Wilson, 2013; Rockinson-Szapkiw et al., 2016). Unfortunately, doctoral students' perceived community is often less than desirable (Terrell et al., 2009), resulting in high attrition rates. The purpose of this chapter is to discuss the importance of a scholarly community, collegial support, and integration.

Case Study

Asma is enrolled in a PhD program in physics. She successfully completed her coursework with a high grade point average and selected a dissertation committee consisting of faculty members with whom she had positive relationships as course professors. She emails her committee members each week with multiple questions and moves forward only after she has clear and precise direction.

However, Asma is struggling to complete her dissertation proposal. She feels that part of her problem is due to conflict and miscommunication within her dissertation committee, as well as delays in receiving precise answers to her numerous questions. At times, the feedback she receives reflects conflicting views and priorities, posing questions rather than providing answers to her questions. She no longer feels closely connected to committee members and believes some members may even be avoiding her. Consequently, she is becoming increasingly isolated and less motivated to continue her doctoral studies.

What the Research Says

Learning aspirations are strong enough to attract adults to a higher education program but not to retain them (Ashar & Skenes, 1993). Volition is the mediating force between intentions and behaviors that facilitates learning (Corno & Kanfer, 1993). Accordingly, volition is thoughts and behaviors that are directed toward maintaining one's intention to attain a specific goal in the face of distractions. While motivation initiates and directs action, volition maintains a course of action when obstacles arise. Heckhausen and Kuhl (1985) depicted volition as a psychological state characterized by thoughts about implementing goals into action, emphasizing self-regulation in the context of persistence. Like Ashar and Skenes (1993), Heckhausen and Kuhl (1985) asserted that initial motivation may be sufficient for students to enroll in doctoral programs. However, students may encounter declining motivation, particularly in the face of adversity.

At this point, volitional processes become important in explaining persistence. This theoretical framework posits that doctoral students have psychological needs, and the satisfaction of these needs influences their behavior. A social support system influences how well these needs are met. Although universities have a responsibility to assist students with fulfilling their goals, students also have a responsibility and obligation to take initiative to meet their goals. Being integrated, socialized, and part of a strong, supportive community can help students sustain motivation and complete the doctoral journey.

Terrell et al. (2009) reported doctoral candidates' perceived levels of *connectedness* (a term associated with community, integration, and socialization) and satisfaction in their doctoral programs are often less than desirable, while a strong sense of community and integration are required to enhance student learning and persistence and to sustain volition (e.g., Rovai, 2002; Rockinson-Szapkiw et al., 2019). Strong feelings of community and being integrated help students meet their basic psychological needs for affiliation by providing students with a voice in shaping their environment, positive connections with other members of the academic community, and opportunities for contribution and meaningful social construction of knowledge for better practice and to contribute to the practical, empirical, and theoretical research.

In situations where the sense of community is weak, less will be shared, and students will struggle to persist. For example, Asma's deteriorating feelings of community, place her at risk of becoming a doctoral dropout. In a meta-synthesis, Bair (1999) identified:

> The single most frequently occurring finding... was that successful degree completion is related to the degree and quality of contact between a

doctoral student and her or his advisor(s) or other faculty in the student's doctoral program.

(pp. 67–68)

While positive relationships with faculty can decrease the time to complete the degree (Maher et al., 2004; Wao & Onwuegbuzie, 2011), negative interactions between students and faculty can contribute to dropout. Negative doctoral student-faculty interactions associated with dropout include factors such as a lack of cooperation, inadequate guidance, and unavailability (e.g., Bair, 1999; Golde, 2005; Lovitts, 2001; Spaulding & Rockinson-Szapkiw, 2012; Willis & Carmichael, 2011). The terms rupture and derailment were used by Golde (2000) to highlight how difficult interactions between doctoral students and faculty can lead to students dropping out of the program.

Similar to the need for student-faculty interactions, researchers have suggested that positive student-student (or peer) interactions are very important to program completion (Bair, 1999; Lovitts, 2001; Wao & Onwuegbuzie, 2011). When student-student interactions are of high quality, students persist (e.g., Ivankova & Stick, 2007; Maher et al., 2004; Spaulding & Rockinson-Szapkiw, 2012; Terrell et al., 2012). However, when student-student interactions are described as uncooperative, argumentative, one-way, disrespectful, ignorant of diversity, and competitive, the persistence is weakened (Golde, 2005; Lovitts, 2001). In sum, researchers agree that socialization, integration, and community with not only faculty and peers but also the program, the university, and the discipline are vital to persistence. Below each is briefly discussed.

The process of socialization in the doctoral journey is one "in which the newcomer is made a member of a community—in the case of graduate students, the community of an academic department in a particular discipline" (Golde, 1998, p. 56). Socialization in a doctoral program encompasses understanding the university culture and becoming affiliated with the classroom, faculty, university, and discipline. Socialization generates feelings of community that help satisfy the students' psychological needs for supportive relationships.

Similarly, integration is a key factor associated with doctoral students' decisions to leave or stay in a program. Tinto (1975) posited that social and academic integration are central to persistence in undergraduate education. Later, extending his work to doctoral students, he suggested doctoral student persistence is "shaped by the personal and intellectual interactions that occur within and between students and faculty and the various communities that make up the academic and social systems of the institution" (p. 231). Researchers have applied Tinto's (1975, 1993, 2007, 2012, 2023) work to doctoral education (Wao & Onwuegbuzie, 2011), finding that academic integration and social integration are associated with persistence (Castelló et al., 2017; Ivankova & Stick, 2007; Rockinson-Szapkiw et al., 2016). These constructs are intertwined for doctoral students. Persistence is related to the term *program integration* and is distinguished by the entity with which the integration is made (Holmes & Rockinson-Szapkiw, 2020). In other words, program integration comprises faculty integration, student integration, and curriculum integration.

Faculty integration refers to doctoral students' satisfaction with both the quality and nature of the interaction they have with faculty, including academic interactions (e.g., didactic instruction, receiving timely feedback) as well as nonacademic interactions (e.g., empathy, care). Student integration refers to students' satisfaction with both the quality and nature of peer interactions within the program. Curriculum integration refers to the satisfaction doctoral students have with the quality and relevancy of the doctoral curriculum (Holmes & Rockinson-Szapkiw, 2020).

Finally, sense of community is defined as "a feeling that members have of belonging, a feeling that members matter to one another and to the group, and a shared faith that members' needs will be met through their commitment to be together" (McMillan & Chavis, 1986, p. 9). Doctoral students experiencing a strong sense of community feel connected, possess stronger levels of social support, trust each other, and accept and respect constructive criticism. Such a strong sense of community acts as a buffer against threats, provides a space in which individuals are free to express their identities, and helps them navigate changes and difficulties.

Significant in this research is the idea that doctoral students foster community through the quality, rather than the quantity, of interactions. Excessive interactions can become counterproductive. On the other hand, academic communities are weakened when members are disconnected from one another due to limited interaction, mistrust, or competition. A sense of community in an academic environment is also weakened by the presence of social cliques that reinforce their own identity and exclude others, one-way communication, and the lack of shared common learning goals or values. Academic communities are strong when members feel connected to each other, feel community membership is a benefit to them, share common interests and values, trust and help each other, pursue common goals, actively engage in two-way communications, and manifest the immediate communication behaviors that reduce social and psychological distance between people (Mehrabian, 1971).

Doctoral students and faculty in traditional (i.e., face-to-face) environments engage in such immediacy behaviors, which are communicative behaviors that increase psychological closeness, thereby reducing feelings of isolation. These behaviors include maintaining eye contact, smiling, and generally presenting oneself in a friendly manner. Although such behavior is possible using technologies such as video conferencing, doctoral students and faculty in a text-based computer-mediated communication environment utilize a unique array of immediacy techniques to engage. In this situation, immediacy can manifest itself by collaborative interaction, edification of others, and the general exhibit of interpersonal warmth with reinforcing interpersonal comments.

Faculty and students in doctoral programs become a community of scholars when they actively engage and learn from one another. Community is built when relationships are fair and equitable. For example, faculty members place reasonable demands on doctoral students. Doctoral students engage in collaborative projects with faculty and jointly disseminate research and project findings in appropriate venues, such as departmental colloquia, research forums, in the community, and at conferences. Building and being a part of a community is positively related to cognitive development, motivation, active learning, metacognition, satisfaction, high achievement, and student persistence (Rovai, 2002). The attainment of such a community requires the deliberate implementation of specific supporting strategies.

Strategies for Success

Consideration of the community should begin prior to entry and continue through the Inquiry Stage. Doctoral students eventually transition from the Knowledge and Skill Development Stage (i.e., coursework), where they receive considerable social support and direction, through the Consolidation

Stage (e.g., the comprehensive exam) to the more independent learning environment of the Inquiry Stage (i.e., the dissertation). When program attrition occurs, it is most likely to occur during this latter stage of the doctoral program. Lovitts (2001) described student work in this stage:

> These are complex processes with which most students have little familiarity or prior experience. Students who reach this stage know (or discover) that they must conduct research that distinguishes them from their peers. Most individuals feel inadequately prepared to conduct this type of research and often find themselves unprepared for the writing style required for a dissertation.
>
> (p. 72)

It is at this critical stage of the doctoral program that many students become less connected with other members of the community as they work independently and autonomously. As students transition to the more independent structure of their doctoral journey, accessing social networks (hopefully formed during the Knowledge and Skill Development Stage) and supportive institutional and discipline-specific programs become essential for their success (Ali & Kohun, 2007). The following are strategies you should consider to ensure that the community is a part of your doctoral studies.

Strategy 1: Consider If a Cohort Model Is Right for You

A *cohort model* encompasses a group of doctoral students who progress through the program in a structured manner. All members of a cohort enter the program together and move through it at the same pace. A structured sequence of courses, from which little to no deviation can occur, is followed by all members of the cohort from the beginning to graduation. This model can help reduce stress related to course selection and completion of the required credits for graduation.

Doctoral students participating in a cohort experience tend to have better integration into the program, as fellow cohort members provide both social and academic support throughout (Rockinson-Szapkiw et al., 2019). As students take courses together and move through the doctoral program, you get to know your peers well. Cohort membership can facilitate feelings of belongingness, a sense that you matter to others, and a shared understanding of needs that are often met through collaboration. A doctoral experience is unique. Students in professional doctoral programs often balance their studies with full-time employment, family responsibilities, and other commitments. A PhD (i.e., research doctorate) student entering a residential program may have moved to a new location and decided to devote several years to being a full-time student and graduate assistant.

The doctoral experience, no matter the program model or modality, is an endeavor of a different order that very few grasp. It is hard to understand, except by those peers who are journeying alongside you. The members of a cohort can be a built-in social and academic support system, commiserating with you about frustrating faculty experience, empathizing with you about the toll a doctoral program is taking on your personal life, answering your questions about assignments, helping create study guides for the comprehensive exam, and reminding you to submit your graduation forms by a deadline. Moreover, you are surrounded by a group of individuals in a similar profession or desiring to enter a similar profession. They automatically become a professional network that usually exists well beyond the program. Moreover, the diversity of your cohort members' cultures and experiences can lead to thought-provoking and illuminating in-class or virtual discussions, an ongoing source of professional development.

However, the benefits of being part of a cohort may not be fully realized by only interacting in class. It is essential to connect in other ways, particularly when offering social support. If you are in a distance education program, you may create a channel or stream on a cloud-based team communication platform or plan regular study sessions or social hours (e.g., wine and cheese parties, coffee meetups) using a video conferencing system. Similarly, in a residential program, you may organize meetups such as quarterly dinner parties, family fun events, or coffee dates. Building relationships with peers in your cohort, both in and outside of the classroom, allows you the social and emotional support to persist through the doctoral program. If Asma connected with her peers regularly to share dissertation struggles, she may not feel so isolated.

While there are many benefits to being part of a cohort, participating in a doctoral program with the cohort model can be restrictive, particularly if you have specific course interests or need to deviate from the sequenced course structure to accommodate job or familial responsibilities. The pace of a cohort model is set, so you must keep up or risk being delayed by a year. The success of the cohort and the support it provides is also dependent upon group dynamics and the ability of members to get along. If you struggle to get along with your peers in your cohort, you may become frustrated and stressed, which can demotivate you and hinder your persistence. Because you do not pick your cohort, you cannot ensure positive group dynamics will develop. Being part of a doctoral program with a cohort model has numerous benefits, but also presents challenges. Ultimately, choosing to participate in a cohort is a personal decision.

Strategy 2: Create Communities with Peers Throughout the Doctoral Journey to Increase Persistence

MacNamara (2003) claimed that the heart of the student persistence problem is the institution's lack of structure to support students in building connections and community; therefore, you may need to advocate for more structure or participate in student-initiated community building. Peer collaboration, in the form of peer review, has the pedagogical advantage of encouraging students to define and discuss their terms for what constitutes reasonable inquiry and a well-written dissertation. Peer collaborations can help you develop dissertation ideas, write a well-edited proposal for the dissertation committee to consider, and avoid becoming overly dependent on faculty input to develop the dissertation. Peer review becomes possible when you participate in an expanded community of scholars that includes other doctoral students as well as doctoral faculty. For example, you can meet periodically with selected peers in a library or coffee shop to discuss dissertation work and share inquiry ideas. Alternatively, and in the case of distance education programs, the peer group can interact via computer-mediated communication at regularly scheduled intervals (e.g., weekly or monthly).

Peer groups may also set up social network sites to collaborate. MacNamara (2003) even endorsed a strategy that follows the constructivist model, allowing students to publish their evolving work on a common website established by the institution. In this way, students can provide feedback to one another, thereby helping them identify and rectify problems and receive support and encouragement from their peers.

Joining or developing a research (or inquiry) group is another way to develop community while also broadening knowledge and developing doctoral and research literacy. Participation in a research group is associated with decreased feelings of isolation (Ahmad et al., 2023) and increased feelings of belonging (White & Nonnamaker, 2008). Regularly attending scheduled meetings based on mutual interest to create purposefully scholarly works (e.g., research articles, white papers, local community workshops, conference presentations) and to share repertoires allows for ongoing connection and collaboration (Wenger, 1998). Moreover, participation offers the opportunity to learn research language and become acculturated to your academic community and discipline of study. However, not all research groups are effective, as researchers have noted that effective research groups require an established purpose and "intentional facilitation" (Ahmad et al., 2023; Pyhältö et al., 2009, p. 223), which involves purposeful interaction, scaffolded activities, and a structured approach. For example, participants may discuss five research articles in preparation for writing a review (e.g., an example for a traditional PhD research group) of the literature, or participants may present one evidence-based practice piece in preparation for a workshop for a local community organization (e.g., an example for a professional doctorate inquiry group). Group meetings may be held online, face-to-face, or in a hybrid format (a combination of online and face-to-face), regardless of the program modality, to be more inclusive of students' vocational and familial responsibilities that may hinder solely on-campus or face-to-face involvement (Berry, 2017).

Strategy 3: Recognize the Importance of Community and Its Relationship with Independence in the Context of Creating a Dissertation Committee

Learner autonomy and self-direction do not equate to learning in isolation (see Chapter 14: Transitioning from Autonomous to Self-Directed Learning). The community still plays a crucial role at every stage of the doctoral journey, supporting you in overcoming challenges and persevering in the program. Community provides a place where you can seek assistance with skills (e.g., writing, research, statistics) in which you feel less confident. The foundation of a strong, wise, and resilient community is socialization that fosters a strong community spirit.

In the Inquiry Stage, selecting an appropriate dissertation committee is an important community-building step (see Chapter 17: Identifying and Developing a Relationship with a Dissertation Chair). The proper role of the dissertation committee is to guide candidates in developing ideas rather than instructing them on the specific details they should develop and propose. In other words, the committee neither holds your hand too much nor too little.

A faculty member's level of support is reminiscent of the Zone of Proximal Development (ZPD). Vygotsky (1978) defined the ZPD as "the distance between the actual developmental level as determined by independent problem solving and the level of potential development as determined through problem solving under adult guidance, or in collaboration with more capable peers" (p. 86). ZPD is closely related to the term scaffolding. Once you have mastered a task with the benefit of scaffolding, the scaffolding can be removed so that you can complete the task independently.

Effective dissertation committee members should provide you with a balance between critique and affirmation. Ownership of the dissertation resides with you. You and your dissertation chair should discuss how feedback will be provided, as well as, the frequency and timing of feedback throughout the process. You are the primary author of the project and are ultimately responsible for both its crafting and executing.

Further, dissertation committees are social systems essential to creating and sustaining a strong doctoral community. One helpful strategy is first to identify the chairperson—a choice that you should consider from the very beginning of your program. You need consider the content and research method expertise of each faculty member and how these relate to their work. You should seek the advice of other students in the program, who have experience with dissertation chairs and committee members. You should not approach a potential dissertation chair without first learning about their published research, personal characteristics, and work habits. This information can be discovered not only through discussions with peers but also by actively seeking opportunities to be involved in research teams, communities, and community projects led by faculty, both during coursework and outside of it.

Once a dissertation chair is selected, discuss the committee composition with your chair before inviting others to serve on the committee (Davis et al., 2012) to ensure you build a committee that works well together and is thus likely to foster a sense of collaboration and, ultimately, community. It is a good strategy to draw committee members from faculty with whom you have had classes, thus ensuring a relationship already exists. The selection of dissertation committee members is very personal and should be based on additional criteria that support a strong academic community:

- members with strengths in different areas (content and research methods) who will bring varying abilities to the table,
- members who are accessible and will take time to read drafts and give constructive and timely feedback,
- members who are supportive and interested in your research, and
- members who get along and collaborate well with each other.

For example, interfaculty interactions within the dissertation committee will replicate power relations in the academy. Consequently, power struggles can occur among faculty members in dissertation committees. When they do, you pay the price.

However, you should be aware that a strong academic community does not imply the absence of inconsistent views. The purpose of having a dissertation committee, as opposed to a single advisor, is to obtain multiple views that can enhance your research. The role of the committee chair is to assist you in sorting out conflicting messages and to help maintain a positive and collegial spirit. In the case study, Asma should approach her chair to clarify the role of committee members and to help her sort out the inconsistent views she receives from the committee.

As the committee is formed, discuss what is expected from each committee member, particularly regarding the level of attention they are expected to provide, and ensure a clear understanding of what the committee expects from them. To be successful, make effective use of the committee's time. The case study suggests that Asma may have become too dependent on her committee members. Unreasonable demands on a faculty member's time weaken community spirit.

You require both time and space to pursue dissertation research and writing. A productive dissertation work environment strikes a balance between working independently and autonomously, collaborating with other students, and working collegially with dissertation committee members who provide general direction while avoiding micromanagement of the research. Actively seek constructive criticism, not only from your dissertation committee but also from other doctoral students. Sharing and critiquing each other's ideas, in both research doctoral and professional doctoral programs, is the essence of research development (Grover, 2007; Rockinson-Szapkiw, 2018).

Questions for Reflection

You are encouraged to reflect on the following questions as you consider how to proactively seek to generate a strong community with peers and faculty across all stages of the doctoral journey.

- What opportunities exist to create or become involved in learning communities in order to learn more about research and potential dissertation committee members?
- How can I build a dissertation committee that will foster a sense of community? How can I nurture a mutual sense of community with my committee members?
- How can I nurture a mutual sense of community with peers in the doctoral program?
- What are the unique barriers to community building among a community of learners that I have or will face during my doctoral program?
- How can I nurture both individual autonomy and a psychological sense of community?
- What computer-mediated communication can I use to strengthen my sense of community? What online communication behavior should I avoid?

Recommended Resources

Ali, A., & Kohun, F. (2007). Dealing with social isolation to minimize doctoral attrition: A four-stage framework. *International Journal of Doctoral Studies*, *2*, 33–49.

Anderson, M. S. (Ed.). (1998). *The experience of being in graduate school: An exploration*. Jossey-Bass.

Rovai, A. P. (2002). Sense of community, perceived cognitive learning, and persistence in asynchronous learning networks. *The Internet and Higher Education, 5*(4), 319–332.

References

Ahmad, S., Ansari, A. N., Khawaja, S. & Bhutta, S. M. (2023). Research cafe: An informal learning space to promote research learning experiences of graduate students in a private university of Pakistan. *Studies in Graduate and Postdoctoral Education, 14*(3), http://doi.org/10.1108/SGPE-01-2023-0011.

Ali, A., & Kohun, F. (2007). Dealing with social isolation to minimize doctoral attrition—A four-stage framework. *International Journal of Doctoral Studies, 2,* 33–49.

Ashar, H., & Skenes, R. (1993). Can Tinto's student departure model be applied to nontraditional students? *Adult Education Quarterly, 43*(2), 90–100.

Bair, C. R. (1999). Doctoral student attrition and persistence: A meta-synthesis (Doctoral dissertation Loyola University). Retrieved from Dissertation Abstracts International.

Berry, S. (2017). Student support networks in online doctoral programs: Exploring nested communities. *International Journal of Doctoral Studies, 12,* 33–48.

Castelló, M., Pardo, M., Sala-Bubaré, A., & Suñe-Soler, N. (2017). Why do students consider dropping out of doctoral degrees? Institutional and personal factors. *Higher Education, 74,* 1053–1068. doi: 10.1007/s10734-016-0106-9.

Corcelles-Seuba, M., Suñe-Soler, N., Sala-Bubare, A., and Castello, M. (2023). Doctoral student perceptions of supervisory and research community support: Their relationships with doctoral conditions and experiences. *Journal of Further and Higher Education, 47*(4), 481–491.

Corno, L., & Kanfer, R. (1993). The role of volition in learning and performance. *Review of Research in Education, 19,* 301–41.

Council of Graduate Schools. (2005). *The Doctor of Philosophy degree: A policy statement.*

Davidson, C., & Wilson, K. (2013). Reassessing Tinto's concepts of social and academic integration in student retention. *Journal of College Student Retention: Research, Theory & Practice, 15*(3), 329–346. http://doi.org/10.2190/CS.15.3. b

Davis, G. B., Parker, C. A., & Straub, D. W. (2012). *Writing the doctoral dissertation: A systematic approach* (3rd ed.). Barron.

Gardner, S. K. (2008). "What is too much and what is too little?" The process of becoming an independent researcher in doctoral education. *Journal of Higher Education, 79*(3), 326–50.

Golde, C. M. (1998). Beginning graduate school: Explaining first-year doctoral attrition. In M. S. Anderson (Ed.), *The experience of being in graduate school: An exploration* (pp. 55–64). Jossey-Bass.

Golde, C. M. (2000). Should I stay or should I go? Student descriptions of the doctoral attrition process. *The Review of Higher Education*, *23*(2), 199–227.

Golde, C. M. (2005). The role of the department and discipline in doctoral student attrition: Lessons from four departments. *The Journal of Higher Education*, *76*(6), 669–700.

Grover, V. (2007). Successfully navigating the stages of doctoral study. *International Journal of Doctoral Studies*, *2*, 9–21.

Heckhausen, H., & Kuhl, J. (1985). From wishes to action: The dead ends and shortcuts on the long way to action. In M. Frese & J. Sabini (Eds.), *Goal-directed behavior: The concept of action in psychology* (pp. 134–157). Lawrence Erlbaum Associates.

Holmes, J. & Rockinson-Szapkiw, A. (2020). The development and validation of the distance doctoral program integration scale. *Online Learning*, *24*(4). http://doi.org/10.24059/olj.v24i4.1951

Ivankova, N. V., & Stick, S. L. (2005). Collegiality and community-building as a means for sustaining student persistence in the computer-mediated asynchronous learning environment. *Online Journal of Distance Learning Administration*, *8*(3), 1–18.

Ivankova, N. V., & Stick, S. L. (2007). Students' persistence in a distributed doctoral program in educational leadership in higher education: A mixed methods study. *Research in Higher Education*, *48*(1), 93–135. http://doi.org/10.1007/s11162-006-9025-4

Lovitts, B. E. (2001). *Leaving the ivory tower: The causes and consequences of departure from doctoral study*. Rowan & Littlefield Publishers.

Lovitts, B. E. (2005). Being a good course-taker is not enough: A theoretical perspective on the transition to independent research. *Studies in Higher Education*, *30*(2), 137–54.

MacNamara, L. A. (2003). *Navigating the journey: A case study of participants in a dissertation support program* (Doctoral dissertation). ProQuest Dissertations & University of Pennsylvania Theses (PQDT) database. (UMI No. 3084866)

Maher, M. A., Ford, M. E., & Thompson, C. M. (2004). Degree progress of women doctoral students: Factors that constrain, facilitate, and differentiate. *Review of Higher Education*, *27*(3), 385–408.

McMillan, D. W., & Chavis, D. M. (1986). Sense of community: A definition and theory. *Journal of Community Psychology*, *14*(1), 6–23.

Mehrabian, A. (1971). *Silent messages*. Wadsworth.

Meschitti, V. (2019). Can peer learning support doctoral education? Evidence from an ethnography. *Studies in Higher Education, 44.* doi: 10.1080/03075079.2018.1427711

O'Keeffe, P. (2020). PhD by publication: Innovative approach to social science research, or operationalization of the doctoral student… or both? *Higher Education Research and Development*, *39*(2), 288–301.

Owens, A., Brien, D. L., Ellison, E. & Batty, C. (2020). Student reflections on doctoral learning: Challenges and breakthroughs. *Studies in Graduate and Postdoctoral Education, 11*(1), 107–122.

Pyhältö, K., Stubb, J. & Lonka, K. (2009). Developing scholarly communities as learning environments for doctoral students. *International Journal for Academic Development, 14*(3), 221–232.

Rockinson-Szapkiw, A. (2018). The development and validation of the Scholar–Practitioner Research Development Scale for students enrolled in professional doctoral programs. *Journal of Applied Research in Higher Education, 10*(4), 478–492. https://doi.org/10.1108/JARHE-01-2018-0011

Rockinson-Szapkiw, A. J., Holmes, J., & Stephen, J. S. (2019). Identifying significant personal and program factors that predict online EdD students' program integration. *Online Learning, 23*(4), 313–335. http://doi.org/10.24059/olj.v23i4.1579

Rockinson-Szapkiw, A. J., Spaulding, L. S., & Spaulding, M. T. (2016). Identifying significant integration and institutional factors that predict online doctoral persistence. *The Internet and Higher Education, 31*, 101–112.

Rovai, A. P. (2002). Sense of community, perceived cognitive learning, and persistence in asynchronous learning networks. *The Internet and Higher Education, 5*(4), 319–332.

Spaulding, L., & Rockinson-Szapkiw, A. (2012). Hearing their voices: Factors doctoral candidates attribute to their persistence. *International Journal of Doctoral Studies, 7*, 199–219. https://doi.org/10.28945/1589

Terrell, S. (2005). Supporting different learning styles in an online learning environment: Does it matter in the long run? *Online Journal of Distance Education Administration, 8*(2).

Terrell, S. R., Snyder, M. M., & Dringus, L. P. (2009). The development, validation, and application of the Doctoral Student Connectedness Scale. *The Internet and Higher Education, 12*(2), 112–116. http://doi.org/10.1016/j.iheduc.2009.06.004

Terrell, S. R., Snyder, M. M., Dringus, L. P., & Maddrey, E. (2012). A grounded theory of connectivity and persistence in a limited residency doctoral program. *The Qualitative Report, 17*(31), 1–14.

Tinto, V. (1975). Dropout from higher education: A theoretical synthesis of recent research. *Review of Educational Research, 45*(1), 89–125.

Tinto, V. (1993). *Leaving college: Rethinking the causes and cures of candidate attrition* (2nd ed.). The University of Chicago Press.

Tinto, V. (2007). Research and practice of student retention: What next? *Journal of College Student Retention: Research, Theory & Practice, 8*(1), 1–20.

Tinto, V. (2012). *Completing college: Rethinking institutional action*. University of Chicago Press.

Tinto, V. (2023). Reflections: Rethinking engagement and student persistence. *Student Success, 14*(2), 1–7. https://doi.org/10.5204/ssj.3016

Vygotsky, L. S. (1978). Mind in society: The development of higher psychological processes. In M. Cole, V. John-Steiner, S. Scribner, & E. Souberman (Eds.), *Interaction between learning and development* (pp. 79–91). Harvard University Press.

Wao, H. O., & Onwuegbuzie, A. J. (2011). A mixed research investigation of factors related to time to the doctorate in education. *International Journal of Doctoral Studies, 6*, 115–134.

Wenger, E. (1998). Communities of practice: Learning as a social system. *Systems Thinker, 9*(5), 2–3.

Wenger, E.C. & Snyder, W.M. (2000). Communities of practice: The organizational frontier. *Harvard Business Review, 78* (1), 139–146.

White, J. & Nonnamaker, J. (2008). Belonging and mattering: How doctoral students experience community. *Journal of Student Affairs Research and Practice, 45*(3), 676–98

Willis, B., & Carmichael, K. D. (2011). The lived experience of late-stage doctoral student attrition in counselor education. *The Qualitative Report, 16*(1), 192–207.

10 Overcoming Statistics Anxiety

Lawrence M. Lesser, PhD

In addition to anxiety (Chi et al., 2023), statistics anxiety is quite common, affecting an estimated 66–80% of graduate students in the social and behavioral sciences (Onwuegbuzie & Wilson, 2003). Devaney (2010) indicated that anxiety levels are even higher when students take statistics via a distance education course, a delivery method that is becoming more common as doctoral programs are being increasingly offered at a distance.

So, if you are a doctoral student, you're not alone if you feel anxious about taking a statistics course, which most professional practice and research doctoral programs require. While statistics anxiety is helpful when it motivates students to learn and complete projects, it is unhelpful when it is debilitating (Martin et al., 2003), affects performance, decreases self-efficacy, or impedes course taking or overall progress toward degree completion (Devaney, 2010; Williams, 2010). In this chapter, statistics anxiety and literature-based strategies to mitigate it during coursework, dissertation, and beyond is discussed.

Vignette

While taking a graduate statistics course from a mathematics department, I found the level of abstraction, notation, and theory difficult. The textbook may have been a classic reference in the field but was not friendly for first learning the material.

It became frustrating and stressful to be at the lectures as I hurriedly copied decontextualized terse mathematics from the chalkboard. I hoped those matrices and subscripts in my notes would somehow make sense later. Though I knew I was not the only student feeling lost, I began to experience anxiety about successfully completing the course.

I decided to take responsibility for my success and seek resources outside of the lectures and textbooks. To understand the statistical topics covered in class and in the text, I went to my university's library to find books covering the same statistical topic for a broader or more applied audience (e.g., "statistics for educators" or "statistics for health professionals").

I found helpful statistics books that used a nonacademic familiar context of personal interest, such as playing cards (Knapp, 1996), sports (Albert, 2003; Tabor & Franklin, 2019), or diversity (Frankfort-Nachmias et al., 2021). After finding real-world examples and less dense notation, I returned to the official course textbook with more understanding and confidence.

I also learned the importance of peer support. My statistics course classmates and I formed a study group called "Students Of Statistics" (SOS!). We met weekly to discuss projects and prepare for exams. We even registered as an official student organization at our university, sponsoring social hours and lectures. Peer support and academic community continue to help me as a professor, and I have been a member of research and writing groups within and beyond my discipline and campus.

Even with my statistics training, I can encounter data issues beyond my expertise. When this occurs, I seek input from a colleague or my university's statistical consulting lab. Statisticians enjoy collaboration, as reflected in the John Tukey quote: "The best thing about being a statistician is that you get to play in everyone's backyard" (Leonhardt, 2000).

What the Research Says

A classic definition of *anxiety* is the expectation of a nonspecific threat that is accompanied by fear and worry (Szuhany & Simon, 2022). If doctoral students experience *statistics anxiety*, they may expect a negative or painful consequence related to taking a statistics course, conducting statistical analyses, or even reading about analysis. This expectation of negative consequence, fear, or worry often results in avoidance behaviors.

Statistics anxiety includes the fear of failing and negative attitudes toward statistics and can also include test anxiety and math anxiety (Benson & Bandalos, 1989). The various facets of statistics anxiety are highlighted by instruments such as the Statistical Anxiety Rating Scale (STARS), the Statistics Anxiety Measure (SAM), and the Statistical Anxiety Scale (SAS). STARS has six subscales: (a) worth of statistics, (b) interpretation anxiety, (c) test and class anxiety, (d) computational self-concept, (e) fear of asking for help, and (f) fear of statistics teachers (Chew et al., 2018; Cruise et al., 1985; Cruise & Wilkins, 1980). SAM identifies five components: (1) anxiety, (2) attitude toward class, (3) fearful behavior, (4) attitude toward math, and (5) performance (Earp, 2007). SAS tracks anxiety in three aspects: (1) examination, (2) asking for help, and (3) interpretation (Vigil-Colet et al., 2008).

Statistics anxiety is linked to numerous factors. Slootmaeckers (2012) suggested that factors inducing statistics anxiety can be classified as situational (e.g., prior knowledge, course grade, etc.), dispositional (e.g., students' attitudes and perceptions), or person-related (e.g., students' gender, age, etc.).

Negative personal experiences in prior mathematics or statistics coursework can result in feelings of helplessness, lack of academic self-confidence or self-efficacy, and the perception that success in statistics is unlikely (Fiore, 1999; Jackson & Leffingwell, 1999; Kelly et al., 2020; Zeidner & Safir, 1989). These associated feelings and perceptions can be further influenced by cognitive, affective, and social factors (Zeidner & Safir, 1989), including: lack of skills (e.g., poor quantitative reasoning skills); self-depreciating, destructive thought processes; feelings of fear; and lack of support.

Understanding the facets of statistics anxiety, their origin, and what perpetuates them is helpful, as interventions need to be aimed strategically. Doctoral students can use the listed components of statistical anxiety instruments to identify what aspects of statistics are the most anxiety-inducing, and then seek extra support or attention accordingly, as I did in the vignette. By becoming aware of and responding to the particular component of statistics anxiety that are salient, doctoral students can become proactive in navigating the doctoral journey with a sense of empowerment and mitigate high anxiety.

Strategies for Success

Literature-informed strategies (informed by experience and the academic literature) can be employed to set you up for success at every stage of the doctoral journey. In addition to these general strategies, you can seek discipline-specific literature discussing techniques for combating statistics anxiety, such as the *Teaching Sociology* articles noted by DeCesare (2007) or the counterpart bevy of papers in *Teaching of Psychology*. You may also gain support in a community of practice as described in Chapter 9: Creating a Scholarly Community.

Identify Program Expectations

Most professional practice and research doctoral programs require at least one statistics course; some require multiple courses. Gathering information about a program's requirement prior to enrollment can help ensure that the program is a good fit for you. You can examine the course requirements. You can browse recent dissertations or publications that have come out of the program to see if any patterns exist in how quantitative methodologies and analyses are used (see Chapter 12: Understanding Quantitative Inquiry). Many institutions have an online repository of dissertations. Once enrolled, this browsing may also inform whom you ask to be your chair and who is best able to support a specific methodology (e.g., parametric vs. nonparametric statistics, observational data vs. experimental data, mixed-methods study).

Embrace the Need for Statistical Literacy and Competence

During the coursework, the Knowledge and Skill Development Stage of the doctoral journey, it is important to develop confidence and skills needed to become a successful scholar or scientist. Building a repertoire to evaluate or conduct a broad range of inquiries is important because questions and corresponding hypotheses may require a variety of statistical analyses, even when using qualitative methods (e.g., Creswell, 2013).

Even if you plan to have a statistical consultant assist with the most technical parts of your dissertation inquiry, you still need a critical mass of background knowledge to ask the right questions, ensure optimal analyses, and interpret and communicate the results during your proposal and dissertation defenses. Even if not required by your program, taking coursework in statistical methods helps make you a more informed consumer and producer of research.

Preparing for Classes

Because statistics anxiety can be triggered if you believe you have a weak or outdated mathematics background, you would be wise to consult the syllabus and prepare in advance for your analysis courses. At a minimum, you need to be ready to handle order of operations, exponents/radicals, summation notation, graphs, linear equations and inequalities, basic set theory, and combinatorics (counting rules). Books have been written for this very purpose (see Brent & Mueller, 1999; Shiffler & Adams, 1996) and work is being done (e.g., Chow et al., 2024) to provide education tailored to each student's knowledge gaps. Because mathematics anxiety can be a trigger for statistics anxiety, reviewing or learning basic mathematical procedures and formulas before taking a doctoral analysis course can build self-confidence or self-efficacy.

Because statistics anxiety can also include verbal reasoning when interpreting data and statistical outcomes (Baloğlu, 2004; Williams, 2010), you can work to understand the big ideas and concepts of statistics with conceptual analogies (e.g., Lesser, 2016; Martin, 2003). You can also use statistical books that use everyday context and deemphasize or simplify formulas and theorems, such as Field (2013), Keller (2005), Rowntree (2004), Utts (2025), Vogt (2007), and the *Statistics for Dummies* series. O'Dwyer and Bernauer (2014) also provide a gentle and insightful introduction to statistics, articulating many big picture components of qualitative and quantitative methodologies.

Additionally, you can further your understanding of basic statistics concepts by exploring applets that many universities and statistics textbook authors host. A list is found in the introduction of Lu (2023). Video streaming sites such as YouTube also offer collections of statistics videos and tutorials for free.

In addition to statistics being anxiety provoking, using statistical technology and programs can also increase anxiety. You can be proactive prior to starting a statistics course by becoming familiar with the technologies (e.g., graphing calculator, statistical software, R, Python, SPSS, SAS, etc.) that are allowed or required. Give yourself time to access and explore technology options (e.g., Shepherd & Richardson, 2024) and learn to use them by watching free online videos about usage. Pedagogical articles (e.g., Shilane et al., 2024) for instructors can help you orient to the technology, too.

If you are anxious that a statistics course has too much to memorize, you may include in your course preparation statistics mnemonics (Lesser, 2011; Mocko et al., 2017; Mocko et al., 2024). If you are an emergent bilingual, you may appreciate online statistics glossaries and applets in multiple languages (see Lesser 2020b).

You may also find it helpful to learn from the experience of past statistics students, such as content challenges (e.g., sampling distribution, variance, hypothesis testing, and how to write conclusions) and unproductive behaviors (technology distractions, procrastination, skipping practice problems, not reading textbook in a timely or thorough manner, missing class, sleep habits) reported by students of McGrath (2014).

Use Humor or the Arts

Despite preparation with resources and the strategies already mentioned, you may still feel statistics anxiety. Because research indicates that humor can lower anxiety that obstructs learning, you may appreciate conceptually-oriented books that employ irreverence or humor (e.g., Field, 2013; Gonick & Smith, 1993; Klein & Dabney, 2013; Norman & Streiner, 1986; Pyrczak, 1998; Runyon, 1977; Salkind, 2014). Consider reading books that explicitly target students with statistics anxiety (e.g., Jaisingh, 2000; Kranzler, 2011).

Art is another form of humanizing statistics, which Field (2010), Lesser (2007, 2008, 2020a), Neumann et al. (2009), and others do. There is also a curated searchable collection of more than a thousand edutainment items at CAUSEweb.org/fun.

Humor can also serve to build community among fellow students (and even professors), thus decreasing feelings of isolation and anxiety. Feeling part of a community of learners and scholars may help you feel more comfortable asking questions and seeking help.

Use Stress Management Techniques

To mitigate your statistics anxiety, you may find it helpful to employ math anxiety reducing strategies such as deep muscle relaxation, meditation, healthy diet and exercise, journaling, desensitization, assertiveness training, improving time management skills and study habits, and adopting a "Math Anxiety Bill of Rights" (Ayers-Nachamkin, 1992; Rodell, 1994; Tobias, 1995;

Wolcott, 2013) (see Chapter 7: Creating a Personal Wellness Plan and Chapter 8: Overcoming Stress and Burnout for more stress management techniques). Also, try using positive self-talk such as, "Getting help will assist me in building a solid foundation for my dissertation" and "I will save so much time and stress by finding out if any changes are needed *before* I start all the work of data collection" may reduce anxiety.

Synthesize Material Across Courses

Your statistics courses provide a broad set of techniques for you to connect to each other and ultimately to your research. For example, you might learn separately about regression and analysis of variance (ANOVA) and should also learn that the latter is a special case of the former (Nelson & Zaichkowsky, 1979). Asking faculty how courses, statistical techniques, and research connect can be helpful. You can also be self-directed by forming peer groups to discuss connections and analyses (see Chapter 14: Transitioning from Autonomous to Self-Directed Learning).

Use a Quantitative Analysis Expert

When you enter the Inquiry Stage, you are responsible for the inquiry for your dissertation and for assembling a dissertation committee. Collectively, the members of your committee need areas of expertise inclusive of content and methodology.

If you are conducting a quantitative dissertation, you should include at least one member who is experienced with statistical analysis to consult with about design, data collection, and analysis. You may also, if institutional policies permit, hire a statistical consultant to assist you with running and interpreting your statistical analysis. This person should be a support and assist you in further understanding statistical analysis and not simply do the analysis for you. Remember that the inquiry you make for your dissertation is yours and you need to understand and explain it during your dissertation defense.

Do not let anxiety keep you from finding a statistical expert for your committee or to consult in a timely manner. More anxiety and pitfalls exist when bringing in a statistics expert *after* time has been spent designing a proposal and collecting data.

Participate in a Research Community

Support groups, as discussed in the vignette, can validate your anxiety and help you prepare for coursework and dissertation inquiry. The process of preparing and presenting your work for different audiences generates new insights (e.g., various questions or feedback) and helps you visualize successful proposal and dissertation defenses.

Your department or university may host seminars, colloquia, journal club meetings, or graduate student research expositions that are excellent avenues to connect and form communities with peers and others. Professional organizations also offer opportunities such as fellowships and conferences where community with others can be formed. As you look ahead to publishing articles, note that some journals now expect you to reference what software you used, control for multiple comparisons, provide access to reproducibility materials (e.g., deidentified raw data), report effect sizes, and not misuse *p*-values or significance testing (Wasserstein & Lazar, 2016).

Questions for Reflection

- What are my available resources for gaining knowledge and confidence, in statistical procedures?
- What ideas and strategies from this chapter are most helpful or useful for me to reduce my anxiety related to statistical analysis? Develop a plan to implement three strategies.
- What negative thought patterns (e.g., "I am not a numbers person," "I am not smart enough to succeed in statistics") do I have? Write each one down and replace it with a positive one.
- Outside your committee, what resources for statistical analysis, internal and external to the institution, are available to me?
- What course(s) in statistics do I need to enhance my academic or career pathways?

Recommended Resources

Chew, P. K. H., & Dillon, D. B. (2014). Statistics anxiety update: Refining the construct and recommendations for a new research agenda. *Perspectives on Psychological Science*, *9*(2), 196–207.

Ellis, A. (2000). *How to control your anxiety before it controls you*. Citadel.
Field, A. P. (2013). *Discovering statistics using IBM SPSS statistics* (4th ed.). Sage.
Kanji, G. K. (2006). *100 statistical tests* (3rd ed.). Sage.
Pallant, J. (2013). *SPSS survival manual: A step-by-step guide to data analysis using SPSS for Windows* (5th ed.). Open University Press.
Tabachnick, B. G., & Fidell, L. S. (2019). *Using multivariate statistics* (7th ed.). Pearson.
Warner, R. M. (2020). *Applied statistics II: Multivariable and multivariate techniques* (3rd ed.). Sage.

References

Albert, J. (2003). *Teaching statistics using baseball*. Mathematical Association of America.
Ayers-Nachamkin, B. (1992). A feminist approach to the introductory statistics course. *Women's Studies Quarterly, 20*(1 & 2), 86–94.
Baloğlu, M. (2004). Statistics anxiety and mathematics anxiety: Some interesting differences. *Educational Research Quarterly, 27*(3), 38–48.
Benson, J., & Bandalos, D. (1989). Structural model of statistics test anxiety. In R. Schwarzer, H. M. van der Ploeg, & C. D. Spielberger (Eds.), *Advances in test anxiety research* (Vol. *6*) (pp. 611–624). Erlbaum.
Brent, R. I., & Mueller, G. (1999). *Just enough algebra for students of statistics*. Addison Wesley Longman.
Chew, P. K. H., Dillon, D. B., & Swinbourne, A. L. (2018). An examination of the internal consistency and structure of the Statistical Anxiety Rating Scale (STARS). *PLoS One, 13*(3), 1–12. https://doi.org/10.1371/journal.pone.0194195
Chi, T., Cheng, L., & Zhang, Z. (2023). Global prevalence and trend of anxiety among graduate students: A systematic review and meta-analysis. *Brain and Behavior, 13*(4), 1–16. doi: 10.1002/brb3.2909. PMID: 36852520; PMCID: PMC10097092.
Chow, S-M., Lee, J., Park, J. J., Kuruppumullage P. D., Hammel T., Hallquist, M. N., Nord, E. A., Oravecz, Z., Perry, H. L., Lesser, L. M., & Pearl, D. K. (2024). Personalized education through Individualized Pathways and Resources to Adaptive Control Theory-Inspired Scientific Education (iPRACTISE): Proof-of-concept studies for designing and evaluating personalized education. *Journal of Statistics and Data Science Education, 32*(2), 174–187.
Creswell, J. W. (2013). *Research design: Qualitative, quantitative, and mixed methods approaches* (4th ed.) Sage.
Cruise, R. J., Cash, R. W., & Bolton, L. D. (1985). Development and validation of an instrument to measure statistical anxiety. In *Proceedings of the Joint Statistical Meetings, Section on Statistical Education* (pp. 92–98). American Statistical Association.

Cruise, R. J., & Wilkins, E. M. (1980). *STARS: Statistical Anxiety Rating Scale*. Unpublished manuscript. Andrews University.

DeCesare, M. (2007). "Statistics anxiety" among sociology majors: A first diagnosis and some treatment options. *Teaching Sociology*, *35*(4), 360–67.

DeVaney, T. A. (2010). Anxiety and attitude of graduate students in on-campus vs. online statistics courses. *Journal of Statistics Education*, *18*(1), 1–15.

Earp, M. A. (2007). *Development and validation of the Statistics Anxiety Measure*. Unpublished doctoral dissertation. University of Denver. Retrieved from https://iase-web.org/documents/dissertations/07.Earp.Dissertation.pdf

Field, A. P. (2010). Non-sadistical methods for teaching statistics. In D. Upton & A. Trapp (Eds.), *Teaching psychology in higher education* (pp. 134–163). Wiley-Blackwell.

Field, A. P. (2018). *Discovering statistics using IBM SPSS statistics* (5th ed.). Sage.

Fiore, G. (1999). Math-abused students: Are we prepared to teach them? *Mathematics Teacher*, *92*(5), 403–06.

Frankfort-Nachmias, C., Leon-Guerrero, A. Y., & Davis, G. (2021). *Social statistics for a diverse society* (9th ed.). Sage.

Gonick, L., & Smith, W. (1993). *The cartoon guide to statistics*. HarperCollins.

Huberty, C. J. (2000). Judgment in quantitative research. *The Mathematics Educator*, *10*(1), 5–10.

Jackson, C. D., & Leffingwell, R. J. (1999). The role of instructors in creating math anxiety in students from kindergarten through college. *Mathematics Teacher*, *92*(7), 583–86.

Jaisingh, L. R. (2000). *Statistics for the utterly confused* (2nd ed.). McGraw Hill.

Keller, D. K. (2005). *The Tao of statistics: A path to understanding (with no math)*. Sage.

Kelly, S., Romero, A., Morrow, J. A., Denton, Z., & Ducking, J. (2020). Instructor misbehaviors and math anxiety. *Communication Reports*, *33*(1), 27–40.

Klein, G., & Dabney, A. (2013). *The cartoon introduction to statistics*. Hill and Wang.

Knapp, T. R. (1996). *Learning statistics through playing cards*. Sage.

Kranzler, J. H. (2011). *Statistics for the terrified* (5th ed.). Pearson.

Leonhardt, D. (2000, July 28). John Tukey, 85, statistician; coined the word "software". *The New York Times*, *149*(51463), A19. https://www.nytimes.com/2000/07/28/us/john-tukey-85-statistician-coined-the-word-software.html

Lesser, L. (2006). Engaging the intuition in statistics to motivate. Paper presented at the 50th national Advanced Placement Conference. https://apcentral.collegeboard.org/courses/ap-statistics/classroom-resources/engaging-intuition-statistics-motivate

Lesser, L. (2007). Learning stats is fun… with the right mode. *STATS: The Magazine for Students of Statistics*, *48*, 7–11, 21, 26–28.

Lesser, L. (2008). Even more fun learning stats. *STATS: The Magazine for Students of Statistics*, *49*, 5–8, 19, 27.

Lesser, L. (2011). On the use of mnemonics for teaching statistics. *Model Assisted Statistics and Applications, 6*(2), 151–60.

Lesser, L. (2016). More statistics education literature on analogies. *The American Statistician, 70*(4), 434.

Lesser, L. (2020a). Statistical poetry. *Journal of Humanistic Mathematics, 10*(1), 533–39.

Lesser, L. (2020b). Redesigning a statistics literacy course to help prepare pre-service teachers to teach (statistics to) English language learners. In L. C. de Oliveira & M. Civil (Eds.), *Teaching mathematics to English language learners: Preparing pre-service and in-service teachers* (pp. 27–46). Palgrave Macmillan.

Lesser, L., & Melgoza, L. (2007). Simple numbers: ANOVA example of facilitating student learning in statistics. *Teaching Statistics, 29*(3), 102–105.

Lu, Y. (2023). Web-based applets for facilitating simulations and generating randomized datasets for teaching statistics. *Journal of Statistics and Data Science Education, 31*(3), 264–272.

Martin, M. A. (2003). "It's like... you know": The use of analogies and heuristics in teaching introductory statistical methods. *Journal of Statistics Education, 11*(2), 1–28.

Martin, A. J., Marsh, H. W., & Debus, R. L. (2003). Self-handicapping and defensive pessimism: A model of self-protection from a longitudinal perspective. *Contemporary Educational Psychology, 28*(1), 1–36.

McGrath, A. (2014). Content, affective, and behavioural challenges to learning: Students' experiences learning statistics. *International Journal for the Scholarship of Teaching and Learning, 8*(2), article 6, 1–21.

Mocko, M., Lesser, L., Wagler, A., & Francis, W. (2017). Assessing effectiveness of mnemonics for tertiary students in a hybrid introductory statistics course. *Journal of Statistics Education, 25*(1), 2–11.

Mocko, M., Wagler, A. E., Lesser, L. M., Francis, W. S., Blush, J. M., Schleicher, K., & Barrientos, P. S. (2024). What they remember may not be what they understand: A study of mnemonic recall and performance by introductory statistics students. *Journal of Statistics and Data Science Education, 32*(4), 416–431.

Nelson, L. R., & Zaichkowsky, L. D. (1979). A case for using multiple regression instead of ANOVA in educational research. *The Journal of Experimental Education, 47*(4), 324–30.

Neumann, D. L., Hood, M., & Neumann, M. M. (2009). Statistics? You must be joking: The application and evaluation of humor when teaching statistics. *Journal of Statistics Education, 17*(2), 1–16.

Norman, G. R., & Streiner, D. L. (1986). *PDQ statistics*. B. C. Decker, Inc.

O'Dwyer, L. M., & Bernauer, J. A. (2014). *Quantitative research for the qualitative researcher*. Sage.

Onwuegbuzie, A. J., & Wilson, V. A. (2003). Statistics anxiety: Nature, etiology, antecedents, effects, and treatments—A comprehensive review of the literature. *Teaching in Higher Education, 8*(2), 195–209.

Pyrczak, F. (1998). *Statistics with a sense of humor*. Pyrczak Publishing.
Rodell, L. M. (1994). Math anxiety bill of responsibilities. *The Teaching Professor, 8*(1), 3.
Rowntree, D. (2004). *Statistics without tears: A primer for non-mathematicians*. Allyn and Bacon.
Runyon, R. (1977). *Winning with statistics: A painless first look at numbers, ratios, percentages, means, and inference*. Addison-Wesley.
Salkind, N. J. (2014). *Statistics for people who (think they) hate statistics* (5th ed.). Sage.
Shepherd, M. A., & Richardson, E. J. (2024). Opting for open-source? A review of free statistical software programs. *Teaching Statistics, 46*(1), 53–63.
Shiffler, R. E., & Adams, A. J. (1996). *Just the basics, please: A quick review of math for introductory statistics*. Duxbury Press.
Shilane, D., Di Crecchio, N., & Lorenzetti, N. L. (2024). Some pedagogical elements of computer programming for data science: A comparison of three approaches to teaching the R language. *Teaching Statistics, 46*(1), 24–37.
Slootmaeckers, K. (2012). Too afraid to learn?! Attitudes toward statistics as a barrier to learning statistics and to acquiring quantitative skills. Paper presented at 4th International Conference on Education and New Learning Technologies (EDULEARN12). Barcelona.
Szuhany, K. L., & Simon, N. M. (2022). Anxiety disorders: A review. *Journal of the American Medical Association, 328*(24), 2431–2445. doi:10.1001/jama.2022.22744
Tabor, J., & Franklin, C. (2019). *Statistical reasoning in sports* (2nd ed.). W. H. Freeman.
Tobias, S. (1995). *Overcoming math anxiety* (revised ed.). W. W. Norton & Company.
Utts, J. M. (2025). *Seeing through statistics* (5th ed.). Cengage.
Vigil-Colet, A., Lorenzo-Seva, U., & Condon, L. (2008). Development and validation of the Statistical Anxiety Scale. *Psicothema, 20*(1), 174–180.
Vogt, W. P. (2007). *Quantitative research methods for professionals*. Pearson.
Wasserstein, R. L., & Lazar, N. A. (2016). The ASA Statement on *p*-values: Context, process, and purpose. *The American Statistician, 70*(2), 129–133.
Williams, A. S. (2010). Statistics anxiety and instructor immediacy. *Journal of Statistics Education, 18*(2), 1–18.
Wolcott, F. L. (2013). Contemplation in mathematics. *Journal of Humanistic Mathematics, 3*(1), 74–95.
Zeidner, M., & Safir, M. P. (1989). Sex, ethnic, and social differences in test anxiety among Israeli adolescents. *Journal of Genetic Psychology, 150*(2), 175–185.

11 Understanding Qualitative Inquiry

James A. Swezey, EdD

Introduction

Qualitative research continues to grow in scope, depth, and popularity among doctoral candidates. More than two decades ago, Patton (2015) wrote, "Qualitative dissertations, once quite rare, have become increasingly common as the criteria for judging qualitative contributions to knowledge have become better understood and accepted. But those criteria are not absolute or universally agreed on" (p. 18). This trend only continues to accelerate. Qualitative research grew nearly 50% faster than the rest of the research industry between 2019 and 2021 (ESOMAR, 2024). In their search of Scopus's comprehensive, multidisciplinary abstract and citation database, Thelwall and Nevill (2021) reviewed studies that employed interviews, focus groups, case studies, and ethnographies that produced unstructured non-numeric data suitable for qualitative research, irrespective of the analysis method used. They found qualitative research increased substantially in 27 broad fields between 1996 and 2019. Doctoral candidates should find qualitative approaches to be viable options for their studies depending upon their research area and the proclivities of their dissertation committee members.

Despite its growing recognition and acknowledged contributions to human knowledge and understanding, qualitative research remains an enigma to many and is often misunderstood by veteran and novice researchers alike. Despite being veiled in mystery to some, if conducted properly, qualitative designs are a valid and robust means of research and program evaluation. "Qualitative research is not intended to be scary or beyond the grasp of novices and doctoral students" (Cypress, 2017, p. 261), but it often is. This chapter is designed to demystify qualitative research for both doctoral program models: the research-scientist and the scholar-practitioner models.

The doctoral candidate who selects a qualitative design chooses to embark on a highly complex dissertation journey. Due to its complex nature, qualitative research will challenge the candidate's resilience and persistence to complete the final leg of the doctoral journey. To find success, the qualitative researcher must be both tenacious and patient.

While qualitative and quantitative studies both employ rigorous research methodologies, characterized by systematic procedures for selecting participants and collecting and analyzing data, they are markedly different in their assumptions about reality, knowledge, values, and the role of the researcher. The purpose of this chapter is to briefly describe the following approaches to inquiry and their distinct purposes: case study, phenomenology, narrative, grounded theory, and ethnography. The chapter concludes by walking the reader through some strategies for developing a qualitative research study.

Case Study

Mateo López was ecstatic when he received word that he passed his comprehensive exam because he knew he was now about to embark upon the next stage of the doctoral journey: the dissertation. Mateo enrolled in an EdD that utilized the scholar-practitioner program model. In his program, Mateo was expected to develop the research skills needed to inform educator practice in the K–12 setting. If he had selected a PhD program with a research-scientist program model, Mateo would have needed to conduct research that contributed to the advancement of scientific knowledge. During his course of studies, he grew increasingly passionate about a topic he thought would prove highly practical within his own community. Mateo was the principal of a large urban high school with a growing Latinx population, and he was concerned about the persistent academic achievement gap between Latinx and Caucasian students all across the city.

While he was excited about his proposed topic, Mateo found it difficult to pin down his problem statement and his dissertation chair told him this would be one of the keys to unlocking which research design would best suit his study. If Mateo articulated the problem as a search for cause and effect or a correlation between certain factors, he would likely find a quantitative design more fitting. If Mateo expressed the problem as an effort to discover why the gap existed or what the gap meant to his Latinx students or how it affected them, he would find qualitative designs that met his needs.

It was not a debate about whether or not quantitative or qualitative designs are better or more valid than the other; it was all about which design would best fit his problem statement and the research questions that evolved from it. Since both methods were equally valid depending upon the problem statement, Mateo even briefly considered conducting a mixed methods dissertation drawing on both quantitative and qualitative designs. But his chair cautioned him against what his chair deemed an overly ambitious plan for a novice researcher.

What the Research Says

Qualitative research has been sometimes viewed with suspicion and associated with pejorative terms such as "soft science" or even as unscientific, which "is peculiarly damning in an era when scientific knowledge is generally regarded as the highest form of knowing" (Mays & Pope, 1995, p. 109). Qualitative research has been criticized as subjective, lacking rigor, reproducibility, and generalizability. While quantitative studies depend upon the validity of instrument construction, with qualitative research, the researcher is considered the human instrument (Patton, 2015). Despite these concerns, not every type of data can be properly addressed using a quantitative approach, and human behavior cannot always be reduced to a numerical representation. There are complex data surrounding people's attitudes, beliefs, emotions, and perceptions that necessitate the stories behind them to truly understand the *why's* and *how's* of certain phenomena.

Those concerned with the validity of qualitative research might argue, "The research is so personal to the researcher that there is no guarantee that a different researcher would not come to radically different conclusions" (Mays & Pope, 1995, p. 109). To address this concern, doctoral candidates must display the expertise, competence, and rigor needed to support their findings. Various checklists, which are designed to enhance the rigor of qualitative research, can serve as useful tools for doctoral candidates. The

Consolidated Criteria for Reporting Qualitative Research (COREQ), created by Tong et al. (2007), is a 32-item checklist for the "explicit and comprehensive reporting of qualitative studies" (p. 349) and is available in a reportable format online (Elsevier, 2024). Another helpful tool is the Standards for Reporting Qualitative Research (SRQR), which is designed to "improve the transparency of all aspects of qualitative research by providing clear standards for reporting qualitative research" (O'Brien et al., 2014, p. 1245).

A recent trend that must be considered by qualitative researchers is the role of artificial intelligence (AI) as a means of data analysis. Traditionally, qualitative data analysis employed some method of coding. *Coding* is "the process of aggregating text or visual data into small categories of information, seeking evidence of the code from different databases being used in a study, and then assigning a label to the code" (Creswell & Poth, 2025, p. 478). In the past, the researcher or researchers were tasked with painstakingly reviewing all the data collected and identifying specific codes that reflected the ideas contained in the data. The ability of AI to analyze huge qualitative datasets in seconds is truly a potential game-changer. But it does come with certain limitations. Morgan (2023) used ChatGPT to reinvestigate two datasets that had been analyzed using traditional methods. He found that ChatGPT "was less successful at locating subtle, interpretive themes, and more successful at reproducing concrete, descriptive themes" (p. 1).

The selection of a particular qualitative design by doctoral candidates is largely dependent upon the research problem and the accompanying questions they seek to address. In traditional qualitative research, there are five approaches addressed by Creswell and Poth (2025) in the fifth edition of their widely acclaimed text, *Qualitative Inquiry and Research Design: Choosing Among Five Approaches*. These approaches are case study, phenomenology, narrative, grounded theory, and ethnography. Additionally, and particularly useful to the scholar-practitioner, are more applied research methodologies that often employ qualitative data collection and analysis methods. These applied methodologies include action research, participatory action research, improvement science, evaluation, and needs assessment. In the following sections, we present an overview of the traditional methodologies and an explanation of the applied methodologies.

Case Study

The case study design is among the most ubiquitous within qualitative research (Priya, 2020). Gall et al. (2007) defined case study "as (a) the in-depth study of (b) one or more instances of a phenomenon (c) in its real-life context that (d) reflects the perspectives of the participants involved in the phenomenon" (p. 447). The unit of analysis for a case study can be a single person, a group of persons, an event, a program, a school, or any other entity such as a decision or a process.

A common mistake of novice researchers is to convolute whether the case is a person (or persons) or an entity. Therefore, the key for the researcher is to carefully and succinctly identify the case being studied as well as its boundaries. According to Yin (2013), case studies are the preferred method when researchers are asking questions regarding "how" and "why" a phenomenon occurs when the researcher has little control over events. Stake (1978) explained case studies are useful for creating understanding, extending experience, and increasing conviction regarding what is known.

Case studies may be descriptive, exploratory, or explanatory (Yin, 2013). The *descriptive* case study simply seeks to describe a phenomenon within its real-life context, while the *exploratory* study seeks to probe the initial phenomenon to develop hypotheses or propositions. *Explanatory* case studies seek to shed light on existing theories.

Various types of case studies also exist. Single case, multiple case, explanatory, intrinsic, holistic, and embedded are all potential case study designs. For instance, Mateo might choose a single (holistic) student or a single (holistic) class section to study or he might conduct a cross-case analysis of two (embedded) single case studies (e.g., one male and one female). There are many permutations for case study designs depending on the goals of the researcher.

For example, Mateo might conduct a descriptive, multiple case study to provide a thick depiction of the experiences of Latinx students from a particular perspective (e.g., gender, socioeconomic status, or grade point average). Case study methodology will give him the opportunity to capture a holistic picture of the situation and its context for a purposely chosen selection of Latinx students.

Phenomenology

"Phenomenology is the study of the world as it appears to individuals when they lay aside the prevailing understandings of those phenomena and revisit their immediate experience of the phenomena" (Gall et al., 2007, p. 495). Drawing upon the ideas of Edmund Husserl, researchers such as Moustakas (1994) explained phenomenology as an "act" which is a lived experience from which the participant derives meaning. Based on this understanding, participant perception is viewed as the primary source of knowledge as derived from both sensation and perceived intention (Moustakas, 1994).

Data for phenomenological studies are typically collected through participant interviews during which participants articulate their lived experiences regarding the phenomena being studied. The key to analyzing data reported by participants is the researcher's ability to *bracket* the distinct experiences of both participant and researcher (Gall et al., 2007, p. 496). Moustakas (1994) used the more arcane Greek term, *Epoche*.

> *In the Epoche, we set aside our prejudgments, biases, and preconceived ideas about things. The world is placed out of action, while remaining bracketed. However, the world in the bracket has been cleared of ordinary thought and is present before us as a phenomenon to be gazed upon, to be known naively and freshly through "purified" consciousness.*
>
> *(Moustakas, 1994, p. 85)*

There are a variety of approaches to phenomenological research: *hermeneutic, heuristic*, and *transcendental*. A hermeneutic study "involves the art of reading a text so that the intention and meaning behind appearances are fully understood" (Moustakas, 1994, p. 9). This approach requires a reflective interpretation of the interview transcript during which the researcher considers and examines his or her own biases and presuppositions to avoid imposing personal views on the participant's experience. While a hermeneutic study is inherently interpretive, a transcendental study focuses on "pure description" (Dowling, 2005, p. 134) of the phenomenon. In contrast, a heuristic study seeks to discover human experience in a meaningful way. Moustakas (1994) described a heuristic study as

> *a process of internal search through which one discovers the nature and meaning of experience and develops methods and procedures for further*

> *investigation and analysis. The self of the researcher is present throughout the process and, while understanding the phenomenon with increasing depth, the researcher also experiences growing self-awareness and self-knowledge.* (p. 17)

Depending upon his research questions, Mateo might consider conducting a phenomenological study. This type of study would lend itself to the question, "What is the lived experience of Latinx high school students in regard to their academic achievement?"

Narrative

Narrative research is often confusing for doctoral candidates because it is both a qualitative research design and a term used to describe a method of data analysis. For example, Mateo might select a phenomenological design to study the lived experiences of Latinx students and yet draw upon *narrative analysis* to examine the texts of his interviews.

A *narrative* design, however, centers on the collection of stories or counterstories from individuals about their lived experiences. Delgado (1989) explained, "Counterstories can open new windows into reality, showing us that there are possibilities for life other than the ones we live" (p. 2414). Espinoza's (2024) dissertation, *Leading Towards Racial Justice: Counterstories of TK-12 Latinx Men Administrators* provides a good example of narrative design. In his dissertation, Espinoza conducted two extensive semi-structured interviews with six male, Latinx administrators.

Creswell and Poth (2025) described several types of narrative designs—biographical, life history, biography, oral history, and autoethnography. A *biographical study* attempts to simply record the life experiences of another person. A key to conducting this form of study is to select an appropriate framework through which the narrative can be interpreted. A *life history* examines an individual's entire life. A *biography*, on the other hand, might only deal with a certain aspect or time period of a person's life (e.g., the playing career of a professional athlete). An *oral history* involves the recorded personal reflections of participants regarding their perceptions of events.

The final type of narrative research is *autoethnography*, sometimes called autobiographical. Autoethnography is the creation of personal narratives informed by the writer's own experiences (Poulos, 2021). While it is a valid form of narrative research, challenges exist, and some universities might not encourage or permit this form of research among doctoral candidates. Among the challenges are an overemphasis on self in isolation from others; the unsupported, negative portrayal of others; and overreliance on personal recollections, which could be inaccurate or misleading. Autoethnographies are categorized by some researchers as a subcategory of ethnography (Merriam & Grenier, 2019). Data for narrative research can be analyzed thematically, structurally, or dialogically (Creswell & Poth, 2025).

Grounded Theory

The aim of grounded theory research is to move past a simple description of events to develop a unified model or theory that explains a process or action (Creswell & Poth, 2025). The new or revised theory is figuratively "grounded" in the data collected from study participants who experienced the process or action. Among the most widely recognized pioneers of grounded theory are Glaser and Strauss (see *The Discovery of Grounded Theory: Strategies for Qualitative Research*, 1999). Strauss was later joined by Corbin and the two (Strauss & Corbin, 1990; Corbin & Strauss, 2015) are among the leading advocates for a systematic approach to grounded theory. Charmaz (2014), Clarke (2005), and Mills et al. (2006) have since introduced an alternative, constructivist perspective.

According to Strauss and Corbin (2015), "Two of the criteria for evaluating the value and effectiveness of a grounded theory are its fit and applicability to teaching, research, and practice" (p. 367). *Fit* refers to the ability of a theory to make sense in everyday experience. To be *understood*, it must be comprehensible to participants and researchers alike. Regarding *generality*, a quality theory will be based on a broad enough spectrum of data to be applicable to a variety of similar circumstances. Finally, a theory must be *controlled* in that the specific conditions under which it operates are clearly defined and articulated.

As a novice researcher, Mateo's committee might be hesitant to suggest grounded theory as it is one of the most complex qualitative designs. But if his research problem and questions require this design, theorists like Strauss and Corbin (2015) provided systematic procedures for collecting and analyzing data. For instance, instead of conducting a narrative study where Mateo hoped to capture the counterstory of his participants, he might propose to explain how those administrators internally and externally constructed their narratives to explain how their narratives took shape.

Among the most difficult tasks for the novice researcher using a grounded theory design is the collection of data, which requires achieving data *saturation*. Saturation occurs when the researcher ceases to find additional data that informs the process or action being studied. Also, difficult and cumbersome is the data analysis process, which is often labeled as the constant comparative method (Creswell & Poth, 2025). This iterative process includes open coding, axial coding, and selective coding. Strauss and Corbin (2015) added a fourth step requiring the development of a theoretical model or conditional matrix, with the goal of "translating abstract ideas into an easily understood diagram" (p. 163).

Ethnography

An ethnographic study is the examination of a culture-sharing group of people in their natural environment (Creswell & Poth, 2025). At first glance, doctoral candidates might be tempted to dismiss an ethnographic design due to their concern that such a study would involve far too large a population. While ethnographic studies can and do include large populations (macro-ethnography), a culture-sharing group could include several teachers or a group of students (micro-ethnography).

As is the case of other qualitative designs, ethnographers seek to examine the lived experiences of the participants within a natural context. Thus, researchers develop a detailed, complete, and complex description of the shared culture and then seek patterns such as rituals and customs or shared ideas and beliefs (Creswell & Poth, 2025). Attempting to describe a culture is not to be treated lightly. Rather,

> It carries quite serious intellectual and moral responsibilities, for the images of others inscribed in writings are most assuredly not neutral. Ethnographic writings can and do inform human conduct and judgment in innumerable ways by pointing to the choices and restrictions that reside at the very heart of social life.
>
> (Van Maanen, 2011, p. 1)

As with other qualitative designs, various approaches to ethnographic studies exist such as confessional, feminist, visual, life history, and autoethnography. Creswell and Poth (2025) identified two particularly popular forms: realist and critical ethnography. *Realist ethnography* is an attempt to provide an objective, third-person account of the cultural context being studied sans personal bias and presupposition. *Critical ethnography* reflects its critical theory underpinnings and advocates for those marginalized by society. Critical ethnography sets out to critique social ills such as inequality, repression, victimization, oppression, and asymmetrical power relations to work toward the emancipation of marginalized groups (Creswell & Poth, 2025).

Two primary hurdles facing the ethnographer are (a) gaining entry or access to the culture and (b) collecting data. Gaining entry into a culture can be particularly difficult for ethnographers because these studies typically require wide-ranging and sometimes intrusive access to the group. Van Maanen (2011) explained collecting data often requires extensive fieldwork. He posited this process might require living *with* the participants being studied full-time, for an indeterminate, extended period of time, as well as living *like* them.

As a doctoral candidate, it would be quite a feat (although not impossible) for Mateo to maintain a full-time job as a school administrator and conduct an ethnographic study. In addition to having to work to gain access to and trust from the students' Latinx culture, Mateo would need to schedule extensive periods of time to conduct fieldwork among the population of students.

Applied Research Methodologies

Qualitative designs may also be employed as part of mixed methods research (see Chapter 13: Understanding Mixed Methods of Inquiry) or used for or as a part of *applied research methods*. Applied research methods are meant to enact some kind of change and are particularly useful scholar-practitioner dissertations because they tend to focus on *problems of practice* (POP). A POP is "a persistent, contextualized, and specific issue embedded in the work of a professional practitioner, the addressing of which has the potential to result in improved understanding, experience, and outcomes" (CPED, 2010). Scholar-practitioners, like Mateo, tend to enter doctoral programs like the EdD concerned about the problems they see in their workplace. They want to go beyond simply studying the problem, seeking instead to improve or fix the problem and the lives of those impacted by it. Applied research methodologies can do just that.

Action research and *participatory action research* have been around for some time. Its purpose is to bring about change in specific contexts, like schools (Parkin, 2009). Mertler (2021) explained that action research is a process that improves a context "by incorporating change and involving educators working together to improve their own practices" (p. 1). In this way, action research involves introducing a change idea, working collaboratively with others to test the idea and gather data, and determining the impact of the change in a reflective way. Most importantly, it is conducted by those who are involved with and have direct access to the problem and means to fix it.

Improvement science, which is new in education fields (Bryk et al., 2015), also introduces change to address POPs but does so with an emphasis on changing the system that generated the problem. Systems thinking (Meadows, 2008) plays an important role in defining the aspects of organizations that generate the problem and in determining where in the system is the best place to begin addressing the POP with the goal of shifting the way the system works. Improvement science might be a good methodology for Mateo if his goal is to reduce the achievement gap between Latinx and Caucasian students. Both action research and improvement science employ a process often called a Plan-Do-Study-Act or Plan-Do-Check-Act iterative cycle where a plan to introduce the change is developed, then implemented. Data are gathered to answer research or inquiry questions that frame the change idea, and those data are studied to determine if the change worked or needs to be adjusted and tried again. This iterative process can often go beyond the dissertation to become a continued effort in the student's workplace. Each of these methodologies prepares the scholar-practitioner with skills in applying research to change practice, skills they will continue beyond graduation.

Other applied methods include evaluation and needs assessment. An *evaluation* seeks to use data gathering tools like those found in qualitative research (i.e., interviews, focus groups, document analysis) to determine if an existing program or intervention in an organization has worked. The logic model, developed by the W.K. Kellogg Foundation, provides a framework that guides the types of data that should be gathered to determine the resources, activities, outputs, outcomes, and impact of the program or intervention. It is a practical model that offers a backwards look to determine the value of the program or intervention and backing that value judgment with evidence. A *needs assessment* is exactly what it sounds like and is something that a scholar-practitioner might undertake to better determine the need to put resources towards fixing a problem. A needs assessment is "a process for figuring out how to close a learning or performance gap... by determining what the important needs are and how to address them" (Sleezer et al., 2014). Both methodologies often look to existing organizational data (e.g., reports, statistics) but also will employ the tools of qualitative research to learn more about the program, intervention, or issue being studied. Again, these two methodologies are very practical and will be used beyond the dissertation process.

Strategies for Success

Bloomberg (2012) reminds us, "A dissertation is an extensive, challenging, and rigorous scholarly endeavor. As such, completing represents the pinnacle of academic achievement" (p. 242). As with any journey, lessons in life come along the way, not in reaching the journey's end. The following are recommendations for doctoral candidates contemplating a qualitative investigation.

Strategy 1: Determine Program Acceptance and Faculty Expertise in Qualitative Inquiry

The introduction to this book presented five stages doctoral candidates must navigate to successfully complete their journeys. When selecting a program during the Entry Stage, a candidate interested in conducting a qualitative study should review the background of the program to see if there is bias against qualitative designs. The prospective candidate must examine faculty curriculum vitae to see if any have an interest in or have published qualitative research.

The student should also check if specific qualitative design courses are offered. Potential course titles might be *Qualitative Research Methods* or *Qualitative Data Analysis*. If no such courses are available, the candidate will know upon entering the program that, while it is still possible to successfully complete a qualitative study, it will certainly be more difficult to navigate the Knowledge and Skill Development Stage. Without these classes, it will become even more imperative that the candidate find faculty mentors familiar with qualitative designs.

Strategy 2: Align Design with Focus of Inquiry

Selecting the proper design is one of the most important decisions a qualitative researcher makes and must properly align with the problem statement and research questions. Within the field of qualitative research, this can be more difficult than it seems. Mateo is an excellent example of how this process unfolds. His interest in the academic achievement gap among Latinx high school students began to grow during a course on educational leadership. The topic resonated with Mateo because of his own experiences as a school principal, and he began to read widely on the topic.

Mateo's research bore fruit as he began to learn more and more about the experiences of Latinx and other minority students. Mateo's close relationship with several Latinx students at his school inclined him toward questions that best aligned with a phenomenological design, as his desire was to describe their lived high school experiences.

When the focus is to explain a process or generate theory, grounded theory is the most suitable approach. When the phenomenon of study is clearly bounded to a specific context or setting, case study may be most fitting. If the purpose is to describe a phenomenon within the context of a culture-sharing group, ethnography would be appropriate. Narrative research is most appropriate when the researcher seeks to tell the life story of one or two individuals with significant experience with the phenomenon being investigated. However, if the goal is to improve the state of an existing problem of practice, one of the applied methodologies might be the best option.

Strategy 3: Construct a Rigorous Design

Rigor in qualitative research is judged by a different set of criteria than in quantitative studies. One parallel framework for increasing rigor in qualitative studies is Guba and Lincoln's (1986) *trustworthiness* criteria. To increase *credibility* (akin to internal validity) qualitative researchers can employ the following strategies: prolonged engagement in the field and persistent observation of participants, triangulation (multiple forms of data collection), peer debriefing, negative case analysis, and conducting member checks with participants.

Transferability (akin to external validity) is increased when the researcher provides thick, rich, descriptions of the context of the study so those reading the findings can judge whether to apply all or part of the findings elsewhere. In qualitative investigations the reader determines the transferability of findings, as opposed to the researcher generalizing findings to a population in quantitative investigations.

Dependability (akin to reliability) and *confirmability* (akin to objectivity) are enhanced through the establishment of an audit trail (documentation of data collection and analysis procedures employed, typically in appendices) and "the carrying out of an audit by a competent external, disinterested auditor" (Guba & Lincoln, 1986, p. 19).

Strategy 4: Plan for Extensive Time in the Field

Mateo did not know it at the time, but his dissertation journey was going to take him longer than he had initially envisioned. The dissertation process in general, but especially for researchers employing qualitative designs, often takes more time than expected. The data collection methods typically employed in qualitative inquiry (e.g., individual interviews, focus groups, observations, reflective journaling, etc.) are often more challenging to schedule and more time-consuming than anticipated, especially for doctoral candidates who frequently hold down full-time jobs while also meeting family and other social obligations.

Conclusion

This chapter explains the strengths and benefits of qualitative methods for conducting research. Qualitative research can be rigorous, reliable, and valid if design methods are properly followed. There are unique advantages to both quantitative and qualitative designs depending upon the nature of the problem being studied and the research questions asked. It is a false argument to claim that one design is inherently superior to the other. As qualitative research becomes more pervasive, it is incumbent upon doctoral candidates and their committees to strive toward rigorous methodologies to ensure all research is conducted with excellence.

Questions for Reflection

You are encouraged to reflect on the following questions and consider them in light of your specific research problem and research questions:

- What is the problem I hope to study and how do I craft the central question of my research?
- What is my goal for the problem—to learn more and produce more knowledge about the problem or to improve or fix the problem and the system that is generating it?
- How is my dissertation better served by using a qualitative rather than a quantitative design?
- What factors will shape which qualitative design I select?
- Who are the faculty in my program who possess expertise in qualitative research?
- What steps will I take to enhance the trustworthiness of my findings?

Recommended Resources

Many sources are available to aid the qualitative researcher. While Creswell and Poth (2025) provided a sound overview of the five qualitative research designs presented in this chapter, other designs (e.g., historical) can be employed depending on the nature of the problem investigated. Texts like Creswell and Poth (2025) and Wolcott (1994) can aid in the understanding of the nature of qualitative inquiry and are very helpful with selecting the appropriate research design, but when it comes time to write the methodology section of the dissertation and actually execute the proposed research it is prudent for doctoral candidates to utilize the primary source texts specific to the selected research design to find the depth and detail needed to conduct doctoral-level research. Below is a sample of general methodology and design-specific texts.

Qualitative Research

Bloomberg, L. D. (2022). *Completing your qualitative dissertation: A road map from beginning to end* (5th ed.). SAGE.

Creswell, J. W., & Poth, C. N. (2025). *Qualitative inquiry and research design: Choosing among five approaches* (5th ed.). SAGE.

Denzin, N. K., Lincoln, Y. S., Giardina, M. D., & Cannella, G. S. (Eds.). (2024). *The SAGE handbook of qualitative research* (6th ed.). SAGE.

Guba, E. G., & Lincoln, Y. S. (1986). But is it rigorous? Trustworthiness and authenticity in naturalistic evaluation. In D. Williams (Ed.), *Naturalistic Evaluation: New Directions for Evaluation* (pp. 73–84). Jossey-Bass.

Merriam, S. B., & Tisdell, E. J. (2015). *Qualitative research: A guide to design and implementation* (4th ed.). Jossey-Bass.

Wolcott, H. F. (1994). *Transforming qualitative data: Description, analysis, and interpretation*. Sage.

Case Study

Stake, R. (1995). *The art of case study research*. SAGE.

Yin, R. K. (2013). *Case study research: Design and methods* (5th ed.). SAGE.

Phenomenology

Moustakas, C. (1994). *Phenomenological research methods*. SAGE.

Van Manen, M. (1990). *Researching lived experience: Human science for an action sensitive pedagogy*. State University of New York Press.

Narrative Research

Clandinin, D. J., & Connelly, F. M. (2000). *Narrative inquiry: Experience and story in qualitative research*. Jossey-Bass.

Denzin, N. K. (1989). *Interpretive biography*. SAGE.

Grounded Theory

Charmaz, K. (2014). *Constructing grounded theory*. SAGE.

Corbin, J., & Strauss, A. (2015). *Basics of qualitative research: Techniques and procedures for developing grounded theory* (4th ed.). SAGE.

Strauss, A., & Corbin, J. (1990). *Basics of qualitative research: Grounded theory procedures and techniques*. SAGE.

Ethnography

LeCompte, M. D., & Schensul, J. J. (2010). *Designing and conducting ethnographic research* (2nd ed.) Alta Mira.

Wolcott, H. F. (2008). *Ethnography: A way of seeing* (2nd ed.). Alta Mira.

Applied Research Methodologies

Kellogg, W. K. (2004). *Using Logic Models to Bring Together Planning, Evaluation, and Action: Logic Model Development Guide.* WK Kellogg Foundation.

Mertler, C. A. (2024). *Action research: Improving schools and empowering educators.* Sage Publications.

Perry, J. A., Zambo, D., & Crow, R. (2020). *The improvement science dissertation in practice: A guide for faculty, committee members, and their students.* Myers Education Press.

Sleezer, C. M., Russ-Eft, D. F., & Gupta, K. (2014). *A practical guide to needs assessment.* John Wiley & Sons.

References

ATLAS.ti. (2024). *The ultimate guide to qualitative research—part 2: Handling qualitative data.* https://atlasti.com/guides/qualitative-research-guide-part-2/data-coding

Bloomberg, L., D. (2012). Afterword. In L. D. Bloomberg & M. Volpe (Eds.), *Completing your qualitative dissertation: A road map from beginning to end* (2nd ed. p. 242). SAGE.

Bryk, A. S., Gomez, L. M., Grunow, A., & LeMahieu, P. G. (2015). *Learning to improve: How America's schools can get better at getting better.* Harvard Education Press.

Charmaz, K. (2014). *Constructing grounded theory.* SAGE.

Clarke, A. E. (2005). *Situational analysis: Grounded theory after the postmodern turn.* SAGE.

Corbin, J. & Strauss, A. (2015). *Basics of qualitative research: Techniques and procedures for developing grounded theory* (4th ed.). SAGE.

CPED (2010). *Design Concepts.* Carnegie Project on the Education Doctorate.

Creswell, J. W., & Poth, C. N. (2025). *Qualitative inquiry and research design: Choosing among five approaches* (5th ed.). SAGE.

Cypress, B. (2017). Rigor or reliability and validity in qualitative research: Perspectives, strategies, reconceptualization, and recommendations. *Dimensions of Critical Care Nursing, 36*(4), 253–263. https://doi.org/10.1097/DCC.0000000000000253

Delgado, R. (1989). Storytelling for oppositionists and others: A plea for narrative. *Michigan Law Review, 87*(8), 2411–2441. https://doi.org/10.2307/1289308

Dowling, M. (2005). From Husserl to von Manen. A review of different phenomenological approaches. *International Journal of Nursing Studies, 44,* 131–142.

Elsevier. (2024). *ÇOREQ (COnsolidated criteria for REporting Qualitative research) Checklist.* https://cdn.elsevier.com/promis_misc/ISSM_COREQ_Checklist.pdf

ESOMAR. (2024). *Global market research.* https://esomar.org/global-market-research

Espinoza, P. (2024). *Leading towards racial justice: Counterstories of TK–12 Latinx men administrators.* Chapman University ProQuest Dissertations Publishing. 30989871.

Gall, M. D., Gall, J. P., & Borg, W. R. (2007). *Educational research: An introduction* (8th ed.). Pearson.

Guba, E. G., & Lincoln, Y. S. (1986). But is it rigorous? Trustworthiness and authenticity in naturalistic evaluation. In D. Williams (Ed.), *Naturalistic evaluation: New directions for evaluation* (pp. 73–84). Jossey-Bass.

Guba, E. G., & Lincoln, Y. S. (1994). Competing paradigms in qualitative research. In N. K. Denzin & Y. S. Lincoln (Eds.) *Handbook of qualitative research* (pp. 105–17). SAGE.

Kellogg, W. K. (2004). *Using Logic Models to Bring Together Planning, Evaluation, and Action: Logic Model Development Guide.* WK Kellogg Foundation.

Mays, N., & Pope, C. (1995). Rigour and qualitative research. *British Medical Journal, 331*(6997), 109–12.

Meadows, D. H. (2008). *Thinking in systems: A primer.* Chelsea Green Publishing.

Merriam, S. B., & Grenier, R. S. (2019). *Qualitative research in practice: Examples for discussion and analysis* (2nd ed.). Jossey-Bass.

Mertler, C. (2021). Action research as teacher inquiry. *Practical Assessment, Research & Evaluation, 26*(19), 1.

Mills, J., Boner, A., & Francis, K. (2006). The development of constructivist grounded theory. *International Journal of Qualitative Methods, 5*(1), 1–10.

Morgan, D. L. (2023). Exploring the use of artificial intelligence for qualitative data analysis: The case of ChatGPT. *International Journal of Qualitative Methods, 22,* 1–10.

Moustakas, C. (1994). *Phenomenological research methods.* SAGE.

O'Brien, B. C., Harris, I. B., Beckman, T. J., Reed, D. A., & Cook, D. A. (2014). Standards for reporting qualitative research: A synthesis of recommendations. *Academic Medicine, 89*(9), 1245–1251. http://doi.org/10.1097/ACM.0000000000000388

Parkin, P. (2009). *Managing change in healthcare: Using action research.* SAGE

Patton, M. Q. (2015). *Qualitative research and evaluation methods* (4th ed.). SAGE.

Poulos, C. N. (2021). Conceptual foundations of autoethnography. In C. N. Poulos, *Essentials of autoethnography* (pp. 3–17). American Psychological Association.

Priya, A. (2020). Case study methodology of qualitative research: Key attributes and navigating the conundrums in its application. *Sociological Bulletin, 70*(1), 94–110. https://doi.org/10.1177/0038022920970318

Saldana, J. (2021). *The coding manual for qualitative researchers.* SAGE.

Sleezer, C. M., Russ-Eft, D. F., & Gupta, K. (2014). *A practical guide to needs assessment*. John Wiley & Sons.

Stake, R. E. (1978). The case study method in social inquiry. *Educational Researcher, 7*(2), 1–10.

Strauss, A., & Corbin, J. (1990). *Basics of qualitative research: Grounded theory procedures and techniques*. SAGE.

Thelwall, M., & Nevill, T. (2021). Is research with qualitative data more prevalent and impactful now? Interviews, case studies, focus groups and ethnographies. *Library & Information Science Research, 43*(2). https://doi.org/10.1016/j.lisr.2021.101094

Tong, A., Sainsbury, P., & Craig, J. (2007). Consolidated criteria for reporting qualitative research (COREQ): A 32-item checklist for interviews and focus groups. *International Journal for Quality in Health Care, 19*(6), 349–357. https://doi.org/10.1093/intqhc/mzm042

Van Maanen, J. (2011). *Tales of the field: On writing ethnography* (2nd ed.). University of Chicago Press.

Yin, R. K. (2013). *Case study research: Designs and methods* (5th ed.). SAGE.

12 Understanding Quantitative Inquiry

Amanda J. Rockinson, EdD, PhD
Rebecca LaFountain, EdD

Introduction

Quantitative and qualitative research methods are both valid approaches for conducting an inquiry; however, they differ significantly in their philosophical assumptions and purpose (Creswell & Creswell, 2023). It is important to understand the assumptions and purpose of quantitative methods as you make decisions and conduct research for coursework, your dissertation, and for publication.

Consider that, before any great building is constructed, the builder analyzes the situation and chooses the building type. Once the type of building is identified, the builder begins sketching out the plans, setting a schedule, and obtaining the needed permits and materials. This was what Frank Lloyd Wright did with *Fallingwater*. Wright did not just start stacking brick upon brick and arrive at his creation. Instead, he analyzed the various landforms, identified the type of building he wanted to build, and designed the building on paper before the first stone was laid. The genius of the building had already been realized prior to construction. Before conducting research, you need to identify the research method (quantitative, qualitative, or mixed methods) for your study. Then, design or structure to begin "sketching" your inquiry plan (e.g., sampling, data collection, etc.). That is, you need to choose a method and design. These elements guide decisions that need to be made about conducting the research. They guide:

- Your research questions
- What data to gather and from whom

- When and how often to collect data
- How to analyze the data

To help you better understand quantitative research, this chapter outlines the philosophical assumptions that underpin it. The chapter addresses when it is appropriate to conduct quantitative research, particularly in the Inquiry Stage (i.e., dissertation). The four goals of quantitative research as presented by Shaughnessy et al. (2012) are explained, and the major quantitative designs proposed by Campbell and Stanley (1963) and Creswell and Creswell (2023) are considered in this review.

Case Study

Sammie, a PhD candidate in Counsellor Education and Supervision, felt a weight lifted off her shoulders after she selected her dissertation topic. After much exploration, she found an article about college students with attention-deficit/hyperactivity disorder (ADHD) experiencing interpersonal issues on campus. The authors noted a gap in the empirical research motivated the need to examine interventions related to the problem.

Finding this empirical gap (i.e., as a PhD candidate in a research program she knew she needed to fill a theoretical or empirical gap in the literature with her dissertation), coupled with her experiential knowledge that many students with ADHD lack social skills, Sammie wondered if social skills training based in a cognitive behavioral (CB) approach could assist students in adjusting to college. She was excited when she realized that she had found a "missing link" in the research or "gap in the literature" to which she could contribute with an independent research study of her own.

Sammie developed a research hypothesis—college students diagnosed with ADHD who are involved in a social skills CB group will have fewer interpersonal problems than those who do not receive the treatment. Because she had formulated a hypothesis with an operationally defined independent variable (the social skills CB group) and dependent variable (interpersonal skills), and because she enjoyed working with numbers and wanted to examine the effectiveness of a treatment, she decided to conduct a quantitative study for her dissertation.

What the Research Says

When taking research courses during the Knowledge and Skill Development Stage, doctoral students often approach the course by reading the material chapter by chapter to learn and grasp an understanding of various terms and concepts. This process is known as the knowledge and comprehension levels developed in Bloom's (1959) seminal work on learning domains. However, as doctoral students approach the Inquiry Stage and have the daunting task of developing and proposing their dissertation study, new skills are required. At this juncture, they examine quantitative research from the more advanced domains of application, analysis, synthesis, and evaluation (Bloom, 1959) to make decisions about inquiry. Doctoral students who tend to see the world as comprised of observable, measurable facts, as opposed to a world that is complex and socially constructed, are likely to be drawn to quantitative research.

To further explain, quantitative research is situated within a *positivist* paradigm for viewing the world (Campbell & Stanley, 1963; Hoyle et al., 2009). Those who adhere to a positivist paradigm embrace the ontological assumption that a single, tangible reality exists, and this reality can be understood, identified, and measured. Furthermore, they adopt the epistemological assumption that knowledge is developed objectively, free from the biases and values of doctoral candidates or participants. Thus, the primary goal of positivist inquiry is to generate explanatory associations or causal relationships to predict or explain phenomena. Doctoral candidates who construct a deductive, linear literature review, develop research questions and corresponding null and alternative hypotheses, and seek to examine the relationship or difference among *variables* (i.e., a characteristic or number that can be measured) are likely to adopt a quantitative method of inquiry for dissertation.

In the case of Sammie, she aims to explain the difference in social skills between students who participate in social skills intervention and those who do not. She desires to obtain knowledge derived from direct observation and make logical inferences based on her observation. As such, a quantitative method is an appropriate choice for her dissertation. Once the decision to adopt a quantitative research method is made, Sammie needs to identify the *research design*(s) she will employ to answer her research questions.

Quantitative Research Designs

Summarizing all quantitative research designs is beyond the scope of this chapter, as researchers and theorists describe and organize them in different ways. However, designs can be categorized in terms of the four goals of quantitative research: (a) description, (b) prediction or association, (c) explanation, and (d) application (Creswell & Creswell, 2023; Shaughnessy et al., 2012) (see Figure 12.1).

Description

In *descriptive research*, a doctoral candidate describes the distribution of the variables in question throughout a sample population (Creswell & Creswell, 2023; LaFountain & Bartos, 2002). Descriptive researchers provide a detailed description of an occurrence or population using numerical data. *Survey research*, for example, is one descriptive approach. Survey research involves the use of a predetermined, carefully selected set of questions. Using survey research, doctoral candidates can examine the distribution of a variable among segments of the population at a given point in time. This type of

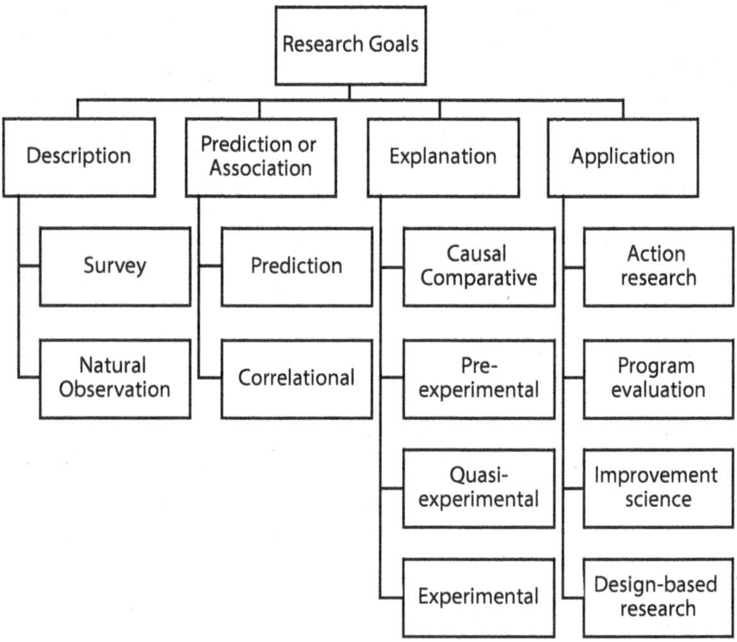

Figure 12.1 Goals of Research.

survey is called *cross-sectional* (Creswell & Creswell, 2023). Likewise, doctoral candidates can explore possible changes in the distribution of the variable over time in *longitudinal surveys. Cross-sequential studies* combine methods from cross-sectional and longitudinal approaches (Creswell & Creswell, 2023). If Sammie were to employ this design, she might gather survey data from a group of students with ADHD, examining their social skills each year they are in college (e.g., first-year, second-year, junior, senior). She may analyze data each year and describe the differences in her participants' social skills over the course of each year of college.

Another descriptive approach involves gathering data to support direct or indirect conclusions. Direct observation in a natural setting without any intervention is called *natural observation*. Observation with an intervention is referred to as participant observation, structured observation, or field experiments (Creswell & Creswell, 2023). For example, Sammie might survey college students with ADHD to determine which social skills inhibit the students' academic achievement the most. This data would assist her in identifying what specific social skills may need to be the focus of an intervention that she develops.

Prediction

A second goal of quantitative inquiry is *association or prediction*, which involves forecasting outcomes based on observed patterns or describing the relationship between variables (Creswell & Creswell, 2023; Shaughnessy et al., 2012). Studies that involve association are often referred to as *correlational research designs* (LaFountain & Bartos, 2002) and describe *what* is happening. They do not describe why it is happening. Doctoral candidates cannot make statements about any cause-and-effect association because they do not know the direction of the cause and cannot guarantee that another variable is influencing the outcome. This is why statisticians often emphasize, "Correlation does not equal causation!"

The variables in a prediction study are referred to as the *predictor* and the *criterion* as doctoral candidates are concerned about whether one or more variables can predict another variable. The variables in an association study are referred to as *variables of interest*, as doctoral candidates are concerned with *how* the variables under study relate to each other (Rovai et al., 2013). When doctoral candidates discover variables that covary, they can make predictions about behavior, adding *covariates* (i.e., variables that may affect variables of interest, the criterion, predictor, or other variables). For example, Sammie may want to examine if ADHD symptoms are associated with cumulative GPAs, participation in extracurricular activities, or levels of test anxiety to better understand how ADHD symptoms influence college outcomes.

Explanation

The third goal of quantitative research is to answer the question, *"Why is it happening?"* Doctoral candidates are concerned with understanding why inquiries seek to identify the underlying causes by examining patterns and causal connections. For example, if employing an explanatory study, Sammie might investigate the effect of a CBT social skills intervention on the social skills of college students with ADHD. Moreover, "why" inquiries are usually accomplished by employing group comparison studies.

In a seminal text, Campbell and Stanley (1963) purported that there are causal comparative studies and three types of experimental group comparison studies: (a) pre-experimental, (b) experimental, and (c) quasi-experimental. A *causal comparative design* is *ex post facto* research—a non-experimental design that is often used for exploratory purposes. In this approach, an event or intervention is studied after the fact, that is, after it has occurred naturally or has already been manipulated. *Pre-experimental designs* are not discussed in depth here, as Campbell and Stanley (1963) deem them worthless due to the inherent, severe threats to internal validity.

Experimental and *quasi-experimental* designs enable doctoral candidates to move beyond merely describing existing data to generating new data that can be manipulated and analyzed to establish cause-and-effect relationships. Experimental and quasi-experimental research studies are accomplished by exposing at least one or more experimental groups to one or more treatment conditions and comparing the results (e.g., within group or time-series designs) or comparison or control groups (e.g., between group designs). *Control* (i.e., a comparison group that does *not* receive the experimental treatment) and *manipulation* (i.e., introduction of the independent variable to the experimental group and withholding from the control group and observing the effect on the dependent variable) are distinguishing elements of these designs (Creswell & Creswell, 2023).

Randomization is the unique characteristic of the actual experimental design. Through *random sampling*, a subset of the population is randomly selected for the study. That is, each member of a population has an exactly equal chance of being selected for the inquiry. By forming groups through *random assignment*, researchers can assume that participant characteristics are evenly distributed across groups from the beginning of the experiment. Suppose the groups have different outcomes after the manipulation, given that all other conditions were held constant. In that case, it is presumed that the independent variable (e.g., treatment or intervention) is responsible for the difference.

The illustrations (Tables 12.1–12.3) depict several pre-experimental, quasi-experimental, and experimental designs. The notations used in the illustration are based on those in Campbell and Stanley's (1963) text and are widely adopted in other research texts.

X reflects exposure to treatment.

O reflects the observation or measurement.

Multiple rows reflect multiple groups.

R reflects that the group(s) were randomly assigned.

Table 12.1 *Illustrations of Pre-experimental Designs*

- One-shot case study
    - X O
- One group pretest-posttest
    - O X O
- Post-test only non-equivalent group design
    - X O
    - O

Table 12.2 *Illustrations of Quasi-experimental Designs*

- Interrupted time-series design (with and without control)
  - O O X O O
  - O O   O O
- Pretest posttest non-equivalent control group design
  - O X O
  - O   O
- Counterbalanced design
  - X(1)O X(2)O X(3)O
  - X(2)O X(3)O X(1)O
  - X(3)O X(2)O X(1)O

Table 12.3 *Illustrations of Experimental Designs*

- Post-test only design
  - R X O
  - R   O
- Pre-test post-test equivalent control group design
  - R O X O
  - R O   O
- Solomon four
  - R X O
  - R   O
  - R O X O
  - R O   O

Although the experimental group design controls for most threats to validity due to participant characteristics being spread evenly across groups, Campbell and Stanley (1963) refer to designs where random assignment is not possible as *quasi-experimental*, including the *nonequivalent control group* design (e.g., a between-group design where two different groups are compared) and the *time-series design* (e.g., a within-group design where one group is compared across time; also called *repeated-measures* design). In the nonequivalent control group design, groups that are not necessarily equivalent prior to treatment are compared using pretest and posttest measures. In a *time-series design,* doctoral candidates examine one group across different times (e.g., before and after a treatment). In other words, it is a design where participants serve as their controls, participating in both the experimental and control conditions (Shaughnessy et al., 2012).

For example, Sammie realized that her desire to study two groups of college students who had been diagnosed with ADHD (where the experimental group would receive a social skills treatment, and the control group would receive no treatment) would classify her dissertation research as a group comparison study. Since she could not use random assignment but intended to manipulate the independent variable and have a control group, Sammie hoped to conduct a quasi-experimental design, specifically a *nonequivalent control group* design. Since there are a variety of different types of quasi-experimental designs, Sammie read a research text most closely associated with her discipline (e.g., Campbell & Stanley, 1963; Creswell & Creswell, 2023; Gall et al., 2007, 2015, aligned with the educational field; Shaughnessy et al., 2012, written for psychology students) to define and justify her specific design for her dissertation.

The designs discussed above require large sample sizes (discussed in Other Considerations below). Doctoral candidates may wonder about their options when working with small samples, especially when dealing with specialized populations (e.g., individuals with personality disorders, students receiving special education services). In these cases, doctoral candidates may consider other experimental designs such as *single-case designs*, also referred to as *single-subject designs* (Kazdin, 2020; Kennedy, 2005; Kratochwill, 1976). Single-case designs are more suitable for testing a single participant (or at most a few participants) than other designs.

The most frequently used of these designs are the *ABAB* and the *multiple baseline*. With both designs, researchers collect baseline data from participants on an individual basis before introducing the intervention. The purpose of these designs is to verify whether each participant exhibits behavior change as a result of the intervention. These designs are briefly mentioned in this chapter but warrant further study if chosen for inquiry related to a course or dissertation.

It is also noteworthy to mention that additional quantitative research designs focus on collecting numerical data to analyze statistically, including but not limited to *instrument development* (e.g., creating a measure to examine variables of interest) or *content analysis* (e.g., systematically coding and quantifying content for patterns).

Application

The final goal of quantitative research, according to Shaughnessy et al. (2012), is *application*. This approach is often used by candidates in professional doctoral programs who seek to examine a problem of practice (POP), a persistent, contextualized, and specific problem within the work environment, which, by addressing, can improve understanding and solve the issue. The goal of application research is to use one or more research designs to address a problem in one's professional practice. For example, if Sammie were an EdD rather than a PhD candidate, she might approach her dissertation inquiry by examining a problem she sees at the university counseling center. The Counseling Center may offer a counseling group to students with ADHD, but the group's effectiveness in reaching its intended purpose—improving social skills—has never been examined. Therefore, for her dissertation, she may decide to use one or several quantitative designs to evaluate the effectiveness of the group, employing an applied method to inform the counseling center's services and enhance their offerings, rather than contributing to theoretical or empirical knowledge.

It is essential to emphasize that quantitative designs are employed as part of or in conjunction with applied research methods (e.g., action research, improvement science, program evaluation, needs assessment, design case research) or mixed-methods approaches (see Chapter 13: Understanding Mixed Methods of Inquiry). There are many applied research methods, which are too numerous to cover in this chapter; however, it is noteworthy to define two of the most commonly used approaches: action research and program evaluation (see Chapter 18: Understanding the Different Types of Dissertations).

Action research, also known as *participatory action research* (PAR), community-based study, action science, reflective action research, transformative research, or action learning, is an application approach used to improve conditions and practices in an environment (Reason & Bradbury, 2008; Whitelaw et al., 2003). Action research "is a form of applied research whose primary purpose is to increase the quality, impact, and justice of… practice" (Gall et al., 2007, p. 597). Per Bradbury (2015), "action research brings together action and reflection, as well as theory and practice, in participation with others, in the pursuit of practical solutions to issues of pressing concern" (p. 1). Its focus is problem-solving. The purpose of action research is to bring about change in specific contexts (Whitelaw et al., 2003) or to generate shared knowledge on how to address problems by bridging the theory-practice gap (Bourner & Brook, 2019). This type of application research involves a cyclical process of planning, implementing, reflecting, and adjusting based on the data (Kemmis & McTaggart, 2005).

Program evaluation is a systematic applied approach for collecting, analyzing, and applying data to address the effectiveness and efficacy of a project, policy, or program (What Works Clearinghouse, 2020). It is the "process of making judgments about the merit, value, or worth of a... program" (Gall et al., 2007, p. 559), to provide information for decision-making and improvement of programs. After understanding various purposes and designs in quantitative research, it is vital for doctoral candidates employing quantitative methods in their inquiries to understand a few other elements.

Validity

When identifying a design and developing the methods section of the dissertation (typically Chapter 3 in a traditional dissertation for a research doctorate), doctoral candidates need to consider validity, especially in cases where they may not be able to conduct their study with the control necessary for a proper experimental design. This condition may be due to factors such as the setting in which they are required to implement their research or the method of sampling they use. For example, Sammie may not be able to assign her participants randomly and must instead use existing groups formed prior to her involvement (e.g., sections of courses determined through course registration, rather than randomization). This would result in nonequivalent groups, introducing threats to the validity of her study, which she would need to minimize or control for in order to ensure her study has internal validity. *Internal validity* addresses whether the outcome of a study results from the variable under study or from some factors not controlled.

Doctoral candidates also need to minimize extraneous (systematic) errors and random (unpredictable) errors. They need to be aware of the classic research by Campbell and Stanley (1963), which identified seven extraneous variables that are potential threats to internal validity in experimental studies. These threats to validity are outlined here; however, doctoral candidates should also be aware that research books within their field may outline additional threats to validity (e.g., see Kazdin (2021) for a discussion about construct validity).

History occurs when participants experience an external event, beyond the exposure to the treatment, which may affect the dependent variable. A solution for doctoral candidates is to include more than one group in the study. As stated previously, random assignment increases the likelihood that characteristics are distributed evenly across both groups from the beginning of the experiment. Additionally, it ensures that all participants have an equal opportunity to be exposed to external events.

Maturation is the psychological or physiological process that may change within participants during treatment, potentially affecting their responses. Doctoral candidates can best control for maturation by including more than one group. Additionally, the use of random assignment will ensure that everyone experiences maturation equally, and any differences can be attributed to the independent variable rather than natural development.

Testing, such as pretesting, can sensitize participants and possibly serve as a learning experience, ultimately affecting internal validity. When using an experimental design with randomization, testing should be used only as a dependent variable. The use of more than one group is also recommended to minimize this threat.

Instrumentation refers to all types of measurement used in the study. In addition to using more than one group, the researcher must ensure that all groups are subjected to the same instruments and procedures.

Statistical regression is a concern when extreme scores are involved, either in the selection of participants (e.g., selecting only gifted students) or in the administration of a measure. Extreme scores tend to regress toward a mean. This threat is avoided by including individuals in the study with a wide range of scores rather than extreme scores, unless justified by the research hypothesis.

Selection is an issue when the method of assigning participants to groups results in systematic differences in the groups. Random assignment is the best means of control for this threat; however, if randomization is not possible, it is necessary to administer a pretest to determine if the groups differ initially on the dependent variable.

Attrition, also referred to as *mortality*, refers to the loss of participants during a study. Pretesting would help doctoral candidates assure themselves whether dropouts and nondropouts differ in their initial status on the dependent variable.

Although internal validity is of primary concern when designing a quantitative study, doctoral candidates also need to be concerned about threats to external validity. *External validity* refers to the extent to which the findings can be generalized to the broader population. Campbell and Stanley (1963) identified four factors that can threaten external validity: (a) interaction between testing and treatment, (b) interaction between selection and treatment, (c) reactivity (participants' awareness they are in a study), and (d) multiple treatment interference (when the same subjects are exposed repeatedly to two or more treatments).

Other Considerations

When doctoral candidates begin to consider their research method and design, several other considerations arise. Although not every consideration is discussed here, a few important ones are introduced.

First, doctoral candidates must consider the population they wish to study. A *population* is defined as all members of any well-defined class of people (e.g., first-year college students diagnosed with ADHD). Because it is usually not possible to recruit an entire population, doctoral candidates must identify that portion of the population to which they have access. This condition is referred to as the *accessible population*.

Doctoral candidates will draw their *sample*, which is the group selected to be included in the study (LaFountain & Bartos, 2002) from the accessible population. Doctoral candidates must use the most significant sample possible when conducting quantitative research; however, finances and time often restrict the number of participants that can be studied. Gay and Airasian (2003) suggested a minimum sample of thirty participants for a causal comparative design. Others recommend a minimum of fifteen for experimental designs and a minimum of fifteen participants for causal-comparative research (Creswell & Creswell, 2023; Gall et al., 2007). In survey research, at least one hundred participants should be studied in each minor subgroup.

As quantitative inquiry often involves hypothesis testing and statistical analysis, *statistical conventions, in addition to research conventions, must be considered when determining* sample size. Cohen's (1988) formula is often used, considering several elements. First, the statistical analysis being used is considered. For example, a doctoral candidate may use a one-tailed *t-test*. Cohen's formula for a one-tailed t-test is used. Included in the formula are the hypothesized effect size, typically a moderate effect size ($d = 0.50$), the alpha level, usually 0.05, and the desired power, typically 0.80. These numbers are used to calculate an appropriate sample size. For example, a doctoral candidate using a one-tailed t-test requires a sample size of approximately sixty-four for their dissertation. Numerous researchers have established both necessary research and statistical conventions for sample sizes, most of which recommend large ones.

Doctoral candidates need to consider the populations to which they have access, so that they do not find themselves with an excellent proposal in hand, but few or no participants with whom to implement it. For example, it probably would not be possible for Sammie to recruit every college student with an ADHD diagnosis. However, she could still carry out her research if she had connections with a large university from which she could draw a sample of participants. She would need to select a representative sample of the population (e.g., students with ADHD attending one specific Southern university). Sampling is just one of the considerations Sammie needs to address in her quantitative inquiry. She will need to take time to read quantitative research texts to ensure all the details of a quantitative research plan are addressed. Finally, a recent trend that must be considered in quantitative research is the role of artificial intelligence (AI), particularly as a means of data analysis, a topic discussed further in Chapter 10: Overcoming Statistics Anxiety.

Strategies for Success

Writing a dissertation is a significant commitment in terms of time and energy. You must select a research method and corresponding design that aligns with your research purpose and research questions. If quantitative research is the route that aligns with your purpose and research questions, then demonstrating an understanding is particularly important. While some doctoral candidates may view the dissertation as merely a culminating process for their doctoral degree, it can also be the beginning of a research agenda that will extend long into their academic career or the start of investigating and solving problems within their professional practice.

Strategy 1: Ensure the Program and Faculty Support Quantitative Research

During the Entry Stage of the doctoral journey, if you are interested in conducting a quantitative study for the dissertation, you need to ensure the faculty in your chosen program holds expertise in and experience with quantitative research. Surveying faculty curriculum vitae and asking questions about faculty expertise and interest during the admissions process is one way to ensure you will have support. Additionally, reviewing recently published dissertations from the program can help determine whether the program has a preference for quantitative or qualitative research methods.

As a prospective student, you should also review course requirements and electives to ensure the curriculum and university support services provide sufficient quantitative research design and analysis courses to support skill and knowledge development in these areas. During the Knowledge and Skill Development Stage, take as many quantitative research and analysis courses as possible, while seeking opportunities to work with faculty who are experts or, at a minimum, have experience with quantitative design and analysis to develop methodological and analysis skills that are needed for the dissertation.

Strategy 2: Align the Design with the Purpose Statement and Research Question(s)

Using a quantitative design is appropriate if (a) the research problem and questions are quantitative, (b) the variables can be measured quantitatively, (c) you feel a philosophical match with the quantitative approach, and (d) you have an accessible population available. Once a quantitative approach is selected, a specific design (or designs) needs to be chosen. Your research design will serve as the architectural blueprint for your dissertation.

The discussion in this chapter on quantitative research designs is only a brief overview. The information contained herein may help determine the basic purpose of the study (e.g., description, prediction, explanation, or application) and in determining whether a descriptive, correlational, group comparison, single-case, or other design is appropriate for your research; thus, providing a general direction for further research. To further explore quantitative research, read texts within your discipline that will support a deeper understanding and provide additional support (see also Recommended Resources below).

Strategy 3: Conduct Rigorous Research

As discussed in this chapter, several considerations must be made to develop a rigorous quantitative research plan, extending beyond the identification of the design. One of these considerations is internal validity. To evaluate whether a study has internal validity and the degree of internal validity the study possesses, you must ask questions such as, "*Is the change in the independent variable responsible for the differences observed in the dependent variable?*" Moreover, "*to what degree can alternative explanations of changes in the variable under study be ruled out?*" Ask these questions to evaluate the internal validity of the study (Heppner et al., 2015).

Several procedures may be undertaken to control for internal validity. These include the following: (a) randomly assigning participants to groups, (b) determining the measurement, and (c) manipulating the independent variable (Hepner et al., 2015). For a comprehensive understanding of these concepts, as well as other relevant considerations, it is essential to thoroughly read and consult relevant research texts.

Questions for Reflection

The following questions can help you apply what is presented in this chapter:

- Who are the faculty members in my program who possess quantitative expertise?
- What opportunities do I have during the Knowledge and Development Stage to increase quantitative skills and knowledge?
- Are my philosophical beliefs about research in line with the quantitative method: Do I see the world as comprised of observable, measurable facts that can be quantified?
- In my research, do I prefer to answer "What is going on?" or "Why is it going on?" and what is my goal in doing quantitative research: description, prediction, explanation, or application?
- How comfortable am I with statistical analysis?

- Who is my population? What is the sample size needed for the chosen research design? What procedure will I use to calculate the needed sample size to ensure a statistical power? Be mindful that large sample sizes are required for causal-comparative studies, in the order of thirty participants per group (or more) (Gay, 1987); whereas, calculating the needed sample size for a *t*-test using Cohen's (1988) formula, sixty-four per group is needed to ensure strong statistical power. Do I have access to the population and sample size I will need to use the research design and statistical analysis I would like to employ?
- What research design(s) are best suited for my study? What procedures can I reasonably and ethically conduct? (e.g., Can I manipulate the independent variable? Can I randomly assign?) Which design(s) would be the most appropriate?
- Based on my chosen design(s), which threats to validity is my study more susceptible to? How can I control for them?

Recommended Resources

Research Books

Campbell, D. T., Stanley, J. C., & Gage, N. L. (1963). *Experimental and quasi-experimental designs for research.* Houghton, Mifflin and Company.

Fraenkel, J. R., Wallen, N. E., & Hyun, H. (2023). *How to design and evaluate education research.* McGraw-Hill.

Heppner, P. P., Kivlinghan, D. M. & Wampold, B. E. (2015). *Research design in counseling* (4th ed.). Cengage Learning.

Kazdin, A. E. (2021). *Research design in clinical psychology* (5th ed.). Cambridge University Press.

Single Case or Subject Design

Barlow, D. H., Nock, M. K., & Hersen, M. (2009). *Single case experimental designs* (3rd ed.). Pearson.

Horner, R. H. et al. (2005). The use of single-subject research to identify evidence-based practice in special education. *Exceptional Children, 72*(2), 165–179.

Kazdin, A. E. (2020a). *Single-case research designs.* Oxford University Press.

Applied Research

McNiff, J. (2017). *All You Need To Know About Action Research*. SAGE.
Romero-Hall, E., Hsiao, E., & Gao, F. (2018). The (re) adaptability of research methodologies in the instructional design & technology field. *Tech Trends, 62*(5), 424–426.
What Works Clearinghouse. (2020). Standards handbook (Version 4.1). U.S. Department of Education, Institute of Education Sciences, National Center for Education Evaluation and Regional Assistance. https://ies..gov/ncee/wwc/handbook
Winter, R. & Munn-Giddings, C. (2001). *A Handbook for Action Research in Health and Social Care*. Routledge.

References

Bloom, B. L. (1959). Ecologic factors in the WAIS Picture Completion Test. *Journal of Consulting Psychology, 23*(4), 375. https://doi.org/10.1037/h0043221
Bloom, B. S. (1956). *Taxonomy of educational objectives, Handbook I: The cognitive domain*. David McKay.
Bourner, Tom., Brook, C., & Mertler, C. (2019). Comparing and contrasting action research and action learning. In C. A. Mertler (Ed.), *The Wiley Handbook of Action Research in Education*, 185–205. doi: 10.1002/9781119399490.ch9.
Bradbury, H. (2015). Introduction: How to situate and define action research. In H. Bradbury (Ed.), *The Sage Handbook of Action Research* (3rd ed.). Sage Publications.
Campbell, D. T., & Stanley, J. C. (1963). *Experimental and quasi-experimental designs for research*. Rand McNally.
Cohen, J. (1988). *Statistical power analysis for the behavioural sciences*. Lawrence Erlbaum Association.
Creswell, J. W., & Creswell, J. D. (2023). *Research design: Qualitative, quantitative, and mixed methods approaches* (6th ed.). SAGE.
Crowl, T. K. (1993). *Fundamentals of educational research*. Brown & Benchmark
Gall, M. D., Gall, J. P., & Borg, W. (2007). *Educational research*. Pearson/Allyn & Bacon.
Gall, M. D., Gall, J. P., & Borg, W. R. (2015). *Applying educational research: How to read, do, and use research to solve problems of practice* (7th ed.). Pearson.
Gay, L. R. (1987). *Educational research competencies for analysis and application* (3rd ed.). Merrill Publishing Company.
Gay, L., & Airasian, P. (2003). *Educational Research: Competencies for Analysis and Application* (7th ed.). Pearson International Edition.
Heppner, P. P., Wampold, B. E., Owen, J., Thompson, M. N., & Wang, K. T. (2015). *Research design in counseling*. Cengage Learning.

Hoyle, R. H., Harris, M. K., & Judd, C. M. (2009). *Research methods in social relations.* Wadsworth.

Kazdin, A. (2020b). *Single-Case Research Designs.* Oxford University Press.

Kemmis, S., & McTaggart, R. (2005). Participatory action research: Communicative action and the public sphere. In N. K. Denzin & Y. S. Lincoln (Eds.), *The Sage handbook of qualitative research* (3rd ed., pp. 559–603). Sage.

Kennedy, C. (2005). *Single-case designs for educational research.* Allyn & Bacon.

Kratochwill (Ed.) (1976). *Single subject research: Strategies for evaluating change.* Academic Press.

LaFountain, R. M., & Bartos, R. B. (2002). *Research and statistics made meaningful in counseling and student affairs.* Brooks/Cole.

Reason, P. & Bradbury, H. (2008). *The SAGE Handbook of Action Research: Participative Inquiry and Practice* (2nd ed.). SAGE.

Rockinson-Szapkiw, A. J. (2013). Quantitative research process. Retrieved from http://amandaszapkiw.com/resources/tutorials-and-instructional-materials/quantitativeresearch-process/

Rovai, A. P., Baker, J. D., & Ponton, M. K. (2013). *Social science research, design, and statistics.* Watertree Press.

Shaughnessy, J. J., Zechmeister, E. B., & Zechmeister, J. S. (2012). *Research methods in psychology* (9th ed.). McGraw-Hill.

What Works Clearinghouse. (2020a). Standards handbook (Version 4.1). U.S. Department of Education, Institute of Education Sciences, National Center for Education Evaluation and Regional Assistance. https://ies.ed.gov/ncee/wwc/Docs/referenceresources/WWC-Standards-Handbook-v4-1-508.pdf

What Works Clearinghouse. (2020b). Procedures and Standards Handbook (version 4.1). https://ies.ed.gov/ncee/wwc/Handbooks

Whitelaw, S., Beattie, A., Balogh, R. & Watson, J. (2003). *A Review of the Nature of Action Research.* Welsh Assembly Government.

13 Understanding Mixed Methods of Inquiry

Dao Nguyen, PhD

Mixed method refers to the integration of both qualitative and quantitative methods in one research study (Creswell, 2022). This chapter provides an understanding of the fundamental principles of mixed methods and the procedures in research practices, especially during the Inquiry Stage (i.e., dissertation or applied research project process). Strategies for success are also included to help doctoral students better prepare for their EdD journeys.

Case Study

Emerson, a doctoral candidate in an EdD program in Educational Leadership, has a research interest that stems from her background as a math teacher at a secondary school, where she later became an assistant principal and was subsequently promoted to principal at a different school in the same state. Both her former and current schools have a diverse student population, with nearly 50% identifying as nonwhite, including African American, Hispanic, Asian, Native American, Native Hawaiian, Pacific Islander, and multi-race non-Hispanic, and over 40% of students from low-income families. The socioeconomic backgrounds of her school's students mirror those of all the state school districts on average.

Earlier this year, Emerson was invited to join the state's STEM Advisory Council, where she is responsible for providing insights into the math achievement gap among high school students and proposing policies and interventions to address this disparity. As a doctoral candidate and an experienced educator and school administrator, Emerson understands the importance of data-based decision-making and policymaking. To better serve her current roles as a principal and STEM advisory council member, she anticipated that her doctoral thesis would focus on a problem closely related to her work practice. She wanted to use her dissertation findings to address the issue that her school and state have struggled with in the achievement gaps between student groups, particularly in mathematics at the secondary education level.

Emerson decided her doctoral research topic would be *mathematics achievement at the secondary school level*, and her research questions would be: (a) *What are the key contributors to student math achievement?* (b) *What policy and practice are most effective in improving math achievement, especially for low-achieving students?*

To seek rigorous answers to these research questions, Emerson needed to identify the best methodological approach for obtaining data. Based on her knowledge of the research methods she learned in coursework, she weighed the merits of quantitative or qualitative methods but ultimately felt both stopped short in their capacity to address the full complexity of the issue. She also thought about the possibility of integrating both approaches but wondered if it was essential or worth doing in terms of time and energy investment. She shared her wavering thoughts with her academic adviser about which method would best fit her topic and research questions. The subsequent sections pertain to the insights she received from her advisor regarding the mixed methods approach for her consideration.

What the Research Says

The concept of mixed methods research first emerged in 1959 when Campbell and Fisk used multiple methods to study psychological traits in humans. However, in the early 1990s, mixed methods evolved into a systematic approach for integrating quantitative and qualitative data across diverse research designs to answer research questions. A researcher might adopt a mixed methods design to address the biases and weaknesses inherent in each data source. That is, by using both quantitative *and* qualitative data, the researcher might better understand the research problem from a "collective strength" in analysis and interpretation (Creswell & Creswell, 2023; Creswell, 2022, p. 2).

Since its inception, mixed methods research has been seen as a third methodology alongside quantitative and qualitative methods. Such a determination has emerged from various perspectives, including philosophical and theoretical approaches, methodological orientations that focus on different phases of the research process, and a transformative perspective aimed at fostering change in communities or among groups.

Mixed methods research offers an effective approach for conducting comprehensive investigations. By gathering both quantitative (closed-ended, numeric) and qualitative (open-ended, textual) data, researchers can integrate or combine the two. This integration enables the drawing of inferences, termed *meta-inferences*, which provide valuable insights that surpass the scope of either quantitative or qualitative data on their own (Creswell, 2022, p. 2). Before delving further into the fundamentals of mixed methods designs, it is important to identify the underlying philosophical assumptions that inform mixed methods research.

Philosophical Worldviews

Creswell and Creswell (2023) use the term *worldview* to refer to "a basic set of beliefs that guide action" (Guba, 1990, p. 17). In the extant literature on research philosophy, the nuance of worldview is associated with different terminologies used by different research methodologists. For instance, Lincoln, Lynham, and Guba (2011) and Mertens (1998) used the term "paradigm" to imply a framework for understanding the nature of knowledge. Crotty (1998) employed a broader range of descriptors, including *philosophical assumptions, epistemologies*, and *ontologies*, to reflect the multifaceted dimensions guiding research methods. Neuman's (2009) *research methodology* highlighted the intricate relationship between the nature of knowledge and the methods by which it is pursued and validated. Despite the varying terminologies, *positivism, constructivism*, and *pragmatism* embody three fundamental philosophical worldviews that influence quantitative, qualitative, and mixed methods approaches, respectively. This chapter focuses on exploring pragmatism as a crucial worldview framework for the mixed methods approach.

Pragmatic Worldview

The philosophical framework of pragmatism, initially developed by John Dewey and Donald Davidson, emphasizes practicality in research endeavors (Schrauf, 2016). Pragmatic researchers "reject the dogmatic either/or choice between quantitative and qualitative approaches and believe that the truth is 'what works' best for understanding a particular research problem" (Ivankova, 2014, p. 16). Under a pragmatic worldview, researchers prioritize the research problem and question over the methods, using all available approaches to understand the problem (Rossman & Wilson, 1985). They employ diverse methods, often a combination of quantitative and qualitative approaches, to collect data related to the focal issue of their research inquiry. In other words, they can freely choose research methods, techniques, and procedures that best align with their needs and purposes without being confined to any specific philosophical or ontological framework (Creswell & Creswell, 2023).

Within the realm of pragmatic research, distinguished scholars like Cherryholmes (1992), Morgan (2007), Murphy (1990), and Patton (1990) have made significant contributions. In recent years, notable figures such as Creswell (2022), Creswell and Clark (2018), Hitchcock and Onwuegbuzie (2022), Mertens (2010), and Poth (2023) have emerged as leaders in the field of mixed methods research, contributing to its growing prominence.

Returning to the case study presented earlier, after comprehending the pivotal assumptions of the pragmatist worldview in research, Emerson acknowledged that her research study necessitated being grounded in this philosophical stance to seek the most viable solutions to the problem of persistent mathematics achievement disparity among secondary school students across her state's school districts. Both quantitative and qualitative data were indispensable to investigating her research questions. On one hand, quantitative data would constitute an objective source for determining significant contributors to math achievement. On the other hand, qualitative data would represent a subjective source, enabling her to gain insights into the challenges encountered by students, teachers, and administrators in their respective roles of learning, teaching, and leading.

In essence, qualitative data would originate from the direct voices of stakeholders involved in math learning and teaching within the school environment. Emerson expected their voices would also provide valuable input for effective bridging strategies. Having established the worldview position of her research (pragmatism) as requiring mixed methods, Emerson pondered upon research design and procedure, specifically when and how to collect, analyze, integrate, interpret, and draw meta-inferences from the combined results.

Three Core Mixed Methods Research Designs

In mixed method research applications, fifteen mixed methods designs have been identified and grouped into two main categories—*core* and

Table 13.1 *Core Designs and Implementation Procedures*

Core Design	Implementation Procedures
Convergent Parallel	Quantitative Strand + Qualitative Strand = Converge Results
Explanatory Sequential	Quantitative Strand → Qualitative Strand = Explain
Exploratory Sequential	Qualitative Strand → Quantitative Strand = Explore

complex—(Creswell & Clark, 2018; Fetters, 2020). This chapter focuses solely on the three core designs—*convergent parallel, explanatory sequential,* and *exploratory sequential*—which serve as the fundamental designs of mixed methods research (see Table 13.1). Regardless of which core design a mixed methods study employs, the implementation procedure typically includes four steps—(1) data collection, (2) analysis, (3) integration, and (4) interpretation and meta-inference. The designs generally vary in the sequence of quantitative and qualitative data collection and analysis, as well as in the integration points.

To facilitate the immediate understanding of the main procedure and intent of each core design, a conceptualized description is provided in the form of a mathematical formula following the design name. The content in this section is mainly adapted from Creswell and Clark (2018).

Convergent Parallel Design: Quantitative Strand + Qualitative Strand = Converge Results

This design involves collecting and analyzing two independent strands of quantitative and qualitative data in a single phase, merging the results of the two strands, and then looking for convergence, divergence, contradictions, or relationships between the two databases. This design seeks a full understanding of a research problem by collecting a variety of data using both quantitative and qualitative tools (close-ended and open-ended, respectively). By combining the strengths of quantitative and qualitative methods, this core design aims to ensure strong validation of the research findings.

Doctoral candidates can choose this design when there is limited time for collecting data in the field, but both quantitative and qualitative information from every participant is needed. This design allows gathering both data types, typically in one visit. With this design, candidates are required to have knowledge and research skills in both quantitative and qualitative research methods. See the previous chapters—Chapters 11: Understanding Qualitative Inquiry and Chapter 12: Understanding Quantitative Inquiry—for specific tenets and strategies of each method. In this design, the doctoral candidates are able to effectively reflect participant voices and report statistical trends. This design is also an ideal option for leveraging the expertise of a diverse research team with varying strengths in quantitative and qualitative research.

Assuming Emerson faced time constraints for her research project—only six weeks for data collection and analysis—and that she is proficient in both quantitative and qualitative methods, she could opt for this convergent parallel design for her mixed methods study. She would follow four typical steps, as outlined in the introduction to the three core designs above. First, she concurrently collected quantitative data mined from her state's math score database and qualitative data from semi-structured interviews with the math teacher and student participants. Second, Emerson analyzed these two datasets separately and independently. Third, once she had the results in hand, she began to merge or integrate the results of the two datasets, comparing the analyzed results in one of the following formats: comparative table or joint display table (see columns one and two of Table 13.2 in the next section as an example), graphical joint display, or passages organized by major topics. Finally, as the last step, she interpreted and drew meta-inferences about what she learned from the comparison.

Following this design, Emerson became aware of some potential challenges, including uneven sample sizes, gaps between numeric and text databases, and discrepancies in results. To address these challenges, she collected a sizeable qualitative sample. In a qualitative study, there is no clear rule for the sample size. However, she followed Lincoln and Guba's (1985) suggestion—the sample size should be determined based on *thematic saturation* or informational redundancy. This means that the sampling can stop when gathering more data does not provide any new information. For example, if the initial qualitative sample has fewer than 10 participants, she could consider upsizing it to more than 10, for instance, 15, 20, or even more, provided that the new sample size helped her reach thematic saturation.

Alternatively, if using uneven sample sizes, the qualitative sample should be a subset of the quantitative sample. Ensuring that the concepts for both data types are consistent is an effective way to minimize the gap when merging textual/audio/visual and numeric databases. In case of discrepancies in analytical results, Emerson could collect additional data or reexamine existing data to identify the critical causes.

Explanatory Sequential Design: Quantitative Strand → Qualitative Strand = Explain

This design involves collecting and analyzing quantitative data first, followed by collecting and analyzing qualitative data. The qualitative data provides a deeper understanding of the quantitative findings. The intent of this design is to use qualitative strands to explain initial quantitative results. The researcher forms group(s) of potential participants based on quantitative results and follows up with qualitative research. The quantitative results guide purposeful sampling for the qualitative phase. This design helps explain mechanisms through qualitative data that shed light on the quantitative results.

Back to the case of Emerson, she was stronger in quantitative research methods, and she had the necessary instruments to measure the correlation between variables (average math scaled score of 10th graders of her state's school districts in 2023, average proportion of Black, Indigenous, and People of Color students and teachers, average proportion of students from low-income families, teacher salary, the presence of hired vocational education teachers, and per-pupil expenditure in the school district). However, Emerson had limited resources, where only one type of data was collected and analyzed at a time. She could collect qualitative data from teacher and student participants later. Moreover, she preferred a straightforward implementation procedure and a clearer structure for her dissertation. Based on those elements, this explanatory sequential design was best suited. She proceeded with her mixed methods research under this design with the following steps.

Step 1 was to design and implement the quantitative strand. She followed the procedural rule as guided in Chapter 12 of this book. Once having obtained the quantitative results, she moved to Step 2—identifying which results needed to be explained, using these quantitative results to refine the pre-determined qualitative and mixed methods questions, deciding which participants would be selected for the qualitative sample, and designing qualitative data collection protocols. Step 3 was conducting the qualitative strand. Chapter 11 of this book provides a good guide for completing the qualitative strand. Last, Step 4—interpretation and meta-inferences of the connected results.

In accordance with these steps, Emerson first summarized and interpreted the quantitative results. Then she summarized and interpreted the qualitative results. Finally, she discussed the extent to which and in what ways the qualitative results help to explain the quantitative results. Figure 13.1 below depicts her general procedure of data collection and analysis.

It is important to note that there were two integration points for Emerson's two datasets. The first point occurred after Emerson completed the quantitative data analysis and connected the selected quantitative results to a qualitative data collection plan. The second point was after the qualitative phase was completed, and when the two sets of connected results were combined to draw integrated conclusions about how the qualitative results explain and extend specific quantitative results. Table 13.2 shows the results of data integration, interpretation, and meta-inferences of the combined findings.

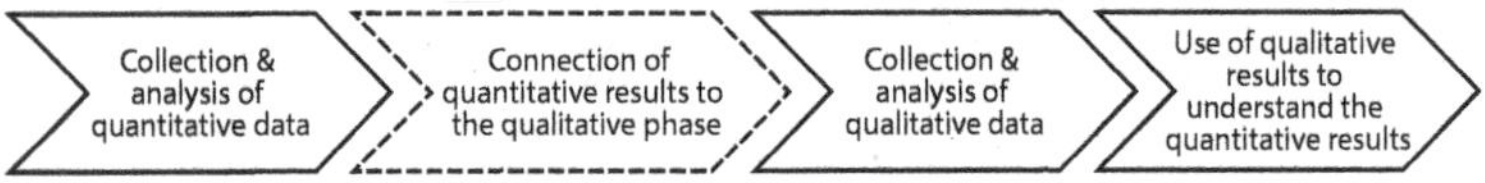

Figure 13.1 The procedures of data collection and analysis under the explanatory sequential design.

Table 13.2 *Joint Display of Quantitative and Qualitative Integrating Results and Meta-inferences*

Quantitative results	**Qualitative follow-up interviews explaining qualitative results**	**Meta-inference (How qualitative results helped explain the selected quantitative results)**
The poverty of 10th-grade students' families negatively influenced math achievement	Theme 1: Parent time and attention Theme 2: Parent expectation for children postsecondary education	The qualitative data from the interviews with 10th-grade students, math teachers, and administrators help explain how/in what ways the poverty badly impacted student math performance
The hiring policy of vocational education teachers positively contributed to the math scores	Theme 3: Inclusion of math in vocational education curriculum Theme 4: Student awareness of math position in their future academic plan. Theme 5: Skill building	The qualitative results help explain how the hiring policy of vocational education teachers in school districts could contribute to improving 10th graders' math scores.

Within this explanatory sequential design, Emerson faced challenges that are not uncommon in mixed methods studies. As her qualitative data collection protocols were not able to be finalized until *after* she analyzed the data collected from the quantitative phase of her study, it was necessary for her to gain additional Institutional Review Board (IRB) approval for the procedures outlined for the qualitative phase. She also added two more student and teacher participants in each of the school samples for a better understanding of how poverty influenced the math achievement. As such, the time for her completion of the whole study was more than she planned (eight weeks instead of six weeks).

Exploratory Sequential Design: Qualitative Strand → Quantitative Strand = Explore

This design involves collecting and analyzing qualitative data first, followed by collecting and analyzing quantitative data. The quantitative data is used to test or further explore the qualitative findings. Its purpose is to develop and apply quantitative measures based on qualitative data to explore phenomena without measures or instruments. From qualitative findings, the researcher develops and test new instruments, then identifies variables for the quantitative study component, assessing the generalization of qualitative results and testing aspects of emergent theories. The final purpose is to explore phenomena in-depth and measure prevalence.

The Exploratory Sequential Design is selected when doctoral candidates and their research problem are more focused on qualitative aspects, requiring an inductive approach, and when it is necessary to develop a culturally sensitive product (e.g., an instrument, intervention materials, or a digital tool). Another reason to consider this design is a particular interest in the transferability and generalization of newly developed products. This design allows for the identification of new research questions based on small-sample qualitative results and determining what can be best tested with a large quantitative sample. Emerson could choose this design based on those conditions. In sum, the design fits the situation in which candidates have time for three distinct research phases: (a) qualitative, (b) development, and (c) quantitative.

With this design, Emerson first designed and implemented the qualitative strand. Chapter 11's Understanding Qualitative Inquiry would be helpful for her to conduct a rigorous qualitative research component. Based on the qualitative results, she designed and piloted a test for a quantitative data collection instrument, then refined quantitative research questions, hypotheses, and the mixed methods questions. The next step was to collect quantitative data. The last step involved interpreting the connected results and drawing meta-inferences with the following procedures: first, Emerson summarized and interpreted the qualitative results, then summarized and interpreted the quantitative results, and last, discussed to what extent and in what ways the quantitative results generalized or tested the qualitative results.

In this Exploratory Sequential Design, the integration of the two datasets has two points: (1) *after the initial qualitative results*, the integration involved using these initial qualitative results to build a new quantitative tool, such as an instrument, intervention, measure, web-based application, or other, that will be tested quantitatively; and (2) *after the final quantitative phase* was completed, integrated the two sets of connected results and drew an integrated conclusion about how the quantitative results were built on the qualitatively informed instrument or materials.

With this design, Emerson understood she needed to prepare for certain challenges. First, she needed to allocate extra time to complete the three phases of the research. Obtaining IRB approval might be difficult because of the unpredictability of the quantitative phase. To deal with this, she planned a tentative direction or considered submitting two separate applications for IRB approval. Another possible challenge was the potential need for two different samples in case the initial qualitative sample does not yield convincing results for creating a new measure or if the initial quantitative data is not statistically significant. Ideally, both samples should be from the same population. Moreover, determining which qualitative results were used to develop a new quantitative instrument and ensuring its validity was not an easy task. But it could be made on the foundations of not only the qualitative results but also on the literature review and theoretical framework.

Applied Research in Education

The mixed methods approach is workable for multiple forms of applied research, such as evaluation, action, and design-based research. In education, *evaluation research* aims to assess the effectiveness of educational programs, policies, or interventions (Mills & Jordan, 2023). In other words, it is commonly employed in the fields of education policy and practice. There are two types of evaluation research—formative and summative evaluation. In the *formative* type, this evaluation is conducted during the development or enhancement of a program or product, with the aim of providing constructive feedback. In the *summative* type, this evaluation occurs following the implementation phase to assess the outcomes or overall impact of the initiative. A mixed methods design could be effective in both types of evaluation research. For example, Atkins et al. (2010) used mixed methods to evaluate the integration of mental health services in schools. These researchers used surveys and behavioral assessments to measure the impact (quantitative), and interviews with school staff, students, and families (qualitative) to assess implementation challenges and stakeholder perspectives. Their study illustrates how mixed methods help evaluate both outcomes and processes in a complex, real-world setting.

Action research in education refers to a systematic inquiry carried out by teacher-researchers, principals, school counselors, and other stakeholders within the teaching-learning environment. This process entails collecting information (data) about the operations of their specific schools, the methods teachers employ, and the ways students learn. The primary aim of action research is to equip educators with a framework for addressing problems of practice within their classroom, school, or school district, ultimately improving both student learning and teacher instructional performance as well as leading effectiveness. As Mills and Jordan (2023) highlighted, "Qualitative data collection techniques are more often applied to action research problems than are quantitative methods and designs" (p. 389). This statement implies that mixed methods could be used in action research. Bell's (2010) mixed method action research is among many educational studies using a mixed methods design to examine the impact of project-based learning (PBL) on student engagement in a middle school science class. Quantitative data were collected via pre- and post-intervention engagement surveys, while qualitative data included teacher reflections and student interviews. The results showed increased student motivation and deeper content understanding. The researcher insisted that the triangulation of data sources from his mixed method design strengthened the validity of the findings.

Design-Based Research (DBR) is a methodological approach used by instructional designers. It is different from action research but shares some similarities. DBR is commonly applied in education to improve teaching practices. This approach involves a process of analyzing, designing, developing, and implementing educational strategies repeatedly. It focuses on teamwork between researchers and educators to solve real-world problems or educational practice problems while generating new ideas and theories (Design-Based Research Collective, 2003). With these two main goals, a DBR research study often uses mixed methods to understand the complexity of educational settings.

Wang and Hannafin (2025) conducted their mixed methods study applying DBR to the design of inquiry-based science instruction supported by digital tools. Their methods involved analyzing student achievement data (quantitative) alongside ethnographic field notes (qualitative). This iterative process guided both teaching practices and theoretical frameworks for technology integration. Another example, Collins et al. (2004) developed a digital tool aimed at enhancing writing skills among middle school students. Their study employed a mixed methods approach, which involved analyzing quantitative writing assessment scores in conjunction with qualitative evaluations of student drafts and teacher interviews. The iterative cycles facilitated adjustments to the tool based on feedback and performance data, ultimately leading to improved writing instruction strategies.

The objectives and empirical examples of evaluation, action research, and design-based research (DBR), discussed above, highlight the widespread application of the mixed methods research approach in various forms of applied educational research. This approach enhances the validity and, consequently, the reliability of mixed methods research, contributing to the pursuit of effective solutions and improvements in educational policy and practice.

Strategies for Success

While professional doctoral programs typically encourage students to conduct applied research rather than basic research, programs across disciplines differ in their requirements in terms of duration and final research report (dissertation in practice, thesis, or research project). The following are strategies for doctoral candidates considering a mixed methods approach in the Inquiry Stage of their doctoral journey.

Strategy 1: Navigate Program Acceptance and Faculty Expertise in Mixed Methods Inquiry

Doctoral candidates should engage in a thorough brainstorming process to develop a robust methodological approach tailored to their specific research topic and objective. If you are considering a mixed methods approach—a combination of qualitative and quantitative research—it is crucial for you to navigate the extent to which your program supports this approach. Review your program's curriculum requirements to ensure alignment with your methodological preferences.

It is also crucial to assess the availability and expertise of faculty members who have experience with mixed methods research, whether through their past scholarly work or their current research interests. To facilitate this consideration, examine recent dissertations or applied research project reports produced within the program, as these documents may highlight the faculty's experience and the institution's commitment to mixed methods inquiry. Additionally, reviewing faculty resumes or CVs available on your school's website can offer valuable insights into the research backgrounds, publications, and areas of specialization of individual faculty members. This information ultimately helps you align your research goals with the strengths and expertise of the department faculty. Having mixed methods mentorship is always vital for supporting candidate research success!

Strategy 2: Decide Specific Procedure Design

By nature, mixed methods research combines the strengths of both quantitative and qualitative methods; however, the distinctive procedures for collecting data, analyzing data, integrating results, and interpreting and making multiple inferences from combined findings set mixed methods apart from traditional quantitative or qualitative approaches as presented in previous chapters. A notable number of doctoral candidates who embark on mixed methods research lack a comprehensive and meticulous description of their design procedures within their mixed methods research plans and reports. In a mixed methods study, the selection of the research design profoundly influences the collection and analysis procedure, and integration points of quantitative and qualitative data, as well as the nuanced interpretation and complex meta-inferences that arise from the combined findings. Therefore, it is imperative for you to cultivate a deep understanding of the strengths and challenges inherent in each design before determining the most appropriate approach for your specific research inquiry, experiences, participant recruitment conditions, timelines, and other pertinent factors. In light of this, this chapter offers guidelines for each core design, thereby equipping you to thoughtfully select the most suitable design for your research objectives and inquiries.

Strategy 3: Conduct Rigorous Research

Consider the measures to ensure the validity of the qualitative and quantitative components in your mixed methods research. Chapter 11, Understanding Qualitative Inquiry and Chapter 12 Understanding Quantitative Inquiry, are good resources for mapping out plans and actions for validating the qualitative and quantitative data collection instruments and protocols (respectively), and analysis procedures. In a mixed methods study, you need more than that to ensure the rigorous quality. In the chosen specific design, you need to integrate quantitative and qualitative results, complying with the particular procedure of the design selected (e.g., convergent parallel, explanatory sequential, or exploratory sequential). Interpreting and drawing meta-inferences from a joint display should be implemented carefully and presented in detail in the Methods chapter of your dissertation. It is best practice that your meta-inferences be connected to related literature and theory.

To showcase the rigorous quality of mixed methods research, in the report, Creswell (2022) advises candidates need to "state the added value of using mixed methods beyond the quantitative and qualitative results" (p. 132). Candidates conducting mixed methods research cannot skip identifying ethical issues associated with the mixed methods design. A specific plan to avoid or control them is essential to guarantee the rigorous quality of their research. For more on ethical considerations in research, see Chapter 22: Understanding the IRB Process.

Strategy 4: Plan Additional Time for Qualitative and Quantitative Components

As discussed in Chapter 11, Understanding Qualitative Inquiry, and in the Three Core Mixed Methods Research Designs section of this chapter, collecting qualitative data may require an increase in sample size to ensure thematic saturation along with follow-up data collection efforts. These measures are essential for gaining deeper insights and achieving a comprehensive understanding of the data. Such adjustments may also require modifications to the IRB application to ensure adherence to ethical standards.

In the quantitative component, particularly within an exploratory sequential design, you may need additional time to conduct a pilot study or perform consistency testing for the designed instrument(s). Therefore, it is crucial to allocate sufficient time for these adjustments within the study timeline. Careful planning for extra time is necessary in a mixed methods study to ensure robust and meaningful research outcomes.

Conclusion

This chapter serves as an introductory guide to the foundational principles of mixed methods and the practical procedures for utilizing a designated design approach. The case study emphasizes the significance of employing mixed methods to address real-world challenges through both open-ended (qualitative) and closed (quantitative) instruments. The integration of qualitative and quantitative data, the interpretation of analytical results, and the derivation of meta inferences from the combined findings are fundamental features that distinguish a mixed methods study from standalone quantitative or qualitative research. Engaging in mixed methods research is essential for practitioners, policymakers, and individuals who seek to gain a comprehensive understanding of the issues they encounter in their professional and work contexts. Such deep insight ultimately empowers one to formulate the most effective solutions. Furthermore, this chapter examines the extent to which the mixed method approach has been applied in educational research and outlines strategies for facilitating mixed methods dissertations, theses, or research projects.

Questions for Reflection

- Which primary philosophical worldview is the framing for my intended study?
- What are my research objective(s) and research questions?
- What mixed methods core design do I plan to use in my research? Or do I plan to use a combination of the core designs to form a complex design?

- What sample(s) will be recruited for my quantitative and qualitative strands?
- What types of data sources will be collected for the quantitative and qualitative strands?
- When and how will the datasets be integrated?
- How will I draw meta-inferences?
- What values will be added to my study results, which are integrated by the quantitative and qualitative data analyses?
- How will I disseminate my research? Will I present it to a conference, submit to a journal, or any other forms?

Recommended Resources for Mixed Methods Research

Creswell, J. W. (2022). *A concise introduction to mixed methods research* (2nd ed.). SAGE.

Creswell, J. D., & Clark, V. L. (2018). *Designing and conducting mixed methods research* (3rd ed.). SAGE

Creswell, J. W., & Creswell, J. D. (2023). *Research design: Qualitative, quantitative, and mixed methods approaches* (6th ed.). SAGE.

Fetters, M. D. (2020). *The mixed methods research workbook: Activities for designing, implementing, and publishing projects*. SAGE.

Greene, J.C., Caracelli, V. J., & Graham, W. F. (1989). Toward a conceptual framework for mixed method evaluation designs. *Educational Evaluation and Policy Analysis, 11*(3), 225–274.

Gutterman, T. C., Fetters, M. D., & Creswell, J. W. (2015). Integrating quantitative and qualitative results in health science mixed methods research through joint displays. *The Annals of Family Medicine, 13*(6), 554–561.

Hitchcock, J., & Onwuegbuzie, A. (2022). *The Routledge handbook for advancing integration in mixed methods research* (1st ed.). Routledge.

Lyman, T., Danmayyanti, R., Titaley, C. R., Suharno, N., Bradley, M., & Krentel, A. (2020). Reframing integration for mixed methods research. *Journal of Mixed Methods Research, 14*(3), 336–357.

Mertens, D. M. (2010). *Research and evaluation in education and psychology: Integrating diversity with quantitative, qualitative, and mixed methods* (3rd. ed.). SAGE.

Poth, C. (2023). *The Sage handbook of mixed methods research design* (1st ed.). SAGE.

Tashakkori, A., & Teddlie, C. (Eds.). (2010). *SAGE handbook of mixed methods in social & behavioral research* (2nd ed.). SAGE.

Venkatesh, V., Brown, S., & Sullivan, Y. (2024). *Conducting mixed-methods research: From classical social sciences to the age of big data and analytics*. Virginia Tech Publishing. https://doi.org/10.21061/conducting-mixedmethods-research

References

Atkins, M. S., Hoagwood, K. E., Kutash, K., & Seidman, E. (2010). Toward the integration of education and mental health in schools. *Administration and Policy in Mental Health and Mental Health Services Research*, *37*(1–2), 40–47. https://doi.org/10.1007/s10488-010-0299-7

Bell, S. (2010). Project-based learning for the 21st century: Skills for the future. *The Clearing House: A Journal of Educational Strategies, Issues and Ideas*, *83*(2), 39–43. https://doi.org/10.1080/00098650903505415

Cherryholmes, C. H. (1992, August–September). Notes on pragmatism and scientific realism. *Educational Researcher*, 13–17.

Collins, A., Joseph, D., & Bielaczyc, K. (2004). Design research: Theoretical and methodological issues. *The Journal of the Learning Sciences*, *13*(1), 15–42. https://doi.org/10.1207/s15327809jls1301_2

Creswell, J. W. (2022). *A concise introduction to mixed methods research* (2nd ed.). SAGE.

Creswell, J. W., & Clark, V. L. (2018). *Designing and conducting mixed methods research* (3rd ed.). SAGE.

Creswell, J. W., & Creswell, J. D. (2023). *Research design: Qualitative, quantitative, and mixed methods approaches* (6th ed.). SAGE.

Crotty, M. (1998). *The foundation of social research: Meaning and perspectives in the research process*. SAGE.

Design-Based Research Collective. (2003). Design-based research: An emerging paradigm for educational inquiry. *Educational Researcher*, *32*(1), 5–8. https://doi.org/10.3102/0013189X032001005

Fetters, M. D. (2020). *The mixed methods research workbook: Activities for designing, implementing, and publishing projects*. SAGE.

Guba, E. G. (1990). The alternative paradigm dialog. In E. G. Guba (Ed.), *The paradigm dialog* (pp. 17–30). SAGE.

Guba, E., & Lincoln, Y. (1985). *Naturalistic inquiry*. SAGE.

Hitchcock, J., & Onwuegbuzie, A. (2022). *The Routledge handbook for advancing integration in mixed methods research* (1st ed.). Routledge.

Ivankova, N. V. (2014). *Mixed methods applications in action research: From methods to community action*. SAGE.

Johnson, R. B., & Christensen, L. (2017). *Educational research: Quantitative, qualitative, and mixed approaches* (6th ed.). SAGE.

Lincoln, Y., & Guba, E. (1985). *Naturalistic inquiry*. SAGE.

Lincoln, Y. S., Lynham, S. A., & Guba, E. G. (2011). Paradigmatic controversies, contradictions, and emerging confluences. In N. K. Denzin & Y. S. Lincoln (Eds.), *The Sage handbook of qualitative research* (4th ed., pp. 97–128). SAGE.

Mertens, D. M. (1998). *Research methods in education and psychology: Integrating diversity with quantitative and qualitative approaches*. SAGE.

Mertens, D. M. (2010). *Research and evaluation in education and psychology: Integrating diversity with quantitative, qualitative, and mixed methods* (3rd ed.). SAGE.

Mills, G., & Jordan, A. (2023). *Educational research: Competencies for analysis and applications* (13th ed.). Pearson.

Morgan, D. (2007). Paradigm lost and pragmatism regained: Methodological implications of combining qualitative and quantitative methods. *Journal of Mixed Methods Research*, *1*(1), 48–76.

Murphy, J. P. (1990). *Pragmatism: From Peirce to Davidson*. Westview.

Neuman, W. L. (2009). *Social research methods: Qualitative and quantitative approaches* (7th ed.). Allyn & Bacon.

Patton, M. Q. (1990). *Qualitative evaluation and research methods* (2nd ed.). SAGE.

Poth, C. (2023). *The Sage handbook of mixed methods research design* (1st ed.). SAGE.

Rossman, G. B. & Wilson, B. L. (1985, October). Numbers and words: Combining quantitative and qualitative methods in a single large-scale evaluation study. *Evaluation Review*, *9*(5), 627–43.

Schrauf, R. (2016). *Mixed methods: Interviews, surveys, and cross-cultural comparisons*. Cambridge University Press.

Wang, F., & Hannafin, M. J. (2005). Design-based research and technology-enhanced learning environments. *Educational Technology Research and Development*, *53*(4), 5–23. https://doi.org/10.1007/BF02504682

Part 3
The Consolidation Stage

14 Transitioning from Autonomous to Self-Directed Learning

Michael K. Ponton, EdD

Introduction

Success in coursework requires doctoral students to engage in autonomous learning; however, success in a doctoral program, whether it be a research (e.g., PhD) or professional (e.g., EdD, DNP, DBA) degree, ultimately requires candidates—students in the inquiry phase of their program—to engage in self-directed learning. The necessary transition from autonomous to self-directed learner requires doctoral students (i.e., you) to understand (a) the difference between the two manifestations of personal agency in learning, (b) the importance of this transition, and (c) methods to develop self-directedness during coursework. This chapter presents a discussion of these requirements and their application at various stages of the doctoral journey.

Case Study

Sara had always been a model student in her coursework. She diligently read assigned material, submitted well-prepared deliverables by deadlines, asked her professors questions when they arose, and participated in informal study groups with her classmates. Her faculty recognized her studiousness as indicated by her near-perfect grade point average throughout her entire doctoral journey.

Sara is now in the dissertation process and struggling. In fact, she has not been able to construct a viable proposal for any research. Her dissertation chair has told her that all she needs to do is read the literature to support the importance of a research question—a question that should be of interest to her in her field—and then design an appropriate study to address this question. It all seems so simple, yet Sara cannot get it done. If only someone would tell her what and how much to read or even what question to pursue, she knows she could do it.

However, Sara needs to perform as an independent researcher throughout the dissertation process and must make her own decisions. Sara has never had to direct her learning, which is why she is so frustrated with having to self-direct the learning necessary to develop a dissertation.

What the Research Says

Autonomous learning is an agentic process that represents, quite simply, intentional action enlisted to accomplish some desired level of learning. Autonomous learners can exhibit *agency* in learning by intentionally learning from aspects of imposed environments (e.g., while taking a course, a student intentionally learns from some aspect of the course as it was designed), selecting learning opportunities from available environments (e.g., a student selects a course to take), or creating entirely new learning activities (e.g., a learner identifies a book to read about something of personal interest) (Ponton, 2016).

In addition, personal agency can be manifested through three distinct modes of action: collective, proxy, and individual (Bandura, 2006). Thus, within the context of learning, (a) *collective agency* occurs when a student intentionally forms a group and learns from the group's performance, (b) *proxy agency* occurs when a student intentionally enlists someone else with requisite knowledge or skills to perform an action that facilitates the student's learning, and (c) *individual agency* occurs when a student intentionally performs alone.

The doctoral stages of Entry, Knowledge and Skill Development, and Consolidation are replete with students engaging in autonomous learning through all its various modes of action; however, engaging in autonomous learning does not ensure that these students will develop as self-directed learners. That is, being able to exert agency in enlisting the help of others does not develop the agentic ability to act alone.

Before initial enrollment, prospective students canvass doctoral programs to select one that addresses their instructional, social, academic, and professional needs. After enrollment, students engage in a similar selection process except at the course or section level. In these selection processes, students do not create the programs, courses, or sections but rather rely on others to design learning activities based upon requisite expertise; however, students still exhibit their own personal agency by intentionally choosing from a multitude of available learning options. This selection process can be done via individual agency (i.e., the student makes their own selection without the input of others), proxy agency (i.e., the student intentionally seeks and follows the advice of others), or collective agency (i.e., the student intentionally works with others to determine a selection).

During the Knowledge and Skill Development Stage (i.e., coursework), successful doctoral students who are autonomous learners choose to attend to course prescriptions (individual agency); ask questions of their faculty and learn from their responses (individual agency); solicit direction from their faculty and follow subsequent guidance (proxy agency); create study groups (collective agency); and seek additional sources of information apart from assigned readings, faculty guidance, and the input of others (individual agency).

In preparation for the Consolidation Stage (where the comprehensive examination is administered), doctoral students not only study alone but also often create study groups with their classmates. High performing doctoral students learn from imposed environments—that is, the courses, study guides, and exam as designed—but also select and create opportunities to learn either independently or with the help of others. Often such learning transcends that which is required to merely satisfy the learning objectives of coursework and the comprehensive examination.

Being an autonomous learner is necessary to maximize the depth and breadth of learning that occurs during the knowledge and skill development and consolidation stages (or, generally, in life); however, being a self-directed learner is necessary to complete a dissertation (research or dissertation in practice, see Chapter 18: Understanding the Different Types of Dissertations) and become a doctor. Thus, even though high grades may be earned during coursework, doctoral students who engage in all modes of autonomous learning may limit their development as self-directed learners thereby threatening ultimate program completion.

Unfortunately, success in coursework is not typically predicated upon fostering self-directedness in learning, as Sara from the case study discovered. Students who enter doctoral programs have already taken many courses and earned outstanding grades; thus, they are master course takers. Typical collegiate courses—even at the doctoral level—are designed to include prescribed readings, activities, assessments, and follow a prescribed schedule. In addition, doctoral students are generally encouraged to consult their professors should subject matter questions arise.

Students who are autonomous learners study assigned readings, ask their professors questions, create study groups to facilitate learning, and exhibit high levels of desire, initiative, resourcefulness, and persistence in their learning (cf. Confessore, 1992); that is, master course takers are typically master autonomous learners. Holders of graduate degrees exhibit higher levels of learner autonomy than those who hold undergraduate degrees (Ponton & Carr, 2016a), and limited data suggest that full professors have higher levels of self-efficacy in autonomous learning than the US population of nontraditional adults (i.e., age range 25–; Ponton, 2018). Learner autonomy is, thus, arguably related to success for increased levels of education up to and including graduate programs.

Autonomous learning occurs "in imposed, selected, or created learning environments and exercised via collective, proxy, or individual agency" (Ponton, 2016, p. 55); however, *self-directed learning* refers to the situation in which the learner exhibits personal agency individually in the creation of learning activities. This definition comports with the definition provided by the International Society for Self-Directed Learning (2021): "self-directed learning is an intentional learning process that is created and evaluated by the learner" (Self-Directed Learning section, para. 2). Doctoral students need to understand the ultimate level of personal development required to complete a dissertation so that they can understand how to develop appropriately before entering the Inquiry Stage of the doctoral journey.

The main premise of this chapter is that completing the Inquiry Stage of the doctoral program requires self-directed learning, which is a subset of the modes of personal agency associated with autonomous learning (Ponton, 2016). This premise is built upon the notion that the doctoral degree represents to society that the holder can independently and competently address a research question or problem of practice via self-directed study, research, analysis, and interpretation; that is, perform the work of an independent academic scholar or scholar practitioner in consuming, producing, and applying research. Even though the doctor may never engage in such scholarly work after graduation, being entitled to hold the doctoral degree is dependent upon an adequate demonstration by the candidate that the requisite self-directedness in learning to produce competent scholarship exists.

Quite simply, then, to complete the dissertation, doctoral candidates must be able to self-direct personal learning. In the Inquiry Stage of a doctoral program, doctoral candidates must be able to completely regulate personal learning that involves self-diagnosing deficiencies in knowledge or skills, self-creating learning activities (including identifying appropriate resources) to alleviate such deficiencies, self-motivating participation in these activities, self-reflecting upon whether or not desired levels of learning are being realized, and self-creating any necessary adjustments to the activities.

In addition, doctoral candidates must also be self-directed in constructing the dissertation, conducting the research, analyzing the data, interpreting the findings, writing the manuscript, and preparing for an adequate oral defense of the work as well as managing personal time to fulfill all of these tasks in a timely manner. The locus of action is the "self" throughout the process. Self-directed learners work individually to create learning activities that answer personal questions rather than relying on others to design activities or provide immediate answers.

In addition, self-directed learners do not limit their learning to someone else's standards (e.g., the scope of knowledge imposed by a course design or expected by a course assessment); rather, they seek out information until personally desired levels of learning are achieved. Self-directed learners enter courses with the goal of learning the subject matter to a degree that is *personally* satisfying rather than entering with the perfunctory goal of earning a high grade. In contrast, autonomous learners may choose others to help direct personal learning and assess the adequacy of achievement.

Thus, the developmental requirement for a doctoral student is to transform from an autonomous learner to a self-directed learner, which begins during the Knowledge and Skill Development and culminates in the Consolidation Stage. In fact, the way this is done is by engaging in self-directed learning as often as possible. To this end, faculty can facilitate this transformation by requiring the exercise of subskills associated with self-directed learning (i.e., related to the individual creation of learning activities) in coursework (Ponton, 2021). Engaging in self-directed learning not only develops the requisite skill to independently direct learning activities but also fosters a feeling of self-efficacy (i.e., perceived ability) that is necessary to maximize the motivation (cf. Bandura, 1997) to engage in this type of learning; that is, people are more likely to engage in self-directed learning if they believe they can do so successfully.

Strategies for Success

The following strategies are offered to engage you in the necessary transition from an autonomous to a self-directed learner.

Strategy 1: Identify Personal Rationale for Obtaining a Doctorate Degree

The first step for you to become a self-directed learner is to understand why holding a doctoral degree is *personally* important. You cannot commit to becoming a self-directed learner, already argued as being necessary to earn the right to hold the doctoral degree, unless you are committed to becoming an academic doctor. Thus, you must reflect upon your individual reasons—that is, define your life goals—for being in a doctoral program in the first place.

Strategy 2: Develop Learning Goals Consistent With Life Goals

The second step to becoming a self-directed learner is to determine your learning interests that support your life goals. The point of this recommendation is for you to focus on continuing your learning during coursework until you are satisfied *independent of professorial expectations.* This puts the responsibility to define what constitutes sufficient learning on you rather than your professors' shoulders as a course design cannot possibly satisfy all individual interests or degrees of understanding for all students.

Thus, fostering self-directedness involves pursuing learning guided by your personal interests and limited only by your personal satisfaction, which may be completely independent of course requirements. For example,

Sara typically stops studying when she feels she has learned the assigned material to the professor's expectations even though the topic is particularly important to her career aspirations and recognizes that more can be learned. Sara should focus on her interests and work to satisfy her learning needs.

Strategy 3: Generate Personal Questions and Individually Seek to Solve Problems

A pervasive opportunity to develop as a self-directed learner involves individually seeking out answers to one's own questions. Regardless of the genesis of questions (e.g., from assigned readings, personal readings, professional practice, classroom discussions, or emergent thinking), another step for you to become a self-directed learner is to create learning activities that answer questions generated during coursework. Too often doctoral students perceive the professor as being the "answer person" for content-related questions, which is a carryover from earlier educational paradigms that place the professor as the proverbial "sage on the stage."

However, to develop self-directedness, you must avoid the expeditious path of asking questions that, thus, limit learning to the knowledge and availability of others and instead pursue the more arduous yet developmentally important path of answering questions for yourself. While Sara has always asked her professors questions, she should begin to diligently attempt to answer them for herself and seek out credible sources of information so that her learning is under her control and does not rely on the presence of others.

Strategy 4: Develop a Personal Work Schedule

Course schedules are typically part of any course design and include dates for assigned activities, deliverables, and tests; however, there can be great variation with respect to when students perform course-related work. Thus, an important step to become a self-directed learner is to develop a personal work schedule *and adhere to it*.

As doctoral students are adults with disparate demands on their time (e.g., due to variations in work, family, church, community, etc.), no one can create an appropriate schedule for you. Thus, by considering your individual demands that inform the creation of a personal schedule, you increase the likelihood of following your schedule and regulating effort to accomplish learning goals.

Strategy 5: Seek Unique Learning Opportunities Related to Personal and Professional Learning Goals

Even though courses typically prescribe learning activities, in doctoral work there are often opportunities to interject personal and professional learning interests into and sometimes supplant such activities, and professors are often amenable to such changes as they recognize the importance of students taking control over their learning, particularly at this level of academe. Thus, another step to become a self-directed learner is to creatively transform prescribed course activities into individually designed learning activities.

As a simple example, a course on the history of US higher education may require a group of students to prepare a class presentation outlining the development of colonial colleges. However, you may have an interest in conducting future dissertation inquiry on curriculum issues and, thus, negotiate with the professor a curricular focus for the assignment—albeit still within the colonial period—for an individual presentation along with an accompanying written literature review. These new deliverables will require self-directed learning as you work independently in their preparation.

Another important aspect of regulating learning is to determine if chosen activities are, in fact, facilitating desired levels of learning. Doctoral curricula often provide opportunities for elective courses, and even required courses may be replaced with other courses or professional credits (usually contingent upon a faculty advisor's approval).

Whether courses are elective, substituted, or in excess of minimum programmatic requirements, an important step to become a self-directed learner is for you to reflect upon whether or not the curriculum itself is satisfying your learning interests and, if not, make appropriate adjustments. The developmental goal is for you to learn to take control over your learning activities in light of desired personal and professional levels of learning.

Strategy 6: Be Selective in Choosing Activities Unrelated to the Doctoral Program

To state the obvious, time is finite. As such, there are myriad possible activities that vie for a doctoral student's time and energy. Some of these activities are personal (i.e., related to family or friends), some are professional (i.e., related to work), and some are academic (i.e., related to one's doctoral journey), and choice is influenced by the relative value an individual ascribes to the possible activities at any given moment. Invoking Strategies 1 and 2 supports self-control in decision-making—anticipating future rewards, prioritizing values, and delaying immediate gratification (Rosenbaum, 1989)—thus, choosing academic activities over nonacademic, discretionary ones (Ponton & Carr, 2016b).

However, there are also myriad academic activities that must be chosen as well. Doctoral students are often presented with opportunities such as attending professional meetings, coauthoring publications, assisting in teaching and research, and serving on committees, and these activities can play an important role in securing future academic appointments after graduation. Because of this, you must carefully exert agency in choosing all activities—academic or nonacademic—unrelated to the doctoral program itself as such activities will lessen the time for program-related work. Self-directed learners make all required decisions in their learning activities; thus, developing intentionally in choosing what to do and what not to do supports your development as a self-directed learner.

Questions for Reflection

In summary, reflect on the following questions to assess whether or not you are developing as a self-directed learner:

- What life goals do I want to accomplish through obtaining this doctoral degree?
- What personal and professional interests support these life goals? Do I use these interests to guide the extent of my learning?
- Do I develop learning activities to answer my own questions instead of relying on others?
- Do I identify opportunities to transform required course activities into personal learning activities?
- Have I created a personal work schedule? If so, am I following it?
- Do I reflect upon curricular choices in light of my learning interests and make appropriate adjustments?
- Do I choose activities that support degree completion and minimize those that do not?

By using these questions to catalyze personal action, you will quickly realize that you can successfully direct your own learning. When this realization occurs during coursework, you will transform from an autonomous into a self-directed learner who is better prepared for the demands of candidacy and will more expediently earn a doctoral degree.

Recommended Resources

Bandura, A. (1997). *Self-efficacy: The exercise of control.* W. H. Freeman and Company.

Bandura, A. (2006). Toward a psychology of human agency. *Perspectives on Psychological Science, 1*(2), 164–80. https://doi.org/10.1111/j.1745-6916.2006.00011.x

Confessore, G. J., & Confessore, S. J. (Eds.). (1992). *Guideposts to self-directed learning: Expert commentary on essential concepts.* Organization Design and Development.

Ponton, M. K., & Carr, P. B. (Eds.). (2016). *Autonomous and self-directed learning: Agentic perspectives.* Watertree Press.

References

Bandura, A. (1997). *Self-efficacy: The exercise of control.* W. H. Freeman and Company.

Bandura, A. (2006). Toward a psychology of human agency. *Perspectives on Psychological Science, 1*(2), 164–80. https://doi.org/10.1111/j.1745-6916.2006.00011.x

Confessore, G. J. (1992). An introduction to the study of self-directed learning. In G. J. Confessore & S. J. Confessore (Eds.), *Guideposts to self-directed learning: Expert commentary on essential concepts* (pp. 1–6). Organization Design and Development.

International Society for Self-Directed Learning. (2021). *About us.* https://www.sdlglobal.com/about-us

Ponton, M. K. (2016). An agentic perspective contrasting autonomous learning with self-directed learning. In M. K. Ponton & P. B. Carr (Eds.), *Autonomous and self-directed learning: Agentic perspectives* (pp. 49–61). Watertree Press.

Ponton, M. K. (2018). Self-efficacy in autonomous learning: A preliminary study of full professors. *International Journal of Self-Directed Learning, 15*(1), 31–42. https://www.sdlglobal.com/journals

Ponton, M. K. (2021). A teaching strategy based upon a model of agentic learning. *Journal of Studies in Education, 11*(1), 1–11. https://doi.org/10.5296/jse.v11i1.18125

Ponton, M. K., & Carr, P. B. (2016a). The possible role of higher education in developing learner autonomy: A quantitative exploration. *International Journal of Self-Directed Learning, 13*(1), 12–25. https://www.sdlglobal.com/journals

Ponton, M. K., & Carr, P. B. (2016b). Understanding and promoting autonomy in self-directed learning. In M. K. Ponton & P. B. Carr (Eds.), *Autonomous and self-directed learning: Agentic perspectives* (pp. 17–31). Watertree Press.

15 Consolidating Learning Across the Doctoral Program

David Holder, PhD

Amanda J. Rockinson, EdD, PhD

Lucinda S. Spaulding, PhD

Introduction

Doctoral programs typically include three fundamental elements: coursework, the comprehensive examination, and the dissertation or cumulative project. Each course is a piece of a larger program designed to prepare students for a successful transformation from autonomous learners to self-directed learners to scholars in their field.

The comprehensive exam serves as a benchmark to assess skills, knowledge, and dispositions essential for the successful completion of the dissertation or cumulative project in the Inquiry Stage of the degree. In essence, it is designed to allow students to demonstrate their readiness for the dissertation or cumulative project. It is in the Inquiry Stage of the doctoral journey that the candidates transition from learners to researchers or scholar-practitioners; the defense is the natural culmination of this transformation. This chapter explores the relationship between coursework, comprehensive examinations, and the dissertation or culminating project, as illustrated through two case studies.

Case Study

John

John is a doctoral student in a PhD program. With his employer pressuring him to complete the coursework, in addition to mounting financial pressures, John pushes himself to the limit and blazes through the doctoral degree phase of his coursework. Nearing the completion of his coursework, the comprehensive exam and the dissertation proposal suddenly loom on the horizon.

John is motivated, does good work, meets deadlines, and is generally a successful student. When he looks into the comprehensive exam, he realizes he is clueless as to what will be on it. He failed to prepare for it throughout his coursework. Further, he realizes he has not conceptualized or developed a viable dissertation proposal. John starts to panic.

Megan

Megan is enrolled in a distance education EdD program. Before registering, she spoke with advisors and discussed the entire process, including coursework, the comprehensive exam, and the Dissertation in Practice (DIP). Once Megan had a good idea of what was involved with earning a doctoral degree, she sat down with her family, set realistic goals, worked out a plan, and divided up familial duties. She began coursework, paced herself, took good course notes to serve as study guides for her comprehensive exam, and built relationships with her peers and faculty. As she finished each course, she archived her papers, her notes, and her resources.

When the comprehensive exam drew near, Megan reviewed her course notes and outlines, as well as identified overlapping areas of skills and knowledge across courses. She experienced minimal stress and anxiety as the day of the exam drew near. She also had a well-conceptualized topic for her DIP. Throughout the coursework phase of her degree, Megan had a goal and a plan, and she followed it. Megan is prepared.

What the Research Says

Coursework

In the Knowledge and Skill Development Stage, doctoral students complete coursework. The coursework can typically be divided into two groups: (a) core and (b) research.

Core Courses

Core courses address the primary knowledge needed in the field. Core courses address the knowledge necessary to establish a foundation for building a bridge between current knowledge and the generation of new knowledge to inform practice or empirically extend existing research in the discipline. The doctoral core curriculum is markedly different than the undergraduate core. Its purpose is to create an opportunity for the student to become a subject matter expert; it is less concerned with the liberal arts. The core courses expose doctoral students to the foundational knowledge and prevailing theories relevant to their discipline. Typically, each course, along with its goals and objectives, is carefully selected by the core faculty. A good program will have classes with minimal overlap that build on previously learned material and expand knowledge in the discipline.

As doctoral students progress through their coursework, they need to identify connections between courses and synthesize the information as they prepare for the comprehensive exam during the Consolidation Stage. Doctoral students who use metacognitive strategies, strategies to "think about their thinking" (Brown, 1978; 1987; Flavell, 1976; 1979), will start to see trends and patterns. They will begin to identify the major authors and theorists in the discipline.

Staying focused and becoming well-read in the field will also be of great value in the Inquiry Stage. While doctoral students should have an open mind and explore new ideas, it would be beneficial for them to identify, early in the program, the subject areas and theories that interest them the most. They should plan to develop assignments that focus on this area of interests. The study of the complexities and various theories within the field will produce a mastery of the content. Identifying a specific focus within the field helps students pinpoint gaps in the literature and problems of practice that warrant additional research for the Inquiry Stage of the doctoral degree.

Research Courses

Research courses equip doctoral students with the skills necessary to apply discipline-specific information and employ scientific reasoning to design investigations that extend knowledge or inform and improve practice. While participation in core courses helps students identify trends, problems, and gaps in the literature within the discipline, participation in research courses exposes them to the various methods, instruments, and tools needed to develop investigations.

As students progress through the Knowledge and Skill Development Stage of their degree, they are wise to exercise their knowledge of the core and research by identifying studies closely related to their topic of interest, while also cataloguing the methods and designs researchers employed to investigate the topics.

According to the case study, John saw courses as simply hoops to jump through. John completed satisfactory work on all assignments, but made few connections across topics or courses, and consequently; was not prepared for his comprehensive exam. As he neared completion of his courses and the looming exam, he was filled with anxiety and trepidation. John did not approach the comprehensive exam with a deliberate strategy. He did not organize class notes and catalog information on researchers and theorists, did not take the time to reflect on and make connections across courses, and struggled to identify areas in the empirical literature where findings were limited or contradictory. Thus, when his comprehensive exam arrived, he struggled to articulate the empirical significance of his proposed study, namely, how it would address a gap in the literature and make an original contribution to his discipline.

Megan, on the other hand, approached the comprehensive exam with a deliberate strategy. From her organized class notes and cataloged information on researchers and theorists, Megan was also able to make connections across courses and identify how both theory and research could help her solve her problem of practice. Megan, who had been deliberate in her program, felt prepared as she approached the exam and dissertation proposal.

By the conclusion of the Knowledge and Skill Development Stage (i.e., coursework), doctoral students should have been exposed to the foundational knowledge and essential skills, both core and research, to become research scientists or scholar-practitioner. At this point, doctoral students are reaching the Consolidation Stage, where they begin to synthesize knowledge and transition from autonomous course takers to self-directed learners (see Chapter 14: Transitioning from Autonomous to Self-Directed Learning).

Not only is it important for doctoral students to use their coursework to gain discipline and research knowledge but also to gain the skills and dispositions of a self-directed learner. Excellent course takers do not necessarily possess the higher-order thinking skills required to create new material and utilize synthesized material in a meaningful way, especially if they fail to develop these skills throughout the Knowledge and Skill Development Stage of their coursework.

The Comprehensive Exam

Success on the comprehensive exam depends on the student's mastery and synthesis of the core content as well as their ability to reason scientifically in the field. The comprehensive exam marks the Consolidation Stage of the doctoral program and serves two purposes: (a) it shows the student's ability to know and demonstrate lucidly within the core concepts of the field, and (b) it reveals the ability to synthesize observations and findings into sound research. There are various types of exams, and each program has its assessment process, which is discussed in more depth in Chapter 16: Navigating the Comprehensive Exam.

Every discipline and every program within each discipline is unique, and there is no set standard format or content of the comprehensive exam. Traditionally, the comprehensive exam serves as a benchmark to assess the understanding, synthesis and application of the goals and objectives of a particular program. In essence, it is designed to enable the doctoral student to demonstrate *readiness* for the expectations of the Inquiry Stage (Capello, 2023; Golde & Dore, 2001). Upon passing the comprehensive exam, most programs consider students doctoral candidates.

Dissertation (or Cumulative Project)

The doctoral dissertation or cumulative project is the final academic requirement in the doctoral process, designed to evaluate the candidate's capabilities in conducting research within their academic discipline. The final recommendation for degree conferment depends on the completion and defense of the dissertation or project.

The doctoral candidate demonstrates their understanding of the literature on a specific topic, ability to execute research, and ability to write about the research in a scholarly manner. Therefore, the doctoral candidate is expected to be a self-directed learner responsible for identifying the "gap" in the literature or the problem of practice to solve (see Chapter 19: Choosing Your Research Topic: Literature Gap vs. Problem of Practice), making an argument they wish to contribute to the field, independently designing and conducting the research, analyzing the data, and producing an original, written report.

In some disciplines, this may be the first time a doctoral candidate is tasked with producing new content and understanding, which can be daunting. For many, the dissertation or cumulative project can be intimidating and anxiety-producing (Arnkoff & Glass, 1992; Cirasella & Thistlethwaite, 2017; Sachs, 2002; Russell-Pinson & Harris, 2019; Waheed et al., 2021). However, through strategic planning through coursework in the Knowledge and Skill Development Stage, these effects can be minimized.

Strategies for Success

The comprehensive exam can be exceptionally (though not always entirely) demystified through a clear understanding of the goals and intended outcomes of the program and the role of coursework in preparing the doctoral student to meet these goals and outcomes. The following are a few strategies to assist in this preparation:

Strategy 1: Understand the Purpose of Coursework

You should view each core course as a piece of a larger picture, which represents the current state of knowledge in your field. Courses are not "hoops" to jump through or hurdles to overcome and move past. Instead, each course provides the opportunity to grow in understanding of the field and identify areas in the literature that are lacking or problems in practice that need further investigation.

Strategy 2: Choose a Research Interest Early in the Program

From the first course in the program, read the literature with a focus on identifying your dissertation or cumulative project topic. Focus on this research interest, both broad (discipline) and in-depth (research interest), and read every course note, text, and article to identify a viable problem to address for your dissertation or cumulative project.

Strategy 3: Be Organized

Develop effective strategies for organizing course material and building a comprehensive understanding of the literature in your discipline. This process involves developing course outlines, archiving course notes and study materials; and cataloging texts, articles, and materials in an organized and accessible manner. Discussed in Chapter 6: Becoming a Digital Scholar, leverage technology to assist in this process! Pay special attention when a professor states "this is seminal work" or "an excellent literature review," and be prepared to discuss the major players in your field.

Strategy 4: Approach Research Courses as Training for the Dissertation

You are wise to view research courses as preparation for designing and executing your dissertation or project during the Inquiry Phase. As such, maximize the opportunities presented in your program's research classes and be diligent in developing an understanding of research methods (qualitative, quantitative, mixed methods) and corresponding designs.

When reading topical articles for assignments in core classes, actively seek to identify and understand the methods and analyses used to generate the findings. Be a critical and discriminating consumer of knowledge by evaluating research designs, being mindful of factors that influence external and internal validity (quantitative) or credibility and dependability (qualitative). Moreover, as your topic of inquiry becomes more crystallized, begin to conceptualize the research methods that are appropriate for your inquiry.

Strategy 5: Gather Information about the Comprehensive Exam

Since there are numerous ways to assess a comprehensive understanding of program objectives, it is essential to gather information about the specific assessment for your program upon entry. Keep the assessment in mind, knowing that you will be required to demonstrate a comprehensive competency-related understanding of the core content as well as readiness for the Inquiry Phase of your doctoral journey. Through the application of core courses to individual areas of interest and a solid understanding of research courses, you will be well-prepared to demonstrate a comprehensive understanding and application of program objectives.

Strategy 6: Preparation Should Start Early and Be Ongoing

The comprehensive exam is a benchmark of your mastery of coursework in your program and should be prepared for from the first course. The comprehensive exam is *not* something that can be "prepped" for in a month or two; it must be integral to a plan of study from the Entry Stage of the program. From the first class in the Knowledge and Skill Development Stage of the program, you should understand what the comprehensive exam is and begin to prepare by seeking out people in your program who have already passed the exam and discussing the strategies they used to prepare.

John powered through his coursework, took minimal notes, and did not keep his texts or any other materials from the classes. As the comprehensive exam approached, he felt frustrated and anxious about the coming exam and subsequent dissertation phase. Megan, on the other hand, had notes from her reading in the texts and from the professors' lectures. She archived them with the class syllabi and reviewed them in preparation for her exam. She worked hard, felt prepared, and looked forward to the opportunity to demonstrate her consolidation of skills and knowledge in the field, as well as her readiness to begin her cumulative project in her EdD.

Strategy 7: See the Comprehensive Exam as an Opportunity to Demonstrate Readiness for the Dissertation/Cumulative Project

By focusing on core courses and using them as a catalyst to explore topics of interest fully, you will be "well-read" in the field. By researching similar studies and applying the knowledge gained through research courses, you will be prepared to synthesize observations and insights into a cohesive study and successfully execute it.

The core and research courses provide the knowledge and skills needed for the comprehensive exam. The comprehensive exam is used to determine readiness for the dissertation. With focus and perseverance, you will have a clear direction and purpose in your research agenda, leading to a successful product in the Inquiry Phase of your degree, and ultimately, be ready to transition from student to researcher or scholar-practitioner.

You would be wise to keep your topic of interest as the focus during the program. When possible, use every paper to deepen your understanding of the topic. Do not underestimate the time required to develop a comprehensive understanding of the topic and its supporting literature. Be prepared for your dissertation topic to evolve throughout your coursework and the Inquiry Phase. Do not stubbornly hold onto an early conception of the study and ignore what the literature reveals or guidance given by faculty.

Questions for Reflection

This chapter discusses the relationship between coursework, the comprehensive exam, and the dissertation or cumulative project, and how each phase prepares you for the successful completion of your program. You need to recognize the connections between your coursework, the comprehensive exam, and your dissertation or cumulative project. The following questions are provided for reflection:

- Do I have a realistic plan for my doctoral journey? Is it fast and furious like John? Or methodical and intentional like Megan? Am I looking at the program holistically, like Megan? Or am I approaching it in isolated segments, like John? In other words, am I seeing how the courses and assignments serve to build and develop my understanding in the field, or am I approaching them as just tasks to be completed?

- What type of comprehensive exam does my program have? What is my strategy for preparing for it? Who can I contact for guidance as I begin my program?
- Am I maximizing the learning opportunities from my courses? What is my plan for archiving my notes, textbooks, and most importantly, my understanding of the learning objectives?
- Am I using my review of the literature in core courses to identify an empirical gap in the literature or solve a problem of practice? Am I identifying the significant theorists and seminal researchers in my field? Am I using my research courses to develop the research skills and knowledge necessary to conduct my research?

Recommended Resources

Champagne, R., Boyle, P., & Pires, C. B. (2021, October). Prepping for your comprehensive exams. *CSA News.* https://doi.org//10.1002/csan.20580

Childress, H. (2016). *The PhDictionary: A glossary of things you do not know (but should) about doctoral and faculty life.* University of Chicago Press. https://press.uchicago.edu/ucp/books/book/chicago/P/bo23151250.html

Dingfelder, S. (2004). Preparing for your comprehensive exams. gradPSYCH Magazine, *2*(2). Retrieved from http://www.apa.org/gradpsych/2004/04/comps.aspx

Grover, V. (2007). Successfully navigating the stages of doctoral study. *International Journal of Doctoral Studies, 2,* 9–21.

References

Anderson, W. P., Krauskopf, C. J., Rogers, M. E., & Neal, G. W. (1984). Reasons for comprehensive examinations: An evaluation. *Teaching of Psychology, 11*(2), 78.

Arnkoff, D. B., & Glass, C. R. (1992). Cognitive processes, anxiety, and performance on doctoral dissertation oral examinations. *Journal of Counseling Psychology, 39*(3), 382.

Bourke, B., Bray, N. J., & Horton, C. C. (2009). Approaches to the Core Curriculum: An exploratory analysis of top liberal arts and doctoral-granting institutions. *Journal of General Education*, *58*(4), 219–40.

Brown, A. L. (1978). Knowing when, where, and how to remember: A problem of metacognition. In R. Glaser (Ed.), *Advances in instructional psychology* (pp. 77–165). Erlbaum.

Brown, A. L. (1987). Metacognition, executive control, self-regulation, and other mysterious mechanisms. In F. E. Weinert & R. H. Kluwe (Eds.), *Metacognition, motivation, and understanding* (pp. 65–116). Lawrence Erlbaum.

Capello, S. A. (2023). Linking assessments to program outcomes in practitioner-oriented EdD programs: An alternative to comprehensive examinations. *Journal of Adult and Continuing Education*, *29*(1), 25–40. https://doi.org/10.1177/14779714221093091

Cirasella, J., & Thistlethwaite, P. (2017). Open access and the graduate author: A dissertation anxiety manual. In K. A. Smith & K. L. Dickson (Ed.), *Open Access and the Future of Scholarly Communication* (pp. 203–225). Rowman and Littlefield.

Flavell, J. H. (1976). Metacognitive aspects of problem solving. In L. B. Resnick (Ed.), *The nature of intelligence* (pp. 231–235). Erlbaum.

Flavell, J. H. (1979). Metacognition and cognitive monitoring: A new area of cognitive-developmental inquiry. *American Psychologist*, *34*, 906–911.

Golde, C. M., & Dore, T. M. (2001). *At cross purposes: What the experiences of doctoral students reveal about doctoral education*. The Pew Charitable Trusts. www.phd-survey.org

Loughead, T. O. (1997). The doctoral comprehensive examination: Fine-tuning the process. *Counselor Education & Supervision*, *37*(2), 140.

Russell-Pinson, L., & Harris, M. L. (2019). Anguish and anxiety, stress and strain: Attending to writers' stress in the dissertation process. *Journal of Second Language Writing*, *43*, 63–71.

Sachs, J. (2002). A path model for students' attitudes to writing a thesis. *Scandinavian Journal of Educational Research*, *46*(1), 99–108. doi:10.1080/00313830120115633

Schulte, I. J., Isley, E., Link, N., Shealy, C. N., & Winfrey, L. (2004). General practice, primary care, and health service psychology: Concepts, competencies, and the Combined-Integrated model. *Journal of Clinical Psychology*, *60*(10), 1011–25. doi: 10.1002/jclp.20032

Waheed, S. A., Gilani, N., Raza, M., & Ahmad, F. (2021). The beginning of more worries: Doctoral candidates' untold stories after submission of the dissertation. *Frontiers in Psychology*, *11*, 537366.

16 Navigating the Comprehensive Exam

Jennifer Fellabaum-Toston, PhD
Jeni Hart, PhD

Introduction

Golde and Dore (2001) noted "the most common features of doctoral programs are coursework and examinations designed to determine if students are ready to advance to the next stage of doctoral study" (p. 40). The examinations may be called preliminary examinations, qualifying examinations, general examinations, oral examinations, or as we will use throughout this chapter—comprehensive examinations (exams for short; or colloquially, comps). These examinations date back to thirteenth-century Europe (Furstenberg & Nichols-Casebolt, 2001; Krsmanovic & Foster, 2023). In the United States, the comprehensive exam began as an oral exam in 1861 at Yale (Kennan & Stewart-Wells, 2021; McAdams et al., 2013; Stewart-Wells & Keenan, 2020); the written exam was introduced at Harvard in 1871 (Furstenberg & Nichols-Casebolt, 2001). It was not until the 1930s, however, that comprehensive exams became more widespread due to efforts to standardize graduate education in the United States (Cassuto, 2015; Estrem & Lucas, 2003; Schafer & Giblin, 2008).

When a student passes their comprehensive exams, they advance from doctoral *student* to doctoral *candidate*. This transition, or admission to candidacy, means that "in the judgement of the faculty, the doctoral student has an adequate knowledge of the field and the specialty, knows how to use academic resources, has potential to do original research autonomously, and presumably will complete the dissertation" (Council of Graduate

Schools, 2005, pp. 28–29). It is also evident in the extant literature that the comprehensive exam stage is often one of the most stressful, anxiety-inducing points along the doctoral degree journey for many students (e.g., Capello, 2023; McAdams et al., 2013; Sverdlik & Hall, 2020). Colón Semenza (2010) described it as "the graduate school equivalent of a midlife crisis," and going as far as to name it "comps burnout" (p. 152). Finally, Estrem and Lucas (2003) stated "The comprehensive exam not only comes at a crucial point in a student's graduate career but is also imbued with a sense of institutional and programmatic selection conjoined with high rates of attrition" (p. 400).

Given the prevalence of high-stakes comprehensive exams in doctoral education and the potential for increased stress, burnout, and attrition, we seek to mitigate these outcomes by shedding light on these exams. In so doing, we provide insights into what students, like Jennifer in the vignette introduced below, should consider as they approach this important phase of their degree program. Our objectives for this chapter include the following:

- Defining the purpose(s) of comprehensive exams
- Recognizing the variations in structures/formats of comprehensive exams
- Discussing the role of faculty (i.e., advisor, committee) in the comprehensive exam process
- Increasing awareness of self-efficacy in writing as it relates to comprehensive exams
- Identifying strategies for success during the comprehensive exam process

Vignette

Jennifer has just finished the first semester of their PhD program. They pride themselves on being organized and prepared throughout their graduate program. Although their cohort received an overview of their program and milestones during orientation, there are details about which Jennifer would like to know more, especially the comprehensive exam process. They anticipate that information will help them be more strategic in future classes and better prepared for the exam once they finish coursework. Jennifer schedules a meeting with their mentor to discuss comprehensive exams.

What the Research Says

It is common practice for doctoral programs to have a variety of milestones to mark progress toward the degree. One of those milestones is the comprehensive examination. Much of the extant literature around comprehensive exams is focused on the purpose and/or structure of the exams, and in some instances, within certain disciplines (e.g., adult education; counseling psychology; marketing; science, technology, engineering, and mathematics [STEM]). In this section, we provide an overview of four themes from the literature on comprehensive exams: purpose, variation in structure and format, role of faculty, and self-efficacy.

Purpose of Comprehensive Exams

As noted in the introduction, comprehensive exams are referred to by several names, including preliminary or qualifying exams (Furstenberg & Nichols-Casebolt, 2001). It is noteworthy, however, that some programs make a distinction and have both a qualifying or preliminary exam *and* a comprehensive exam. As such, "the lack of a clear title may suggest the lack of a clear purpose" (Cassuto, 2015, p. 82). Thus, it is not surprising a dedicated student, like Jennifer in the vignette, would have questions about how the exams are administered in their program.

Historically, doctoral program faculty used comprehensive exams to determine whether a student had the depth and breadth of knowledge in the field or discipline; the ability to think critically; and the requisite skills to complete the program, including an assessment of their ability to conduct independent scholarship (Capello, 2023; Cassuto, 2015; Childress, 2016; Estrem & Lucas, 2003; Freer, 2022; Nolan, 2002). In this way, some consider these exams to promote student development, as it facilitates student advancement to the next phase in their career, especially if the goal is to pursue the professoriate (Self et al., 2023). Because doctoral education is not a monolith, and prepares students for a variety of career outcomes, there is some question about whether these purposes are relevant for every doctoral degree program, such as professional doctorates like the EdD or PsyD. Therefore, exams themselves should have different purposes and structures. Emphasizing that one size does not fit all, Capello (2023) stated:

> *It may be that PhD students transition from students to scholars through their programs, but many EdD students enroll in their programs already established in their careers. They may not need to go through a process of becoming but rather go through a process of developing and refining practitioner knowledge and skills and synthesizing that knowledge and skill with scholarly knowledge.* (p. 36)

Whatever the purpose of a comprehensive exam, if a student is not successful, traditionally, they are dismissed from their program. This decision to dismiss a student can signal they are not equipped to represent the discipline or field (Cassuto, 2015; Champagne et al., 2021; Self et al., 2023). However, in their study, Self et al. (2023) found contemporary comprehensive exams often allow remediation, suggesting the goal is to help students pass the exam. With this opportunity to remediate and retake the exam, very few students are dismissed from their programs. Despite these changes, the comprehensive exam process remains time consuming and stressful for most doctoral students (Cahn, 2024; Furstenberg & Nichols-Casebolt, 2001).

Variation in Structure and Format of Comprehensive Exams

Once Jennifer has a better understanding of the purpose of the comprehensive exams, talking with their advisor about the structure, format, and assessment is a good next step. Comprehensive exam structure and format vary across discipline, degree program, and institution (Furstenberg & Nichols-Casebolt, 2001). However, some aspects of the process are generally followed. For example, students often take their exams after they have finished coursework and upon completing a successful written and oral exam, students become *doctoral candidates* (Capello, 2023). The exam is typically prepared by a student's faculty advisor or in conjunction with a committee of three to five faculty, and centers around several broad questions about the discipline or field of study. In some cases, students are asked a question specific to their intended dissertation topic. Then, students respond to the questions without the use of notes or resources over one or multiple days in a campus location, sometimes with other students who are completing their exam at the same time (Ponder et al., 2004; Schafer & Giblin, 2008). Students next present their exam to the committee, who then determines whether they passed, failed, or need remediation (Capello, 2023; Estrem & Lucas, 2003).

Recognition of the stress for students and faculty, variations in disciplines, as well as the changing nature of doctoral education has led to an increase in new forms of assessment to replace the high-stakes and high-pressure comprehensive exams (Capello, 2023; Estrem & Lucas, 2003; Freer, 2022). Examples of other formats programs have used to structure the examination include:

- original paper,
- paper on an area of specialization,
- concept paper,
- literature review,
- article critique,
- portfolio,
- take-home exam with extended time (Freer, 2022; Nolan, 2002; Ponder et al., 2004).

In addition to varied formats, assessment of the exam may not involve the student's committee but rather rely on reviews by other faculty members in the department who remain anonymous to the student (Estrem & Lucas, 2003).

Whatever the design of the comprehensive exam, it should be based on each individual doctoral program's learning outcomes (Capello, 2023; Furstenberg & Nichols-Casebolt, 2001). Because this is not always the case, scholars have critiqued the purpose and format of these exams for decades (Mayhew, 1972; Nolan, 2002; Self et al., 2023). By focusing on learning outcomes, programs can ensure they are designing comprehensive exams as more authentic and humane (Capello, 2023; Kennan & Stewart-Wells, 2021; Ponder et al., 2004; Self et al., 2023), which can improve retention (Wollast et al., 2018), self-efficacy (Krsmanovic & Foster, 2023), and provide salient exercises that can advance students' careers (McAdams et al., 2013; Stewart-Wells & Keenan, 2020). In this vein, Nolan (2002), Schafer and Giblin (2008), and Cannon (2020) left readers with salient rhetorical questions that can challenge faculty to rethink more traditional positivist approaches to comprehensive exams:

- "If knowledge is dynamic and ever shifting rather than static, how would a student benefit from synthesizing what the literature says about a field of study?" (Nolan, 2002, p. 42)
- "Why would knowing anything about the history of the field in which they plan to work benefit them?" (Nolan, 2002, p. 42)

- Are "exams more important because of the process students experience vs. actual answers they produce?" (Schafer & Giblin, 2008, p. 286)
- "[How do] they *function* (emphasis in original) to produce subjects in academia?" (Cannon, 2020, p. 40)

Likely with such questions in mind, Capello (2023) identified a series of benchmark assessments that may be salient for doctoral programs (e.g., proposing a paper and presenting at a conference, writing a book chapter or grant proposal). These sorts of activities intentionally contribute to students' career goals and program outcomes. Moreover, it is possible to include several smaller benchmark assessments as the comprehensive exam, which serves to reduce the high-stakes high-pressure formats of some exams (Capello, 2023). Regarding their efficacy, faculty who engage an authentic benchmark approach report that students demonstrate stronger writing, problem-solving, research, and organizational skills than in more traditional exams (Kennan & Stewart-Wells, 2021).

Role of Faculty in Comprehensive Exams

First and foremost, as suggested above, the role of faculty and the program should be to interrogate the purpose, structure, and format of the comprehensive exam so that it aligns with program learning outcomes and values. Once the program faculty establish these principles for the exam, a student's advisor serves as the liaison between the student and department (Barnes & Austin, 2009). This means that they are crucial players in articulating what the exam is and how students should prepare for it. Without strong advising and mentoring relationships, students may not have the necessary guidance to be successful throughout their graduate program, including with their comprehensive exams (Barnes & Austin, 2009).

Moreover, when students critique the exam process, they often point to feeling unprepared, reinforcing the importance of the faculty advisor (McAdams et al., 2013). There are other ways advisors can and should intentionally support students. For example, they can convey confidence in the students' abilities, create a space where students can comfortably and candidly discuss their feelings about the exam, prepare to intervene if committee questions are irrelevant, and provide honest assessment of the written and oral exams (Bargar & Mayo-Chamberlain, 1983, p. 414, as cited in Gardner & Barnes, 2014;

Klocko et al., 2015). All students, like Jennifer, should talk with their advisor about what support is available, both through the program/institution and from the advisor themselves. It would also be beneficial for students to learn what role the committee plays in the exam process in their program.

In addition to the important role faculty advisors play, doctoral students often have a faculty committee that can assist them in the comprehensive exam process. The committee can help students prepare for comprehensive exams and provide useful feedback to the students through questions they may pose during the oral defense to help identify areas to remediate, if necessary, and better position them for the next phase in their degree process (Capello, 2023; Estrem & Lucas, 2003). Thus, having a supportive, helpful, and congenial committee can be vital to student success (Barnes & Austin, 2009). In addition, each member of the committee has the potential to serve as an additional advisor or mentor to help students develop interdisciplinary knowledge, support their well-being, and meet other program goals for which a single advisor lacks capacity and/or expertise (National Academies of Sciences, Engineering, and Medicine (NASAM), 2018).

Although not specifically tied to the comprehensive exam process, there is substantial evidence that mentor networks and multiple mentor models help students develop more quickly as scholars because of the added support (NASAM, 2019). It then follows that if a committee can function as a mentor network, doctoral students will be more likely to thrive throughout their degree program, including their comprehensive exams.

Self-Efficacy and Comprehensive Exams

Another important topic receiving increased attention in scholarship about doctoral education is *self-efficacy*. Bandura (1982) defined self-efficacy as "judgments of how well one can execute courses of action required to deal with prospective situations" (p. 122). Importantly, self-efficacy differs from *self-esteem*, which "is concerned with judgments of self-worth" (Bandura, 1982, p. 11). Given this definition of self-efficacy, Krsmanovic and Foster (2023) found "students' attitudes toward both comprehensive exams and capstone are significantly correlated with their self-efficacy and perceived program outcomes" (p. 19); with higher self-efficacy, "more favorable a students' perspective will be toward their comprehensive exam and capstone" (p. 19).

Designing exams with the intention of enhancing self-efficacy can be critical to student success because during a doctoral program, "the lowest self-efficacy levels were observed in students who were completing their comprehensive exams" (Sverdlik & Hall, 2020, p. 115), compared with other phases like the Knowledge and Skill Development Stage (i.e., coursework) or the Inquiry Stage (i.e., the dissertation). In many cases, this influence on self-efficacy could be attributed to the transition from seeing self as student to seeing self as an independent scholar when moving from what Gardner (2009) termed Phase II (Integration) to Phase III (Candidacy).

Self-efficacy in writing, or what Schmidt and Alexander (2012) called *writerly self-efficacy,* is one way self-efficacy is explored in the literature around doctoral education. In their discussion, Naidoo et al. (2023) indicated "writing promotes student engagement by activating self-efficacy and helping students develop a scholarly identity" (Section 1.2. Writing Self-Efficacy). Naidoo et al. (2023) also noted the benefits of writing self-efficacy include "increasing writing performance and achievement, higher course grades, and increasing student engagement" and can also "alleviate writing anxiety and increase confidence" (Section 4.6 Writerly Self-Efficacy and Student Belonging, para. 3). Given that writing is a major component of comprehensive exams and the Inquiry Stage that follows, no matter the structure or format used, investing in the development of one's own *writerly self-efficacy* would certainly be worthwhile.

Strategies for Success

Based on this discussion of the literature, here are five big picture strategies for you to consider as you prepare to be successful in your comprehensive exams:

Strategy 1: Invest in understanding expectations ahead of time

As Champagne et al. (2021) wrote, "careful preparation and a mindful approach to exam day will help reduce the anxiety associated with comps, so you can showcase your competency with confidence" (p. 52). While you may have opportunities throughout coursework to prepare for your comprehensive exams (e.g., assigned readings, literature review assignments, annotated bibliographies, portfolio activities), ensuring you understand the purpose, format, and the how and who of evaluation are also important parts of preparation. These expectations are most often covered in program handbooks, through conversations with an advisor/program faculty, and/or in program orientations.

Strategy 2: Establish peer mentoring/support:

In alignment with the benefits of peer feedback/editing that the participants in Klocko et al. (2015) noted, Colón Semenza (2010) encouraged avoiding *Desert Island Syndrome* (p. 152). Naidoo et al. (2023) provided a few examples of what this peer support, or avoiding the Desert Island Syndrome, can look like: "social groups, writing groups, peer writing partners, as well as comprehensive examination preparation groups" (p. 9). These peer networks may develop organically, growing out of relationships built along the way during coursework, or via an intentional structure established by the program. While cohort-based programs may provide more opportunities for peer support to grow, students in non-cohort programs might find options for such experiences through graduate student organizations at their institution or through the professional associations relevant to their discipline.

Strategy 3: Build self-efficacy in writing:

In addition to seeking out programmatic and institutional supports related to writing, students may also consider Klocko et al.'s (2015) recommendations centered around time, feedback and clear expectations, anxiety, and writing mechanisms:

- Scheduling regular meetings with advisor;
- Identifying tools to develop goals and skills;
- Engaging in peer feedback, editing, and/or writing groups;
- Seeking clear and consistent expectations from faculty;
- Soliciting examples of successful writing; and
- Taking opportunities to practice writing (e.g., revise course papers based on feedback) (pp. 28–29).

Strategy 4: During the written exams:

Colón Semenza (2010) implored students to "make sure [they] answer the question" (p. 160), and with some minor adjustments, this advice could apply to other exam formats as well (e.g., portfolios, article critiques). This recommendation addresses two potential pitfalls that can occur as a student responds: (a) they change the question to the point where they are no longer answering what was asked; and/or (b) they overshare or incorporate far more than is needed to show they know a lot (p. 160), often referred to as the kitchen sink approach. If a student is unsure of a question's intent, they should ask for clarification. If not, Colón Semenza recommended they "begin [their] response by articulating exactly how [they] interpret the question (e.g., 'My understanding is...') and then proceed" (p. 160).

Strategy 5: During the oral exams:

When it comes to the oral comps (often referred to as the defense), it is rare that a common set of questions is used for all students. While there are more common approaches to questions (e.g., questions about literature reviewed, questions about how they made this or that decision), there will also likely be questions intended to push at the boundaries of what the student knows about the topic(s) addressed in their written exams. This is when it is important to "be willing to say, 'I don't know'" (Colón Semenza, 2010, p. 164).

In sum, students should consider the oral questions as opportunities to demonstrate: (a) some of what they had potentially hoped to include in the written portion but were not able to due to time constraints or other reasons; and (b) the reflecting and thinking skills they have built along the way. It can also be a chance to dialogue with committee members, learning from how they might respond to the question asked. As Colón Semenza (2010) stated, "Always remember that a thoughtful response will go over better than a clever, evasive one" (p. 164).

Questions for Reflection

As you embark on your journey the comprehensive exam, take time to reflect on what is discussed in this chapter. Below are a set of questions to prepare for your exams:

- After learning the purpose of comprehensive exams in my doctoral program, what goals might I set for myself to get the most out of this process?

- Recognizing the importance of the relationship between advisor and student, what are 3–5 aspects I hope will be incorporated into my relationship with my advisor?
- What tools and resources related to writing are available to me? Will I want to invest in external resources (e.g., an editor) as well? Are there policies that limit the use of external resources, including generative artificial intelligence that I must consider before investing in them?
- Based on who I am as a student, what additional supports will I want to make sure to have in place as I go through the comprehensive exam process?
- Beyond my advisor, what relationships do I have or need to develop to ensure I do not experience *Desert Island Syndrome* (Colón Semenza, 2010)?
- If I receive critical feedback throughout the process, how do I best address and incorporate it to further develop as a thinker and knowledge producer?

Recommended Resources

The following resources provide useful tips related to the comprehensive exam process. They can also be helpful for faculty to review as they advise students and design exams centered on program learning outcomes.

For those interested in learning more about the history of comprehensive exams, check out pages 27–29 of Capello's (2023) article *Linking Assessments to Program Outcomes in Practitioner-Oriented EdD Programs: An Alternative to Comprehensive Examinations.*

Champagne et al. (2021, October), doctoral candidates/students at the time, wrote *Prepping for Your Comprehensive Exams.* This brief magazine article includes several tips, and at the end, they recommend these resources:

- From the University of Nebraska—Lincoln: Eight Ways to Prepare for Comprehensive Exams
- From the Department of History at the University of Washington: 20 Tips for the Ph.D. Exam
- From Stephanie Hedge in *Inside Higher Ed*: Surviving Studying for Comprehensive Exams

Additionally, there are five other articles from *Inside Higher Ed* that may be of interest:

- Surviving Writing Comprehensive Exams, by Stephanie Hedge (2012, June 7)
- Deconstructing the Written Comprehensive Exam, by K. D. Shives (2013, March 21)
- 5 Strategies for Organizing Notes for Comprehensive Exams, by Emily VanBuren (2014, February 18)
- Surviving and Thriving During Quals, by Natascha Chtena (2016, January 14)
- A Qualifying Exam Proposal Checklist, by Megan Poorman (2017, March 16)

A post by Libby Natola (2022, May 27) from the *Advice to a Scientist* website provides some additional insights, entitled How to Study for Oral Comprehensive or Qualifying Exams. Although written with a focus on exams in the sciences, much of the advice can apply across disciplines. At the end of this post, Natola also shared the University of Nebraska-Lincoln resource noted above, as well as three web resources that focus on preparing for oral exams:

- From *Education Corner*, a post by Becton Loveless, as of publication of this chapter was last updated in April 2024: Best Oral Exam Preparation Tips
- From *ThoughtCo.*, a post by Grace Fleming, as of publication of this chapter was last updated in September 2019: Preparing for an Oral Exam
- From the *STUWO* blog, a post by Christina Pichler, written in January of 2021: Oral Exams: These Tips Will Help you Master Even the Toughest Questions

To learn more about one intentional approach to peer mentoring/support, communities of practice, we encourage you to review:

- Adkisson, A., Coffman, K., Galloway, C., Jefferson-Evans, A., Miller-McCollum, K., Olszewski, C. A., Spivey, D. A., & Znamenak, K. (2020). Peer mentoring and communities of practice: Reflections from newly minted PhDs. *New Directions for Adult and Continuing Education, 167–168*, 107–118. https://doi.org/10.1002/ace.20402

References

Adkisson, A., Coffman, K., Galloway, C., Jefferson-Evans, A., Miller-McCollum, K., Olszewski, C. A., Spivey, D. A., & Znamenak, K. (2020). Peer mentoring and communities of practice: Reflections from newly minted PhDs. *New Directions for Adult and Continuing Education, 167–168*, 107–118. https://doi.org/10.1002/ace.20402

Bandura, A. (1997). *Self-efficacy: The exercise of control.* W.H. Freeman, 122–147.

Barnes, B. J., & Austin, A. E. (2009). The role of doctoral advisors: A look at advising from the advisor's perspective. *Innovative Higher Education, 33*, 297–315. https://doi.org/10.1007/s10755-008-9084-x

Cahn, S. M. (2024). *From student to scholar: A candid guide to becoming a professor* (2nd ed.). Resource Publications.

Cannon, S. O. (2020). Making kin with comprehensive exams: Producing scholar in intra-action. *Qualitative Inquiry, 26*(1), 36–50. https://doi.org/10.1177/1077800419869962

Capello, S. A. (2023). Linking assessments to program outcomes in practitioner-oriented EdD programs: An alternative to comprehensive examinations. *Journal of Adult and Continuing Education, 29*(1), 25–40. https://doi.org/10.1177/14779714221093091

Cassuto, L. (2015). *The graduate school mess: What caused it and how we can fix it.* Harvard University Press.

Champagne, R., Boyle, P., & Pires, C. B. (2021, October). Prepping for your comprehensive exams. *CSA News.* https://doi.org//10.1002/csan.20580

Childress, H. (2016). *The PhDictionary: A glossary of things you don't know (but should) about doctoral and faculty life.* The University of Chicago Press.

Colón Semenza, G. M. (2010). *Graduate study for the twenty-first century: How to build an academic career in the humanities* (2nd ed.). Palgrave Macmillan.

Council of Graduate Schools in the U.S. (2005). *The Doctor of Philosophy degree: A policy statement.* https://eric.ed.gov/?id=ED331420

Estrem, H., & Lucas, B. F. (2003). Embedded traditions, uneven reform: The place of the comprehensive exam in composition and rhetoric PhD programs. *Rhetoric Review, 22*(4), 396–416.

Freer, J. (2022). Assessing doctoral candidacy: The development of an assessment tool for comprehensive portfolios. *Canadian Journal of Education, 45*(3), 703–721.

Furstenberg, A. L., & Nichols-Casebolt, A. (2001). Hurdle or building block: Comprehensive examinations in social work doctoral education. *Journal of Teaching in Social Work, 21*(1–2), 19–37. https://doi.org/10.1300/j067v21n01_03

Gardner, S. K. (2009). The development of doctoral students: Phases of challenge and support. *ASHE Higher Education Report, 34*(6). https://doi.org/10.1002/aehe.3406

Gardner, S. K., & Barnes, B. J. (2014). *Advising & mentoring doctoral students: A handbook*. CreateSpace Independent Publishing.

Golde, C. M., & Dore, T. M. (2001). *At cross purposes: What the experiences of doctoral students reveal about doctoral education*. The Pew Charitable Trusts. Retrieved from www.phd-survey.org

Keenan, K. M., & Stewart-Wells, A. G. (2021). Moving beyond comprehensive exams: Implementing authentic assessments to enhance doctoral student learning. *Christian Higher Education*, *20*(1–2), 69–86. https://doi.org/10.1080/15363759.2020.1851815

Klocko, B. A., Marshall, S. M., & Davidson, J. F. (2015). Developing practitioner-scholar doctoral candidates as critical writers. *Journal of Higher Education Theory and Practice*, *15*(4), 21–31.

Krsmanovic, M., & Foster, H. A. (2023). Best practices for EdD comprehensive exams and capstone projects: Students' attitudes and perspectives of outcomes in an online program. *Impacting Education: Journal on Transforming Professional Practice*, *8*(3), 15–22. https://doi.org/10.5195/ie.20223.397

Mayhew, L. B. (1972). *Reform in graduate education* (Vol. *18*). SREB Monograph. Southern Regional Education Board.

McAdams, C. R. III., Robertson, D. L., & Foster, V. A. (2013). Doctoral oral examinations and contemporary counselor education: Are they compatible? *Counselor Education & Supervision*, *52*, 270–283. https://doi.org/10.1002/j.1556-6978.2013.00042.x

Naidoo, K., Quaynor, L., & Shen, Y. (2023). Doctoral students' experiences, self-efficacy, and send of belonging related to academic writing in an online program. *Education Sciences*, *13*(11). https://doi.org/10.3390/educsci13111097

National Academies of Sciences, Engineering, and Medicine. (2018). *Graduate STEM education for the 21st century*. The National Academies Press. https://doi.org/10.17226/25038

National Academies of Sciences, Engineering, and Medicine. (2019). *The science of effective mentorship in STEMM*. The National Academies Press. https://doi.org/10.17226/25568

Nolan, R. E. (2002). How graduate students of adult and continuing education are assessed at the doctoral level. *The Journal of Continuing Higher Education*, *50*(3), 38–43. https://doi.org/10.1080/07377366.2002.10401203

Ponder, N., Beatty, S. E., & Foxx, W. (2004). Doctoral comprehensive exams in marketing: Current practices and emerging perspectives. *Journal of Marketing Education*, *26*(3), 226–35. https://doi.org/10.1177/0273475304268778

Schafer, J. A., & Giblin, M. J. (2008). Doctoral comprehensive exams: Standardization, customization, and everywhere in between. *Journal of Criminal Justice Education*, *19*(2), 275–289. https://doi.org/10.1080/10511250802137648

Schmidt, K. E., & Alexander, J. E. (2012). The empirical development of an instrument to measure writerly self-efficacy in writing centers. *Journal of Writing Assessment, 5*(1). Retrieved from https://escholarship.org/uc/item/5dp4m86t

Self, K. J., Kroke, P. C., Waters, A. J., Goodie, J. L., & Bennion, L. D. (2023). Comprehensive and qualifying examinations: A qualitative review of APA-accredited doctoral psychology programs. *Training and Education in Professional Psychology, 17*(4), 391–399. https://doi.org/10.1037/tep0000438

Stewart-Wells, A. G., & Keenan, K. M. (2020). Assessing doctoral students: A background on comprehensive and authentic assessments. *The Journal of Continuing Higher Education, 68*(2), 84–100. https://doi.org/10.1080/07377363.2020.1743950

Sverdlik, A., & Hall, N. C. (2020). Not just a phase: Exploring the role of program stage on well-being and motivation in doctoral students. *Journal of Adult and Continuing Education, 26*(1), 97–124. https://doi.org/10.1177/1477971419842887

Wollast, R., Boudrenghien, G., Van der Linden, N., Galand, B., Roland, N., Devos, C., De Clerq, M., Klein, O., Azzi, A., & Frenay, M. (2018). Who are the doctoral students who drop out? Factors associated with the rate of doctoral degree completion in universities. *International Journal of Higher Education, 7*(4), 143–156. https://doi.org/10.5430/ijhe.v7n4p143

Part 4
The Inquiry Stage

17 Identifying and Developing a Relationship with a Dissertation Chair

Sharon M. Pratt, EdD

Lucinda S. Spaulding, PhD

Introduction

A significant factor associated with doctoral student persistence is the quality of the candidate–chair relationship (Rademaker et al., 2016; Burkholder & Bidjerano, 2023; Waalkes et al., 2022). The *dissertation chair* (sometimes also referred to as director, advisor, or supervisor) serves as a guide and mentor during the doctoral candidate's progression through the Inquiry phase of the degree program. The relationship between the dissertation chair and candidate is one that ideally begins during coursework (i.e., student–professor/student–advisor), develops until completion of the program (i.e., candidate–chair), and continues to grow after the degree is complete (i.e., colleagues in the discipline). Both chairs and students play a role in the transition from mentorship to collegial relationship within the research and professional doctoral program.

In this chapter, research on mentorship and developing professional relationships is presented, followed by a discussion of specific strategies and recommendations for establishing a positive relationship, whether within a research or professional doctoral program model. Questions for reflection focus on key behaviors and attitudes that influence the successful navigation of this relationship that is so integral to doctoral persistence. The case study below illustrates how students can build a successful, collaborative partnership within a research doctoral program.

Case Study

Jackie, a PhD student, reflected on her doctoral experience. While she progressed through the Knowledge and Skill Development Stage, she worked with different professors. As she learned about each of their research endeavors, she found Dr. Wang had research interests similar to her own.

Dr. Wang was also impressed with Jackie's astuteness and abilities, so he initiated a mentorship relationship with her by inviting her to collaborate on a research study he was working on. As they worked together, they discussed avenues to publish and present. They submitted proposals for several conferences and manuscripts for publication. By the time Jackie reached the Inquiry Stage of her degree, she and Dr. Wang had published four articles and presented at three conferences together. She felt well prepared to begin her dissertation journey.

For her dissertation research, Jackie decided to extend a topic she had been researching with Dr. Wang. As they discussed her ideas, he expressed interest in her research direction and volunteered to chair her dissertation committee. Jackie enthusiastically accepted his offer, and under his guidance, selected her committee members, individuals they both respected and with whom Dr. Wang had a strong working relationship. Jackie sought advice from Dr. Wang on research question development, data collection, and analysis. Their conversations were consistently marked by respect and consideration of each other's opinions and experience. Their collaboration prepared her to execute her research and successfully defend her dissertation.

Dr. Wang and Jackie's professional relationship continued beyond the conferment of her degree. Dr. Wang's instrumental mentorship helped Jackie secure a tenure-track faculty position with a research university upon graduation. As colleagues in the field, Jackie and Dr. Wang continue to coauthor publications and present their research at conferences. Jackie also appreciates Dr. Wang's continued mentorship as she works toward achieving tenure.

What the Research Says

Prior to the implementation of formal schooling, *apprenticeship* was the primary way individuals learned new skills. Individuals would work alongside an expert for the purpose of becoming skilled like the expert (Collins et al., 1989). Though current doctoral programs, both face-to-face and distance, have replaced this historic apprenticeship model of teaching and learning, seminal research on student attrition and retention has highlighted the importance of interacting with and establishing a positive relationship with faculty (Tinto, 1975, 2023).

Research indicates candidates are more likely to persist when they have positive relationships with their dissertation chair, and when the chair communicates clear expectations (Gittings et al., 2018; Hanson et al., 2022; Hill & Conceição, 2020; Mosyana et al., 2022; Sparkman & Doran, 2019; Sverdlik et al., 2018). When chairs facilitate interaction and collaboration, they promote the development of strong scholarly community, which involves engagement, trust, dedication, and often results in persistence (Rademaker et al., 2016). Sense of connectedness supports persistence (Kumar et al., 2023). When chairs engage with candidates, candidates' sense of belonging and self-efficacy with respect to the dissertation increases (Varghese & Finkelstein, 2021), also positively influencing persistence (Brill et al., 2014).

The Mentor Relationship

For the purpose of this chapter, *mentorship* is defined as a "professional, working alliance in which individuals work together over time to support the personal and professional [and academic] growth, development, and success of the relational partner through the provision of career and psychosocial support" (Dahlberg & Byars-Winston, 2019, p. 37). Further, mentor relationships may be formal, informal, passive, or active (Ensher & Murphy, 2011).

In some doctoral programs, faculty advisors are assigned to students at the Entry Stage. These mentors play an integral role in socializing students to the doctoral program as well as to the nature of academia and the discipline. Other mentor/mentee relationships develop naturally during the Knowledge and Skill Development Stage as students and faculty interact through coursework and around scholarly activities, like Jackie's relationship with Dr. Wang. Conversely, proactive students may seek and request mentorship by a chosen faculty member early in their program. Yet other mentor relationships evolve as opportunities arise for students to collaborate with faculty on projects, or support faculty scholarship through doctoral assistantships or fellowships.

Irrespective of how or when the mentor relationship is initiated, the relationship generally provides the mentee with benefits inclusive of (a) scholarly growth and development, (b) guidance with professional aspirations, and (c) emotional support and encouragement (Groman & Paquette, 2023; Kumar et al., 2023). For example, Jackie enrolled in a PhD program (i.e., a research doctorate model) and was assigned a faculty mentor who assisted with her development of research competencies. Within a scholar-practitioner model, faculty mentors support advisees in applying evidence-based practices, such as applying research to find solutions to problems that exist.

Though the mentoring relationship initially tends to benefit the mentee through gaining new skills and knowledge, research suggests over time the relationship becomes mutually beneficial as the mentor also develops scholarly leadership skills that include being authentic in interactions, being facilitative rather than directive, being visionary in looking toward long-term goals, and in improving personal areas of deficiency (Flora, 2017).

From Mentor to Chair

Relationships initiated in the Knowledge and Skill Development Stage, whether formally assigned or informally developed, often result in a Chair/Candidate relationship in the Inquiry Stage. This natural progression, as the case study highlights, is the ideal experience for both a doctoral student and their dissertation chair. Unfortunately, however, the maturing, positive, and productive relationship between Jackie and Dr. Wang is not the norm for many doctoral candidates and their chairs.

Research on doctoral attrition indicates poor relationships with faculty is a common reason doctoral students leave a doctoral program (Desphande, 2016; Gittings et al., 2018; Hanson et al., 2020; Hill & Conceicao, 2020; Ruud et al., 2016). A meta-analysis of research on doctoral student attrition published from 2020 to 2017 found the most frequently occurring reason for doctoral candidate attrition was poor rapport with their dissertation supervisor (Sverdlik et al., 2018). Research across disciplines indicates a primary challenge doctoral students face in their relationship with their faculty mentors is a lack of communication and accessibility, which can cause the student to feel isolated, particularly in online doctoral programs (Deshpande, 2016; Sparkman and Doran, 2019). Other issues can occur when there is misalignment in doctoral candidate and faculty mentor research interests, values, communication styles, and expectations (Devos et al., 2016). Lack of vested interested in the candidate's research topic or personal well-being are also challenges that frequently occur (Groman & Paquette, 2023).

Doctoral student characteristics and actions can also weaken relationships with faculty. Specifically, doctoral faculty mentors cite procrastination, dependency, and unwillingness to take feedback constructively to improve one's work as undesirable traits in doctoral students (Burkholder & Bidjerano, 2023; Goldman & Goodboy, 2017; Howells et al., 2017). When doctoral students demonstrate low levels of intrinsic motivation and initiative it can create a strain between the candidate and faculty member (Burkholder & Bidjerano, 2023), increasing students' pessimism toward the process coupled with a decreased self-efficacy in their ability to meet expectations (Orsini and Coers, 2022; Splinter et al., 2022).

While adverse relationships with faculty are associated with attrition, a positive relationship between the doctoral candidate and their dissertation chair has long been understood as one of the most important contributing factors to successful completion of the doctoral degree (Acharya & Rajendran, 2023; Gardner, 2009; Gittings et al., 2018; Hanson et al., 2020; Hill & Conceição, 2020; Mosyana et al., 2022; Sparkman & Doran, 2019; Sverdlik et al., 2018). Further, a good relationship with advisors or dissertation chairs also has a positive effect on time to degree completion (Devos et al., 2016; Sparkman & Doran, 2019; Sverdlik et al., 2018). Supportive relationships are marked by the student's ability to access the faculty member, frequent communication between the faculty member and student, and a mentor's willingness to provide more than just procedural information, providing a meaningful mentoring relationship that goes beyond a dissertation defense (Hill & Conceição, 2020; Kumar et al., 2023; Lim et al., 2019; Rademaker et al., 2016).

Within a professional doctoral program model, a supportive relationship also includes the faculty member supporting their mentee students in learning how to relate research to solving real-world problems within their field (Deshpande, 2016), whereas in a research doctoral program, a supportive relationship includes the faculty member providing guidance in scholarly research and disseminating results to contribute knowledge to the specific discipline (Hill & Conceicao, 2020), as evident in the case study with Jackie and Dr. Wang.

Doctoral candidates should consider both academic and interpersonal skills when choosing dissertation chairs (Jorgensen & Wester, 2020) as dissertation chairs are not only depended on to provide guidance on the technical aspects of the dissertation, but also on career guidance, publishing, and equally important—psychosocial support when self-doubt and anxiety arise (Ari et al., 2022; Bottomley et al., 2020; Harsoor et al., 2022; Splinter et al., 2022).

When doctoral faculty members consider chairing and mentoring students through the dissertation process, they may identify several desirable qualities and characteristics in potential mentees. For example, they may look for students who are successful in their program and show evidence of transforming from autonomous course takers to self-directed learners (see Chapter 14: Transitioning from Autonomous to Self-Directed Learning) who are seeking to take ownership of their research interests (Sverdlik et al., 2018). Additionally, faculty seek to mentor students who are motivated and committed to the academic process, evidenced by a student's abilities in goal setting, coping strategies, and effectively managing personal and professional obligations to meet their academic goals (Goldman & Goodboy, 2017; Howells et al., 2017). Interpersonal skills of respect, positivity, gratitude, intellectual humility, and a willingness to listen to constructive feedback are also important student dispositions that support positive relationships with one's dissertation chair (Albertyn & Bennett, 2021; Burkholder & Bidjerano, 2023).

Strategies for Success

The case study presented in this chapter highlights a highly functioning professional relationship between a doctoral student and her faculty mentor.

However, the student–faculty and chair/candidate relationship can all too often be fraught with challenges that make the student consider leaving the program (Deshpande, 2016; Gittings et al., 2018; Hanson et al., 2020). The following strategies can be used to successfully navigate and build a strong professional relationship with your chair that transforms from professor during coursework, to mentor, to dissertation chair, and finally, to colleague in the field upon doctoral completion.

The key to all successful professional working relationships is their dual nature, which involves equal participation, investment, and commitment (Sverdlik et al., 2018). Knowing the responsibilities and applying the strategies for developing positive relationships will help you not only complete your degree in a timely manner but also build a curriculum vitae evidencing skills and experiences necessary for obtaining a faculty position, like Jackie, or advance in a professional practitioner role (for more on this topic see Chapter 23: Publishing and Presenting and Chapter 24: Transitioning from Student to Professor).

Strategy 1: Seek Faculty Mentors Early in the Program

As faculty mentorship is the most influential factor in completing a doctoral program (Sverdlik et al., 2018), you should seek out faculty mentors early in your program. At the Entry Stage, when searching for and considering possible doctoral programs, you should inquire about the opportunities to receive mentorship from faculty in both the program and the school or college of study. You might ask if the program offers formal mentorship opportunities such as those where faculty are assigned to new students from the onset of the program or if students are given opportunities to join research teams. Additionally, you might ask about assistantships or fellowships, which often offer opportunities for mentorship. If enrolling in a professional doctoral program, you might ask about opportunities to work alongside faculty in field experiences or internship opportunities that connect doctoral students with practitioners working in field settings.

If the program of study does not have a formal mentor program, the mentor relationship needs to be initiated by either the faculty member or the student. Some faculty are *talent seekers* (DeAngelo, 2010) and initiate mentorship relationships with students. You should become aware of the characteristics specific faculty seek in mentees, such as being proactive, evidence of self-directed learning, taking responsibility for the research, and strong self-management skills in terms of goal setting and time management. You should assess your abilities in these areas and, if necessary, develop and model these desirable characteristics consistently in all interactions with all your program faculty. If these characteristics are not personal strengths, seeking support from a faculty mentor in a proactive fashion to develop these attributes will go a long way in demonstrating your willingness to grow professionally.

Be proactive and initiate seeking a dissertation chair (Gittings et al., 2018). If enrolled in a research doctorate like Jackie, become well acquainted with the nature and focus of your program faculty's scholarly work by researching their academic profiles and curriculum vitae, reading their existing scholarship, and seeking any online videos or materials the faculty have posted. Proactively seek ways to support or collaborate with faculty whose research interests align with your own by reaching out to them before or during your program and inquiring about research team positions. You might also mention specific faculty in your admissions application. Ask thoughtful questions during class discussions. If enrolled in a professional doctoral program, look for faculty who have experience or partnerships in the field that match their interests and future career goals.

Further, be cognizant that your needs will change as you progress through the various stages of your doctoral journey. Seek mentors who demonstrate they are adaptable to students' changing needs as they navigate the various stages of the doctoral journey. Faculty who can provide guidance for professional development and networking opportunities for research and applications of practice into the field will be invaluable as you move beyond your dissertation (Gonzalez, 2024) and enter the collegial stage of your chair/candidate relationship.

Finding and building a supportive mentor-mentee relationship is important to all doctoral study. Mentors have been described as role models and sponsors, with the goal of promoting scholarly development and support through instructing, challenging, and modeling scholarship and professionalism in the field (Gittens, 2013). In essence, faculty mentoring serves to socialize the doctoral student to not only the program, but in the case of the professional doctorate also into their chosen discipline and this mentor has the potential to become the candidate's dissertation chair. In the case of the professional doctorate, faculty mentoring serves to socialize you into the program as well as into how to apply scholarship and inquiry to transform your field of practice.

Strategy 2: Choose a Chair Wisely

Just as finding a mentor is important, you should also choose your chair wisely. When considering who to ask to chair your dissertation committee, choose someone you believe will be knowledgeable about your research topic and research design. Additionally, when choosing a chair, think about faculty members who are encouraging, provide substantive feedback, and ask for improvement in your work. Receiving only praise might leave good feelings but does not help stretch your current abilities to learn something new or reach for a higher standard of quality. Because conducting formal research is uncharted territory for most doctoral students, obtaining good guidance and feedback will be necessary when proceeding with the doctoral program and dissertation research. For this reason, Hill and Conceicao (2020) encourage doctoral candidates to seek faculty mentors who are visionary "to not only see them for who they are but also for who they can become" (p. 42). In sum, you want a chair who sees your potential and will challenge you to grow through the research process.

Since doctoral candidates work closely with their chair, it is also important to consider schedules, personality, and communication styles when determining suitability (Sparkman & Doran, 2019). Reflecting on past experiences with professors in coursework, assistantships, or research teams can all be helpful in choosing a chair. Initiate conversations with faculty to discuss the possibility of chairing your research. During such conversations, ask about their advising process, communication style, feedback timelines, and availability to determine compatibility.

Strategy 3: Become a Self-Directed Learner

To ensure a positive relationship with your dissertation chair, you need to take personal responsibility for your research. After all, this is your research work and your future. Chapter 14 discusses the importance of doctoral students transitioning from autonomous learners during the Knowledge and Skill Development phase to self-directed learners in the Inquiry phase of the doctoral journey. As a doctoral candidate, it is important that you search for and locate resources that will aid in developing your dissertation (e.g., developing the literature review, constructing the research design, analyzing and interpreting data) rather than asking your chair to provide them to you.

For research doctorates, it is also helpful to read other dissertations, become a member of a professional research organization (e.g., the American Educational Research Association), and attend conferences where empirical research is presented. These activities provide examples and experiences from which to learn needed skills and abilities. If enrolled in a professional doctorate, it will be helpful to read practitioner journals that relate research to practice and review reports resulting from grants that explored effective practices in the field. Additionally, attending professional conferences can support learning how to apply research to practice.

For both types of programs, joining or creating small study groups with peers is also recommended. Building community among your fellow students can support your learning, well-being, and endurance in the program (see Chapter 9 for more on community). Finally, and most important, no matter professional goals, you should select a topic of inquiry that is important and personally meaningful to you to ensure you are intrinsically and independently motivated to answer your research or inquiry questions and advance learning for your discipline (research doctorate) or field (practitioner doctorate). After all, you will spend significant time with this topic.

Strategy 4: Establish Goals and a Timeline

One frequent challenge doctoral candidates face is gaining access to their chair when they have questions or need advice (Gittings et al., 2018; Hanson et al., 2020). To address this challenge, it is helpful to establish goals and set a timeline with your chair for the completion and submission of various tasks associated with the dissertation process, such as the literature review, first draft of the proposal, revisions to the proposal, and so forth (Groman & Paquette, 2023). A timeline should be detailed and clear to both you and your chair. Timelines often include all the tasks you, your chair, and other committee members will accomplish with dates for submission and feedback. Not only will the timeline help keep you moving through the process, but it will also communicate to all involved the anticipated length of time for completing the research.

Furthermore, you should solicit chair and committee member feedback on goals and a corresponding timeline to ensure alignment with your professional and personal responsibilities throughout the year. It is important for you to consult your dissertation chair to determine time frames that are both workable and realistic for all parties for the many steps involved in the process. Faculty members can provide recommendations for how long each step of the process can take (e.g., revisions on the dissertation proposal). Additionally, consider university deadlines for graduation and how those fit with timelines. It is not uncommon for programs to require a final defense to take place approximately a month before graduation, building in time for post-defense revisions and a final edit.

Strategy 5: Communicate Regularly

Communicate regularly with your dissertation chair by providing systematic updates throughout the process. This communication should include at least monthly contact with your chair to discuss current and future stages of the dissertation work, though some suggest weekly (Kumar et al., 2023; Sparkman & Doran, 2019). Communicate and update your chair regularly through email, video conferencing, or scheduled phone calls. Both timing and format should be discussed and agreed upon between you both early in the candidate/chair relationship. As meetings arise, be prepared by having questions and ideas noted ahead of time (Groman & Paquette, 2023), thus showing your chair you value their time. Keep running notes in one place so you have a clear record of the goals and the outcomes of each meeting to keep both on track. Do not be surprised if your faculty chair does the same.

The ubiquity of virtual mentorship, whether the program is face-to-face or online, provides doctoral candidates and their faculty mentors with a variety of modes of communication to ensure a collaborative relationship. Both synchronous and asynchronous methods can be valuable to building trust and achieving set goals, as well as combating feelings of isolation and disconnection (Deshpande, 2016; Rademaker et al., 2016). Faculty mentors and doctoral candidates have reported using email, video conferencing, content management systems, online document sharing, and virtual file sharing as means to stay in communication during the dissertation process (Groman & Paquette, 2023; Kumar et al., 2023). Further, online document sharing allows one to comment and use track changes to reflect suggestions or revisions. Virtual file sharing sites (e.g., DropBox or OneDrive) are more streamlined methods for storing, editing, and developing ideas in writing. Following up on written feedback with a virtual meeting can be helpful for ensuring a common understanding. Video conferencing can be particularly helpful for synchronous conversations for reading reactions of the other person, sharing files, and sharing one's screen and allows for both you and your chair (and committee members) to work from various locations.

Be aware of these resources and technologies and discuss how to use them with your dissertation chair. As different technologies are used in communications between faculty and students, initiate discussion of expectations with your chair for the type of communication to avoid conflict or misunderstanding. For more information about leveraging available technologies during the doctoral journey see Chapter 6.

Strategy 6: Be Politely Assertive

Some students experience frequent or overbearing criticism as they work with their dissertation chairs, which may result in them believing they are not able to complete any tasks effectively. While keeping an open line of communication with your chair is important for ensuring the research is progressing appropriately, you may at some point need to be politely assertive in communications with your dissertation chair. Doctoral inquiry should include student ownership with support given by the dissertation chair (Sverdlik et al., 2018). Candidates can address ownership of their study by asking questions about bigger issues, while holding opinions on more minor issues (Goldman & Goodboy, 2017; Lim et al., 2019; Rademaker et al., 2016). For example, while developing her literature review, Jackie identified a new potential theory to inform her research allowing her to examine the issue from a different lens than she and Dr. Wang used in their prior research. Jackie read widely on the theory, including work by the primary theorist and peer-reviewed research by other researchers who used the theory to inform their work. Jackie made an appointment to talk with Dr. Wang, made a strong oral and written argument for the new theory, and Dr. Wang supported her decision.

There may, however, be times when your dissertation chair sees a situation differently, causing a difficult conversation. In these instances, you should listen to each other while at the same time consulting what is known in the discipline or field as well as respected research methods within the discipline and type of program (research versus professional doctorate). If a disagreement occurs with your chair, you should explain your position politely and be sure to back up dissent of your chair's position with supporting literature or field of practice. Going back to the literature will help move the personal conflict that may be building back to solving the issue. In some cases, it may be beneficial to broaden the discussion to include committee members to invite additional perspectives and arrive at a consensus among the full committee.

Finally, it is important to be mindful that your academic work is not only a reflection of you, but also a reflection of your chair and committee members who will "sign off" and officially endorse the dissertation at completion. If the issue is not one that causes you to compromise your morals, values, or ethics, it is prudent to defer to your chair and committee members and trust their expertise. Dissertation chairs do not seek to extend your time-to-degree completion, but rather, seek to ensure the final product is a positive reflection of all involved.

Strategy 7: Welcome Edits and Revisions

Not all criticisms or requests for revisions should be considered negative. You should expect multiple rounds of revisions and should consider edits and revisions as learning opportunities that offer positive improvements to your work (Sparkman & Doran, 2019). When you look at edits more objectively, you will find your feelings are not as easily hurt because you see the higher standard of quality the finished dissertation will hold and how this will ultimately benefit your future, whether seeking to advance in academia or professional practice.

Strategy 8: Seek Opportunities to Collaborate

As Jackie finished her degree, she continued to nurture the relationship with her dissertation chair not only to complete her degree successfully, but also long term as a collaborative working relationship. While her chair was an important mentor as she began a professional career with her new degree, ultimately this relationship should become mutually beneficial (Flora, 2017; Murphy & Kram, 2014). In research doctorates, candidates and chairs should look for common interests to collaborate on research studies, coauthored articles, and presentations. In professional programs, candidates and their chairs can look for common interests in applying research in their field and sharing it with practitioners to improve practice. Ultimately, the relationship you have with your dissertation chair will be mutually fulfilling and long lasting if both you and your chair are able to contribute and learn from each other.

Questions for Reflection

With negative student-faculty relationships being the most cited factor associated with doctoral attrition (Deshpande, 2016; Gittings et al., 2018; Hanson et al., 2020; Hill & Conceiçao, 2020; Ruud et al., 2016), developing a positive mentor relationship with a faculty member who has the potential to transform into a candidate–chair relationship is essential to your persistence and timely completion. You would be wise to reflect on the following questions to proactively foster a positive student–faculty relationship.

Applying to Doctoral Programs

- Does the department have a formal mentor program where I am assigned a faculty member from the onset of the program?
- What kind of opportunities exist for me to join research teams to collaborate with faculty and peers on scholarly activities?
- Are there opportunities for assistantships or fellowships?

Developing a Mentor Relationship

- What faculty member has similar research interests as me?
- How can I support the scholarly activities of my doctoral faculty?
- Who has provided timely and quality feedback on my work in different courses?
- How can I demonstrate the qualities faculty members seek in mentees?

Choosing a Dissertation Chair

- What characteristics would a faculty member have to be a good match for my topic of inquiry and design?
- What characteristics would a faculty member have to be a good match for my interest in applications of research to practice?
- Who has a similar work ethic or motivation for completion?
- Who has a good record of time-to-degree with their doctoral candidates?

While Working Together

- How will we establish goals and a timeline that will cover all responsibilities for each person (candidate, dissertation chair, and committee members)?
- How will I keep my chair regularly updated on my progress (emails, phone calls, video conferencing, online file sharing)?
- How will we structure regularly (e.g., weekly, monthly) scheduled meetings with each other?
- What are questions I should ask my chair (versus a peer) and what are issues I should self-study and develop a position based on literature?

Nearing Completion and Following Graduation

- What common interests do my chair and I hold for coauthored articles, presentations, or applications of research into practice?
- What conferences would be good places for us to present research together?
- How can we support each other in future research areas?

Recommended Resources

Howells, K., Stafford, K., Guijt, R., & Breadmore, M. (2017). The role of gratitude in enhancing the relationship between doctoral research students and their supervisors. *Teaching in Higher Education*, *22*(6), 621–638.

Lim, J., Covrig, D., Freed, S., De Oliveira, B., Ongo, M., & Newman, I. (2019). Strategies to assist distance doctoral students in completing their dissertations. *International Review of Research in Open and Distributed Learning, 20*(5), 192–210.

Murphy, W., & Kram, K. E. (2014). *Strategic relationships at work: Creating your circle of mentors, sponsors, and peers for success in business and life.* McGraw-Hill Press.

References

Acharya, V., & Rajendran, A. (2023). A holistic model of resources to enhance the doctoral student's well-being. *International Journal of Educational Management, 37*(6/7), 1445–1480. https://doi.org/10.1108/IJEM-11-2022-0457

Albertyn, R., & Bennett, K. (2021). Containing and harnessing uncertainty during postgraduate research supervision. *Higher Education Research & Development, 40*(4), 661–675. https://doi.org/10.1080/07294360.2020.1775559

Ari, F., Vasconcelos, L., Tang, H., Grant, M., Arslan-Ari, I., & Moore, A. (2022). Program evaluation of an online Ed. D. in learning design and technologies: Recent graduates' perspectives. *Tech Trends, 66*, 699–709. https://doi.org/10.1007/s11528-022-00744-7

Bottomley, K., Schumacher, J., Burleigh, C., & Lindsay, P. (2020). Supporting online doctoral students to increase persistence and completion. *Online Journal of Distance Learning Administration, 23*(4), 1–9.

Brill, J. L., Balcanoff, K. K., Land, D., Gogarty, M., & Turner, F. (2014). Best practices in doctoral retention: Mentoring. *Higher Learning Research Communications, 4*(2), 26–37.

Burkholder, G. J., & Bidjerano, M. (2023). Getting them done: A qualitative study of characteristics of mentors successful in graduating online students in a distance education context. *Mentoring & Tutoring: Partnership in Learning, 31*(4), 489–511. https://doi.org/10.1080/13611267.2023.2225393

Cochran, J. D., Campbell, S. M., Baker, H. M., & Leeds, E. M. (2014). The role of student characteristics in predicting retention in online courses. *Research in Higher Education, 55*(1), 27–48.

Collins, A., Brown, J. S., & Newman, S. E. (1989). Cognitive apprenticeship: Teaching the crafts of reading, writing, and mathematics. In L. B. Resnick (Ed.) *Knowing, learning, and instruction: Essays in honor of Robert Glaser* (pp. 453–494). Lawrence Erlbaum Associates.

Dahlberg, M. N., & Byars-Winston, A. (Eds.) (2019). *The Science of Effective Mentorship in STEMM.* National Academies of Sciences, Engineering, and Medicine; Policy and Global Affairs; Board on Higher Education and Workforce; Committee on Effective Mentoring in STEMM. National Academies Press.

DeAngelo, L. (2010). Preparing for the PhD at a comprehensive institution: Perceptions of the "barriers." *Journal of the Professoriate, 3*(2), 17–33.

Deshpande, A. (2016). A qualitative examination of challenges influencing doctoral students in an online doctoral program. *International Education Studies, 9*(6), 139–149.

Devos, C., Boudrenghien, G., Van der Linden, N., Frenay, M., Azzi, A., Galand, B., & Klein, O. (2016). Misfits between doctoral students and their supervisors: (How) are they regulated. *International Journal of Doctoral Studies, 11*, 467–486.

Earl-Novell, S. (2006). Determining the extent to which program structure features and integration mechanisms facilitate or impede doctoral student persistence in mathematics. *International Journal of Doctoral Studies, 1*, 45–57.

Ensher, E. A., & Murphy, S. E. (2011). The mentoring relationship challenges scale: The impact of mentoring stage, type, and gender. *Journal of Vocational Behavior, 79*(1), 253–266.

Flora, J. D. (2017). The doctoral mentoring relationship: The phenomenology of scholarly leadership. *International Journal of Doctoral Studies, 12*, 219–249.

Gardner, S. K. (2009). Student and faculty attributions of attrition in high and low completing doctoral programs in the United States. *Higher Education, 58*, 97–112.

Gittens, C. B. (2013). The McNair Scholars Program as an agent of socialization in the doctoral experience. ProQuest LLC.

Gittings, G., Bergman, M., Shuck, B., & Rose, K. (2018). The impact of student attributes and program characteristics on doctoral degree completion. *New Horizons in Adult Education and Human Resource Development, 30*(3), 3–22.

Goldman, Z. W., & Goodboy, A. K. (2017). Explaining doctoral students' relational maintenance with their advisor: A psychosocial development perspective. *Communication Education, 66*(1), 70–89.

Gonzalez, C. A. (2024). *Dr. Who? Trials and triumphs of first-generation doctoral students, Identifying support systems for successful completion of doctoral degrees* (Publication No. 31140884) [Doctoral dissertation, UCLA]. ProQuest Dissertations & Theses Global.

Groman, M. & Paquette, K. (2023). Achieving a terminal education degree: An Interpretative phenomenological analysis of doctoral student graduates' and faculty mentors' perceptions. *Education, 143*(3), 100–116.

Hanson, J., Loose, W., & Reveles, U. (2022). A qualitative case study of all-but-dissertation students at risk for dissertation noncompletion: A new model for supporting candidates to doctoral completion. *Journal of College Student Retention: Research, Theory & Practice, 24*(1), 234–262.

Harsoor, S. S., Panditrao, M. M., Rao, S., Bajwa, S. J. S., Sahay, N., & Tantry, T. P. (2022). Dissertation writing in post graduate medical education. *Indian Journal of Anaesthesia, 66*(01), 34–65. https://doi.org/10.4103/ija.ija_1106_21

Hill, L. H., & Conceição, S. C. (2020). Program and instructional strategies supportive of doctoral students' degree completion. *Adult Learning*, *31*(1), 36–44.

Howells, K., Stafford, K., Guijt, R., & Breadmore, M. (2017). The role of gratitude in enhancing the relationship between doctoral research students and their supervisors. *Teaching in Higher Education*, *22*(6), 621–638.

Jorgensen, M. F., & Wester, K. L. (2020). Aspects contributing to dissertation chair success: Consensus among counselor educators. *Journal of Counselor Preparation and Supervision*, *13*(3), 2.

Kumar, S., Bollinger, D., & Roumell, E. A. (2023). Technologies, strategies, and supports helpful to faculty in the e-mentoring of doctoral dissertations. *Online Learning*, *27*(3), 1–22.

Lim, J., Covrig, D., Freed, S., De Oliveira, B., Ongo, M., & Newman, I. (2019). Strategies to assist distance doctoral students in completing their dissertations. *International Review of Research in Open and Distributed Learning*, *20*(5), 192–210.

Mosyana, A. U., Ukoha-Kalu, B. O., Isah, A., Umeh, I., Amorha, K. C., Ayogu, E. E., & Ubaka, C. (2022). Factors associated with the timely completion of doctoral research studies in clinical pharmacy: A mixed-methods study. *PloS ONE*, *17*(9), e0274638.

Murphy, W., & Kram, K. E. (2014). *Strategic relationships at work: Creating your circle of mentors, sponsors, and peers for success in business and life*. McGraw-Hill Press.

Orsini, J., & Coers, N. (2022). Leaders and scholars: How faculty mentoring behavior influences the development of leadership self-efficacy. *Journal of Leadership Education*, 1–24. https://doi.org/10.12806/V21/I1/R8

Rademaker, L. L., Duffy, J. O. C., Wetzler, E., & Zaikina-Montgomery, H. (2016). Chair perceptions of trust between mentor and mentee in online doctoral dissertation mentoring. *Online Learning*, *20*(1), 57–69.

Rockinson-Szapkiw, A. J. (2012). Investigating uses and perceptions of an online collaborative workspaces for the dissertation process. *Research in Learning Technology*, *20*(3), 267–82.

Ruud, C. M., Saclarides, E. S., George-Jackson, C. E., & Lubienski, S. T. (2016). Tipping points: Doctoral students and consideration of departure. *Journal of College Student Retention: Research, Theory & Practice*, *20*(3), 1–22.

Sparkman, D., & Doran, C. (2019). Affective challenges faced by doctoral students: Supporting them to completion. *Journal on Educational Psychology*, *13*(1), 14–23.

Splinter, L. A., Pool, A. M., Schmuldt, L. M., & Bluemlein, J. S. (2022). Dissertation completion experience in online CACREP-accredited counselor education programs: A phenomenological inquiry. *Journal of Counselor Preparation and Supervisor*, *15*(3). https://digitalcommons.sacredheart.edu/jcps/vol15/iss3/5

Sverdlik, A., Hall, N. C., McAlpine, L., & Hubbard, K. (2018). The PhD experience: A review of the factors influencing doctoral students' completion, achievement, and well-being. *International Journal of Doctoral Studies*, *13*, 361–388.

Tinto, V. (1975). Dropout in higher education: A theoretical synthesis of recent research. *Review of Educational Research*, *45*(1), 89–125.

Tinto, V. (2023). Reflections: Rethinking engagement and student persistence. *Student Success*, *14*(2), 1–7. https://doi.org/10.5204/ssj.3016

Varghese, L., & Finkelstein, L. (2021). An investigation of self-efficacy crossover between mentors and proteges within mentoring dyads. *Annals of the New York Academy of Sciences*, *1483*, 80–97. https://doi.org/10.1111/nyas.14324

Waalkes, P. L., DeCino, D. A., Jorgensen, M. F., & Somerville, T. (2022). Counselor educators' experiences of dissertation-chairing relationship dynamics. *Professional Counselor*, *12*(2), 123–137. https://doi.org/10.15241/plw.12.2.123

18 Understanding the Different Types of Dissertations

Amanda J. Rockinson, EdD, PhD

Introduction

The dissertation is the final academic requirement for the doctoral degree and is designed to evaluate a doctoral candidate's capabilities as a researcher. Final recommendation for the degree depends strongly upon the dissertation and approval of the manuscript by the doctoral candidate's committee. Through the dissertation, candidates demonstrate their understanding of the literature, their ability to execute research, and their skills at writing in a scholarly manner. The candidates hold the primary responsibility for identifying the problem to be investigated, the knowledge that they wish to contribute to the field, and producing an original piece of research. The candidates are also independently responsible for designing, conducting, analyzing, and presenting the research and ensuring their final manuscript is written in a scholarly manner. The role of their committee is to facilitate and support candidates through this process. The dissertation phase is a critical time in the doctoral journey, and one phase where many students decide to withdraw from their program (The Council of Graduate Schools, 2015).

This chapter is designed to help students better understand the dissertation and the process of successfully completing it (Terrell, 2023). A first step is to understand that many different types of dissertations exist. This chapter supports the doctoral candidate in understanding the traditional five-chapter dissertation process, which is often used in research doctoral programs. However, to support professional doctoral students, an overview of the Dissertation in Practice (DiP) and a few alternative dissertation project models are presented.

Case Study

Dave, a PhD student in psychology, just passed his comprehensive exam. Throughout his coursework, he has heard faculty and peers talk about the dissertation process. They talk about Chapters 1, 2, and 3, saying he should consider these chapters throughout his coursework. During the first two years of his doctoral journey, Dave was too embarrassed to ask what each chapter entailed as it seemed like all his peers understood the dissertation. Now, he realizes, he should have asked more about the dissertation process. He is enrolled in a dissertation course but does not know how to begin a dissertation. He feels alone and wonders if he will be able to complete his degree.

Robert, an EdD student completing a degree in counseling, is entering the dissertation process after successfully passing his comprehensive exam. Throughout each year of the program, he has been developing his Dissertation in Practice (DiP). Through his dissertation, he plans to develop an intervention that will address why adolescent boys fail to seek help for affective mental health issues, a problem he has observed in practice for many years in his role as a school counselor. As he enters the dissertation process, he feels confident that he can complete the process within a year because his program has embedded the development of his proposal (i.e., Chapters 1, 2, and 3) draft throughout coursework.

What the Research Says

The Traditional Dissertation

Chapter 1: Introduction

The traditional dissertation, which is often required in the research doctorate such as the one Dave is pursuing, consists of five chapters. This dissertation begins with a proposal manuscript that consists of the first three of the five chapters—Chapters 1, 2, and 3. Chapter 1 provides the foundation for the dissertation, including an introduction to the topic, a problem statement, and a purpose statement. Creswell (1994) noted, "A problem might be defined as the issue that exists in the literature, theory, or practice that leads to a need for the study" (p. 50). For a research doctorate, the problem typically addresses a gap in theoretical, empirical, methodological or content knowledge, the evidence base, or research population (Miles, 2017; Muler-Bloch & Kranz, 2014; Robinson et al., 2011) (see Table 18.1).

The problem for the dissertation study is summarized in a problem statement that clearly provides the background and significance of the problem (Creswell & Creswell, 2023). Within the statement, the doctoral candidate explains the "So what? Who cares?" of the study. This statement usually begins with "The

Table 18.1 *Types of Research Gaps Identified in a Problem Statement*

Evidence Gap	Existing research is contradictory and needs further investigation to explain why the contradiction exists (e.g., some research argues that distance education is more effective than residential education, while other research demonstrates that residential education is more effective than distance education).
Knowledge Gap	Research does not exist and is needed on a specific topic or phenomenon (e.g., the use of artificial intelligence in mentoring practices has not been researched).
Methodological Gap	An alternative method needs to be employed to further understand a phenomenon or topic (e.g., the nonreporting of rape has only been examined via survey research; therefore, a qualitative study that gives voice to nonreporting survivors is needed).
Empirical Gap	Research findings or propositions need further validation using more rigorous research methods (e.q., initial research using a quantitative, pre-experimental design demonstrates that a specific teaching method may be effective; however, more rigorous designs need to be employed).
Theoretical Gap	Theory is needed to explain a phenomenon or topic (e.g., theory exists to explain the persistence of undergraduate students, but the theory is not applicable and needs to be further developed to explain doctoral student persistence).
Population Gap	A population is not adequately represented in the research (e.g., a specific gender, race, ethnicity, or age).

problem is…" and spans one to two paragraphs. A purpose statement often follows the problem statement. A purpose statement provides "a specific and accurate synopsis of the overall purpose of the study" (Locke et al., 1987, p. 5). At a minimum, the purpose statement includes a brief description of the research method(s) that will be used in the study (i.e., qualitative, quantitative, or mixed), the research design(s), the variables (i.e., independent, dependent, variable of interest, covariate) or phenomenon (i.e., the particular focus about the problem to investigate), and the specific population (Creswell & Clark, 2018). Creswell and Poth (2025) offered a template for writing the purpose statement. Here are the example templates adapted from Creswell and Poth (2025) for both quantitative and qualitative methods.

Qualitative Purpose Statement Template:

The purpose of this ________ (narrative, phenomenological, grounded theory, ethnographic, case) study (is, was, will be) to ____________ (understand, describe, develop, discover) the ____________ (central phenomenon of the study) for ____________ (the participants) at __________ (the site). At this stage in the research, the __________ (central phenomenon) will be generally defined as _______________ (a general definition of the central concept). The theory guiding this study is ______________ (identify theory and cite theorist) as it ______________ ________________ (explain the relationship between the theory and the focus of inquiry).

Quantitative Purpose Statement Template:

The purpose of this __________________(true experimental, causal comparative, correlational, pretest-posttest control group) study is to examine (compare, relate) the __________ (independent variable, variable of interest) to ______________________(dependent variable), controlling for ____________________ (control variables) for __________________ (participants) at ______________________ (the research site). The independent variable(s)/One of the variables of interest ____________________ will be generally defined as ______________________ (a general definition). The dependent variable(s)/Other variables of interest will be generally defined as ____________________ (a general definition), and the control and intervening variables(s), ________________ (the control and intervening variables), will be statistically controlled in this study.

These statements are central to doctoral candidates work as all preceding writing within the manuscript should be funneled through the problem and purpose statements.

Finally, the introduction chapter usually lists the study's research questions (and hypotheses, if quantitative) and provides a list of definition of terms that are central to understanding the study. A typical dissertation study contains two to five research questions. The research questions need to be derived from the problem and purpose statements, which represent the determined and well-articulated problem. The research questions should be feasible (i.e., investigating and gathering data to answer these questions is doable and within your capacity), clear, significant, and ethical. The questions should also clearly identify the sample population. They should imply the method, design, and analysis. More specifically, qualitative questions should ask about meaning, process, perceptions, or behavior, whereas, qualitative questions are usually broader and become more specific as the doctoral candidate moves into the actual data collection and analysis process. Research questions that are quantitative in nature should ask about the relationship between two or more variables and be testable (i.e., possible to collect data to answer the question). They should include a statement about what is hypothesized as research or null hypotheses. Finally, a list of terms that are pertinent to the study should be included and clearly defined in the final section of Chapter 1. Citations should be provided for each definition and referenced in the reference list or bibliography. Chapter 1 is included in both the dissertation proposal and final dissertation manuscript.

Chapter 2: Review of Literature

Chapter 2 is inclusive of the review of literature (see Chapter 19: Choosing Your Research Topic: Literature Gap vs. Problem of Practice). The review of literature is the written *synthesis*—not a summary—of the literature, arranged around themes from the doctoral candidate's critical perspective. Chapter 2 is a coherent argument establishing the need for the dissertation study and a detailed explanation of the conceptual framework that will shape the proposed research. Writing this part of the document requires engaging in the literature search process. According to Maxwell (2005), "the point is not to *summarize* what has already been done in the field. Instead, it is to ground the problem and the investigation in the relevant previous work, and to give the reader a clear sense of your... approach to the phenomena that... [you wish to] study" (p. 123). Thus, a literature search is "a systematic and thorough search of all types of published literature in order to identify as many items as possible that are relevant to a particular topic" (Bawden, 2000, p. 1). Most doctoral candidates review 1,000–2,000 articles in this process. However, in their dissertation reference list, they may only include 10%–20% of what is reviewed. Doctoral candidates often report that this is the hardest chapter to complete and takes the longest. While the organization of sections may differ, Chapter 2 is generally comprised at minimum of (a) an Introduction, (b) the Review of the Literature, (c) the Theoretical Context/ Framework, and (d) Summary. Chapter 2 is included in both the dissertation proposal and final manuscript.

Chapter 3: Method

Chapter 3 presents the research methods that the doctoral candidate plans to conduct the study. The method and the plan are described in sufficient detail to allow replication. In the proposal, the doctoral candidate describes the planned methods in future tense. While in the final dissertation, the doctoral candidate describes what was done (i.e., past tense). This chapter typically includes the methods, design, settings, participants, instrumentation or data collection methods, data collection procedures, analysis, and methods for increasing trustworthiness (qualitative) or validity and reliability (quantitative), as well as ethical considerations (e.g., informed consent, confidentiality, etc.).

In the research design section, the candidate clearly identifies the research *method* (i.e., qualitative, quantitative, or mixed) and *design* (i.e., phenomenological, basic qualitative, ethnographic, case study, grounded theory, quasi-experimental, pretest-post test control group design, causal comparative) for investigating the problem. The explanations of both the method and design need to be specific enough that any reader clearly understands and can follow along easily. The identified design needs to be exact. It is not sufficient to state that a quantitative, quasi-experimental study was conducted. It would be more appropriate to state that a pretest-posttest nonequivalent control group design was conducted. If selecting a phenomenological study, it would be most appropriate to state that a hermeneutic-phenomenological study was conducted.

In addition to identification of the method and design, in Chapter 3, the candidate provides a concise rationale for why the method, as well as the design, is most appropriate for the study. In other words, the candidate addresses questions such as: What is the method? What is the design? What is the purpose of the design? When is it used? Why is it the most appropriate choice for the present study?

In the participants section of Chapter 3, the population, sample size, type of sample (e.g., purposive, criterion, theoretical), and sampling procedures or techniques (e.g., convenience sampling, snowball sampling) are explained. In appropriate quantitative studies, the type of assignment (e.g., random assignment, matching, or blocking; only if a quantitative, experimental study) is also described and includes an in-depth discussion of how the sample is identified from the population, who selected the sample, and how the study is introduced to the sample, including gaining participation. The sample selection procedures (who, what, when, where, how) are explained. For example, David is describing "who," his sample is, describes the characteristics (e.g., age, ethnicity, gender, skill, experience, education, etc.). Real names for people and locations are never used. The candidate uses pseudonyms for people and descriptors when necessary to protect confidentiality. Further, the needed sample size (e.g., 64 per group for a statistical power of .8; 30 for a grounded theory qualitative design) for the chosen research design and analysis is specified. Each decision is supported by citations.

In the setting section, the candidate describes the investigation's setting or context, where the study takes place (e.g., geographic location, testing location, school system, specific course or program for the treatment and control groups, etc.). The candidate describes not only the key characteristics of the setting (e.g., classroom, computer lab, office, web-based, online, etc.), but also, where applicable, the resources (e.g., devices, software, etc.) and constraints. The candidate addresses questions such as: Why was this site/ setting chosen for this project? What does the organization look like? What does the setting include?

In the instrumentation or data collection methods, section the instrument(s) used (or planned for use) to measure each variable or phenomenon are identified and described. The instruments may include tests, surveys, questionnaires, observational protocols, semi-structured interview protocols, or other measurement methods. For clarity and to demonstrate deep understanding of the research process, a candidate may demonstrate via a table or figure how each data point or instrument is used to answer each posed research question. If, for example, the candidate is going to use survey questions 3–8 to answer Research Question 1, then it is stated and demonstrated in a figure or table.

In a case where an instrument or data collection protocol is created for the purpose of the investigation, the candidate describes the procedures followed in developing the item. If a validated instrument (one that already exists, has undergone validity and reliability testing and has been used in many studies in the discipline area) is being used to collect data, the candidate clearly describes the instrument including its content, its origin, and its appropriateness.

If applicable in quantitative studies, scoring information for the composite and subscales is included (e.g., range of possible scores and interpretation of scores) as well as validity information and reliability statistics. In some cases, reliability statistics are reported for the data in the present study. For each validated instrument, the following ideas are discussed: (a) A description of the instrument, its content, and its origin. (b) Is the instrument appropriate? (c) What support exists for use with the population selected for the study (e.g., adults, adolescents, etc.)? (d) What support exists for use in the setting selected for the study (e.g., online)? (e) Does the instrument conceptualize the construct in the manner that the candidate conceptualizes it? (f) An explanation of the scoring information for the composite and subscales—What are the possible range of scores? What scores are considered high, medium, and low? In other words, how are scores interpreted? (g) What are the measurement characteristics? Validity? Reliability? Structure (subscale, instrument items, etc.)? How will the reliability for the data be reported? (h) How was permission gained to use the instrument? (i) What tool(s) was used to administer the instrument (e.g., SurveyMonkey, Google Forms, paper and pencil, etc.)?

The procedures section clearly outlines the steps planned (for the proposal) or taken (for the final dissertation manuscript) for the investigation. Examples of important steps include: securing IRB approval, recruiting participants for the study, conducting a pilot study, training individuals to implement the treatment, administering the procedures, gathering data, and recording procedures. The procedures are described in a chronological, step-by-step format providing enough detail that the study could be replicated by others. If qualitative inquiry is part of the investigation, the candidate often uses subsections that detail different data-collection methods. These sections may include, but are not limited to, interviews, focus groups, observations (participant and/or direct), document analysis (e.g., archival records, journals, letters), artifact analysis (e.g., photographs), and researcher field notes. These data collection procedures should follow the recommendations of established qualitative researchers in the field.

All procedural materials (e.g., protocol, training manual) are included in the appendices. Such materials may include, but are not limited to; IRB application/approval letter, needs assessment, intervention plans, informed consent form, list of interview questions or interview guide, observation protocols or templates, instruments, a letter of support from the research site with identifying information removed, etc.

In the analysis section, the candidate explains how the data will be analyzed (for the proposal) or were analyzed (for the final dissertation manuscript). When using a statistical analysis in a quantitative study, the chosen statistical procedure is identified and a concise rationale for it is provided. The candidate explains how the chosen statistical procedure is consistent with the research questions, hypotheses, and type of data collected (as outlined in Chapters 1 and 3). In other words, why is the chosen analysis the most appropriate choice to test the hypothesis? The rationale needs to be supported by the extant literature. For each identified analysis, all assumption tests and how they are tested, the statistic used to report the effect size, the convention used to interpret it, and the alpha value (p-value) used are discussed. The software used to analyze the data is identified. In this section, a statistical procedure for each hypothesis is needed. Thus, most candidates, implementing quantitative designs, organize the quantitative analysis procedures around the hypotheses.

In sum, for each hypothesis and corresponding analysis, the candidate uses the following questions: (a) What analysis is used to test the hypothesis? (b) What is the rationale for this based on the literature? (c) What descriptive analyses will be used? (d) What assumption tests are conducted? How will each assumption be tested? (e) How is the effect size reported and what convention is used to interpret it? (f) What significance/alpha level is used? And (g) What statistical software is used to run the analysis, if applicable (e.g., AMOS, SPSS, etc.)?

For qualitative data analysis, the candidate identifies and explains the procedures, providing a concise rationale for each type of analysis. These data analysis procedures are related to the data collection protocols identified for each research question and follow the recommendations of established qualitative researchers in the field as well as seminal qualitative sources (e.g., Erlandson et al., 1993; Lincoln & Guba, 1985; Merriam, 1988; Miles & Huberman, 1994; Patton, 1980, 1990).

Often in Chapter 3, the candidate discusses limitations, delimitations, and ethical considerations. The candidate describes the *delimitations* of the study (decisions made to narrow the focus and scope of the research), if applicable, and the *limitations* of the study (weaknesses to the study that cannot be controlled). The weaknesses of the study may be related to the design (e.g., lack of randomization, bias), the analysis, the instruments, and the sample (e.g., gender, age, ethnicity, geographical location). In a quantitative study, the candidate discusses limitations, including threats to both internal and external validity by identifying the type of threat and describing it in light of the present investigation. A discussion should ensue about how the limitation could impact the study, and the steps, if any, to be taken or were taken to mitigate the threat.

The candidate should also discuss any ethical considerations or implications of the research. These might include gaining informed consent, data storage and usage, protecting confidentiality (e.g., use of pseudonyms), and any other potential issues that might arise and how they will be addressed. The ethical principles that candidates should consider are those set forth in the Belmont Report developed for human subject research (National Commission for the Protection of Human Subjects of Biomedical and Behavioral Research, 1979). For example, (a) doing good (i.e., beneficence) and (b) doing no harm (i.e., non-malfeasance). Chapter 3 is included in both the dissertation proposal and final manuscript.

Chapters 4 and 5: Results and Conclusions

After the study is completed, the doctoral candidate writes Chapters 4 and 5 for the final dissertation manuscript. The purpose of Chapter 4 is to present the results of the investigation and include the basic findings generated from the data analysis process.

Chapter 5 goes into a deeper discussion where the doctoral candidate (Dave, in this example), answers the research question(s) in plain language, discusses the results of the study in light of the literature (reviewed in Chapter 2) noting consistencies and differences with prior studies and using prior studies to explain results, provide implications related to theory, practice, policy, or method; notes limitations; and suggests ideas for future research. Chapter 5 consists of at least five sections: (a) Introduction and Summary of the findings, (b) Discussion (of the findings; e.g., What are the results and what do they mean?), (c) Implications (for practice; e.g., How do the results inform practice?), (d) Recommendations (for future investigations that are a logical extension of the findings and limitations of the present study), and (d) Conclusion (i.e., succinctly summarizes the primary findings and concludes the manuscript).

Within a research doctorate, two defenses are typically required. For example, Dave discovered that his PhD program requires both a proposal defense and a final dissertation defense. For his proposal, Dave must write Chapters 1, 2, and 3, and then orally defend his research proposal. For the final defense, he must complete the entire manuscript and defend it orally.

Between the writing of each chapter and the defense, the candidate works closely with their dissertation chair on the manuscript to ensure it is clear and presentable to the committee. The candidate may also work closely with a committee member who serves as an expert methodologist to ensure the explanation of the data collection and analysis are appropriate and clear. The candidate will sends the manuscript (proposal or final) to the committee approximately two weeks before the prescheduled defense date to give their committee time to read the document. At the defense itself, the committee comes together either in person or virtual (depending on the institutional rules), the candidate presents the work with a visual (usually a PowerPoint presentation), each committee member will have the opportunity to ask questions and provide feedback, the student will then leave the space (physical or virtual—depending on program modality) while the committee members discuss their collective determination to (a) pass pending few or no revisions, (b) require significant revisions, or (c) fail the defense. Once the committee determines the outcome and requested revisions (if applicable), the candidate is invited to return to receive the committee decision. Often, defenses are open to the public and other students/candidates, faculty, and family can attend. Both the proposal and final defenses may take one to two hours.

The Dissertation in Practice

Professional doctorate programs vary in their approaches to the dissertation, often requiring a culminating project called a Capstone or Dissertation in Practice (DiP). These different types of dissertations align with the distinction between the two types of doctorates. As described elsewhere in this book, the research and professional doctorates "serve distinct purposes," with the purpose of the professional doctorate "to solve… [practical] problems" (Shulman et al., 2006, pp. 25–26). Thus, at least two elements distinguish a professional doctorate dissertation from a research doctorate dissertation: (1) the objective and (2) the audience to whom the document is disseminated. Archbald (2008) purported the professional doctorate dissertation is a distinctive format that demonstrates "developmental efficacy" and "community benefit," while maintaining "intellectual stewardship" and rigor required by academia (p. 704). The research completed for a professional doctorate dissertation provides a unique bridge between academic research and real-world practice. The DiP advances professional or practical knowledge, while addressing a complex problem of practice in a localized context inclusive of rigorous and ethical methods, innovative inquiry, and alternative research approaches (Perry, 2016; Perry et al., 2020). The core purpose "should serve the objective of motivating and guiding change with evidence, arguments, and values" (Archbald, 2008, p. 715).

A distinguishing feature of a DiP is its aim to address a *Problem of Practice* (PoP), defined as a persistent, contextualized, and specific issue embedded in the doctoral candidates' professional work (CPED, 2010), referred to as the "practice context." The research conducted for the DiP is both scholarly and practical, intentionally seeking to enhance the understanding, experience, or improvement of a specific professional problem and to generate actionable findings that are specific to the practice context. This aspect distinguishes the DiP from the traditional research dissertation, which seeks to generate generalizable findings rather than create a new theory or knowledge (Everson et al., 2024; Weiler & Virtue, 2024; Willis et al., 2010). DiPs focus on inquiry questions (versus research questions) that are pragmatic (e.g., What happens when an intervention is implemented? What is underlying a specific problem that is occurring in the work context?) (Zambo, 2011), such as the one Robert proposed.

The Problem of Practice (PoP) and aim of the investigation help define the inquiry questions and drive the selection of the research approach, which are often applied in natural, real world environments (i.e., action research, evaluation, improvement science, design-based research). For example, Robert seeks to address a problem that he has observed in practice as a school counselor. Adolescent boys fail to seek affective mental health assistance. As Robert considers how to improve or solve this problem, he defines the problem both through using of extant literature and defining what this problem looks like in his school context. Once he has a clear understanding of the problem in his context, he can consider the best applied research method to address it.

Four primary research approaches are often applied to influence change and make improvements related to the PoP. These approaches include improvement science, action research, evaluation, and design-based research, all of which are often seen in DiPs. *Improvement science* takes a systems lens to understand how the organizational system is generating the problem of practice in the local context. Through a Plan-Do-Study-Act (PDSA) inquiry cycle, the candidate develops and implements a change idea that seeks to improve the system. Qualitative and quantitative data are gathered to evaluate and determine if the change idea resulted in an improvement to the system (Perry et al., 2020). The PDSA cycle is a systematic approach implemented in health care, business, and education settings.

Action research is an iterative research design in which a candidate designs, implements, and then evaluates the efficacy of initiatives aimed at solving problems within their professional practice. This approach is not focused on systems but rather looks more closely at a candidates practice or smaller scale change (i.e., action). Findings from rigorous studies of initiatives often impact local practice and policy in professional settings, as they provide evidence for best practices (Herr & Anderson, 2015; Stringer & Ortiz Aragón, 2021).

Evaluation research is a systematic inquiry that examines the feasibility, efficacy, and impact of a specific program, practice, or policy. Inquiry may be conducted prior to, during, and after the implementation of the initiative to determine whether it should be continued, modified, or discontinued. Evaluations follow a systematic approach such as the Logic Model design that investigate the design of the program, practice or policy, how it was implemented, and the impact it had on those involved and the organization.

Design-based research, another iterative process, focuses on using research and data to design solution-focused intervention. Whereas the improvement science and action research seek to understand the impact of an intervention, design-based research seeks to gather data for the design of the invention. This approach is often employed in the field of learning sciences (Anderson & Shattuck, 2012) where stakeholder behaviors and needs help to frame the design of the intervention. DiPs using this approach develop locally informed interventions that seek to improve practice and motivate change. As a result, the audience for the dissertation extends beyond the dissertation committee to community stakeholders and is often disseminated to relevant audience (i.e., administrators in the workplace, other professionals) for longer-term use in professional settings.

Other Dissertation Models

In this chapter, the traditional five-chapter dissertation, used in research doctorates like Dave is enrolled in, and its components were discussed. Moreover, the Dissertation in Practice (DiP) was discussed, which is often required for a professional doctorate like Robert's program. However, both professional and research doctorates sometimes adopt alternative dissertation formats. Although not exhaustive, Table 18.2 provides defining features of various alternatives to the dissertations described in this chapter. Doctoral candidates should review their institution's dissertation policies and handbooks to determine the model or models that are acceptable for their program. Additionally, suppose they are interested in an alternative format, but these policies and handbooks do not mention it. In that case, candidates might discuss these options with their advisor to see if an alternative format is possible.

Table 18.2 *Other Types of Dissertation Models*

The Three-Article Dissertation (TAD)	Comprises three or more published or publishable manuscripts, with an introductory and a summary chapter that explain how the three or more articles are linked. The manuscripts typically focus on a single, coherent topic. Moreover, doctoral candidates are usually required to be the sole or first author on published or publishable pieces.
A group-based or collaborative dissertation	An inquiry may be conducted and written in traditional or alternative formats in partnership with other doctoral students. Hamilton (2022) provides a great overview of the group-based Dissertation in Practice, which is an article worth reviewing if engaging in this type of alternative dissertation.
A library-based dissertation	It is essentially a literature review. The doctoral candidate analyzes and synthesizes existing research and data, rather than collecting new, original data. This type of dissertation focuses on evaluating, compiling, and critically examining literature to build a comprehensive understanding of a topic

Strategies for Success

"A dissertation is an extensive, challenging, and rigorous scholarly endeavor. As such, completing it represents the pinnacle of academic achievement" (Bloomberg, 2012, p. 242). The following are recommendations for you to think about and engage in the dissertation process.

Strategy 1: Determine the program's dissertation process and acceptable types of dissertations.

Before entering the program, identify information about the dissertation process, including the types of dissertations that are acceptable. Determine if, like Robert's program, you will build your dissertation throughout courses. Identify if you are required to complete a traditional five-chapter dissertation or if alternative dissertation types are allowed or expected.

Strategy 2: Ask questions throughout the doctoral process about the dissertation.

If you have questions about the dissertation, ask the faculty and peers. Locate and read program or dissertation handbooks. Do not wait, like Dave, to ask questions about the dissertation process.

Strategy 3: Understand the contents or components of the dissertation.

Identify the type of dissertation that you will complete and understand each chapter or component. For example, Table 18.3 demonstrates phrases used in a traditional five-chapter dissertation.

Strategy 4: Leverage AI to assist with your dissertation.

AI tools are constantly evolving. For example, AI Tools for Academic Research are consistently assisting with research. AI tools (e.g., ResearchRabbit) can assist you with identifying and evaluating previous researchers' methodologies, designs, and literature. Visualizing helps you identify connections between studies, authors, and research topics. AI tools (e.g., Explainpaper and Consensus) can provide simplified written and visual summaries of complex research findings.

Other AI tools (e.g., Quivr) are helpful for indexing and retrieving research. By the time this book is published, these AI examples may be archaic, but the strategy remains. Identify AI programs that ethically streamline the dissertation process, without compromising the integrity of your research.

Table 18.3 *Phrases Used in a Traditional Dissertation*

Chapter 1: Introduction	The purpose of this study is to examine… in order to address gaps in existing research or address the problem of practice This dissertation aims to…
Chapter 2: Literature Review	Research demonstrates…, but results remain inconsistent. The majority of the literature has focused on… leaving… underexplored. This literature review summarizes…, while demonstrating that… remained unexplored.
Chapter 3: Method	This study used a [qualitative/quantitative/mixed] methodology and [XXX] design, which were appropriate given…. This method and design were used to examine… Data were collected through… and analyzed using… … sample was used to secure a sample that consisted of… participants…
Chapter 4: Results	The results show that… The analysis demonstrates…
Chapter 5: Discussion	The results found… and this provides support for… The study results make a contribution by addressing the gap identified in the literature… These findings are consistent with previous studies that reported… The results differ from earlier work, which suggested… Limitations include…which should be considered when interpreting the results.

Questions for Reflection

Doctoral candidates are encouraged to reflect on the following questions:

- What problem do I hope to study? What type of dissertation is best suited to address the problem I hope to explore?

- What dissertation resources, including handbooks and courses, are available to me as I progress in my dissertation journey? How do these resources inform my dissertation? How can I use courses to inform my dissertation?
- What questions do I have about the dissertation? Who can best answer these questions?
- As AI evolves, how can I leverage it to assist me in the dissertation process?

Recommended Resources

Creswell, J. W., & Creswell, J. D. (2023). *Research design: Qualitative, quantitative, and mixed methods approaches* (6th ed.). SAGE.

Hyatt, L. & Roberts, C. (2023). *The dissertation journey: A practical and comprehensive guide to planning, writing, and defending your dissertation* (4th ed.). Corwin.

Muhammad, R. (2025). *Dissertation literature review sprint: Finish & defend your chapter in 30 days—powered by AI* (English ed.).

Perry, J. A., Zambo, D., & Crow, R. (2020). *The improvement science dissertation in practice: A guide for faculty, committee members, and their students.* Myers Education Press.

Terrell, S. (2023). *Writing a proposal for your dissertation: Guidelines and examples* (2nd ed.). Guilford.

References

Anderson, T., & Shattuck, J. (2012). Design-based research: A decade of progress in education research? *Educational Researcher, 41*(1), 16–25. doi:10.3102/0013189X11428813

Archbald, D. (2008). Research versus problem solving for the Education Leadership doctoral thesis: Implications for form and function. *Educational Administration Quarterly, 44*(5), 704–739.

Archbald, D. (2011). The emergence of the nontraditional doctorate: A historical overview. *New Directions for Adult and Continuing Education,129*, 7–19. https://doi.org/10.1002/ace

Bawden, D. (2000). Book Review: Effective literature searching for research (2nd edition), Sarah Gash Gower, Aldershot, 2000. *International Journal of Information Management, 20*(5), 407–407. 10.1016/S0268-4012(00)00033-5.

Carnegie Project for the Educational Doctorate (CPED). (2010). *Design concept definitions*. Retrieved from http://cpedinitiative.org.

CGS (2015). CGS Report Highlights Completion Trends of Underrepresented Minorities in STEM Doctoral Programs: Findings Suggest New Strategies for Improving Retention and Completion. www.cgsnet.org/sites/default/files/PR_DIMAC_2015-04-06_final.pdf.

Creswell, J. W. (1994). *Research design: Qualitative & quantitative approaches*. Sage Publications, Inc.

Creswell, J. D., & Clark, V. L. P. (2018). *Designing and conducting mixed methods research* (3rd ed.). SAGE.

Creswell, J. W., & Creswell, J. D. (2023). *Research design: Qualitative, quantitative, and mixed methods approaches* (6th ed.). SAGE.

Creswell, J. W., & Poth, C. N. (2025). *Qualitative inquiry & research design: Choosing among five approaches* (5th ed.). SAGE.

Everson, K., Tamim, S., Torres, K. M., & Hemmer, L. (2024). *The importance of the Dissertation in Practice (DiP): A resource guide for EdD students, their committee members and advisors, and departmental and university leaders involved with EdD programs*. Myers Education Press.

Ewell, S. & Childers-McKee, C., Giblin, J., McNabb, J., Nolan, K. & Parenti, M. (2022). Taking Action: The Dissertation in Practice at Northeastern University. *Impacting Education: Journal on Transforming Professional Practice. 7*, 4–8. 10.5195/ie.2022.219.

Hamilton, W. (2022). The group-based dissertation in practice: A journey worth taking. *Impacting Education: Journal on Transforming Professional Practice, 7*. 42–46. 10.5195/ie. 2022.234.

Herr, K. & Anderson, G. (2015). *The action research dissertation: A guide for students and faculty* (2nd ed.). Sage.

Lester, S. (2004). Conceptualizing the practitioner doctorate. *Studies in Higher Education, 29*(6), 757–770.https://doi.org/10.1080/0307507042000287249

Locke, L. F., Spirduso, W. W., & Silverman, S. J. (1987). *Proposals that work: A guide for planning dissertations and grant proposals* (2nd ed.). Sage.

Maxwell, T. W. K. (2009). Producing the professional doctorate: The portfolio as a legitimate alternative to the dissertation. *Innovations in Education & Teaching International, 46*(2), 135–145. Doi: 10.1080/14703290902843760

Miles, D. & Scott, L. (2017). Conference Workshop: Confessions of a dissertation chair: The Six Mistakes Doctoral Students Make with the Dissertation. Black Doctoral Network Conference, Atlanta, GA, United States.

Mueller-Bloch, C. & Kranz, J. (2015). A framework for rigorously identifying research gaps in qualitative literature reviews. Conference: Proceedings of the 36th International Conference on Information Systems (ICIS).

National Commission for the Protection of Human Subjects of Biomedical and Behavioral Research. (1979). *The Belmont report: Ethical principles and guidelines for the protection of human subjects of research.* U.S. Department of Health and Human Services. https://www.hhs.gov/ohrp/regulations-and-policy/belmont-report/read-the-belmont-report/index.html

Perry, J. A. (2016). *The EdD and the scholarly practitioner: The CPED path.* Information Age Publishing.

Perry, J. A., Zambo, D., & Crow, R. (2020). *The improvement science dissertation in practice: A guide for faculty, committee members, and their students.* Myers Education Press.

Robinson, K. A., Saldanha, I. J., & McKoy, N. A. (2011). Development of a framework to identify research gaps from systematic reviews. *Journal of Clinical Epidemiology, 64*(12):1325–1330. doi: 10.1016/j.jclinepi.2011.06.009. Epub 2011 Sep 19. PMID: 21937195.

Rockinson-Szapkiw, A. (2019). Toward understanding factors salient to doctoral student persistence: The development and preliminary validation of the doctoral academic-family integration inventory. *International Journal of Doctoral Studies, 14,* 237–258.

Shulman, L. S., Golde, C. M., Bueschel, A. C., & Garabedian, K. J. (2006). Reclaiming education's doctorate: A critique and a proposal. *Educational Researcher, 35*(2), 25–32.

Smrekar, C., & McGraner, K. (2009). From curricular alignment to the culminating project: The Peabody College EdD capstone. *Peabody Journal of Education, 84*(1), 48–60.

Storey, V. A., & Hartwick, P. (2010). Critical friends: Supporting a small, private university in crafting an innovative scholar-practitioner doctorate. In G. Jean-Marie & A. H. Normore (Eds.), *Educational leadership preparation: Innovative and interdisciplinary approaches to the EdD and graduate education.* Palgrave Macmillan.

Stringer, E. T. & Ortiz Aragón, A. (2021). *Action research* (5th ed.). Sage Publications.

Terrell, S. (2023). *Writing a proposal for your dissertation: Guidelines and examples* (2nd ed.). Guilford.

Walker, G. E., Golde, C. M., Jones, L., Bueschel, A. C., & Hutchings, P. (2008). *The formation of scholars: Rethinking doctorial education for the twenty-first century.* Jossey Bass.

Wergin, J. F. (2011). Rebooting the Ed.D. *Harvard Educational Review, 81*(1), 119–140.

Weiler, J., & Virtue, E. (2024). *The disquisition: An equity-driven capstone for leadership preparation programs.* Myers Education Press.

Willis, J., Inman, D., & Valenti, R. (2010). *Completing a professional practice dissertation: A guide for doctoral students and faculty.* Information Age.

Zambo, D. (2011). Action research as signature pedagogy in an Education Doctorate program: The reality and hope. *Innovative Higher Education. 36*(4), DOI: 10.1007/s10755-010-9171-7

19 Choosing Your Research Topic: Literature Gap vs. Problem of Practice

Elizabeth Zumpe, PhD

Introduction

For doctoral students, selecting a research topic is one of the first milestones on the path to becoming a research scientist or scholar-practitioner. During the Knowledge and Skill Development Stage of the program students complete assigned readings and tasks provided by professors. By the Inquiry Stage of the program, the doctoral candidate transitions from autonomous to self-directed learner as they transition from student to scholar. Now considered a doctoral candidate instead of a doctoral student, the candidate is responsible for selecting the inquiry focus and developing corresponding research questions.

Choosing a topic for inquiry can be a challenging task. Some students, like Kim in the vignette below, start their doctoral journey with a clear idea about—and strong attachment to—what they want to study. However, choosing an initial area of interest is not the same as identifying a research focus. For students who start with an area of interest, determining the focus of their research may be exciting or sobering. What a student initially thinks is a unique idea often has been written about in volumes, making it difficult to defend the significance of yet one more study on the topic. Students who start with a desire to solve a grand societal issue come to realize that researchable questions are usually quite narrow. Other students start their doctoral journeys with wide curiosities and no particular focus. For these students, this step of the journey requires a series of decisions about what is in and what is out. A dissertation (research doctorate) or cumulative project (scholar-practitioner doctorate) is only one study, ideally completed within a year, and thus can only answer a few questions. Students must make choices and set up boundaries so they do not get sidetracked by extraneous wonderings and passions.

Case Study

Kim is a district administrator who serves as a director of programs for multilingual learners in a large urban school district. As a first-generation immigrant who migrated to the United States as a young child and who is now a bilingual adult, Kim is passionate about ensuring all professionals in her district understand their obligations to support students whose first language is not English. About one-fifth of her district serves multilingual students, many of whom are first generation immigrants. Kim also wants to be sure that the district communicates that students' home languages and cultures are valued, while also ensuring students' progress in learning English.

Kim starts her doctoral journey with a determination to find out how to ensure all teachers feel responsible for ensuring the academic success of students whose first language is not English. In her previous role as an English Learner specialist and coach in this district, Kim found inspiration when working with teachers who eagerly sought to learn how to use inclusive practices to develop students' English language skills. Too many teachers, however, seemed resistant to the idea that they needed to adapt their preferred teaching style and their academic content to meet students' needs. During many classroom visits, she observed in horror as teachers largely ignored students who were designated as English Learners. Sometimes, those students were given coloring tasks to keep them quiet while the teacher focused on teaching the rest of the class. When Kim asked the teachers about this, they told her those students were the responsibility of the English Learner specialists. She struggled to figure out how to motivate more resistant teachers to want to improve their practice to support English Learners.

Kim has already decided her dissertation will focus on ensuring educational experiences for emergent multilingual students. Kim is in a doctoral program that has two pathways for completing the dissertation—one for preparing to become a research scientist, and one for becoming a scholar practitioner. The program chair communicated that the choice should depend on whether her long-term career would be in academic research and higher education or in leadership service and practice in the PK–12 educational system. Kim is torn. An academic research pathway might allow her to have a broader influence to change policies and the system in the longer term. On the other hand, advancing in her current career to higher levels of leadership, such as becoming a superintendent, could allow her to make a more immediate impact on students in the system right now.

When Kim shares these thoughts with her dissertation chair, she is relieved to find out that she does not have to make a firm decision about the rest of her career right now. Scholar practitioners can pursue careers in higher education, and research scientists can become superintendents. For now, her chair tells her, the more important question is, for what kind of purpose do you want to undertake dissertation research? Do you want to complete a dissertation that advances general knowledge about factors or practices that enable or hinder educational development for emergent multilingual students? Or do you prefer to spend your effort and time on a dissertation that seeks to improve upon an important problem of practice in your current district? This choice changes how to go about defining your topic and posing research questions.

What the Research Says

To assist readers with successfully navigating dissertation topic selection, this chapter is designed to help you understand how research scientists and scholar practitioners identify a focus for research and key distinctions between them. To differentiate up front, research scientists start with *a general topic of interest* and then narrow their focus as they *read seminal literature* and identify *a gap in the literature*. Scholar practitioners, on the other hand, start with *a broad concern or puzzle in their practice* and then narrow their focus as they *assess needs for improvement* within their local context and *define and frame an actionable problem of practice* with stakeholders.

For Research Scientists

For students completing dissertations in the tradition of research scientists (e.g., a PhD), choosing a research focus begins with determining a general area of interest. Students who begin with a wide array of possible interests need to first select one area from which to develop their research topic. There is not a clear consensus among scholars as to how a doctoral student should go about choosing a topic (Lei, 2009; Olalere et al., 2014). From a survey of doctoral candidates working on their dissertations, Olalere et al. (2014) found five main factors influenced students' topic selections: (a) professional experiences; (b) personal life experiences; (c) relationships; (d) personal interests; and (e) influences from previous classes or readings. The expertise of the faculty member serving as their chair also tends to be a factor for students' choice of topic. Students might consider which areas they are best positioned to study, given their background, their career goals, the faculty they work with, and the program they are in.

At the same time, scholars caution students against choosing a focus for purely convenient or strategic reasons. While being passionate does not guarantee a good research topic, a good scenario is to choose a topic about which both faculty and students have strong interest and curiosity (Single, 2010). Students' level of interest tends to be important for sustaining motivation through the learning journey. For example, Kim initially determined her area of interest—how PK–12 teachers support emergent bilingual students in the classroom—through a combination of her professional and personal life experiences and by considering what she felt most passionate about in her field.

According to Brubaker and Murray (2000), doctoral students may find their initial topics of interest from a variety of sources: (a) *relevance*: a particular urgent concern in the field or society; (b) *methodology:* an idea for collecting data in an innovative way that has not been tried before; (c) *theory:* an interest in developing a new theory or extending an existing theory; or (d) *on-the-job problems*: an issue encountered during previous or current work experiences. Kim's initial topic arises from a combination of relevance and on-the-job problems.

Choosing an initial topic is an important first step, but further steps are needed to translate a broad topic of interest into a research focus. This process follows what scholars often describe through the metaphor of a funnel (Grant & Osanloo, 2014). With one's broad topic of interest at the top of the funnel, students think through a series of considerations and analytic steps to arrive at a more specific and researchable focus within that topic.

After a general topic of interest has been identified, students begin to funnel and hone a research focus by venturing into the existing literature. At this stage, students are encouraged to read deeply and widely within their chosen area of interest. Terrell (2016) suggested students must "read, read, read and then read some more" because "only by knowing the relevant literature in a field will he or she be comfortable in, or capable of, moving forward" (p. 7). Reading widely, however, does not necessarily mean reading anything and everything on the topic. For identifying a research focus, it is helpful to read with purpose and intention. Usually much more has been studied and published about a topic than a doctoral student could initially imagine, but that does not mean that there is nothing more to be discovered. Very little terrain of scientific knowledge has been so thoroughly mapped as to be known with certainty or consensus. The trick is to figure out what is known and not known about the phenomenon of interest. This is the "gap" that your research will address if enrolled in a research doctorate.

A helpful step toward finding a gap in the literature is to identify which books or journal articles seem *seminal* about that topic and read them closely. Seminal publications are defined as groundbreaking studies that influenced many subsequent studies and lines of research, and they tend to be frequently cited (Herrmannova et al., 2018). As students identify and read seminal works, they should also then find later works that build upon these earlier lines of inquiry and trace how research about this topic has evolved over time. Did most of the publications occur within the last five years? Or were most written over 20 years ago? Has the topic gained or lost steam, or has there been a change in terminology? For example, if Kim searches for literature about the topic *emergent bilingual students*, she may find many publications in the past few years, and little before then. The reason for this is that the term is relatively new, first proposed by García (2009), slowly gaining traction among scholars as they worked to debate and clarify the meaning and importance of this concept and term (Turnbull, 2018). To determine a gap in the literature, Kim should also consult works that use previously dominant terms, such as *English Language Learners* or *limited-English proficient* to understand what has and has not been addressed in this field of study.

As students become familiar with the literature, they also seek to pinpoint one or more types of gaps in the literature—what is not yet known. Drawing on a typology created by Miles (2017), three types of literature gaps can be especially relevant for social scientists: (a) a methodological gap; (b) a population gap; and (c) a theoretical gap. To find these gaps, students should read with intention to find out: Through which methodologies has this topic or phenomenon been studied? With which groups of people or populations? Which theories have been applied to understand the issue? It is helpful to keep a log or a spreadsheet to track what you read and find out about these questions. It is also helpful to note: To what extent do studies produce similar findings or come to conflicting conclusions?

A *methodological gap* is when a phenomenon has mostly been studied using only one or two methodological approaches or has not often been studied using other methodologies. For example, Kim might find that the research base on how teachers support emergent bilingual students has tended to use mostly descriptive case studies based largely on qualitative methods, and few studies involving quantitative methods. She could reflect on what she knows about the strengths and limitations of different methodologies. While case studies provide rich description of how a phenomenon operates in a particular context, they usually are not designed in ways that can demonstrate the impact of a particular intervention. Kim could consider whether action research, program evaluation, or experimental research that measures the impact of particular teaching practices on student outcomes might be helpful.

A *population gap* occurs when a phenomenon has not been studied with certain groups or in ways that allow researchers to explore potential differences between groups. One type of population gap is when researchers select participants in ways that obscure or overlook the experiences or outcomes of marginalized or nondominant communities. For example, Kim might find that existing research about emerging bilingual students has focused almost entirely on students whose families are native Spanish speakers, with few studies examining other linguistic and cultural groups. Having grown up in a family that primarily spoke Vietnamese, Kim may consider if new insights might be revealed through research focusing on students whose primary language is neither English nor Spanish. Kim might find another type of population gap if she sees that studies about teachers of emergent bilingual students have focused mostly on preservice or novice teachers, with relatively few studies about experienced or veteran teachers.

A *theoretical gap* is when existing research has not yet used certain theories to explore a particular phenomenon, when two potentially related theories have been used in disconnected ways, or when studies using different theories have yielded conflicting results. For example, Kim might find that existing studies about how teachers support emergent bilingual students have tended to rely on two main theories, both of which focus on how teachers form beliefs about students. Considering her interest in understanding how to support current teachers to better serve students, Kim wonders about the new insights that might be possible if organizing her study around a different theory that may predict or explain how in-service teachers can learn to change their practice (for more on theoretical frameworks, see Chapter 20).

As doctoral students enrolled in research doctorates clarify the gap in the literature, they will also need to satisfy a set of criteria that, according to Brubaker and Murray (2000), most doctoral committees will use when deciding on whether to approve a topic: (a) *scholarly intent*: Does this topic constitute "true research" (p. 59) designed to advance our collective scientific knowledge, as opposed to "propagandizing or salesmanship" (p. 59) to convince the world of their opinion or predetermined belief? (b) *feasibility*: Is this study doable with this methodology? Can it be done in the available time? Does the student have (or can they obtain) the necessary skills, personnel, and equipment? (c) *significance*: Do we need this study? Will the results be important to the field and public?

For Scholar Practitioners

As with research scientists, scholar practitioners may start with specific interests related to their professional experiences, life experiences, and personal interests. They may also find their interests influenced by the classes they take, readings, and their faculty's expertise. However, for scholar practitioners, the primary purpose of inquiry is not to produce generalizable knowledge about a phenomenon. Rather, it is to understand the nature and causes of a problem of practice in a particular local context, and design and test a change process to learn how to improve upon it (Mintrop, 2016; Perry et al., 2020). If designed systematically, insights from such research can and should be applicable to other contexts (Mintrop, 2016).

For scholar practitioners, the initial source of research topics aligns most with Brubaker and Murray's (2000) category of on-the-job problems. Topic selection starts by reflecting on challenges in the workplace: What important problem exists in our organization? Assuming existing research seldom provides certainty about how to solve the complex problems we face in practice, it is often possible for scholar practitioners to address what Miles (2017) describes as a practical knowledge gap. However, for the scholar practitioner, identifying a research focus does not occur by finding a gap in the literature but rather by defining and framing a high-leverage and actionable *problem of practice*.

As defined by Mintrop (2016), "problems of practice deal with *practices* that are entrenched in leaders' own organizations" (p. 24). Practices include how people routinely think about, organize, and carry out their work, and the behaviors through which people routinely interact within an organization. A high-leverage problem of practice is one that is persistent, essential for the core goals and purpose of the organization, and for which there is currently not a clear solution and therefore is worthy of the time and effort entailed in researching it (Hinnant-Crawford & Anderson, 2025; Mintrop, 2016; Perry et al., 2020). An actionable problem of practice is one within the student's sphere of influence to address (Mintrop, 2016; Perry et al., 2020).

Scholar practitioners do not often start out with a clearly defined and actionable problem of practice. According to Herr and Anderson (2014), research questions for scholar practitioners often start out as "puzzles" (p. 92) and fuzzy dilemmas. Puzzles and dilemmas are useful starting points for motivating research, but additional thinking steps are needed to transform these fuzzy concerns into specific inquiries. Puzzles often refer to what the literature on problem solving describes as "ill-structured" problems, meaning it is not clear at the outset what exactly is the problem or how to solve it (Robinson et al., 2021).

Determining a research focus requires steps to move from a fuzzy concern to specifically define and frame the problem. This is an iterative process. According to Mintrop and Zumpe (2016), defining a problem means establishing the difference between "what is and what ought to be" (p. 40). Framing refers to boundaries put up around the problem—similar to a frame around a painting. Frames bring certain aspects of the picture into center view and leave others out of the picture. When we frame problems, we tend to draw upon "worldviews, ideologies,… [and] broader political and normative assumptions" (Mintrop & Zumpe, 2016, p. 41). For this reason, problem frames tend to be contested. Problem framing is important because how we frame a problem tends to include assumptions about what is causing it and how it can be solved. As students learn more about a problem, their framing of the problem often shifts.

For example, Kim begins her doctoral journey with a passion for ensuring the success of multilingual learners. As she turns to the task of defining and framing a problem of practice, Kim may first think about the problems she has faced or observed in the workplace. Perhaps first she may think about her frustrations with convincing teachers to use inclusive practices to support multilingual students in the classroom. In her current role as a director of multilingual learning, Kim may also think about accountability data that tracks English learner outcomes in her district. She may wonder about the extent to which teachers are utilizing the learning offered through the professional development opportunities that her department has organized. These are all various passions and fuzzy concerns that Kim may find important, but it is not yet clear what exactly is an important problem of practice occurring in her district that her dissertation research could help to improve upon. Kim needs more information.

For students conducting research within and about their own organizations, defining and framing a problem can be more difficult than it sounds. As Mintrop (2016) explained, practitioners usually begin with intuitive assumptions about the problem, what is causing it, and how to solve it. On the one hand, intuitive knowledge contains valuable insights about the taken for granted, or tacit, aspects of professional work and one's local context—knowledge that can be quite valuable for problem solving (Davis & Davis, 2003). On the other hand, our intuition is also where potential biases and blinders can arise that short-circuit thinking and constrain our research (Kahnemann, 2011). When thinking about improvement, practitioners who work in fast-paced and complex environments may be used to skipping over the step of clarifying the problem to solve and instead name a solution they think should be implemented (Bryk et al., 2015; Mintrop & Zumpe, 2019).

Preparing to conduct research as a scholar practitioner means making our initial intuitions explicit so we can challenge them with new learning and setting aside our attachments to predetermined solutions to learn from evidence. In this way, defining and framing an actionable and high-leverage problem of practice involves a shift from intuitive to analytical thinking. Mintrop (2016) recommended six principles for moving from a fuzzy concern and intuitive assumptions to a clearly defined and framed problem of practice: (a) *urgency* for the organization (not just for the individual student); (b) *actionability* (within one's sphere of influence); (c) *feasibility* (can be addressed within a limited time with the resources available); (d) *strategic alignment* (is connected to the goals of the larger organization, such as the district); (e) *concreteness* (is narrowed to a set of specific, observable organizational practices that can be targeted for change); and (f) *stretch* (enables the organization to develop into its next level of work). More so than research scientists, scholar practitioners need to consider which problems they are best positioned to study, given their sphere of influence in their organizations.

Hinnant-Crawford and Anderson (2025) offer another related set of principles to guide problem definition with a 5S framework: (a) *significance* (why this problem is important); (b) *source* (what is causing it); (c) *substantive focus* (how might it be addressed); (d) *scale* (who needs to be involved in addressing it); and (e) *scope* (where is the problem located in the organization or system). For example, for Kim, ensuring the success of multilingual learners seems actionable. But does this issue meet the other criteria for a problem of practice? Is the progress of multilingual learners currently a significant problem? Is it something that others in the district are urgently concerned about? Certainly, it has been a concern in Kim's department. However, at recent school board meetings, the superintendent seemed focused on the issue of chronic absenteeism, board members raised concerns about Math performance, and parents were vocal about school facilities. Even though one-fifth of their student population consists of students for whom English is not their primary language, Kim cannot say whether people in her district outside of her office perceive this issue with urgency. Strategically, ensuring the success of multilingual learners aligns with the district's vision of ensuring twenty-first-century skills for all students. But she would be hard pressed to say what is the source, scope, or scale of the problem, or whether it is a feasible and appropriate stretch for her district. To address this, Kim would need to gather more information to define exactly what the problem is and what are the organizational practices that need changing in her district. For this reason, before scholar practitioners can determine their research topic, they need to conduct local needs assessments (Mintrop, 2016).

Whereas research scientists hone their research topic by finding a gap in research literature, scholar practitioners define a problem by identifying a gap between the desired and current state in their local contexts. A good *needs assessment* integrates multiple forms of evidence about organizational strengths and limitations, with an emphasis on evidence about organizational processes and practices—including surveys, interviews, and observations—alongside organizational performance data. As scholar practitioners consult and integrate such evidence, they get closer to defining and framing a problem of practice as they figure out: What appears to be a problem around here? What do people perceive as needs for improvement? Which of these needs appear to be widely shared and can be prioritized as a focal problem for collective learning? What organizational practices—observable beliefs, attitudes, and behaviors—are creating this problem and can be targeted for change?

For example, Kim should conduct a local needs assessment, first, to find out: What is going on with multilingual learners in her district? She might explore performance data, such as: To what extent, and in which areas, are these students developing intellectually and achieving? In which areas has their development or achievement stagnated? To identify a problem of practice, Kim also needs evidence about organizational beliefs and practices, such as: To what extent do principals and instructional coaches currently encourage teachers to focus on emergent bilingual students, and through which kinds of leadership moves and interactions? To what extent are teachers currently directing their teaching effort toward multilingual students, and through which kinds of curriculum or teaching moves? To what extent do these patterns vary across subject areas, grades, and schools?

Another purpose for conducting a local needs assessment is to understand and diagnose the problem. As with the process of identifying a problem, the process of diagnosis may start with intuitive assumptions. However, intuition and common sense alone are not usually sufficient for understanding the problem

While scholar practitioners do not identify a research focus by searching for a gap in research literature, that does not mean scholarly literature is not part of the process. An important step of shifting from intuition to analysis is consulting the scholarly knowledge base (Mintrop, 2016; Perry et al., 2020). One reason why it is important to consult the knowledge base is to situate a local problem into a broader context. High-leverage problems that practitioners perceive to be specific or unique to their local context are often related to a larger challenge in the system. Problems of practice worthy of disciplined inquiry for dissertation research should meet Mintrop's

(2016) criteria of urgency and strategic alignment and Hinnant-Crawford and Anderson's (2025) criteria of significance. Meeting these criteria usually means understanding how a problem of practice is a local manifestation of a broader problem occurring more widely in the system—and therefore that policymakers, researchers, and practitioners across the system are also likely to be concerned about.

The knowledge base is also vital for thinking beyond, and challenging, intuitive assumptions about the problem. As part of defining and framing a problem of practice, scholar practitioners need to engage in diagnosis, similar to a doctor (Mintrop, 2016). When a patient visits a doctor about a physical ailment, the doctor may start by asking patients to describe the symptoms, but their prognosis and treatment do not focus on the symptoms alone. Rather, doctors seek out additional information to determine root causes. This often includes considering multiple diagnostic data points (such as family history, mental health, blood work, and scans). In a similar way, scholar practitioners, in the shift from intuitive to analytical thinking, need to consider a variety of data points. Data alone is not enough, however. To effectively interpret and draw inferences from data, doctors draw upon theoretical knowledge of how the human body works and potential disorders or diseases that can affect it. Likewise, scholar practitioners need to become familiar with useful theories and empirical evidence in the research knowledge base that can help them identify the root causes of their problems of practice and, equally important, identify evidence-based practices and treatments to ameliorate the problem.

The iterative process of honing a research topic for scholar practitioners depends upon collaboration. While dissertation research is usually the product of a doctoral candidate, the tasks of defining and framing actionable problems of practice are not best pursued by an individual on their own. Most problems in organizations are not the result of one person or one group but are rather products of systems of interacting processes and practices (Bryk et al., 2015). Thus, identifying, understanding, and intervening into problems all typically require the involvement of multiple people in varying roles. Involving others is also important because improving upon high-leverage problems of practice requires sustained motivation and learning; generating such motivation is not likely accomplished by simply telling people what to implement (Mintrop & Zumpe, 2019). Thus, scholar practitioners should lead the inquiry but also need to think about how to involve others as collaborative problem solvers (Hinnant-Crawford & Anderson, 2025) and co-designers (Mintrop, 2016). In particular, doctoral students are advised to engage "users" in the organization—the people who most directly experience the problem or whose practices are the targets of change—by allowing their experiences and voices to shape the problem-solving process (Bryk et al., 2015; Hinnant-Crawford & Anderson, 2025).

Strategies for Success

For Research Scientists

- Begin by identifying a broad area of interest in your field that excites you and you are well-positioned to study, given your background and the faculty you work with.
- Funnel down from this broad area of concern to a narrower research focus
- Read literature about this topic widely—and with intention
- Begin by reading seminal literature; then trace the studies that followed to understand how the study of this topic has evolved over time
- Search for a methodological, population, or theoretical gap in the literature

For Scholar Practitioners

- Begin by identifying a challenge facing your organization
- Tap your intuition; then iteratively challenge it with analytical thinking
- Think like a doctor: move past symptoms of the problem to identify root causes
- To shift from intuition to analysis, conduct local needs assessments about outcomes, processes and practices
- Consult the research knowledge base to: (a) situate your local problem in a broader context and establish its significance; and (b) draw upon theory and evidence to identify the root causes of the problem.

- Involve multiple people—especially those who experience the problem most directly or whose practices are the target for change—in identifying and diagnosing the problem
- Define and frame a problem of practice that is (a) *urgent*; (b) *actionable*; (c) *feasible*; (d) *strategically aligned*; (e) *concrete*; and (f) *offers stretch* for the organization

Questions for Reflection

For Research Scientists

- Which topic in my field meets the following criteria: It is interesting to you, important in the field, and relevant to my dissertation committee or chair?
- What are the most influential works published about this topic?
- What are the gaps in the literature about this topic when it comes to methodologies used, populations studied, or the theories applied?
- What is a feasible aspect of this gap that I can study within my available time, resources, and expertise, and that would also make a significant contribution to the field?

For Scholar Practitioners

- What do I think most urgently needs improving in my workplace?
- To what extent do others also see this as an urgent issue?
- Which organizational practices do I hear and see people doing or saying that demonstrate this problem?
- What does the evidence from my organization say about this problem and what might be causing it? What does evidence and theory from scholarly literature say about this problem and what might be causing it?
- Whose voices and perspectives need to be involved to understand this problem?

Recommended Resources

Bonney, E. N., Capello, S. A., & Yurkofsky, M. (Eds.) (2024). *Improvement science in the field: Cases of practitioners leading change in schools*. Rowman & Littlefield.

Burnett, J. (2009). *Doing your social science dissertation*. Sage Publications.

Coghlan, D. (2019). *Doing action research in your own organization* (5th ed.). Sage Publications.

Perry, J. A. (2023). *Reclaiming the education doctorate: A guidebook for (re)designing EdD programs*. Myers Education Press.

Roberts, C. M. (2010). *The dissertation journey: A practical and comprehensive guide to planning, writing, and defending your dissertation* (2nd ed.). Corwin.

Robinson, V. (1992) Why doesn't educational research solve educational problems? *Educational Philosophy and Theory, 24*(2), 8–28.

References

Brubaker, D., & Murray, T. R. (2000). *Theses and dissertations: A guide to planning, research, and writing*. Praeger.

Bryk, A. S., Gomez, L. M., Grunow, A., & LeMahieu, P. G. (2015). *Learning to improve: How America's schools can get better at getting better*. Harvard Education Press.

Davis, S. H., & Davis, P. B. (2003). *The intuitive dimensions of administrative decision making*. Scarecrow.

García, O. (2009). *Bilingual education in the 21st century: A global perspective*. Blackwell.

Grant, C., & Osanloo, A. (2014). Understanding, selecting, and integrating a theoretical framework in dissertation research: Creating the blueprint for your "house." *Administrative Issues Journal, 4*(2), 12–26.

Herr, K., & Anderson, G. L. (2014). *The action research dissertation: A guide for students and faculty*. Sage Publications.

Herrmannova, D., Patton, R. M., Knoth, P., & Stahl, C. G. (2018). Do citations and readership identify seminal publications? *Scientometrics, 115*, 239–262.

Hinnant-Crawford, B., & Anderson, E. (2025). 5S framework for defining problems addressed through improvement research in education. In D. J. Peurach, J. L. Russell, L. Cohen-Vogel, & W. R. Penuel (Eds.), *The foundational handbook on improvement research in education* (pp. 297–324).

Kahnemann, D. (2011). *Thinking, fast and slow*. Farrar, Strauss and Giroux.

Lei, S. A. (2009). Strategies for finding and selecting an ideal thesis or dissertation topic: A review of literature. *College Student Journal, 43*(4), 1324–1333.

Miles, D. A. (2017, August). A taxonomy of research gaps: Identifying and defining the seven research gaps. In *Doctoral student workshop: Finding research gaps—research methods and strategies.*

Mintrop, R. (2016). *Design-based school improvement: A practical guide for education leaders.* Harvard Education Press.

Mintrop, R., & Zumpe, E. (2016). Defining and framing problems of practice. In R. Mintrop, *Design-based school improvement: A practical guide for education leaders* (pp. 31–42). Harvard Education Press.

Mintrop, R., & Zumpe, E. (2019). Solving real-life problems of practice and education leaders' school improvement mind-set. *American Journal of Education, 125*(3), 295–344.

Olalere, A., Aldarbag, A. M., & Erdener, M. A. (2014). The dissertation topic selection of doctoral students using dynamic network analysis. *International Journal of Doctoral Studies, 9,* 85–107. http://ijds.org/Volume9/IJDSv9p085-107Olalere521.pdf

Perry, J. A., Zambo, D., & Crow, R. (2020). *The improvement science dissertation in practice: A guide for faculty, committee members, and their students.* Myers Education Press.

Robinson, V., Meyer, F., Le Fevre, D., & Sinnema, C. (2021). The quality of leaders' problem solving conversations: Truth-seeking or truth-claiming? *Leadership and Policy in Schools, 20*(4), 650–671.

Single, P. G. (2010). *Demystifying dissertation writing: A streamlined process from choice of topic to final text.* Routledge.

Terrell, S. R. (2016). *Writing a proposal for your dissertation: Guides and examples.* The Guilford Press.

Turnbull (2018) Reframing foreign language learning as bilingual education: Epistemological changes towards the emergent bilingual. *International Journal of Bilingual Education and Bilingualism, 21*(8), 1041–1048. DOI: 10.1080/13670050.2016.123886

20 Understanding the Conceptual and Theoretical Framework

Lucinda S. Spaulding, PhD
Amanda J. Rockinson, EdD, PhD
James A. Swezey, EdD

The theoretical framework and conceptual framework are foundational to doctoral students' inquiry in the Inquiry Stage. These frameworks guide the writing of the problem, purpose, and questions, which in turn lead to choosing the appropriate research method(s) (i.e., qualitative, quantitative, or mixed methods) or application. This chapter defines the theoretical and conceptual framework and discusses how they inform the inquiry process.

Case Study

June is a PhD student in educational leadership, nearing the completion of her coursework. She is also a newly appointed assistant principal of a large, urban high school. In her new position, she is tasked with two primary roles: (a) facilitating and overseeing the professional learning communities (PLCs) in her school, and (b) finding ways to close achievement gaps between groups of students in her school. The National Center for Educational Statistics (2025) defines achievement gaps as significant differences in achievement scores between two groups of students (i.e., White and Black students, or White and Hispanic students, or male and female students). With a desire to merge her academic and professional demands, June decides to focus her dissertation research on the role of Professional Learning Communities

(PLCs) in equipping teachers with effective teaching strategies to support the academic success of all students.

As June begins to immerse herself in the literature on Professional Learning Communities (PLCs) and achievement gaps, she becomes incredibly overwhelmed. She identifies numerous gaps in the literature that she can address. Moreover, as a Black woman, June is struggling with whether she should take an advocacy approach and represent the voice of individuals who have typically been marginalized, or whether it would be more prudent to take an objective stance to investigate the effectiveness of a program.

After several months of wading through the literature, she becomes frustrated and is no closer to identifying a specific research focus. June makes an appointment with her dissertation chair to discuss her challenges. After attentively listening to her summarize the literature on her desired dissertation topic and potential study ideas, June's chair asks her one simple question: "What is your theoretical framework for your research?"

In the discussion that follows, June realizes that while she has been closely analyzing and synthesizing the empirical literature on her topic, she has also efficiently organized her findings into a detailed outline with key constructs and categories. She has paid little attention to the role of theory in guiding and framing her review of the literature and inquiry approach. She failed to realize the importance of integrating empirical findings with theoretical concepts into an original conceptual framework for her dissertation research.

What the Research Says

Many doctoral students, like June, are unaware of the importance of using a *theoretical framework* to guide their dissertation research (Anfara & Mertz, 2015; Grant & Osanloo, 2014). Although students may be familiar with the term, they are often unsure of its precise definition. This is understandable, as the term *theoretical framework* is often not clearly defined in the literature (Varpio et al., 2020). It is often used synonymously and interchangeably with terms such as *conceptual framework* and *literature review* (Crawford, 2020). However, the conceptual framework and theoretical framework are distinct in their definitions and functions. Rocco and Plakhotnic (2009) contrasted the difference between a theoretical and conceptual framework: "Whereas a *theoretical framework* is used when investigating a specific theory, a *conceptual framework* is made up of theoretical and empirical work relevant to the manuscript's purpose, where the purpose is not to investigate a specific theory further [italics added]" (p. 122).

In essence, the conceptual framework serves as the literature review (typically Chapter 2 in a traditional dissertation, see Chapter 18: Understanding the Different Types of Dissertations). However, it is also worth noting that a literature review is both a product and a process. As Merriam and Simpson (2000) highlighted, the literature review is a process conducted "to develop a conceptual framework" (p. 10). The literature review process involves a literature search. A literature search is "a systematic and thorough search of all types of published literature in order to identify as many items as possible that are relevant to a particular topic" (Gash, 2000, p. 1). Doctoral students can expect to review between 1,000 and 2,000 articles. In the product, however, they may include only 10–20% of what is reviewed. Thus, the literature review, as a product, is a written document that presents a coherent argument leading to a proposed inquiry. It is an argument written from the perspective of doctoral students, which includes a written synthesis of the literature organized around themes from a critical perspective (see Chapter 21: Writing Your Literature Review).

Conceptual Framework

Ravitch and Riggan (2017) defined the conceptual framework as "an argument about why the topic one wishes to study matters, and why the means proposed to study it are appropriate and rigorous" (p. 5). Ravitch and Riggan (2017) further noted that a conceptual framework "is a series of sequenced, logical propositions the purpose of which is to convince the reader of the study's importance and rigor" (p. 7).

That is, a conceptual framework is not a summarization of "what has already been done in the field" (Maxwell, 2005, p. 123), but rather it grounds a proposed inquiry "in the relevant previous work... to give the reader a clear sense of your theoretical approach to the phenomena that you propose to study" (Maxwell, 2005, p. 123).

The conceptual framework should thus serve two purposes: (a) to show how the doctoral students' inquiries fit into what is already known (relationship to existing theory and research) and (b) to show how the students' inquiries contribute, empirically, theoretically, or practically, to the field (i.e., intellectual goals) (Maxwell, 2005). For the professional doctorate, situating the problem of practice within the relevant theory and previous literature is useful. The theory and literature illuminate the problem of practice within a broader context, assisting doctoral candidates in framing or contextualizing the problem, identifying its root causes, informing appropriate interventions, and planning a research and analytical strategy. While using the literature and theory to frame a problem may not be unique to a professional doctoral dissertation, the relationship among these elements differs from that in a research doctorate, where the literature and theory demonstrate how doctoral candidates will fill a knowledge gap. For example, if June were in a professional doctorate program that utilized the scholar-practitioner model, she would use literature and theory to inform practical decisions about addressing the achievement gap. Moreover, rather than using a gap in the literature as a rationale for conducting her study, she would use the existing literature to inform her development of the PLC intervention. In other words, she would use the literature to provide rationale for the intervention decisions she makes to solve her problem of practice. She would use her conceptual framework to develop a research-based solution, a plan for testing it to see how it works within her local school context, and then to guide her discussion about practical, concrete actions for the stakeholders of her dissertation.

The role of a conceptual framework in a research doctorate dissertation, such as the one June is conducting, is to demonstrate the empirical or theoretical significance of the dissertation. Varpio et al. (2020) stated that the conceptual framework is

> *the justification for why a given study should be conducted. The conceptual framework (1) describes the state of known knowledge, usually through a literature review; (2) identifies gaps in our understanding of a phenomenon; and (3) outlines the methodological underpinnings of the research project.*
> *(p. 990)*

In sum, the conceptual framework is an original synthesis of the theoretical, seminal, and empirical literature into a cohesive argument for a dissertation, as depicted in Figure 20.1.

The conceptual framework helps focus and justify the inquiry problem (i.e., shows why the inquiry is important to the field). The conceptual

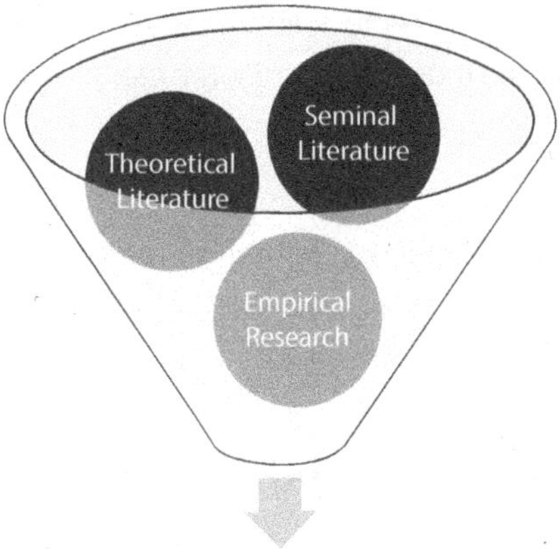

Conceptual Framework:
Underlying Argument for the Study Based on Theory and Previous Research

Figure 20.1 Conceptual Framework.

framework and the theoretical framework(s) discussed guide the proposed questions and the purpose of the dissertation, helping doctoral students identify and justify the type of research method or application needed to answer the inquiry questions.

Theoretical Frameworks

While a conceptual framework comprises both theoretical and empirical literature used to inform the inquiry (Grant & Osanoloo, 2014), the theoretical framework typically includes one or two prominent theories. Common theories used in social science research include social cognitive theory (Bandura, 1986), adult learning theory (Knowles, 1980), attachment theory (Bowlby, 1988), and Maslow's (1954) theory of motivation. The theoretical framework is defined as "a logically developed and connected set of concepts and premises—developed from one or more theories—that a researcher creates to scaffold a study" (Varpio et al., 2020, p. 990). It is part of the conceptual framework (Grant & Osanoloo, 2014). The theoretical framework

> *serves as a structure and support for the rationale for the study, the problem statement, the purpose statement, the significance, and the research questions.*

> *The theoretical framework provides a grounding base, or an anchor, for the literature review, and most importantly, the methods and analysis.*
>
> *(p. 12)*

The theoretical framework is an element of the conceptual framework "that situates the relationships explored in a study into the context of developing or testing formal theories" (Crawford, 2020, p. 38).

Quantitative Research and Theoretical Frameworks

In quantitative studies, where doctoral students use theory deductively and place it at the beginning of the research plan, the theoretical framework provides an overarching explanation for how and why one variable is expected to explain or predict another variable, informing the research questions and hypotheses (Creswell & Creswell, 2023). The theoretical framework is thus central as the inquiry is designed to test the theory. In quantitative studies, doctoral students use theory to identify variables they want to focus on and to generate hypotheses. They collect data to test these hypotheses. Then, they analyze the data and reflect on whether the theory is confirmed or disconfirmed by the results (i.e., the doctoral students reject or fail to reject the null hypotheses).

The theoretical framework also serves as the lens for reviewing and organizing the literature. For example, in her review of the literature, June finds that research is mixed on the effectiveness of Professional Learning Communities (PLCs) in helping teachers develop effective teaching strategies to support the academic success of all students. Some researchers claim that participating in PLCs led to teachers effectively implementing specific strategies, which in turn led to increased student achievement. However, other research suggests PLCs make no difference in teacher behavior or student achievement.

June notes that the PLCs studied have been implemented in various ways, utilizing a range of technologies. June begins to speculate about the mixed results. Upon further research, she comes across communication theory, specifically media richness theory (MRT; Daft & Lengel, 1984). Media richness is defined as the ability of a communication medium to convey the meaning of the message (Daft & Lengel, 1984). A medium's level of media richness is determined by four criteria: (a) the accessibility of instant feedback, (b) the capacity to convey cues such as body language and tone of voice, (c) the use of natural language, and (d) the level of personal focus. MRT assumes that the use of rich media, compared to lean media, results in more effective communication (Daft & Lengel, 1984). Theorists have argued that the richer the communication medium, the more ambiguity and uncertainty are reduced, and the better tasks are performed (Daft & Lengel, 1984).

June wonders, could it be that the effectiveness of the PLC on teachers' behaviors and students' achievement is influenced by the medium through which the PLC is delivered? Some PLCs have been created and implemented using online discussion forums, while others have been established through face-to-face meetings or video conferencing. June methodically reviews the literature on PLCs and media theory; she cannot find any studies that considered the medium used to deliver the PLCs.

Considering the media richness theory, June notes that face-to-face and video conferencing PLCs are more media-rich than online, text-based discussion forum PLCs. Using MRT, June hypothesizes that face-to-face and video conferencing PLCs, when compared to online, text-based discussion forum-based PLCs, will result in more effective communication, learning of new strategies, and ultimately a greater likelihood that teachers will implement the new strategies to improve student achievement.

So, June proposes the following quantitative research question: What difference, if any, exists in teachers' understanding of teaching strategies based on the type of Professional Learning Community (PLC) they participate in (discussion forum-based, video-conferencing-based, or face-to-face)? What difference, if any, exists in teachers' implementation of the teaching strategies based on the type of PLC they participate in (discussion forum-based, video-conferencing-based, or face-to-face)?

June's exploration of the literature and application of theory informs her inquiry problem, purpose, and questions. The questions that she poses are aimed at testing a theory and examining the relationship between variables, which can be quantified and tested using objective, validated measures. Objective knowledge is sought to answer the research questions; thus, this approach is consistent with the positivist paradigm (see Chapter 12: Understanding Quantitative Inquiry), which underlies quantitative research. As a result, her questions led her to adopt a quantitative research design for her dissertation.

Qualitative Research and Theoretical Frameworks

However, as is the case with many research topics, June could also approach her study using a qualitative method of inquiry. While traditionally the use of theory in constructing a qualitative study was discouraged, as theory was considered the *product* of qualitative research, it is now generally accepted that *atheoretical* research is impossible (Anfara & Mertz, 2015). Merriam and Simpson (1998) argued that it is "difficult to imagine a study *without* a theoretical or conceptual framework" (p. 45).

Theory plays several important roles in qualitative studies. Anfara and Mertz (2015) explained that theory "situates qualitative research clearly within the scholarly conversation, adds subtlety and complexity to what appear at first glance to be simple phenomena, and allows for building a repertoire of understandings, diverse perspectives, of the same phenomenon" (p. 190). In addition to helping the researcher demonstrate the scholarly significance of a study, developing a theoretical framework for a qualitative study is helpful as it serves as the "structure, the scaffolding, the frame of the study" (Merriam, 1998, p. 45). Theory also helps researchers narrow down and focus on a specific aspect of a topic (Anfara & Mertz, 2015) and provides an orienting lens to guide the research design, data analysis, and interpretation of findings (Creswell & Creswell, 2023).

For example, June has a clearly identified dissertation focus and compelling problem to investigate, but she is still struggling to hone it in and settle on a problem. After reading several quantitative studies employing rigorous experimental designs that suggest Professional Learning Communities (PLCs) are more effective forms of professional development (PD) than traditional forms of PD, June recognizes that little research exists to describe *how* and *why* PLCs are effective.

After continuing to read and reflect, June recognizes that leadership is central to effective educational endeavors; leaders play a critical role in motivating individuals to reach their full potential (Burns, 1978), and educational leadership may be crucial to understanding the effectiveness of PLCs. While there may be multiple theoretical orientations for her topic (Anfara & Mertz, 2015), June feels that transformational leadership theory (Burns, 1978) is quite fitting as a framework for focusing her research on the leadership role in creating and facilitating effective PLCs dedicated to reducing achievement gaps.

As she investigates a phenomenon within clearly bounded systems (i.e., PLCs), June decides to employ a qualitative, multiple-case study research design for her dissertation, with each PLC serving as her unit of analysis (i.e., the case). As case studies aim to answer *how* and *why* questions (Yin, 2018) and transformational leadership theory focuses on motivating individuals as well as group performance (Burns, 1978), June constructs the following open-ended research questions for her qualitative, multiple study: (a) How do PLC leaders motivate members of the community to implement interventions in their own classrooms? (b) Why is participation in a PLC (small group) an effective form of professional development?

Being true to qualitative inquiry, June refrained from making hypotheses; however, she used theory to guide the formation of her questions. June also draws on theory when she begins to analyze her data, as she can use transformational leadership theory as both a *sieve* (Anfara & Mertz, 2015) and a *lens* (Creswell & Creswell, 2023) as she sorts through and begins to make sense of the wealth of data her qualitative inquiry will generate. During analysis, her theoretical framework will provide June with many of the codes, categories, or conceptual labels she needs to develop a cogent analysis, description, and discussion of the phenomenon.

Further, when June publishes her results, readers may have greater confidence in her findings because they have been alerted to the theoretical lens (i.e., perspective) through which she is analyzing her data, while also knowing she consciously revisited the theory throughout her analysis. Therefore, she has minimized subjectivity and bias inherent in qualitative research. Most importantly, while qualitative studies are limited in terms of generalizability due to their often lacking random sampling procedures, by framing her study with an empirically validated theory, June can situate her research within the "scholarly conversation" (Anfara & Mertz, 2015, p. 192) on the topic across disciplines.

In the qualitative scenario, June's exploration of the literature and application of theory also guided her research questions. The theory shed light on an aspect of PLCs that was previously unknown. This led June to pose open-ended questions aimed at understanding a phenomenon with multiple, individual interpretations, consistent with the post-positivist and constructivist paradigm underlying qualitative research methodologies.

Applied Research and Theoretical Frameworks

In applied studies, which are typically associated with the professional doctorate, doctoral students use theory to provide the background for the study's problem and guide them in developing the research question(s) and their choice of methods (qualitative, quantitative, or mixed). In other words, theories "provide a general explanation of what the researcher hopes to find in a study or a lens through which to view the needs of participants and communities in a study" (Creswell & Poth, 2025). As with other types of dissertations, the theoretical framework is embedded in the literature review and placed within the context of the empirical literature of the problem being studied. Literature reviews within professional doctorates are frequently framed within the study using common learning theories, psychological perspectives, and related frameworks (Kumar et al., 2022).

Baird et al. (2020) noted that students in professional doctoral programs often struggle to apply theoretical frameworks to their studies effectively and postulated that this "may occur because graduate faculty assume students arrived with this skill set, they do not know how to teach the process or they do not believe they have time or should need to teach writing" (p. 722). This lack of faculty guidance likely leads students to use theories inappropriately (i.e., out of context) or misapply theories to their problems of practice.

If June were in a professional doctorate program, she would be seeking a theory that could frame her problem and guide the development of her research question, which in this case would seek to solve a practical problem. Let us say that the problem of practice in this case was poor collaboration between teachers assigned to the professional learning communities. June might select a theoretical framework, such as collaborative learning theory (Bruffee, 1984) or sociocultural theory (Vygotsky, 1978), which encompasses key ideas including social interaction, shared knowledge, cumulative learning, and the institutionalization of knowledge. Based on either of these theories, June might be led to an applied research question such as "How can participants in a professional learning community at a large urban high school improve the practice of social interaction?" or "How can the problem of a lack of shared knowledge be solved among participants in a professional learning community at a large urban high school?"

The Components of Theory

To further understand how theory guides inquiry, it is essential to comprehend what a theory is and the components that comprise it. Kerlinger (1979) defined theory as "a set of interrelated constructs (variables), definitions, and propositions that present a systematic view of phenomena by specifying relations among variables, to explain or predict the phenomena" (p. 64). Every theory has three elements (Anfara & Mertz, 2015): (a) *concepts*: words assigned to events or sensations (e.g., age: amount of time; intelligence: amount of knowledge), (b) *constructs*: cluster of concepts that form a higher unit of thought (e.g., IQ), and (c) *propositions*: expression of the relationship among constructs. Borrowing from Anfara and Mertz's description, Maslow's (1954) theory of motivation is a good example of the relationship between concepts, constructs, and propositions:

> *According to Maslow, human beings have a variety of needs (concepts), some more fundamental than others. Maslow grouped these needs into five basic categories (constructs), arranged them hierarchically from "lower" to "higher" (propositions). Lower needs dominate behavior when they are not satisfied. Higher needs become salient only after the lower needs have been satisfied. From these concepts, constructs, and propositions, Maslow concluded that behavior is an expression of one's drive to reduce deficiencies by gratifying the most salient type of needs theory.*
>
> *(p. xvi)*

Theories address various levels, including the individual (e.g., self-efficacy theory), the group or organization (e.g., family systems theory), or society (e.g., Marxism). According to Agnew and Pyke (1969), good theories are (a) simple, (b) testable, (c) novel, (d) supportive of other theories, (e) internally consistent, and (f) predictive. Anfara and Mertz (2015) quite simply concluded, "A useful theory tells an enlightening story about some phenomenon. It is a story that gives you new insights and broadens your understanding of a phenomenon" (p. xvii).

Additional Considerations in Selecting a Method

As indicated earlier, the theoretical framework provides the lens or the theoretical perspective on a topic and guides the construction of research questions. Often, there may be multiple theoretical orientations for a single topic. For students enrolled in research scientist or PhD programs, gaps in the literature highlighted by the lens may lead to research questions that aim to address knowledge that can be examined quantitatively, qualitatively, or a combination of both. For students enrolled in scholar-practitioner programs, solutions to problems of practice highlighted by the lens may lead to inquiry questions or solutions that can also be addressed quantitatively, qualitatively, or both.

A few other factors should be considered in addition to selecting a theoretical framework for a study, including: (a) the nature of knowledge and paradigms underlying research methodologies, (b) the purpose and feasibility of conducting the inquiry, and (c) individual factors.

Paradigms

Doctoral students need to consider their personally held philosophy about the nature of knowledge and understand the type of knowledge the research questions aim to uncover. These philosophical assumptions need to be considered within the framework of the research paradigms. Gall et al. (2007) suggested that researchers "make different epistemological assumptions about the nature of scientific knowledge and how to acquire it" (p. 31).

It is important to note the distinction between qualitative and quantitative methods is more than the difference between words and numbers: "A more complete way to view the gradations of differences between them is the basic philosophical assumptions researchers bring to the study, the types of strategies used overall in the research… and the specific methods employed" (Creswell & Creswell, 2023, p. 4). In other words, paradigms (and underlying epistemologies) define how researchers approach the world and research, and therefore influence methodological decisions.

Unfortunately, experts in the field continue to argue and debate most aspects of paradigms (also referred to as interpretive frameworks), leaving the novice researcher to struggle through a morass of information. Guba and Lincoln (1994) outlined four paradigms used to guide the discussion here: (a) positivism, (b) post-positivism, (c) critical theory, and (d) constructivism.

As with each of the major paradigms, positivism generates fervent discussion and debate among its adherents and detractors, yet little consensus has been reached regarding its meaning (Lincoln & Guba, 1985). Gall et al. (2007) defined *positivism* "as the epistemological doctrine that physical and social reality is independent of those who observe it, and that observations of this reality, if unbiased, constitute scientific knowledge" (p. 16). Positivist researchers claim that universal principles, rules, or laws can be identified and applied to general settings, regardless of individual experiences, even if those experiences contradict the principle, rule, or law. Individual exceptions are considered "noise" by researchers (Gall et al., 2007, p. 26). The cornerstone of positivism is the concept of objective reality.

Quantitative research is consistent with the idea that knowledge is derived from direct observation and logical inference based on observation. Quantitative researchers are concerned with seeking an objective reality through the isolation and precise measurement of variables, and maintaining a detached, objective stance in research to avoid bias. Statistical methods are used to examine relationships among variables and generalize findings to entire populations.

For example, June could isolate the variable, type of medium, providing teachers with the same PLC intervention delivered in three different mediums. She could then measure the dependent variables using validated instruments and analyze the data using statistical analysis. Although June sees a quantitative study as a potential viable option, she has two concerns. First, she is having difficulty identifying validated instruments to measure her variables, as the accessible population she is planning to study is primarily composed of teachers from racial and ethnic minority groups. Most instruments she found in the literature were normed and validated on primarily White, middle-class populations of teachers.

Second, June believes that knowledge is constructed through the interaction of multiple perspectives, rather than a single objective reality. Thus, positivism—the paradigm on which quantitative research is based—is not consistent with the beliefs June holds. Simply because a researcher has a belief about knowledge, it does not limit their use of a methodology; it simply requires that they struggle with it. Given her belief that knowledge is constructed through interaction and lack of valid measures, June decides to pursue a qualitative research method.

Post-positivism emerged as a paradigm in response to perceived weaknesses and inadequacies with the positivist framework (Lincoln & Guba, 1985). According to Gall et al. (2007), "Postpositivism is an epistemology that assumes an objective reality, but that this objective reality can only be known imperfectly" (p. 16). Post-positivists acknowledge that, despite efforts at neutrality, the researcher inevitably will inject bias into a study. The basis for this claim is that social science research invariably incorporates the researcher's beliefs and values. For instance, as June seeks to focus her research on the role of PLCs in closing the achievement gap between White students and racial and ethnic minority students, she recognizes she brings certain biases to the study as she is a racial and ethnic minority.

Critical theory is a paradigm that posits that oppression of various groups, especially minorities, exists as a result of hegemony (Creswell & Poth, 2025). *Hegemony* is the perspective that "privileged cultural groups maintain domination of other groups through various cultural agencies that exert power" (Gall et al., 2007, p. 510). This paradigm emerged out of several diverse schools of thought in early twentieth-century Frankfurt, Germany.

During the aftermath of World War I, social science researchers began to study the ever-changing forms and roles of social, political, and economic power that enveloped the postwar world. Critical theory has since evolved to encompass feminist theory, critical race theory, and other related perspectives. As June's dissertation addresses the achievement gap, her study may inherently have a critical element to it, as she seeks to bridge the divide between the achievement of minority and majority students.

Constructivism stems from the belief that there is no objective reality, but rather reality is a social construct based on individual interpretations (Lincoln & Guba, 1985). It separates itself from the so-called hard sciences in that it acknowledges that studying human beings is distinct from the study of other natural phenomena (Patton, 2014).

One of the leading proponents of the constructivist framework (especially as it relates to grounded theory) is Kathy Charmaz. According to Mills et al. (2006), Charmaz advocated for the researcher as (a) the coproducer of reality along with participants, (b) who is immersed within the data, and (c) who is an evocative storyteller on behalf of participants. Embracing this paradigm requires researchers to examine their constructions of reality, ensuring that their perspectives are not imposed on those of the study participants.

Constructivism affirms that each participant will construct a different understanding of events because they will each experience them differently. Quantitative research, which aims to discover an objective reality, is not consistent with this paradigm; however, qualitative research is often grounded in constructivism, where knowledge is viewed as relative and socially constructed. As such, qualitative research is concerned with understanding a phenomenon from the perspective of those who live it. The researcher is a *human instrument* (Guba & Lincoln, 1994); that is, all data collected is filtered through and interpreted by the researcher. It is essential for researchers to critically examine their philosophical assumptions about the underlying assumptions of the two research approaches (Creswell & Poth, 2025).

Doctoral candidates must clarify for themselves how they believe knowledge is created, as well as what their research questions aim to uncover, and whether these questions are consistent with the underlying paradigm of each method. For example, June believes that knowledge is constructed through the interaction of multiple perspectives. Her decision to use a qualitative, multiple-case study design to examine an issue from multiple perspectives aligns well with this paradigm. Jane needs to recognize, however, that her reality as a Black female will inherently influence how she conducts her research, analyzes, and interprets her data. As the human instrument in her qualitative study, June needs to articulate her interpretive framework (i.e., paradigm) and its associated assumptions.

In this discussion of paradigms, it would be remiss to overlook the idea of *paradigm wars* (Gage, 1989; Onwuegbuzie, 2002). While some note that the two methodologies are complementary (Creswell, 2023), and mixed methods may be a viable choice for a dissertation (Johnson & Onwuegbuzie, 2004), Levine (2007) discussed the relationship between methods as contentious. Universities and faculty often have strong traditions related to research methods and tend to hold disdain for the opposing method.

Discipline-specific traditions also exist. For example, hard science disciplines (e.g., physics, biology) have strong quantitative traditions (see Delbanko, 2012). Doctoral students are wise to be aware that disagreements between paradigms and methodological traditions exist among faculty and within scholarly communities.

The Purpose and Feasibility of the Research

As discussed, the examination of the literature and application of theory guide the doctoral student to identify the research purpose and research questions. In addition to evaluating the type of knowledge that the research question aims to uncover, considering the purpose of the research and the nature of the questions guides the choice of method, as illustrated in the case of June.

Strauss and Corbin (2015) suggested that qualitative methods can be used to gain a deeper understanding of phenomena about which little is yet known. They can also be used to gain new perspectives on things about which much is already known, or to gain more in-depth information that may be difficult to convey quantitatively. Thus, qualitative methods are appropriate in situations where one needs first to identify the variables that might later be tested quantitatively, or where the researcher has determined that quantitative measures cannot adequately describe or interpret a situation.

Qualitative-focused research questions (a) tend to be broad and more general in terms than quantitative questions as not to delimit the study; (b) are open ended; (c) usually begin with words such as "what" and "how"; (d) do not usually contain directional words such as "effect," "impact," "cause," or "relate"; (e) identify the research site; and (f) ask about people's experiences, the meaning people make of their experiences, or people and their social or interpersonal contexts (Creswell & Creswell, 2023; Patton, 2014). Thus, qualitative methods are feasible when the researcher wants to examine a population in which little research has been done and the assessable population is small.

Quantitative research aims to explain the relationship between or among variables, predict or determine causal relationships, and test a theory or model (Creswell & Creswell, 2023). Quantitative focused research questions are: (a) specific and restricted in scope; (b) involve constructs that are measurable numerically; (c) contain directional words such as "affect," "impact," "cause," "difference," or "relate"; and (d) identifies variables. Variables are typically independent (e.g., groups) or dependent (e.g., test scores, attitudinal survey scores), and (e) ask precisely about the difference or relationship between variables (Creswell & Creswell, 2023; LaFountian & Bartos, 2002).

Quantitative methods are feasible when instruments have been normed and validated to study constructs of interest. Lack of access to large, accessible populations and validated instruments makes the feasibility of quantitative research difficult.

Individual Factors

There are a few additional factors doctoral students need to consider when selecting their research method: (a) time, (b) a desire to work with people versus numbers, (c) writing skills, and (d) a desire to develop skills within a specific methodology. Therefore, doctoral students need to recognize that, due to the nature of data collection (narrative versus numerical), qualitative research can be more time-consuming than quantitative research.

Qualitative research may require more time interacting directly with people; quantitative research is likely to require more time interacting with numbers. Quantitative research requires technical, scientific writing, whereas qualitative research requires more descriptive and narrative writing. Finally, a doctoral student may desire to gain expertise through mentorship within a specific methodology, as this may be the one time in their scholarly career when they have a committee of three people coming alongside to mentor and advise.

Strategies for Success

The following strategies are offered for you to consider and apply as you begin the process of narrowing your research focus and selecting your research method.

Strategy 1: Be Aware of Discipline, Faculty, and Program Paradigm Preferences

As "paradigm wars" exist, social integration within specific scholarly communities (i.e., disciplines or universities) may depend on a doctoral student's interaction with a particular research methodology (Metz, 2001; Pallas, 2001). An examination of university curricula, discipline-specific journals, and interviews with faculty can provide insight for prospective and first-year doctoral students as to whether a specific methodology (qualitative or quantitative) is preferred over another for success in the scholarly community.

Strategy 2: Use Coursework to Learn about Theory and Methods

Throughout the Knowledge and Skill Development Stage, you should read literature and seek to understand the difference between conceptual frameworks and theoretical frameworks, as differentiating among these distinct concepts can help you better organize, conceptualize, conduct, and present and discuss your research. The latter point is not addressed in this chapter; however, the conceptual framework and theoretical framework need to inform not only the inquiry and method choices, but also the discussion of findings, whether for empirical purposes or concrete actions.

Coursework is also the ideal time for you to familiarize yourself with various theories within your discipline and outside of your discipline that could potentially frame your dissertation research or culminating project. You should identify theories used in research studies and presented in textbooks, read seminal theoretical sources as resources for course assignments, and discuss theory with faculty.

The Knowledge and Skill Development Stage is also an opportune time to develop skills in both quantitative and qualitative methods and research applications (e.g., improvement science, action research). Onwuegbuzie and Leech (2005) encouraged training in both methods, and Creswell and Miller (1997) recommended personalizing the curriculum to prepare for methodological choice in the dissertation process.

Strategy 3: Choose a Theoretical Framework and Articulate Its Application

Once you have identified a topic of interest and spent time researching the state of knowledge on the topic (i.e., conducting a review of the literature), you need to identify a theory to frame the reviewed studies and to guide the development of your research questions. You need to be prepared to answer the question June's chair asked: "What is your theoretical framework for your research?"

Once you identify and select the theory(ies) that best address all facets of your research topic, it is then helpful to explain how the theory informs the research questions and constructs being examined. If enrolled in a professional doctoral program, this process will also help you contextualize your problem of practice and develop solutions to solve the problem. If your proposed question is quantitative, you need to explain how the theory informs your choice of variables and the relationship between or among them. Creswell and Creswell's (2023) script is a helpful tool to use to do this: "The theory I will use is (theory name). It was developed by (identify the origin, source, developer of the theory), and it was used to study (identify the topics where one finds the theory being applied)" (p. 62).

Then, you need to identify the central hypothesis of the theory and its adaptation to the study:

> *The theory indicates that (identify propositions or hypotheses in the theory). As applied to my study, this theory suggests that I would expect my independent variable(s) (state-independent variables) to influence or explain the dependent variable(s) because (provide a rationale based on the logic of the theory).*
>
> *(p. 61)*

The theoretical framework also serves as the lens for reviewing literature in Chapter 2 of the dissertation. The theoretical framework is also employed to analyze, interpret, explain, and describe the study's results (Motitswe, 2025).

In qualitative research, finding a fitting theoretical framework can be challenging, even for experienced researchers (Anfara & Mertz, 2015). Read extensively on your topic, note the theories other researchers use to guide their inquiries, reflect, and dialogue with your dissertation chair and committee members. Consider your research paradigm when selecting your theoretical framework and ensure there are no inconsistencies.

As the researcher is the human instrument in the qualitative study (Guba & Lincoln, 1994), if you choose a qualitative research design you need to clearly articulate your theoretical framework, how it informs the construction of research questions, method selection, and most important, how it will serve as a lens to filter the data when analyzing and determining how to represent your findings (typically in Chapter 4). This last point is crucial; qualitative researchers need to acknowledge that while "theories can allow us to see familiar phenomena in novel ways, they can also blind us to aspects of the phenomena that are not part of the theory" (Anfara & Mertz, 2015, p. 193).

Thus, the theoretical framework serves as a *delimitation* to the study (i.e., a researcher decision that serves to focus or narrow the scope of the study) and the limitations that stem from this delimitation need to be clearly acknowledged and explained.

Strategy 4: Choose a Method Consistent with the Nature of Knowledge Being Sought

As a doctoral candidate, you need to allow your exploration of the literature and application of theory to guide your research questions. Once your questions are posed, consider the nature of the knowledge the question is assessing as well as the purpose of the question to identify the most appropriate research method.

If your questions are aimed at testing a theory and examining the relationship between two or more variables that can be quantified and tested using objective, validated measures, then a quantitative method may be most appropriate. If the aim is to understand multiple perspectives and to represent the voice of individuals who experienced a phenomenon, then a qualitative method may be more appropriate.

Strategy 5: Choose a Method That Is Feasible and Aligns with Personal Factors

Doctoral students need to take into consideration (a) time, (b) a desire to work with people versus numbers, (c) writing skills, (d) a desire to develop skills within a specific methodology, and (e) feasibility of the methodology prior to choosing a method. A fear of statistics is not a good reason to avoid quantitative research. In June's case, she plans to examine a problem within a specific context and where the perspective of multiple individuals (e.g., teachers, administrators) is needed to understand the phenomenon. Therefore, the purpose of her research is consistent with qualitative methods.

Further, June has a small accessible population and is studying a population in which very few instruments have been normed and validated, making the feasibility of quantitative research difficult (see Chapter 12: Understanding

Quantitative Inquiry). June also likes to work with people, is a strong writer, and wants to further develop her skills as a qualitative researcher.

Questions for Reflection

The theoretical framework you select significantly shapes the nature and direction of your research, including the research purpose, selection of variables (if quantitative) or phenomenon (if qualitative), and the construction of the research questions. The next essential step is aligning your research method with the nature of your research.

It is important to highlight that the process of selecting your theoretical framework, working it into your conceptual framework for the study, and aligning your method is not always a linear and sequential process; researchers need to continue to read, reflect, and revise throughout the entire process of developing the dissertation proposal, and for qualitative studies, questions may continue to emerge even after the data has been collected. The following questions serve as a guide in this process:

Theoretical Framework

- What is my research topic or problem of practice? What theories are researchers in my discipline using to guide the research on this topic and related topics?
- What key variables, constructs, or concepts will I investigate? If leaning *quantitative*, what theory(ies) inform my predictions (hypotheses) about the relationships between these variables? If leaning *qualitative*, what theory(ies) provide a lens for examining all facets of the issue or phenomenon I want to investigate?

Conceptual Framework

- If in a research doctorate, drawing from the theoretical and empirical literature that I analyzed and synthesized when developing my literature review, what is my overall argument (i.e., your original case) for the need for your study? If in a professional doctorate, drawing from the theoretical and empirical literature that I analyzed and synthesized when developing my literature review, how will I contextualize my problem of practice? What are the root causes of the problem? How does it inform appropriate interventions to solve my problem?

Paradigm

- How do I view the world and the nature of reality? As (a) objective and observable, or (b) as subjective and dependent upon personal experience and perspective?
- What is my role as the researcher? To (a) describe, or (b) to advocate, give a voice, or emancipate?

Method Selection

- Is my goal to (a) test hypotheses about the relationships between two or more operationally defined variables, or (b) to explore a topic to identify variables that may later be evaluated quantitatively?
- Do I seek to (a) gain new perspectives on things about which much is already known, or (b) gain more in-depth information that may be difficult to convey quantitatively?
- Can my variables of interest or key constructs be (a) isolated and manipulated or (b) are they best observed in their natural environment?
- Can I collect data from my sample using (a) normed and validated instruments, or (b) is the data best collected through observation and in-depth interviews?

If my answers to the paradigm and method questions above generally aligned with (a), a *positivist* paradigm, then I probably need to consider a quantitative method; if my answers generally aligned with (b) a *post-positivist* or *constructivist* paradigm, I may need to consider a qualitative method. If I found myself aligning with both (a) and (b), then my inquiry may be well suited to a mixed methods approach. However, it's important to note that mixed methods involve rigorous qualitative *and* rigorous quantitative data collection and analysis methods, may warrant more than one theoretical framework, and depend on the researcher to successfully integrate and combine findings from each design (see Chapter 13: Understanding Mixed Methods of Inquiry). Whether conducting a qualitative, quantitative, or mixed methods study, I need to consider the following in my choice of research approach:

- Nature of the problem
- Accessibility to participants
- Time
- Budget
- A desire to work with people versus numbers
- Writing skills
- A desire to develop skills within a specific methodology
- Overall feasibility of the methodology

Recommended Resources

Anfara, V. A., & Mertz, N. T. (2015). *Theoretical frameworks in qualitative research* (2nd ed.). SAGE Publications.

Grant, C. & Osanloo, A. (2014). Understanding, selecting, and integrating a theoretical framework in dissertation research: Creating the blueprint for your house. *Administrative Issues Journal*, *4*(2), 12–26.

Ravitch, S. M., & Riggan, M. (2016). *Reason and rigor: How conceptual frameworks guide research* (2nd ed.). SAGE Publications.

References

Agnew, N., & Pyke, S. (1969). *The science game: An introduction to research in the behavioral sciences*. Prentice Hall.

Anfara, V. A., & Mertz, N. T. (2015). *Theoretical frameworks in qualitative research* (2nd ed.). SAGE Publications.

Baird, S. B., Kearney, K. S., & Nephew, A. (2020). Writing through theoretical frameworks in the doctoral classroom. *Studies in Graduate and Postdoctoral Education*, *11*(3), 281–294. DOI 10.1108/SGPE-02-2020-0013

Bandura, A., & National Inst of Mental Health. (1986). *Social foundations of thought and action: A social cognitive theory.* Prentice-Hall, Inc.

Bowlby, J. (1988). *A secure base: Parent-child attachment and healthy human development*. Basic Books.

Bruffee, K. A. (1984). Collaborative learning and the "Conversation of Mankind". *College English*, *46*(7), 635–652.

Burns, J. M. (1978). *Leadership*. Harper and Row.

Charmaz, K. (2006). *Constructing grounded theory*. SAGE Publications.

Connelly, L. M. (2014). Research roundtable: Use of theoretical frameworks in research. *Medsurg Nursing*, *23*(3), 187–188.

Crawford, L. (2020). Chapter 3: Conceptual and theoretical frameworks in research. *Foundations in Research Design*. SAGE Publications.

Creswell, J. W. & Creswell, J. D. (2023). *Research design: Qualitative and quantitative, and mixed methods approaches* (6th ed.). SAGE Publications.

Creswell, J. W., & Miller, G. A. (1997). Research methodologies and the doctoral process. In L. Goodchild, K. E. Green, E. L. Katz, & R. C. Kluever (Eds.), *Rethinking the dissertation process: Tackling personal and institutional obstacles* (pp. 33–46). Jossey-Bass.

Creswell, J. W., & Poth, C. N. (2025). *Qualitative inquiry and research design: Choosing among five approaches* (5th ed.). SAGE Publications.

Daft, R. L., & Lengel, R. H. (1984). Information richness: A new approach to managerial behavior and organizational design. In Cummings, L. L., & Staw, B. M. (Eds.), *Research in organizational behavior 6* (pp. 191–233). JAI Press.

Delbanko, A. (2012). *College, what it was, is, and should be*. Princeton University Press.

Denzin, N. K., & Lincoln, Y. S. (2018). *The SAGE handbook of qualitative research* (6th ed.). SAGE Publications.

Gage, N. L. (1989). The paradigm wars and their aftermath. *Educational Researcher*, *18*(7), 4–10.

Gall, M. D., Gall, J. P., & Borg, W. R. (2007). *Educational research: An introduction* (8th ed.). Pearson.

Gash, S. (2000). *Effective literature searching for research*. Gower.

Grant, C. & Osanloo, A. (2014) Understanding, selecting, and integrating a theoretical framework in dissertation research: Creating the blueprint for your house. *Administrative Issues Journal*, *4*(2), 12–26.

Guba, E. G., & Lincoln, Y. S. (1994). Competing paradigms in qualitative research. In N. K. Denzin & Y. S. Lincoln (Eds.) *Handbook of qualitative research* (pp. 105–17). SAGE Publications.

Johnson, R. B., & Onwuegbuzie, A. J. (2004). Mixed methods research: A research paradigm whose time has come. *Educational Researcher*, *33*(7), 14–26.

Kerlinger, F. N. (1979). *Behavioral research: A conceptual approach*. Holt, Rinehart, & Winston.

Kivunja, C. (2018). Distinguishing between theory, theoretical framework, and conceptual framework: A systematic review of lessons from the field. *International Journal of Higher Education*, *7*(6), 44–53.

Knowles, M. S. (1980). *The Modern Practice of Adult Education: From Pedagogy to Andragogy: Revised and Updates*. Association Press.

Kumar, S., Dawson, K., Pollard, R., & Jeter, G. (2022). Analyzing theories, conceptual frameworks, and research methods in EdD dissertations. *TechTrends*, *66*, 721–728. https://doi.org/10.1007/s11528-022-00739-4

LaFountain, R. M., & Bartos, R. B. (2002). *Research and statistics made meaningful in counseling and student affairs*. Brooks/Cole.

Leech, N. L. (2012). Educating knowledgeable and skilled researchers in doctoral programs in schools of education: A new model. *International Journal of Doctoral Studies*, *7*, 19–37.

Levine, A. (2007). Educating researchers. *The Education Schools Project*.

Lincoln, Y. S., & Guba, E. G. (1985). *Naturalistic inquiry*. SAGE Publications.

Maslow, A. H. (1954). *Motivation and personality*. Harper and Row.

Maxwell, J. A. (2005). *Qualitative research design: An interactive approach* (2nd ed.). SAGE Publications.

Merriam, S. B., & Simpson, E. L. (2000). *A guide to research for educators and trainers of adults* (2nd ed.). Krieger.

Metz, M. H. (2001). Intellectual border crossing in graduate education: A report from the field. *Educational Researcher*, *30*(5), 12–18.

Mills, J., Boner, A., & Francis, K. (2006). The development of constructivist grounded theory. *International Journal of Qualitative Methods*, *5*(1), 1–10.

Motitswe, J. M.C. (2025). Chapter 2: Navigating the selection and integration of theoretical frameworks as a lens for exploring social phenomena. In A. A. Midikana, *Enhancing research for academicians in higher education* (pp. 21–35). IGI Global.

National Center for Educational Statistics. (2025). *Achievement gaps*. Retrieved from https://nces.ed.gov/nationsreportcard/studies/gaps/#:~:text=Achievement%20gaps%20occur%20when%20one,than%20the%20margin%20of%20error.

Onwuegbuzie, A. J. (2002). Positivists, post-positivists, post-structuralists, and postmodernists: Why can't we all get along? Towards a framework for unifying research paradigms. *Education*, *122*(3), 518–30.

Onwuegbuzie, A. J. & Leech, N. L. (2005). Taking the "Q" out of research: Teaching research methodology courses without the divide between quantitative and qualitative paradigms. *Quality & Quantity: International Journal of Methodology*, *39*, 267–296.

Pallas, A. M. (2001). Preparing education doctoral students for epistemological diversity. *Educational Researcher*, *30*(5), 6–11.

Patton, M. Q. (2014). *Qualitative research and evaluation methods* (4th ed.). SAGE Publications.

Ravitch, S. M., & Riggan, M. (2017). *Reason & rigor: How conceptual frameworks guide research* (2nd ed.). SAGE Publications.

Rocco, T. & Plakhotnik, M. (2009). Literature reviews: Conceptual and theoretical frameworks. *Human Resource Development Review*, *8*(1), 120–30.

Strauss, A., & Corbin, J. (2015). *Basics of qualitative research: Techniques and procedures for developing grounded theory* (4th ed.). SAGE Publications.

Varpio, L., Paradis, E., Uijtdehaage, S. (2020). The distinctions between theory, theoretical framework, and conceptual framework. *Academic Medicine*, *95*(7), 989–994.

Vygotsky, L. S. (1978). *Mind in society: The development of higher psychological processes*. Harvard University Press.

Yin, R. K. (2018). *Case study research: Designs and methods* (6th ed.). SAGE Publications.

21 Writing Your Literature Review

Jill Alexa Perry, PhD

In academia, the terms *literature* or *extant literature* are often used. However, what do these terms really mean, particularly for students? This chapter examines the central role review of the literature plays in both professional doctorate studies and research doctorate studies. To illustrate the distinction, consider the case of Shonda.

Case Study

When Shonda entered graduate school, she noticed her PhD program faculty continuously referring to "the literature." They would ask in class, "What does the literature say about this?" The first thing that came to mind were pamphlets, the kind that you find at the doctor's office, or in a tourist center at a highway rest stop. "We have plenty of literature on how to manage X illness," she could hear a nurse saying. Shonda wondered what her program faculty were talking about. Her Introduction to Education Policy professor spoke about literature as if it were both a place ("go" search the literature) and an authority ("how is that defined?" by the literature).

As a PhD student, Shonda quickly learned she would have to write a dissertation that would contribute to the "extant literature" by filling in a gap with a topic that had not been researched. It was her first year and her head was spinning. She had no idea how to do that. She got up the nerve to ask a student who was a few years ahead of her what her faculty meant by literature and how she was going to contribute. She learned the literature referred to all that had been written about a specific topic within a specific discipline. Figuring she needed to get her head around this idea, she went to the library on campus to "look at" the literature and figure out what she could contribute. Shonda was overwhelmed. So many books had been written on education policy. The librarian told her she should also look online at the journal articles located in the numerous databases. She instantly felt hopeless, and imposter syndrome set in. Did she have to read all of this? How was she going to contribute to "the literature"? More importantly, how would any of this help her fix the problems she had left behind as a principal in Texas?

What the Research Says

Literature as a Tool

My goal with this chapter is twofold: (a) to guide doctoral students around the notion of literature and eliminate similar anxiety; and (b) to demonstrate how literature can serve you in your doctoral program and professional work no matter if you are in a research or professional practice doctorate. I do this by framing literature as a tool in the process of argument building (Booth et al., 2016). No matter what kind of doctorate they are pursuing, research will require that doctoral students build an argument for what they intend to study or address. First let's start with the definition of literature and what it is used for.

What Is Literature and How Do I Find It?

Literature refers to written works such as books, articles, and essays considered to have artistic or intellectual value. Broadly, literature encompasses a range of genres and forms, including fiction, poetry, drama, essays, and nonfiction. For doctoral study, you will work with literature that relates to your discipline or field of study. In this context, literature generally means the books, journal articles, and other dissertations written about the many topics, issues, and problems found in your discipline or field. Literature can also mean the writings produced by professional organizations.

In truth, the extant (i.e., existing) literature can be overwhelming, as Shonda found standing in the education policy section of her university library with thousands of books and journals in front of her. However, the literature does not have to be all-consuming. Rather, the extant literature can be viewed as a support or tool to help learn more about your topic. For Shonda, rather than feel intimidated and lead with fear and feelings of being overwhelmed, she should read with curiosity and a willingness to broaden her thinking; the literature is an opportunity. For you, recognize that literature is a large part of doctoral study and let yourself go down rabbit holes of learning. But do so with intention, guided by your topic, so you do not get too far off track.

Searching

How do we dive into the literature without getting lost? Firestone et al. (2020) found one of most important elements of teaching scholarly practitioners to use existing literature is to teach them the skills of how to search databases including learning about types of databases, how to conduct keyword searches, and learning to understand and assess different types of literature. The same is true for those studying to be research scientists. The key skills that Firestone et al. (2020) identified are:

- Searching for literature in online databases
- Reading literature in both simplified and detailed manners
- Assessing the validity of articles
- Understanding the contributions and limitations of research studies
- Comparing and contrasting study findings
- Organizing bibliographies of usable knowledge
- Synthesizing to frame the topic or problem
- Communicating their insights to other constituencies

These skills should be taught in your doctoral program and can often be learned as you gather, organize, and evaluate articles that you read.

With the search engine capabilities that exist today, you can start by searching your area of interest to see what comes up. Initial literature searches allow you to see what types of literature focus on your topic, how long the topic has been investigated, what theories have been developed around your topic, and what has been learned about the topic. As articles and books populate your search, look for the abstract that provides an overview of the piece. If the abstract relates and resonates, consider reading more. I tell my students to go from reading the abstract to reading the findings section to determine if the piece relates to your topic. If yes, then reading the full article could support your learning. I then tell my students to look at the literature review section and the bibliography to see who and what the authors cited to begin your path of discovery. It makes sense to use what others have done to guide your search. Plenty of online platforms (e.g., Mendeley, Zotero, Endnote, RefWorks, etc.) allow you to download articles or electronic books to keep these sources organized (both to create citations and references, and to develop summaries and note key take aways) so you can focus on your learning. Often your university will have these organization tools available to you for free.

Mintrop (2020) suggested the literature can help students develop a "robust knowledge base" for understanding and describing their topic or problem. He outlines a robust knowledge base as one that is:

- Based on established and widely accepted theories
- Based in a good number of strong empirical studies
- Condenses multiple empirical studies
- Differs in methods: both in-depth interpretations of qualitative data and generalizations through statistical analysis of quantitative data
- Provides solid reporting on practical applications of research (Mintrop, 2020, p. 82).

Building your knowledge base serves to help you understand your discipline or field and see what and how research has been done.

Another way to begin your search is to speak with a librarian. Many programs will invite the librarian into an introductory course to give an overview of the library systems and explain how to search literature. Beyond that introductory overview, you can reach out to the librarian to help you begin your search by providing them with your topic. Librarians are amazing sources of support and will often kick start your search for you. Do not be afraid to ask!

When searching in the literature, look for seminal work or theories that guide your field or discipline, even if they do not directly relate to your topic of interest. Typically, you will learn about these theories in your coursework as they are the foundation for your discipline or field. For example, if your field is *study abroad in higher education*, you might consider the guiding theories of cultural adaptation, transformative learning, and intercultural competence. These theories are grounded in years of research by their authors and likely used to ground most work in the discipline or field. Once you understand the key theories, look for other pieces that have been written with these theories as guides to learn how the theories are applied. If you are a scholar practitioner, you might also consider how these theories have played out in practice such as in pre-study abroad orientations or courses. As you move from theories to how theories are used in other writings, search by date to see what has been more recently written to have a newer perspective of how theories are being used. For example, social learning theory (Bandura, 1977) is an earlier iteration of Bandura's (1986) social cognitive theory. For a more in-depth discussion on the role of theory in research see Chapter 19.

Once you get into the literature, view it as key to your growth and learning, rather than as a place to become overwhelmed and anxiety ridden, as Shonda did. Generally, students enter doctoral programs to learn more about a question or issue that has bothered them, or to develop skills to fix problems they faced in practice. The literature can be a good tool for both. However, students also come with preexisting notions about their question, issue, or problem. Shonda, for example, arrived at her PhD program wanting to learn more about and research why educational spending was less in rural and poor school districts. She wanted to learn how to highlight how policies were disregarding local context. Ultimately, she wanted to be a professor who taught new or rising educational leaders the importance of policy in K–12 leadership. Shonda had lots of ideas and went into the literature looking to justify her thinking. In addition to being overwhelmed, she was frustrated that "the answer" was not right there in black and white.

Recognize that doctoral study is about growing and transforming into an expert; that is, an expert about a specific topic or an expert who can use literature to lead and change practice. Learning from others through critically reading existing literature is part of the process. Use your background and knowledge to question what authors are presenting and recognize that your current expertise, experience, and curiosity count in this process. Pay attention to how your professors ask questions like, "what does the literature say? Or what is the author's argument?" These questions are meant to teach you to read literature critically. If you get stuck, ask for help or guidance from your faculty, librarian, or other students. What Shonda eventually learned as she talked to her professors, librarians, and peers, was that she entered the doctoral program because she wanted to learn, not because she already knew everything. She settled into the idea that she is a learner, and her previous experience could contribute to that learning experience.

Search Strategies

Learning from the literature should not be a blind endeavor, however. Have a strategy or plan when you read the literature. Once you have found some literature to read, how will you determine if what you find is what you need to be reading? I have told my students to keep their topic written in a notebook and use it as a guide to build "piles" (electronic folders or literal piles, your preference) of literature as they read abstracts and findings—a) definitely read, b) maybe read, and c) not relevant. Spend time getting to know the organization software you will use and all that it can do in terms of helping you cite and summarize each piece. You will never regret taking time to learn your organization software! Take the time to input the details for each citation. Have the program open as you read so you can summarize key points, document quotes you might use and ask questions that might push your thinking (and your literature searches) forward.

You might also consider conducting an annotated bibliography which is another way to systematize your thinking about literature sources. An annotated bibliography includes a summary and an evaluation of each piece of literature you read, provides a comprehensive overview of the research on a particular topic you are investigating, helps you keep your information organized, and demonstrates any relevance the source may have in the broader discipline or field. Table 21.1 below offers an outline for conducting an annotated bibliography.

Table 21.1 *Sample annotated bibliography form*

APA Citation
Purpose (as stated in the work)
Theoretical framework
Conceptual framework
Methods used
Sample and population
Results
Strengths/limitations & suggestions for future research
Relevance to your area of Interest
Notes and quotes (include the page #!)

By treating the literature as an opportunity to learn, you build the knowledge and skills needed to articulate and support your own arguments around the topic. Additionally, as you read, you learn how others in your field write. Pay attention to how articles are formatted, how topics are grounded in other literature, the theories that guide the research, how findings are presented, how abstracts are written, and how reference lists are written. The literature can be a support tool for understanding how to emulate these skills as you become a research scientist or scholarly practitioner.

What Is Literature Used For?

Literature is the foundation for learning in your discipline or field and has many uses. My master's advisor used to say, "Grad students read." That is, your job during your coursework is to read literature to learn about the founding theories, key authors, and existing knowledge in your discipline or field. Additionally, literature can expose you to different research methods and how they are used in different studies, providing context and examples to demystify the research process. Reading will generate your own thinking which will ultimately lead you on your own quest in the literature. This early reading will expand your scope and expose you to new ideas. This immersive process is important to becoming a doctorate holder as it provides the foundation for how to use the literature as a tool for the next time you want to investigate something. You will learn during this early reading that the literature can provide answers and guide you when you are not sure where to take your own work. A professor in my doctoral program was famous for saying, "When you don't know, are unsure, or you feel stuck in your own work, go back to the literature." That is, rather than panic or flounder, go read some more to broaden your thinking and get new ideas flowing. Personally, I have found this advice to be pertinent as much in my personal life as much as my academic work! Knowledge holds the key to helping you move forward.

Strategies for Success

When most people talk about literature in doctoral programs, they think of the dreaded literature review that comes with the dissertation process. Much has been written across disciplines about the role of the literature review in the dissertation process and how to go about creating a literature review (Boote & Biele, 2005; Denney & Tewksbury, 2013). I do not want to reiterate this very sage advice for which I will offer references to review below, but rather hope to help you understand how doing a literature review can serve you as a tool in your research scientist or scholarly practitioner program. To do this, I provide an example of the purpose of the literature review in a PhD in education dissertation and in an education doctorate (EdD) dissertation.

Comparison of Dissertation Literature Reviews

The PhD in education is a research doctorate that culminates with a traditional five-chapter dissertation of which Chapter 2, the literature review, is an important part and is often 75 or more pages. Those who seek a PhD in education typically aim to become a research scientist in education or tenured faculty in a university. PhD student dissertations are usually an original study that demonstrates their understanding of the discipline (i.e., theories, key authors, existing studies) and contributes new knowledge, thereby filling a "gap" in the existing literature.

The EdD, on the other hand, is the professional degree in education which prepares working professional practitioners to use research and inquiry to change educational practice, ameliorate persistent problems in practice, and to lead educational organizations. Those who seek an EdD plan to stay in practice and view the doctorate as a means to learn how to "transform their field" (CGS, 2007, p. 8) through the application of theory and research. The EdD dissertation can take many formats but generally aims to learn about and improve a complex educational problem as it is playing out in the work setting. EdD student dissertations are much more applied and localized, teaching the student how to address problems found in practice with the same research tools that PhD students use. Such dissertations are increasingly known as a dissertation in practice (DiP), or a "scholarly endeavor that impacts a complex problem of practice" as defined by the Carnegie Project on the Education Doctorate (CPED).

In both these dissertation types, each student will use the existing literature, but in different ways. Table 21.2 below (from Perry et al., 2020, p. 73) demonstrates the ways in which these two distinct doctorates use research as a tool in their dissertations.

Table 21.2 *Comparing the Use of Literature in PhD and EdD Dissertations*

PhD Use of Literature	EdD Use of Literature
Set context of research study	Problem identification and rationalization
Situate in scholarly/historical contexts	Situate problem in broader context
Report on existing claims	Identify root causes of problem
Examine research methods	Develop conceptual framework/theory of improvement
Identify a gap in knowledge	Build arguments for improvement
Demonstrate student understanding	Identify what field doesn't know
Frame researcher lens	Frame study of intervention or investigation
Justify research methodology	Serve as analytic starting point

You will see in this table the literature serves different roles for each type of dissertation. Neither is better than the other; rather they serve the goal of the type of student and their career path. For example, Shonda, a PhD student, needs to have a solid grasp of the existing literature in education policy and the claims this literature makes. Her dissertation literature review will demonstrate to her dissertation committee that she has read broadly and is able to stake her work in the existing work in educational policy. Shonda will use the literature to create the context or background for the study she will pursue and demonstrate where her work will add to and potentially fill a "gap" in what has been studied already. In other words, she will demonstrate the empirical significance of her proposed research.

Further, Shonda will use the literature to explain her viewpoints and how she sees the issue she wants to study, establishing herself as part of the research process. She will use the literature to demonstrate credibility for the method (quantitative, qualitative, or mixed-methods) she will choose for her study by discussing what others have done and why her choice is a good fit for her work. All these uses serve the dissertation process. However, in the long term, these uses are preparing Shonda with the skills and knowledge she needs to become a research scientist. That is, the literature review is both a process as well as a final product. Many PhD candidates have the goal of earning a tenure track position in a university where they are expected to continue to do research and publish their work (i.e., establish a research agenda). The dissertation launches this career path by (a) giving them an avenue to generate their first several publishable articles (an expectation for tenured faculty), and (b) establishing a research agenda which will grow as they continue to investigate their research topic and related topics. Shonda will leave her PhD program prepared for the role of assistant professor in educational policy having a firm grasp of the discipline's body of knowledge and having contributed to it.

In contrast, the EdD student is not necessarily going to become an expert on an issue but rather will become a *scholarly practitioner* who knows how to use research and inquiry as a means to address complex problems of practice repeatedly. Their dissertation serves as the *cadaver* (Perry, 2023) upon which they will practice how to combine their professional expertise with scholarly knowledge to name, frame, and improve any problem they encounter. Further, the scholar-practitioner's dissertation work will prepare them to become transformational leaders through the process of applying research to practice. In this sense, the EdD dissertation candidate uses literature as a tool for grounding and expanding their thinking about a localized problem that has been studied more broadly in the literature. Many practitioners come with years of experience, and professional knowledge helps shape the way they think about specific problems. The literature can serve as an opportunity for students to go beyond their own understanding and learn more deeply about the problem so they can think about how they might address it locally. They may use the literature to learn about interventions that have been implemented on a broader scale and consider if those interventions might work more locally. They may use the literature to understand reasons why the problem happens in other contexts. They may also use the literature to develop a conceptual framework or theory of change for how they want to address the problem on a more local level. They do not need to look for gaps or read exhaustively. Rather the literature is a tool for defining and contextualizing their problem and can be used repeatedly as new problems arise in their practice.

Literature is a central component to doctoral study. As you can see above it serves many purposes. However, no matter what kind of program you are in, the literature is a tool at your service for learning, defining, contextualizing, framing, and for building arguments around your own research. In the next section, I explain how to use research in the argument building process.

Argument Building

In 1995, the trio of Booth, Columb, and Williams produced a book called *The Craft of Research*. Geared toward undergraduates, the book is a must read for all doctoral students (check out the 2016 edition). This seminal text provides a clear and understandable overview of the research process, how to write to specific audiences, how to use literature, and how to make research claims and back them with evidence. This last part is where I find opportunity for doctoral students and their literature reviews. Let's look at how to map an argument.

According to Booth et al. (2016), an argument has four parts: (a) *a claim*, (b) *a reason for making the claim*, (c) *evidence to support that claim*, and (d) *an underlying warrant* that ensures the reasons and evidence are logical in connection to the claims. Figure 21.1 below is a map of an argument.

First, a *claim* is your main point. A statement you have made about the topic or the problem you are investigating. You have made that claim because you have been given *reason* either by what you have read, seen, or experienced. You can ground that claim and your reasons in *evidence* from data, experience, or literature. In connecting your reasons and evidence to your claim, you are sure that each reason and each piece of evidence is *warranted* for your claim. That is, you provide a clear connection between your reasons and evidence and the claim you are making. For example, I offer the following argument:

> *When America feels threatened by a particular minoritized group, the government seeks to get rid of them (CLAIM). The United States (US) government has done it before (REASON). For example, during World War II, the US government incarcerated eleven thousand to twelve thousand Americans with Japanese heritage (EVIDENCE). Therefore, there is reason to believe they might do it again (WARRANT).*

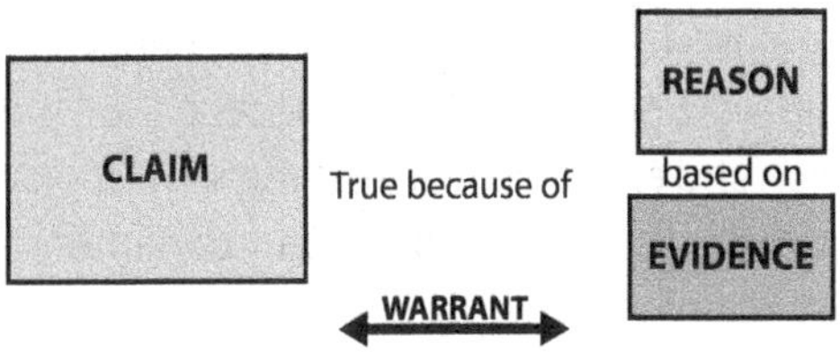

Figure 21.1 Mapping Your Argument

Though it is true that reasons and evidence can be twisted to support a claim, the warrant is the piece that brings logic into the equation. One should ask, when reading or writing an argument, "Do the reasons and evidence logically support the claim?"

Argument building might look different in a research scientist dissertation than in a scholarly practitioner dissertation. Research scientists build arguments for the need to study a particular phenomenon. They gather data to establish that a phenomenon is happening and the impacts of that phenomenon. A scholar practitioner makes a claim about a problem they see playing out in their professional area and work to persuade others that the problem exists and needs to be addressed. Either way, the doctoral student is making a case for their work through building arguments.

An important aspect of building an argument is considering your audience (Booth et al., 2016). An argument is meant to convince or persuade someone that something is true. Defining for whom you are writing is first and foremost. A research scientist writes for their doctoral committee and others in their discipline who are interested in learning more about the phenomenon they are studying. Building an argument as a research scientist requires you to know the language, the theories, the work done in your discipline. In terms of the dissertation, I have mentioned the research scientist is looking to fill a gap and thereby adding to the literature. An important part of your argument will be to see what arguments have already been made in the literature. You can use these arguments and the evidence from other studies to support your claim about what you are studying. Additionally, you will need to consider the opposing viewpoints that are counterarguments in your discipline to ensure your claims are warranted.

For a scholar practitioner dissertation, the claim is made to persuade the reader that a problem exists and needs to be addressed. The audience will be the doctoral committee as well as those practitioners who will learn from what the scholar practitioner seeks to address with their study. The audience might also include stakeholders, or those who are impacted by or generating the problem. In this kind, or dissertation in practice (DiP) the literature serves as a source of reason and evidence whereby the scholar practitioner grounds their claims beyond what they are seeing locally to demonstrate the problem exists within the specific field in many contexts.

Building your argument is an important part of your dissertation experience. Using the literature to support your work is crucial. Moving beyond the dissertation, you will have learned the necessary skills to use literature as a form of evidence in building arguments either in academic writing as a professor or in improving problems of practice as a practitioner.

Conclusion

When approaching your literature review, remember the opportunities you have to (a) broaden your thinking, (b) gather evidence, and (c) build your own arguments. Consider the resources available to support you in your literature search—your university librarian, literature organization programs (which most libraries offer to students for free), dissertations from those who graduated from your program, and any handbooks or directions of what is expected. Use these as you prepare and get started. The literature review experience can not only be a good one but also a process for learning the skills of critically consuming and evaluating literature, developing deeper understanding and considering evidence. Each of these skills will serve you and your doctorate no matter what kind of doctorate or career path.

Questions for Reflection

- How am I feeling about the literature in my field?
- What program materials exist to support me in my literature search?
- Have I reached out to my librarian to ask about literature searches?
- What key search terms will I use, and how will I systematically track the databases searched?
- How will I take and organize my notes from the literature I review?
- How will I build and organize the literature to support my argument and establish the significance of my proposed research through my construction of Chapter 2?

Recommended Resources

Boote, D. N., & Beile, P. (2005). Scholars before researchers: On the centrality of the dissertation literature review in research preparation. *Educational Researcher, 34*(6), 3–15. https://doi.org/10.3102/0013189X034006003

Booth, W. C., Colomb, G. G., & Williams, J. M. (2016). *The craft of research*. University of Chicago Press.

Denney, A. S., & Tewksbury, R. (2013). How to write a literature review. *Journal of Criminal Justice Education, 24*(2), 218–234.

Doucet, F. (2019). *Centering the margins: (Re)defining useful research evidence through critical perspectives.* William T. Grant Foundation.

Perry, J. A., Zambo, D., & Crow, R. (2020). *The improvement science dissertation in practice: Guide for faculty, committee members, and their students.* Myers Education Press.

References

Bandura, A. (1977). *Social learning theory.* Prentice Hall.

Bandura, A. (1986). *Social foundations of thought and action: A social cognitive theory.* Prentice-Hall, Inc.

Boote, D. N., & Beile, P. (2005). Scholars before researchers: On the centrality of the dissertation literature review in research preparation. *Educational Researcher, 34*(6), 3–15. https://doi.org/10.3102/0013189X034006003

Booth, W. C., Colomb, G. G., & Williams, J. M. (2016). *The craft of research.* University of Chicago Press.

Council of Graduate Schools (2007). *CGS taskforce report on the professional doctorate.* Council of Graduate Schools:.

Denney, A. S., & Tewksbury, R. (2013). How to write a literature review. *Journal of Criminal Justice Education, 24*(2), 218–234.

Firestone, W., Perry, J. A., & Leland, A. (2020). Teaching research evidence use through the education doctorate. *Planning and Changing, 49*(3/4), 135–149.

Mintrop, R. (2020). *Design-based school improvement: A practical guide for education leaders.* Harvard Education Press.

Perry, J. A. (2023). *Reclaiming the education doctorate: A guidebook for (re) designing EdD programs.* Stylus Publishing, LLC.

Perry, J. A., Zambo, D., & Crow, R. (2020). *The improvement science dissertation in practice: A guide for faculty, committee members, and their students.* Myers Education Press.

22 Understanding the IRB Process

Fernando Garzon, PsyD
Daniel Hitchcock, PhD
Jessica McCleese, PsyD

Ethical principles are critical in the development of a dissertation that has people as research participants. This chapter highlights how correct application of these principles can reduce problems and unnecessary delays when doctoral students seek institutional review board (IRB) approval of their research studies and dissertation research.

Case Study

Juanita is elated; she just passed her proposal defense. As she begins talking with Dr. Smith about implementing her study, he reminds her of the Institutional Review Board (IRB) process she learned about last year.

"Remember, you'll need to consider the ethical aspects of your study and get IRB approval first," he states.

"You mean the Institutional Review Board? Sure, I remember. But certainly, that will not be an issue since my committee has approved my proposal. Doesn't that mean that my committee feels like I've thought through this process enough?"

"Not exactly," Dr. Smith replies.

"Your committee is supportive of the research that you want to do and can see the value in your dissertation; however, the IRB will take a much closer look at your actual proposed method to make sure there are no potential ethical concerns. Let me give you some examples to help you understand. The following situations all involve unethical research practices. For example, John gave a survey to elementary school teachers at his school to find out how they felt about the level of support they received from school administration. The principal saw some unflattering survey results lying on John's desk, and three teachers with the most negative views 'mysteriously' did not have their contracts renewed the next year."

"That's an obvious blunder. You shouldn't leave your data lying around," Juanita observed.

"Yes, but sometimes ethical violations are more subtle. Mark conducted excellent interviews with recent adolescent male Latino immigrants about their challenges in adjusting to the United States, but he hadn't anticipated a few of them becoming emotionally distressed as they described their experiences. Some even had flashbacks of traumatic experiences. He had no plan in place (like a referral to a mental health professional) to get additional help if something like this occurred. He didn't know how to help them himself, so it was a mess."

"Yikes!" Juanita moaned.

"Susan was surveying tenth graders to find out how the quality of their relationship with their parents impacted career goals. She was shocked when she got several angry calls from parents who complained about not being informed of her study and not giving permission for their children to participate. Do you see what the problem was?"

"Well, sort of. The parents should have known about the research, right?"

"Yes. When minors are involved in research, parents need to know and provide consent under most circumstances. That's a United States federal regulation. You see, the IRB focuses on research ethics in projects like yours that involve human subjects. They help you identify areas that you might inadvertently miss that could produce big ethical problems later. They ask you to think through the safeguards needed in your methodology to protect your participants."

"Okay, that makes more sense. What are the key ethical principles I need to keep in mind and where do I start?" Juanita asked.

What the Research Says

Institutional Review Boards (IRB), also sometimes called human subject review boards, are federally mandated and regulated entities that ensure the rights and welfare of people participating in any research study. As discussed below, IRBs are guided by a set of ethical principles and play an integral role in institutions with faculty and students conducting research with human subjects. Although beyond the scope of this chapter, a similar review process is federally mandated for research involving animals, conducted by an Institutional Animal Care and Use Committee (IACUC). For more information about the oversight of animal research see the guide published by the National Research Council (Albus, 2012).

Key Ethical Principles

The ethical principles that currently guide research involving human subjects were established in response to tragic human experiments. The Nuremberg trials after World War II revealed horrendous studies the Nazis had conducted on people. Even in the United States, we have seen harmful investigations. For example, the Tuskegee Study of Untreated Syphilis in the Negro Male was sponsored by the US Public Health Services over a 40-year-period (1932–1972). This study denied medical treatment (including antibiotic cures) to 399 African Americans in order to "study" the course of the disease. Over one hundred patients died during the study.

Public outrage led Congress to establish a commission to develop basic ethical principles to guide future research with human subjects. As a result, in 1979, the commission released the Belmont Report (National Institutes of Health, 1979). The Belmont Report codified into federal law three basic ethical principles—*respect for persons, beneficence*, and *justice*—which provide the foundation for the functioning of IRBs. The American Education Research Association has also adopted these principles.

The first principle involves *respect for persons* who are involved in research studies. Individuals must be free to make their own decisions, without coercion, about whether they wish to participate in a study, and they must be provided with sufficient information about the study to make a reasonable decision. Those with limited autonomy (e.g., children and people with limited mental capacity) must have extra protections to ensure their rights and safety are maintained.

The second principle focuses on *beneficence* or "do no harm." Research must minimize potential harm to participants and maximize possible benefits. This principle directly relates to how the study is designed, the level of training the researchers possess, and the plan they have in place to address potential risks and problems that could arise for participants during the course of the study.

The third principle examines *justice*. People are equal and should be treated fairly. Experiments should not take advantage of one participant population in the study to have all the benefits of the research given to another population. For example, a breakthrough in instructional techniques for students with problems in math should not be developed on students in poor school districts and then given only to students in wealthy school districts after empirical support is gathered. Vulnerable populations must not be exploited. The burdens and benefits of research studies should be shared equitably.

Institutional Review Boards

Conceptually, IRBs help researchers apply the Belmont ethical principles to their studies. All universities in the United States that have students or faculty conducting federally funded experiments with human subjects must have an IRB. Two Department of Health and Human Services subdivisions (the Office of Human Research Protection and the Food and Drug Administration) are the agencies that regulate the IRB.

IRBs have significant power. They may approve a study, disapprove it, or modify its design to protect participants. They may also observe any aspect of the study's actual implementation, conduct continuing reviews of the study on at least an annual basis, and suspend or terminate a study at any time if the risks to the participants outweigh the benefits (Renteln, 2022). Students, such as Juanita who are working on dissertations or other doctoral research projects that involve people as participants, must submit their research proposal to the IRB for approval before recruiting or collecting data from any participants.

Even when the student is doing action research, a continuous improvement project (CI), or a program evaluation project, submission is normally needed. Sometimes the IRB committee is less familiar with these applied methodologies which can be in a gray area that sometimes qualifies for review and sometimes does not (Hinnant-Crawford et al., 2024). A key IRB review criterion relates to if the study is human subjects research intended to produce generalizable knowledge (Mertens, 2023). Action research, program evaluation, and CI projects are typically focused on inclusive, collaborative efforts aimed at organizational improvement, rather than collecting data to research individuals. The intent is also not to produce generalizable knowledge but rather to result in organizational benefit (Hinnant-Crawford et al., 2024). Consequently, many of these projects do not need IRB review; however, the IRB must make this determination. Current IRB regulations may make the review process for these projects challenging and some have advocated for updates in IRB ethical guidelines to better promote inclusivity, collaborative inquiry, and justice inherent in CI-related research (Hinnant-Crawford et al., 2024).

Severe consequences exist for students who try to by-pass the IRB process. These consequences might include dismissing offending students from their academic programs or canceling their study. At a minimum, in all US universities, doctoral students will not be allowed to use any data in their research that was collected without IRB approval. Depending on the proposed research, a violation of IRB could result in some students starting their dissertation completely over from square one if the data is of the nature that it cannot be collected a second time.

In general, the IRB consists of a committee of at least five persons from differing professions. These individuals serve as reviewers for the research projects. The IRB has three levels of review, depending upon the research design, type of human subjects involved, and the risk level involved in the experiment. Many research projects fall into the two lower levels (*exempt* and *expedited*) rather than the highest level of scrutiny (*full review*).

The term *exempt* does not imply that the doctoral student can skip the IRB application process and review. Rather, the IRB alone determines each project's official status. Projects the IRB may categorize as exempt after the review include research involving normal educational practices that occur in typical educational settings; anonymous surveys, and interviews when these involve nonsensitive subjects; some anonymous cognitive, aptitude, and achievement testing; certain observation studies of public behavior; and some de-identified archival research. Studies classified as *expedited* include recorded interview studies (e.g., video, audio, photographic) and studies examining group characteristics (e.g., perception, cognition, communication, cultural beliefs). Certain medical studies may also be categorized as expedited.

All exempt and expedited projects are deemed to have minimal risk, meaning that the IRB views the stress involved in the studies as no more than would be experienced in daily life or routine medical or psychological examinations. *Full review* projects do not fall into the exempt and expedited categories and often involve higher than minimal risk for participants. A study's specific focus on vulnerable populations (such as children, prisoners, cognitively challenged, and groups with limited economic resources) also influences how the IRB categorizes and reviews a research project.

The review time involved for exempt and expedited reviews is typically shorter than that for a full review, though the time still may be substantial. In all situations, doctoral students must plan in their research timeline sufficient time for the IRB review. The review time will vary depending on the university and the varying responsibilities of the individuals serving on the committee. Additionally, some IRBs may send questions to the research applicant and/or request revisions be addressed prior to providing approval. The timeliness of responses to IRB questions and revision requests are a critical aspect of how long the entire review process takes. Talking with your dissertation committee, other faculty, and the IRB ahead of time can provide a general idea of a potential timeline.

Sometimes an IRB will have two different applications (one for exempt and expedited projects) and another more detailed application for more complex studies that require full review. In those cases, to help students decide which application to use, the university's IRB website will often have decision trees or other helpful guidelines. In other cases, the IRB will have just one application for all three levels of review, so the distinction is less important.

To help researchers and students understand the rationale and process of the review, most IRBs require anyone who wishes to submit an application to first complete a training program called Collaborative Institutional Training Initiative (CITI). This training usually involves several hours of learning about research ethics and IRB procedures, and then passing one or more quizzes about the details.

The IRB Application Review Process

IRB applications are very detailed and reflect the Belmont ethical principles previously discussed. This section describes general components IRBs consider in applications. For more specific information, university IRB websites and federal regulations such as 45 CFR 46 and subpart A, also known as the *Common Rule*, should be reviewed. The main task of the IRB is to review the application for its compliance regarding human ethics. Keep in mind, however, that the IRB is not reviewing the research content, research methods, or design, unless these have any direct bearing on ethical issues and human subjects' participation.

Project Description

IRB applications require the principal investigator (e.g., the doctoral student) to provide a complete description of the proposed research project. The description should be written in nonspecific discipline language so reviewers from different disciplines can easily understand the study. Detailed information is required about who the participants will be, how they will be recruited, how the security, privacy, and confidentiality of their data will be protected, a thorough analysis of the potential risks and benefits of the study, and what the informed consent process will look like during the research investigation. The application must be completed correctly with appropriate grammar and spelling. Failure to complete the application or adhere to the use of correct grammar and spelling may result in the application being returned and not reviewed. Additionally, at the time of this writing, emerging technologies such as artificial intelligence are beginning to impact the IRB application process. Consult with your IRB personnel or website for any guidance on the usage of these technologies.

Informed Consent

Informed consent involves presenting information to research participants about the study's purpose, procedures, risks, benefits, and the participant's rights. These aspects must be presented in a manner readily understandable for the person's cultural background, language, and educational background. Many university IRB websites have templates to assist in the creation of this document. In most exempt or expedited studies in which participants are anonymous, this information is given to participants for them to keep without the researcher retaining a signed consent copy (with IRB permission). Other studies require the researcher to retain a signed informed consent document.

IRBs also have special rules for *deception-based studies* where revealing the purpose of the study in the informed consent could ruin the investigation. Most IRB websites describe these rules. Research involving children or populations with limited mental capacity generally includes guardian informed consent and *child assent*. An assent provides information found in the informed consent but is provided in a manner that is consistent with the individuals' developmental level and mental capacities. Exceptions to the general requirement for parental consent do exist in some types of research on children. For example, educational studies that focus on teaching strategies and curricular development do not need parental consent if the research involves minimal risk to the children.

If doctoral students conduct their research in schools, businesses, religious organizations, government entities, and other readily identifiable organizations, outside of the university, they need to gain permission to conduct their research at the location and may need to supply the IRB with documentation showing that the organizations give permission for the study to be conducted. However, in some cases of research conducted in PK-12 schools, the student may have to apply for IRB at the research location. If the study includes multiple research sites, the students normally need only to secure IRB approval from their sponsoring university and to provide documentation of the approval to any research site IRBs. These other sites have the right to request a full application to their site if they so desire.

The IRB committee also examines the application to determine whether adult or child participants for the research study might be unduly coerced into participating. Consider, for example, how schools will sometimes provide parents the opportunity to "opt out" of participation in research and failure to opt out infers consent. This scenario means some children might participate in the research even though the parent may not actually want their child to be research participants. Employers, teachers, managers, or administrators who seek participants from their organizations must be careful about this aspect.

Further, in any research project, students must include appropriate safeguards to assure potential participants have genuine freedom of choice. This assurance is especially true when incentives or tokens of appreciation are used to enhance recruitment. The IRB carefully reviews such strategies (Largent et al., 2017). Sample questions the IRB will consider include the following:

- Is this a vulnerable population more at risk of manipulation or coercion?
- If volunteers get a reward at work or extra credit in a class for participating in the study, do they have other options to get a reward or extra credit if they choose not to participate?
- Do these other options involve approximately equal time and effort?
- Is the monetary value of any incentive or token of appreciation reasonable and not excessive?
- Are there "unstated but implied" consequences for failing to participate?

Finally, the potential benefits of being in the study (for the participant or society as a whole) are weighed against the potential risks. A sense of justice and fairness in the risks and how the benefits of the study will be shared must be clearly articulated.

Data Protection

For those who choose to participate in the study, the committee will consider how their research data is safeguarded to protect privacy and confidentiality. Safeguards are essential. These might include the way in which data is deidentified such as the use of pseudonyms. The physical storage of data is also considered. Password protection of electronic data files, locked storage of paper surveys, how potentially identifiable individual information is coded, and other strategies are crucial.

Strategies for Success

The following strategies can help you apply what is presented in this chapter to your research study to be successful when planning for and submitting an IRB application for doctoral research.

Strategy 1: Apply Ethical Principles

The key ethical principles described in the Belmont Report are critical for understanding how the IRB review process relates to any research study that involves people. It is important for the doctoral candidate to consider carefully how the Belmont ethical principles apply to the specific design of the study. By doing this, students can avoid the unethical practices like those Juanita's chair outlined in the case study and ensure that the study is ethical.

Strategy 2: Review the IRB Website to Learn the Process and Any Training Requirements

While IRB rules and regulations are the same everywhere, each university has its own set of guidelines for submitting an application and materials to the IRB. The doctoral candidate must know and fulfill any training requirements prior to submitting an application. Generally, the doctoral candidate will find the specific application process at the university's IRB website. Contact the IRB with any questions.

Strategy 3: Always Submit the Project for IRB Review and Plan Sufficient Time for the IRB Review and Approval Process

Doctoral candidates should never try to "bypass" the IRB even when they think a project involving people does not qualify as human subjects research (e.g., action research, CI, or program evaluation research). Severe penalties, such as dismissal from the degree program, exist at all universities. At a minimum, collected data without IRB approval must be discarded and cannot be used in the dissertation. Doctoral candidates should reach out to their IRB to determine if they should submit an application as the IRB is the sole body that can determine if a project needs to be reviewed or not. Additionally, doctoral candidates should remember the IRB process can be lengthy (e.g., several months). Planning sufficient time for the IRB review will alleviate stress and help to plan your work. Talking with the dissertation committee, other university faculty, and the IRB to get an idea of the potential timeline is helpful in the planning process.

Strategy 4: If Doing Applied Research, Discuss with Your Dissertation Chair the IRB's Familiarity with These Types of Projects

IRBs can be less knowledgeable about these types of projects, though this is increasingly changing. They may mistakenly classify them as human subjects research and create significant methodological difficulties with the study's implementation. Having a conversation with your dissertation chair and the IRB chair may be beneficial in assessing the IRB committee's familiarity with how to evaluate whether your project qualifies as human subjects research. Sometimes, education on these types of strategies may be appropriate for the IRB committee before submitting the project for review. Consider sharing Hinnant-Crawford et al. (2024) with your IRB.

Strategy 5: When in Doubt, Ask the IRB

When a question arises, doctoral candidates should ask the IRB. For example, Juanita's planned research involves archival data from children within a school system. She is unsure if she will need to gain parental consent and child assent. Her chair advises her to email the IRB to determine the answer to her question. The chair should be included in all correspondence with the IRB. In fact, some IRBs designate the candidate's chair as the principal investigator for the research they are supervising.

Strategy 6: Gain Organizational Approvals When Needed

Doctoral candidates need to begin working on obtaining any needed organization permissions while they are engaged in the IRB application process. Doing so will support the candidates in knowing whether the organization requires IRB approval before or after it will give approval for gathering data in their space.

In the case study, when Juanita seeks permission from the school system she has selected to serve as a research site, she finds out that the school district has a research ethics board of their own. A representative from the district tells Juanita that she will need to provide documentation of her university's IRB approval. Her chair informs her this request is not uncommon, and in some cases, either the IRB or the study site needs to be willing to provide conditional approval pending the approval of the other entity.

Questions for Reflection

The following questions may be useful in considering how to apply the Belmont ethical principles to your IRB application.

- How do the research methods convey respect for the persons involved in the study?
  - Is the need for participants to have information about the study (the informed consent/assent process) adequately addressed?
  - Is it clear that there is no sense of coercion in the study?
- In what ways does the study reflect beneficence (limiting potential risks while maximizing potential benefits to participants and society)?
  - Are sufficient safeguards for securing and protecting the data collected from participants present?
  - Are the risks sufficiently considered and is there a clear plan should a "worst-case scenario" occur?
  - Are there ways the study can help the participants in the future?
- Does the study reflect justice (treating people equally and fairly)?
- Are any incentives used in the study inappropriate?
  - Is there an "unstated but implied" consequence for not participating? For example, if participation in your study gains you extra credit on a research paper, is there an alternative assignment (that takes approximately the same amount of time as participation) that will earn the same extra credit?
- What is the average review/approval time at the university's IRB and is sufficient time included in the research timeline for this process?

Recommended Resources

Office of Human Research Protection website.

Your university's IRB website.

Amdur, R., & Bankert, E. (2022). *Institutional review board: Member handbook*. Jones and Bartlett Learning.

Hinnant-Crawford, B., Bonney, E. N., Perry, J. A., Bozack, A. R., Peterson, D. S., Crow, R., & Carlile, S. (2024). Continuous improvement, institutional review boards, and resistance to practitioner scholarship. *Educational Researcher*, *53*(1), 46–53. https://doi.org/10.3102/0013189X231208413

References

Albus, U. (2012). Guide for the care and use of laboratory animals (8th ed.). *Laboratory Animals*, *46(3)*, 267–268. https://doi.org/10.1258/la.2012.150312

Hinnant-Crawford, B., Bonney, E. N., Perry, J. A., Bozack, A. R., Peterson, D. S., Crow, R., & Carlile, S. (2024). Continuous improvement, institutional review boards, and resistance to practitioner scholarship. *Educational Researcher*, *53*(1), 46–53. https://doi.org/10.3102/0013189X231208413

Largent, E. A., Joffe, S., & Lynch, H. F. (2017). Paying research participants: Regulatory uncertainty, conceptual confusion, and a path forward. *Yale Journal of Health Policy, Law, and Ethics*, *17*(1), 61–141. https://www.ncbi.nlm.nih.gov/pmc/articles/PMC5728432/

Mertens, D. M. (2023). *Research and program evaluation in education and psychology: Integrating diversity with quantitative, qualitative, and mixed methods* (6th ed.). SAGE Publications.

National Institutes of Health. (1979). *The Belmont report: Ethical principles and guidelines for the protection of human subjects of research*. US Government Printing Office.

Renteln, A.D. (2022). Impact and influence of the institutional review board: Protecting the rights of human subjects in scientific experiments. In L. J. Jussim, J. A. Krosnick, & S. T. Stevens (Eds.), *Research integrity: Best practices for the social and behavioral sciences* (pp. 370–395). Oxford University Press. https://doi.org/10.1093/oso/9780190938550.003.0015

Part 5
The Completion Stage

23 Publishing and Presenting

Michael L. Jones, PhD

Many individuals are motivated to earn a doctoral degree as it is the general prerequisite for a career in academia. Most institutions of higher learning look for candidates who have already established a record of scholarly productivity in their field, or at a minimum, show potential for developing a scholarly research and writing agenda. This chapter highlights the importance of scholarly contribution to the discipline and provides strategies for individuals seeking to become published. The chapter ends with a brief discussion on the use of Generative AI in writing and publishing.

Case Study

Ashley is a good student in a PhD program at a top-ranked university. As Ashley nears the completion of her coursework, she begins reviewing job postings for tenure-track faculty positions at universities to determine what qualifications potential employers will seek when she enters the job market. She quickly notices a common theme accompanying preferred qualifications: an established or very promising record of scholarly contributions to the discipline.

Ashley has already demonstrated high academic performance and has some experience teaching undergraduate courses at her university. However, having not yet submitted a manuscript for publication, much less being published, Ashley determines that help is needed and consults her dissertation chair for advisement on how she should embark on a path that will ensure that she stands a competitive chance at being hired for a tenure-track faculty position in higher education upon completing her degree.

Ashley has begun to realize that such a position will require not only outstanding academic performance but also scholarly productivity. The crucial question for Ashley is, "What is the best way for me to begin to publish articles in reputable journals and maximize my career opportunities upon completing my doctorate?"

What the Research Says

The adage "publish or perish" is as important in academia today as ever. The expectation is not only for tenure-track faculty, however. According to Rawat and Meena (2014), publishing prior to graduation is a growing expectation for doctoral students seeking careers in academia. Early scholarly productivity for doctoral students is positively associated with initial postgraduation career placement as well as a stronger publication record later in their career.

Writing and publishing peer-reviewed articles during the doctoral journey demonstrates to the field, and the prospective employer, three things: (a) students who have published have demonstrated the ability to write at a standard expected by one's discipline, (b) the work of students who are well published is generally highly regarded within its discipline, and (c) the propensity to maintain a scholarly agenda based on the principle that past actions predict future behavior, for "students who publish during their studies are more probable to publish after they graduate".

The publication of peer-reviewed journal articles, independent of or from the dissertation itself, is an essential step to complete, and complete well, before the doctoral student can migrate into the academic workplace.

The advantages of publishing extend beyond securing an academic position. A manuscript submitted to a quality journal will likely receive useful critique that, regardless of the manuscript's acceptance, will enable refinement of the original work and will be useful in increasing scholarly research and writing skills. Further, collaborating with faculty on research throughout the journey and publishing the dissertation manuscript as a peer-reviewed article may result in constructive feedback, training in research, and refinement of skills. This collaboration may also lead to close and enduring research relationships with faculty.

Doctoral students who publish prior to completing their dissertation research often develop skills as independent researchers (Gardner, 2008). The process builds research confidence and self-efficacy, which will be beneficial in completing the dissertation. Publishing an article from the dissertation manuscript similarly evokes confidence and self-efficacy, which are important attributes to launch an academic career and to bring to faculty interviews.

Publishing research benefits not only the individual researcher but also the broader academic community. It offers a valuable way to share new ideas, insights, and discoveries, helping others to learn from and build on that work. Through publication, researchers can contribute to the growth of knowledge in their discipline, support ongoing academic conversations, and promote innovation. In this way, publishing plays a key role in advancing both personal careers and the development of the field as a whole.

This dissemination of knowledge supports the academic philosophy of "standing on the shoulders of giants" and provides a moral and philosophical value-add to society. Finally, accumulating publications builds recognition, and recognition unlocks the door to many other opportunities, including, but not limited to promotion, editorial roles, keynote invitations, and collaboration opportunities.

Despite the importance of scholarly productivity during the doctoral journey and the many benefits of having publications on the curriculum vitae (CV) when applying for positions in higher education, many doctoral students remain reluctant to publish.

The level of student scholarly productivity can be associated with several factors: (a) the availability of specific writing training courses; (b) individual coaching and mentoring sessions; (c) coauthoring strategies; (d) planned writing time; (e) collegial feedback; and (f) collaborative networks.

In addition to the factors cited above, doctoral faculty members play a significant role in socializing doctoral students to the practice of writing for publication. According to Kamler (2008), when faculty fail to initiate the process, many students do not publish. However, when faculty initiates the process and provides mentorship, students are able to develop as researchers and authors.

Coauthoring a manuscript helps doctoral students become familiar with the publishing process and build their confidence to eventually write and submit their own sole-authored work. To support this development, students should actively seek out faculty members with similar research interests and offer to contribute to their research projects.

Strategies for Success

The importance of scholarly productivity and its benefits have been presented. This section discusses the various sources of publication material, and steps that can assist doctoral students in producing and submitting material which will lead to publication.

Planning to Publish: Step 1

The first step in preparing to publish is just that—preparing or having a plan. For example, during the Knowledge and Development Stage, Ashley, from the case study, should have begun researching topics that could be published in parallel with her course assignments. She could have taken the literature reviews she completed for her core coursework, revised them to meet the author's guidelines from the target journal, and submitted them for publication. To identify ways to contribute to the field, Ashley could seek faculty advisement about gaps in the literature and where to publish.

When thinking about publishing from the dissertation, Ashley needs to consider what sections can be published and how they will be published. The literature review section is usually a rich source of up-to-date information on specific bodies of knowledge that are readily accepted by many journals. Relative to the research conducted after completing a doctorate, a literature review from a dissertation tends to be very comprehensive and current. The problem is publications of this kind are less likely to be cited, as other authors will treat them as an index to locate the original publications. Being cited is important for scholarly recognition and credibility in the field.

The findings sections of the dissertation can and should be published. Usually, two or more publications can be written from the findings chapter. The findings section makes a very valuable contribution to the knowledge base within the discipline. Usually, doctoral studies are comprehensive with detailed analyses. Ashley's publications based on her findings will be an opportunity for her to make a meaningful contribution to the academic community.

Step 2: Select an Appropriate Journal

Once *what* to publish is determined, the next step is to consider *where* to publish. A good starting point is to identify which journals publish the majority of the references cited in the manuscript. It is likely that a preponderance of references may come from only a handful of journals, indicating that these journal editors and reviewers may have an interest in the topic of study. Next, target journals should be sorted according to their *impact factors*—this is usually the number of citations per article, per journal, per year and is averaged over one, three, or five years. The best place to find impact metrics is through the Journal Citation Reports (JCR) database, available in most university libraries. JCR provides the Journal Impact Factor (JIF)—a widely recognized measure of journal influence. Top-tier journals typically have an impact factor of 10.0 or higher, while lower-ranked journals may have impact factors closer to 1.0. In addition to JCR, Google Scholar Metrics can serve as a useful and accessible indicator of journal quality. It ranks journals based on the h5-index, which reflects how many highly cited articles a journal has published in the past five years. While not as formal as JCR, Google Scholar is a reputable and widely used tool for assessing journal visibility and reach.

Impact factors are useful for two reasons. First, they indicate the value of a journal according to peer evaluation (i.e., the more it is cited, the higher its rank). Having an article accepted into a highly ranked journal establishes a researcher in his or her field. Second, the impact factor has a high correlation to its rejection rate. A journal with an impact factor of greater than 10.0 may reject 99% of its submissions. On the other hand, a lower-ranked journal (e.g., with an impact of around 1.0) will still have a good relative standing, but they may reject only 75% of articles received.

An additional consideration is how the journal structures its review. Journals can be (a) *double-blind reviewed*—the names of the authors and the reviewers are removed; (b) *blind-reviewed*—the names of the authors are removed; (c) *peer-reviewed*—manuscripts are sent to authors who are currently submitting, or who have previously submitted (this can still be blind or double-blind); and (d) *editorial-reviewed*—the manuscript is reviewed and accepted/rejected by the editor alone.

Usually, manuscripts that have endured the scrutiny of a double-blind review are preferred and held in higher regard. These are likely to contribute significantly more value to an academic's CV. A final consideration is how many issues a journal has each year. A greater number of issues may mean more articles published annually and, therefore, a greater chance of acceptance.

The conventional advice for doctoral students is to publish in low-ranked journals until the student learns the craft. However, some advocate the alternate strategy: a paper should be written for the highest relevant journal and revised for submission further down the list as rejections are received. The value of this strategy is twofold.

First, academics need to become accustomed to rejection and criticism. Deliberately submitting to a journal that may be beyond one's current capacity means that the rejection will be less painful, but the lessons of coping with rejection are still learned. Second, and more importantly, the feedback received from top-ranking journals is usually of a high quality and will assist with the further development of the manuscript. Eventually, the manuscript will find its niche. The cost of this strategy is time—it can take years for the manuscript to be accepted, and time is not a luxury doctoral students can usually afford.

Another strategy to employ is to look for special issues and calls for papers (CFP). Ashley should subscribe to alerts on relevant journals that will monitor for CFPs. The advantage of CFPs is that the rejection rate may be significantly lower, and the fit will be strong.

Step 3: Understand the Mission and Make Sure the Submission is Appropriate

Once a journal is selected, it is important to become familiar with the journal's mission. For example, how do Ashley's topic and methodology fit with the expectations of the journal? To answer this question, Ashley should look at the aims and scope of the journal as well as at what topics the journal has published recently. Ashley needs to find a moderate interest in the topic of the paper.

There should be sufficient existing articles on the topic to justify further publication. However, if the topic is already heavily published, it may be considered saturated, and the manuscript could be rejected for lacking originality. To address this, the author should clearly explain in the cover letter to the editor the unique and meaningful contribution the manuscript makes to the field or discipline.

Step 4: Understand the Submission Guidelines and Follow Them

The next step is for Ashley to go to the journal's website and read the "instructions for authors." The manuscript should then be meticulously prepared according to these guidelines, and all format instructions, word counts, and other advice should be followed carefully. Editors may reject manuscripts simply because of poor formatting. It may also be prudent for Ashley, where possible, to ensure that the manuscript includes several references from the target journal. Doing so will demonstrate alignment with the journal's scope and show that the work is engaging with its scholarly community.

Another strategic move would be to cite the work of the journal's editor or potential reviewers who are active in the topic area. Doing so demonstrates familiarity with key contributors in the field and may increase the manuscript's relevance and appeal to those involved in the review process. Ashley should ensure that the spelling is the right style (e.g., American or British). The writing style of the paper should anticipate the audience of the journal. If it is an international journal, write with a polycentric mindset addressing a universal audience.

Step 5: Clearly State the Article's Contribution to the Field

It is also important to be mindful that the manuscript must contribute to knowledge in the discipline. This contribution should be clearly articulated in the abstract, introduction, and conclusion, ensuring that the significance and originality of the work are evident throughout the manuscript. A good strategy is to include the original contribution in the title, explain it in the abstract, describe it in the introduction and discussion, and then reinforce it in the conclusion. Creating a good article is like selling a product—the reason to buy (read) must be clear.

Finally, it is important to remember that the goal of publishing is not only to have the manuscript accepted—it must also be read and cited. This is also the editor's primary view. The editor will only accept papers that will be cited, as a poorly cited paper reduces the journal's impact. So, market the paper with enthusiasm. The title should be provocative, clear, descriptive, and unambiguous. Take for example this title: "Lone inventors as sources of breakthroughs: Myth or reality?" Here, the topic is clear and specific, using words which work to narrow the focus or delimit the content as the reader progresses through the title. The added section "Myth or Reality" questions assumptions and gives the title a provocative edge.

The abstract needs to create a high hit rate in search engines and databases. A good way to do this is to articulate key impact-rich phrases and then rearticulate them carefully. Keywords are also important and should be broad but specific. See the example below for why this is important.

Example Abstract (paper on remote work productivity)

This study examines the impact of remote work on employee productivity in knowledge-based industries. Drawing on data from a multi-country survey and longitudinal performance metrics, the research identifies key factors that enhance or hinder productivity in remote work environments. Findings suggest that autonomy, digital communication quality, and home-office setup significantly influence outcomes. The study contributes to emerging debates on the future of work, offering practical insights for managers and policymakers adapting to hybrid and remote workforce models.

Why it works: Impact-rich phrases such as "remote work," "employee productivity," "knowledge-based industries," and "future of work" are strategically placed. These phrases are rearticulated in different forms (e.g., "remote work environments,""hybrid and remote workforce models") to boost searchability in databases. Keywords for this abstract might include: Remote work, Productivity, Hybrid workforce, Knowledge work, Future of work.

Using Generative Artificial Intelligence (GenAI) in Writing and Publishing

The integration of GenAI into academic writing and publication has garnered significant attention and discussion over the last couple of years. There is no doubt that AI can help us on many levels in the creation of publishable work.

However, to what extent does using AI constitute plagiarism or just simple cheating? Scholars and journals generally take a spectrum-based approach to either encouraging or discouraging the use of generative AI. For example, AI can be useful in germinating ideas, it can also be invaluable in the process of editing the final paper, especially where authors might struggle with language. When considering the building blocks of most journal articles, GenAI has been seen to be most helpful in the following areas: idea generation, content structuring, literature synthesis, data collection and management, data analysis, and editing (Khalifa & Albadawy, 2024; Xu, 2025).

Ganjavi et al. (2024) conducted a study of the one hundred largest academic publishers and the top 100 highly ranked scientific journals to assess their GenAI usage policies. They found only the journal *Science* explicitly prohibited all use of GenAI tools in creating a manuscript. Most of the journals accepted the use of some AI, but the extent of AI use had to be acknowledged in a pro-forma template that was usually expected to be included in the method section of the paper.

The advice for all doctoral students is to tread carefully and read the target journal's AI policy before using GenAI.

Questions for Reflection

In summary, a consistent and well-planned strategy for publication is good preparation for the postdoctoral stage of an academic's career. This strategy is a plan that should be considered early in the process of the doctorate. The following is a list of questions that may assist you as you consider your own development of a publication record:

- What do I want to attain with a post doctoral degree? Is academia the path for me? What do I want to be known and remembered for?
- Who can I engage to assist me in developing my strategy and helping me unleash my writing potential? This question helps me consider who can assist me in starting the journey. Utilize all of the resources at hand, including members of my dissertation committee.
- Where can I publish? What journals most closely align with my career and research interests? This question helps me to consider my research and publication path. Which journals will be most helpful to my career? After discovering these key journals, set up alerts and

monitor them for new content every month. Become familiar with the content and explore potential publication opportunities, including calls for papers (CFPs) and calls for future research.

- What areas of my dissertation have the most potential for publication, and what is my value-add? This question considers what value I have to offer the world. Ensure I make the most of my research by seeking opportunities to publish as much of my work as possible. Publish my work within my own field, and also consider opportunities for cross-disciplinary collaboration where I may integrate my findings, methods, or literature into other disciplines.

Answering these questions will help you begin your path to publication success. The first question helps to verify that academia is the right place for you. If it is not, then publication may not be the way forward; if it is, then you have no choice—begin the journey, begin it soon, and do it well. What you write is indelible; it is available for all to see—including prospective employers and collaborators—for the remainder of your career. Resist the urge to get a quick (and easy) publication in a low ranked journal—shoot for the stars!

Recommended Resources

Dalcher, D. (2024) The urge to publish: Transforming your dissertation into publications. In B. Pasian & R. Turner (Eds.), *Design Methods and Practices for Research of Project Management* (2nd ed., pp. 289–300). Routledge.

Horta, H., & Santos, J. M. (2016). The impact of publishing during PhD studies on career research publication, visibility, and collaborations. *Research in Higher Education*, *57*, 28–50.

Radford, D. R., Seath, R. J., Davda, L. S., & Potts, G. (2020). Research dissertation to published paper: The journey to a successful publication. *British Dental Journal*, *228*(10), 791–794.

Salmons, J., & Kara, H. (2019). *Publishing from your doctoral research: Create and use a publication strategy*. Routledge.

References

Caffarella, R. S., & Barnett, B. G. (2000). Teaching doctoral students to become scholarly writers: The importance of giving and receiving critiques. *Studies in Higher Education*, *25*(1), 38–51.

Can, G., & Walker, A. (2011). A model for doctoral students' perceptions and attitudes toward written feedback for academic writing. *Research in Higher Education*, *52*(5), 508–36.

Carter, S. (2011). Doctorate as genre: Supporting thesis writing across campus. *Higher Education Research and Development*, *30*(6), 725–36.

Casey, B. H. (2009). The economic contribution of PhDs. *Journal of Higher Education Policy and Management*, *31*(3), 219–227.

Debowski, S. (2006). *Critical times: An exploration of recent evaluations of researcher development needs*. Paper presented at the HERDSA Conference, Perth, Australia, July.

Edwards, D. F., & Thatcher, J. (2004). A student-centred tutor-led approach to teaching research methods. *Journal of Further and Higher Education*, *28*(2), 195–206.

Foster, R. L. (2009). Publishing your dissertation. *Journal for Specialists in Pediatric Nursing*, *14*(1), 1–2.

Friend, J. I., & Gonzalez, J. C. (2009). Get together to write. *Academe*, *95*(1), 31–33.

Ganjavi, C., Eppler, M. B., Pekcan, A., Biedermann, B., Abreu, A., Collins, G. S., Gill, I. S. and Cacciamani, G. E., 2024. Publishers' and journals' instructions to authors on use of generative artificial intelligence in academic and scientific publishing: Bibliometric analysis. *BMJ*, *384*, 1–12.

Gardner, S. K. (2007). "I heard it through the grapevine": Doctoral student socialization in chemistry and history. *Higher Education*, *54*(5), 723–740.

Gardner, S. K. (2008). "What's too much and what's too little?": The process of becoming an independent researcher in Doctoral Education. *Journal of Higher Education*, *79*(3), 326–350.

Green, R. G., Hutchison, E. D., & Sar, B. K. (1992). Evaluating scholarly performance: The productivity of graduates of social work doctoral programs. *Social Service Review*, *66*(3), 441–466.

Hemmings, B. (2012). sources of research confidence for early career academics: A qualitative study. *Higher Education Research and Development*, *31*(2), 171–184.

Kamler, B. (2008). Rethinking doctoral publication practices: Writing from and beyond the thesis. *Studies in Higher Education*, *33*(3), 283–94.

Khalifa, M. and Albadawy, M., 2024. Using artificial intelligence in academic writing and research: An essential productivity tool. *Computer Methods and Programs in Biomedicine Update*, *5*, 100145.

Kwan, B. S. C. (2010). An investigation of instruction in research publishing offered in doctoral programs: The Hong Kong case. *Higher Education*, *59*(1), 55–68.

LaRocco, D. J., & Bruns, D. A. (2006). Practitioner to professor: An examination of second career academics' entry into academia. *Education*, *126*(4), 626–639.

Lee, A., & Kamler, B. (2008). Bringing pedagogy to doctoral publishing. *Teaching in Higher Education*, *13*(5), 511–523.

Leech, N. L. (2012). Educating knowledgeable and skilled researchers in doctoral programs in schools of education: A new model. *International Journal of Doctoral Studies*, *7*, 19–37.

Lei, S. A., & Chuang, N.-K. (2009). Research collaboration and publication during graduate studies: Evaluating benefits and costs from students' perspectives. *College Student Journal*, *43*(4), 1163–1168.

Megel, M. E. (1987). Nursing Scholars, writing dimensions, and productivity. *Research in Higher Education*, *27*(3), 226–243.

Nettles, M. T., & Millett, C. M. (2006). *Three magic letters: Getting to Ph.D.* John Hopkins University Press.

Paglis, L. L., Green, S. G., & Bauer, T. N. (2006). Does adviser mentoring add value? A longitudinal study of mentoring and doctoral student outcomes. *Research in Higher Education*, *47*(4), 451–476.

Perlmutter, D. D., & Porter, L. (2005). Thinking beyond the dissertation. *The Chronicle of Higher Education*, *52*(17), 0–C1,C4.

Rawat, S., & Meena, S. (2014). Publish or perish: Where are we heading? *Journal of Research in Medical Sciences: The Official Journal of Isfahan University of Medical Sciences*, *19*(2), 87.

Stoilescu, D., & McDougall, D. (2010). Starting to publish academic research as a doctoral student. *International Journal of Doctoral Studies*, *5*, 79–92.

Sweitzer, V. B. (2009). Towards a theory of doctoral student professional identity development: A developmental networks approach. *The Journal of Higher Education*, *80*(1), 1–33.

Xu, Z., 2025. Patterns and purposes: A cross-journal analysis of AI tool usage in academic writing. arXiv preprint arXiv:2502.00632.

24 Transitioning from Student to Professor

Mark C. Rehfuss, PhD
Amanda J. Rockinson, EdD, PhD

As discussed in Chapter 1, Choosing the Right Program Model: Research or Professional Doctorate, the degree doctoral students choose prepares them with the skills, knowledge, and dispositions necessary for a specific career trajectory. While doctoral graduates are increasingly choosing to work outside academia, most postgraduate students entering research doctorate programs still intend, or hope to, pursue careers in academia or a research laboratory. As such, this chapter focuses on preparing for a job in academia during a research doctorate program. However, it is also recognized that doctoral education is traditionally structured to socialize and prepare students for future professorial roles (Weidman, 2020). However, the landscape of academia is rapidly changing (i.e., an oversupply of PhDs and a decline in tenure-track positions), meaning graduates must be open to alternative ideas. This chapter discusses the faculty interview preparation, which begins on the first day of the doctoral program. The chapter includes tips for developing a curriculum vitae (CV) and preparing for interviews, including questions applicants should be ready to discuss and questions they should consider asking potential employers. This chapter aims to assist doctoral students in taking steps toward getting an interview and gaining employment in higher education.

Case Study

Evan, a full-time PhD student in business administration, called his dissertation chair in panic:

> *Please help me! I am unsure why I am not receiving any interviews for faculty positions. I have sent my resume to every opening posted, but I have not gotten*

any bites. I am getting nervous; I've passed my proposal defense. I have my dissertation defense scheduled and plan to walk in the spring commencement. What should I do? Can you help me identify what I am doing wrong or not doing? I am starting to freak out!

What the Research Says

Evan's experience is not unfamiliar to doctoral students, especially when they fail to prepare for the interview process from the very beginning of their doctoral program. Preparing for the faculty interview process and a faculty position should begin on the first day of the doctoral program (Davis, 2011).

Obtaining a faculty position is about being the person that the institution not only wants but needs. Suppose a doctoral student's goal is to become a professor. In that case, the focus of the doctoral program should be less about grades and more about using the courses and program opportunities to gain experiences that develop and, in turn, demonstrate the abilities of a faculty member. To achieve this, the doctoral student must seek experiences that align with the desired position, including research (primarily funded research), teaching, and service.

The life of a professor is built on a foundation consisting of research, teaching, and service (Boyer, 1990; Kyvik, 2013; Papin et al., 2022; Sutherland, 2017). Each university or college determines the exact proportions or general ratio of each that is necessary for success as a professor (e.g., teaching institutions vs. research institutions, tenure vs. non-tenure positions). Still, all three are essential for success as a faculty member at any institution. Thus, a doctoral student needs to organize their doctoral program experiences to gain expertise in these three areas.

The easiest way to explain the three is related to the curriculum vitae (CV) and cover letter, which typically form the first step in any higher education application process. It is essential to note that, in addition to the CV and cover letter, institutions may also require an institution-specific application form and ancillary materials (e.g., formal or informal transcripts, letters of recommendation, writing samples, philosophy of education statements, research statements, etc.).

A CV is an academic resume; it is not the same thing as a standard resume. Where a resume is a one- or two-page summary of vocational experiences and education, a CV is a compilation of educational, professional, teaching, scholarly, and service activities related to gaining an academic position. A CV focuses on the training and preparation to be a professor in the field (Formo & Reed, 2011). When doctoral students begins, their CV typically consists of one or two pages, primarily outlining their education and related employment experiences. However, it will grow with the experiences gained throughout the program. A CV should be developed within the first semester of the program and updated at the end of each subsequent semester.

At a minimum, a CV should include contact information, educational background, and professional experience. It is essential when constructing a CV that the doctoral student ensures the contact information is accurate by using an address, email, and phone number that they will maintain after graduation. The CV also needs to include sections that demonstrate professorial skills related to (a) teaching, (b) research, and (c) service, so keeping a record of all accomplishments and involvements during the doctoral program is essential.

Education

The educational training section should begin with the highest degree and then proceed to the undergraduate degree. The graduate needs to include the type of degree earned, focus area, and the department and university. Anticipated defense and graduation dates should be included if the doctoral student has not graduated. Depending on the program, students who have not yet completed their degree but have finished all their coursework and officially begun the dissertation phase can refer to themselves as doctoral candidates.

Teaching

Faculty roles are evolving, becoming increasingly diverse, and shifting their focus to teaching and learning. Some researchers have noted that as much as 40–60% of a faculty role is now devoted to teaching (Culver et al., 2025); yet teaching development (e.g., conceptual understanding, interpersonal skills, and professional attitudes and habits) is rarely a part of doctoral training

(Brew et al., 2011; Maher et al., 2014; Mantai, 2019; Cardoso & Mantai, 2025). Moreover, many doctoral students may not have the opportunity to teach.

Thus, doctoral students should seek opportunities to add teaching to their CVs. The doctoral student should include courses taught at the undergraduate, graduate, or doctoral level, specifying the course, the semester in which it was taught, and the responsibilities held in each course. If the doctoral student is a graduate assistant or teaching assistant, they should include the position title, their supervisor, and the responsibilities associated with the position. Presentation of a special topic for a professor on a course in which they were not enrolled can be listed, including the topic, the course, and the instructor. Additionally, guest lectures may be included.

Research

A primary goal of doctoral education, traditionally, is to train students as professors who can "produce and consume" research (Weidman, 2010, p. 210)—to develop research skills (Mitic & Okahana, 2021).

Thus, doctoral students should seek opportunities to add research to their CVs. The focus of the research section is on publications, presentations, and workshops. It is standard to list publications in peer-reviewed journals first, as they are considered more rigorous and demonstrate potential for future scholarly activity. All doctoral students should aim to publish at least one to two peer-reviewed journal articles before graduating. The easiest place to start publishing is in an association newsletter related to the discipline. Publishing in a newsletter can build confidence; however, it is essential to recognize that university or college interviewers also want to see evidence of scholarly, peer-reviewed articles, as well as funded research (Weidman et al., 2003).

Publishing, and especially publishing original research, for the first time, is challenging, and understanding the process takes mentorship (see Chapter 17: Identifying and Developing a Relationship with a Dissertation Chair). Joining or assisting faculty with a research project is an effective way to gain practical research experience and learn how to conduct research and write for publication. Doctoral students should seek out research mentorship opportunities at the beginning of their degree program. This may involve joining a faculty member on a grant project or collaborating with a research team. At the end of the program, the doctoral student should write at least one article derived from their dissertation.

Presentations also demonstrate scholarship potential. From the program's inception, doctoral students should begin writing and submitting proposals to present at professional conferences within their discipline. There are local and institution-based conferences as well as state, regional, national, and international conferences. Conferences at all levels should be considered, and it is recommended that doctoral students seek out regional, national and international conferences throughout their program. However, institutional-based conferences or symposiums are a significant first step in presenting.

Peer reviewed means that others in the profession have reviewed the presentation material (e.g., paper, outline of the presentation) and found it rigorous enough to present or publish. When considering publishing and presenting during the doctoral program, doctoral students should think about how to "make everything count twice" (i.e., utilize it for both program and professional purposes).

Throughout the Knowledge and Skill Development Stage of the doctoral journey, doctoral students are required to complete numerous course assignments. Assignments, however, can be viewed as more than a task for a grade. This means taking them to the next level. Suppose the doctoral student has a paper to write. In that case, they may focus the paper on something that can be presented at a conference or used as part of a literature review for a possible dissertation or article.

Once the paper is submitted, it can be reorganized and converted into a format suitable for presentation or publication. Although this involves extra time and planning after the assignment is submitted, it can result in new items to add to the CV. Doctoral students should view all coursework and related experiences as opportunities to produce scholarly work that is essential for preparation for and entrance into a professorial role.

Service

Napper-Owen (2012) suggested that doctoral students "too often fail to receive preparation that is well balanced" (p. 136), and service is often not addressed at all. However, service is also essential and can be defined as anything that is done for the discipline, profession, or university. Doctoral students need to join professional, discipline-specific organizations and associations. Many organizations offer opportunities for postgraduate students to serve on committees and contribute to various needs within the organization. Through this they are ready for the kind of leadership that will be required of a faculty member.

Professional organizations also offer opportunities to build relationships and connections that could later lead to a faculty position. Suppose the doctoral student remembers the importance of creating and capitalizing on opportunities in the areas of teaching, research, and service. In that case, they should have a strong CV to submit with their applications for faculty positions.

The Application Process

When applying for a faculty position, a cover letter is essential because it introduces the CV and highlights how the applicant is a good fit for the position. A good cover letter is crucial as it is the first item the search committee chair will see. The cover letter should be a one-page document that highlights how the applicant is the perfect fit for the posted position opening. The key points in the cover letter should align with the position call.

The applicant should write a new letter for each job posting, as each posting will specify the specific qualifications and characteristics required and preferred in the applicant. The letter needs to address those things, but in a manner that makes the reader also want to read the CV. The cover letter is one page in length and does not contain all the information from the CV; it simply provides highlights that demonstrate the applicant is a good fit for the position.

There are several key general ideas that doctoral students should be aware of when seeking a full-time faculty position. A doctoral student's first full-time faculty job may not be their top choice in terms of university or location. As a first-time position is often an entry-level one (e.g., assistant or instructor), the salary level may not be what one expects or desires.

Universities typically do not hire their graduates or graduates from other local programs, so relocation should be expected. Some institutions hire their doctoral students as part-time or adjunct instructors, but typically not as full-time faculty members. Full-time faculty positions are limited in number, as most job openings occur only through the retirement of faculty, their transition into administrative positions, or small expansions in program size.

The doctoral student should begin exploring entry-level faculty positions (e.g., lecturer, instructor, assistant professor) posted during their doctoral program, allowing them to gain knowledge about the types of positions available and what is expected in an application. The doctoral student needs to realize that most departments will have only one open position every few years; therefore, if the doctoral student wants to be at a specific place he or she needs to make the most of his or her chances by gaining the needed experience and demonstrating their qualifications in the cover letter, CV, and eventually the interview process.

The Interview Process

Although the interview process varies across institutions, there are some general steps that most faculty interviews include. After submitting a cover letter, CV, and application (if required), applicants may receive an acknowledgment email. In some cases, no notification is sent. Within a few weeks of the application deadline, the faculty search committee will meet and identify its top three to six applicants. These applicants will be contacted and invited for a phone or virtual interview.

The entire committee, usually present, conducts the interview, which typically consists of three to six faculty members and administrators. These interviews, typically lasting one hour, are used to determine the final two or three applicants who will be invited to campus. When participating in the interview, the applicant must be in a quiet, uninterrupted space. It is also appropriate to inquire about the composition of the interview committee, and it is wise for the applicant to research each committee member thoroughly. The applicant should take note of the interviewers' names and research their areas of expertise and research interests. Additionally, they should discuss how their interests and expertise align with and extend the current faculty's areas of focus.

Preparation for the initial phone or web interview involves two things. First, the applicant needs to research the university to become familiar with its general history and nature (e.g., religious affiliation, notable programs, program vision, and college). The applicant should also be knowledgeable about the various programs or courses of study within the department in which they are interviewing. The applicant must also be prepared to discuss their research agenda and philosophy of education or teaching.

Second, the applicant needs to prepare and practice responses to typical interview questions, such as Why are you applying for this position? What do you think you bring to this position? How do you work with others and provide examples? Tell us about a project you had to complete on time and describe how you successfully achieved this goal. Have you successfully defended your dissertation, or if not, why and when do you plan on having it completed? Tell us three of your strengths and three of your weaknesses. What courses would you like to teach and why? How would your strengths fit with our program, and what do you bring that will make our program better? What area of research and scholarship are you interested in pursuing?

When preparing for these questions, the applicant should remember that this initial interview serves as a screening process to eliminate candidates who appear strong on paper but are not a good fit for the position, program, or university.

Two to three applicants may be invited for an on-campus interview. The travel costs for the visit are typically covered by the university, and meals are provided and usually shared with faculty and students. The campus visit may span one or two days. It will usually involve a full itinerary including individual interviews with faculty, students, the chair of the department, the dean of the college, and often someone from the provost's and human resources departments.

Questions such as the ones posed in the initial phone or web interview are often asked again. However, many others may be asked. In the Recommended Resources section of this chapter, several books are recommended, each with a list of interview questions.

Applicants should also be prepared to give a research or professional presentation to the search committee, college faculty, and students. The presentation usually focuses on original research and is often developed based on the applicant's dissertation research. The presentation is typically slated for one hour, and the applicant should allow time for questions and discussion at the end. Alternatively, applicants may be asked to teach a class.

Presentation attendees may appreciate an accompanying handout of the slides or an outline of the key points. A virtual link or QR code is also appropriate. Applicants should include their contact information on the handout or after the presentation, so attendees can contact them to discuss the presentation further if they wish. Attending professional conferences and presenting also provides networking opportunities. Networking is crucial in recruiting faculty members, as it enhances the visibility of doctoral students within the academic community and demonstrates a commitment to professional growth. It opens doors to new positions and provides resources and support for career advancement.

Applicants should be mindful that the campus visit is an opportunity for everyone to get to know them and determine if they can bring something extra to the faculty and enhance the institution's reputation both locally and nationally. During the visit, the committee observes the applicant's professionalism, interpersonal skills, and leadership abilities.

The campus visit is also an opportunity for applicants to determine if the college or university is a good "fit" for them personally and professionally. It is a time to learn about the faculty, the department, the institution, as well as the local area (it is not uncommon for the itinerary to include a tour around the city or town by a local realtor). During informal times or when provided the opportunity in an interview, applicants should ask questions about the atmosphere and specific expectations for research production, teaching load, grant writing, and service.

It is also a good time to get a sense of the faculty and their attitudes toward the program: Are they happy and motivated, or simply going through the motions until retirement? It may be interesting to inquire about the reason the position is open. It is appropriate to ask about the average salary during this visit (see Recommended Resources). Load expectations for teaching can also have an impact on salary and are important to identify: is it 2/2 or 3/3, is it nine or 12 months? Does it include summer teaching, or is that for extra pay? How many summer courses are available, and are they expected?

Final Considerations

A final crucial quality that makes a doctoral student an effective faculty member is the ability to work both independently and as part of a team. This means that the doctoral student can teach classes, conduct research, and publish independently, as well as with peers. Thus, taking opportunities to demonstrate both the ability to be an independent worker and a team player is important. One of the best ways to achieve this is to assist with completing departmental tasks and to serve on departmental committees.

Strategies for Success

It is noteworthy to consider that this chapter has solely focused on the professional aspects of the research doctoral program. However, the underlying vocational success in academia is also dependent upon the development of a researcher identity integrated with other identity aspects, work-life integration, and self-efficacy among other social and emotional aspects developed through a doctoral program (Rockinson-Szapkiw et al., 2017). Many of these topics are explored throughout this book, which you need to consider in addition to what is highlighted in this chapter.

Therefore, you need to engage in the process of becoming a scholar and professional throughout the entire doctoral journey. These points focus on the steps doctoral students need to take to make the most of their doctoral training.

Strategy 1: Build a CV, Starting Day One of the Program

Throughout the entire program, you should focus on building your CV, encompassing research, teaching, and service. In the case study, Evan's anxiety may have been alleviated had he planned to apply for faculty positions from day one of his program and sought ongoing opportunities to build his CV. Experiences that may assist you in obtaining a faculty position following graduation may include fellowships, teaching experience in higher education, authoring or coauthoring publications, presenting at professional conferences, and serving on committees.

Strategy 2: Write a Focused Cover Letter

When applying for a faculty position, write a one-page cover letter that highlights the match between your capabilities and the position, emphasizing each element required for the job. The letter should be free of spelling and grammatical errors and formatted as a business letter. The cover letter should not detail every item on the CV, but rather, highlight selected skills, knowledge, and experiences that demonstrate you are a good fit for the position.

Strategy 3: Develop Responses to Interview Questions Prior to the Interview

Develop responses to the interview questions posed in this chapter and the resources recommended at the end of this chapter. Evan asks ChatGPT or AI to generate potential interview questions for a faculty interview. Practicing question responses with a peer, advisor, or in a mock interview setting is recommended.

During the interview, you must present yourself honestly, yet in a favorable light. For example, when Evan gets an interview, he is asked the question, "What are your weaknesses?" He does not want to say, "I am always late," knowing that no one wants to hire a perpetually tardy person. He also remembered the recommendation of his chair, "When dealing with questions, seek to assess weaknesses and discuss perceived weaknesses that are strengths." So, he answered, "Well, sometimes I tend to overwork. I could be working on the computer 24/7, answering emails, and refining my presentations, so I must remind myself to practice balance." Overworking is not considered a weakness by an employer.

The key to answering interview questions is to honestly highlight who you are by ensuring the employer knows that if you get the job, you will be the most complex and most brilliant working person in the department. Having numerous concrete examples to support every statement is also important.

Strategy 4: Exhibit Self-Confidence and Professionalism During Interviews

During the phone or virtual interview, consider standing up during the call, as this can add more energy to your voice and the answers you provide. Prior to and during the on-campus interviews, take the initiative to learn the names of those present and remember the interactions and discussions you have with them. Before the interview, thoroughly research the university and program. Be prepared to discuss them comprehensively. Finally, follow up every interview with a thank-you email.

Strategy 5: Apply Broadly, Network, and Seek Mentorship

When seeking a faculty position, pursue open positions and be flexible. Applying broadly for positions helps you secure a first faculty position, which is more important than the location itself. Throughout your doctoral program, seek networking and mentoring opportunities to advance your career.

Strategy 6: Utilize AI Tools to Manage Academic Workload as You Build Your CV

Incorporate AI tools, such as the Listening App and ChatGPT, to manage your academic workload effectively. This Listening App can convert your reading materials into an audio format, allowing you to listen to academic papers and books while cleaning your house, driving, or doing something else. ChatGPT can assist with writing IRB applications or gathering research.

Questions for Reflection

Considering that the process of obtaining an academic position begins upon entry into the doctoral program, developing a strong CV and handling professional interviews effectively are essential. Begin preparing for the first faculty interview by reflecting and acting upon these questions.

- Picturing what is needed on a strong CV, what is one thing I can do today to start the process of expanding it? What is the first step I need to take to make sure I have something significant to add to my CV?
- What is one thing I can do currently to make something in one of my courses relevant to my goal of becoming a faculty member?
- Who can I talk to about assisting with research or developing a research element for my CV?
- What are the organizations on campus or in my profession that I should be engaged with, working for, and presenting at conferences, as well as seeking mentoring and networking opportunities?
- How can I research the steps to apply for a faculty position in my discipline? Have I familiarized myself with the standard timeline for applying (e.g., usually nine to 12 months prior to the starting date)?

Recommended Resources

Bourne, P. E. (2017). Ten simple rules for considering a career in academia versus government. *PLoS Computational Biology, 13*(10), e1005729.

Cahn, S. M. (2024). *From student to scholar: A candid guide to becoming a professor* (2nd ed.). Resource Publications.

Childress, H. (2016). *The PhDictionary: A glossary of things you do not know (but should) about doctoral and faculty life*. University of Chicago Press.

Formo, D. M., & Reed, C. (2011). *Job search in academe: How to get the position you deserve*. Stylus Publishing.

Gardner, S. K. (2008). "What is too much and what is too little?" The process of becoming an independent researcher in doctoral education. *The Journal of Higher Education, 79*(3), 326–350. https://doi.org/10.1080/00221546.2008.11772101

Gardner, S. K. (2010). Faculty perspectives on doctoral student socialization in five disciplines. *International Journal of Doctoral Studies, 5*, 39–53. https://doi.org/10.28945/1310

McAlpine, L., Amundsen, C., & Turner, G. (2014). Identity-trajectory: Reframing early career academic experience. *British Educational Research Journal, 40*(6), 952–969. https://doi.org/10.1002/berj.3123

Noorbhai, H. (2025). *Roadmap of the professoriate: Strategic guide for progression from graduate student to (full) professor*. Kindle.

References

Anderson, L., & Krathwohl, D. (Eds.). (2001). *Taxonomy of learning, teaching, and assessment: A revision of Bloom's taxonomy of educational objectives*. Longman.

Boyer, E. L. (1990). *Scholarship reconsidered: Priorities of the professoriate*. Jossey-Bass Publishers.

Brew, A., Boud, D., & Namgung, S. U. (2011). Influences on the formation of academics: The role of the doctorate and structured development opportunities. *Studies in Continuing Education, 33*: 51–66. https://doi.org/10.1080/0158037X.2010.515575.

Cardoso, S., & Mantai, L. (2025). Global transformations and doctoral agency: Cross-national perspectives on the evolving doctoral experience. *Innovations in Education and Teaching International*, 1–16.

Culver, K., Kezar, A., & Koren, E. R. (2025). Faculty, Academic Careers, and Environments (FACE) Framework: A Guide to Faculty Work for Research, Practice, and Policy. *The Journal of Higher Education*, 1–33. https://doi.org/10.1080/00221546.2025.2466421

Davis, L. J. (2011). What I tell my graduate students. *The Chronicle of Higher Education.*

Kyvik, S. (2013). The academic researcher role: Enhancing expectations and improved performance. *Higher Education 65*, 525–538. https://doi.org/10.1007/s10734-012-9561-0

Maher, M. A., Gilmore, J., Feldon, D., & Davis, T. E. (2014). Connected or conflicted? Doctoral students' evolving perceptions of the teaching-research relationship. *Journal of School Public Relations, 35*(3), 402–425.

Mcinnis, C. (2000). Changing Academic Work Roles: The everyday realities challenging quality in teaching. *Quality in Higher Education, 6*(2), 143–152. https://doi.org/10.1080/713692738

Napper-Owen, G. (2012). Raising the next generation. *Quest, 64*(3), 131–140. https://doi.org/10.1080/00336297.2012.704777

Papin, J. A., Keim-Malpass, J., & Syed, S. (2022). Ten simple rules for launching an academic research career. *PLoS Computational Biology, 18*(12). https://doi.org/10.1371/journal.pcbi.1010689.

Shelton, D. S., Delgado, M. M., Greenway, E. V., Hobson, E. A., Lackey, A. C., Medina-García, A.,... & Horner-Devine, M. C. (2021). Expanding the landscape of opportunity: Professional societies support early-career researchers through community programming and peer coaching. *Journal of Comparative Psychology, 135*(4), 439.

Sutherland, K. A. (2017). Constructions of success in academia: An early career perspective. *Studies in Higher Education, 42*(4), 743–759.

Weidman, J. C. (2010). Doctoral student socialization for research. In S. K. Gardner, & P. Mendoza (Eds.). *On becoming a scholar: Socialization and development in doctoral education* (pp. 45–56). Stylus Publishing

Weidman, J. C. (2020). Conceptualizing student socialization in higher education: An intellectual journey. In *Socialization in Higher Education and the Early Career: Theory Research and Application* (eds. Weidman, J. C. & DeAngelo, L., pp. 11–30) Springer.

Weidman, J. C., Twale, D., & Stein, E. L. (2003). Socialization of graduate and professional students in higher education, a perilous passage? *The Journal of Higher Education, 74*(6), 719. https://doi.org/10.1080/00221546.2003.11780868

25 Transitioning from Student to Scholar-Practitioner

Lucas B. Hill, PhD

Introduction

Whether completing a professional doctorate or a research doctorate, graduates of both programs face the choice of whether to pursue a career as a research scientist in academia or scholar-practitioner in their field of professional practice. While professional doctorates have a distinct focus on application to professional practice, higher education is often tilted to the research scientist track in the conscious and unconscious replication of the university faculty who teach and mentor students and postdoctoral scholars. Yet, for most fields, the job market is much more expansive and needs highly trained professionals who can apply their skills and knowledge to solve real-world problems. The challenge is most students typically only experience the university environment and can be ill-prepared to make the transition from student to scholar-practitioner. The purpose of this chapter is to explore seven key dimensions that aid individuals in thinking about and preparing for the transition to apply their expertise in the field, as opposed to academic careers in higher education (the focus of Chapter 24). The dimensions addressed include identity, socialization, confidence, independence, knowledge and skill, connections, and work-life balance.

Case Study

Hector Lopez is about to graduate with his PhD in biomedical engineering from a state university. He is the first in his family to earn such a degree. Even his bachelor's degree was a major familial accomplishment. Like many students, he entered his PhD program with aspirations to become a faculty member at a research university. However, after his second year, he had the chance to participate in a National Institutes of Health (NIH) T32 training program at his university. Part of the program included a summer internship program at a cancer institute where he had the opportunity to put his knowledge and training to use in the practical application of medical imaging equipment to help in the diagnosis, treatment, and research of various kinds of cancer. He thoroughly enjoyed being able to move out of the sterile research lab environment of his graduate research assistantship and into "hands-on" work that allowed him to flex both his creativity and technical prowess with a surprising level of autonomy. Hector left his T32 experience knowing that while he was earning the credentials to move into academia next, he wanted to become a scholar-practitioner and identified several areas in which he wished to increase his knowledge and skills. Since his internship, he has asked around his department to identify former students who have become scholar-practitioners in his field. Luckily, a few former students were still in the area, so he invited them to grab a coffee. He is unsure what to expect in transitioning from student to scholar-practitioner and is not 100% confident that he is "ready" for the leap into the seemingly unknown. Through his visits with alumni, seven key dimensions in preparing for the transition surface.

What the Research Says

In this section, each of the seven dimensions that aid you in thinking about and preparing for the transition from student to expert-practitioner are explored by considering key literature through the lens of Hector Lopez from the case study. You are invited to imagine being a friend who tags along with Hector to his various coffee dates to get the "scoop" on the transition from student to scholar-practitioner. The following sections synthesize strategies for success, provide key reflection questions, and outline recommended resources.

Identity

Students such as Hector often find themselves asking key questions, "Who am I?" and "What do I want to be when I grow up?" as they transition from being a student to an expert. Graduate and doctoral studies can be a tumultuous time of identity exploration as individuals attempt to weave together what they came into school with; what they receive through training, observation, and experience; and what they will go on to do "in the field" (Colbeck, 2008), which can have an impact on their physical and mental health and their disciplinary identity (Gonzales et al., 2021). Students learn to balance several role-based identities during graduate school (e.g., student, researcher, teaching assistant) which are internalized for that specific context (McAlister et al., 2022), but which are required to evolve and change as they transition out of their terminal degree completion. Ideally, graduate programs should support the development of a distinct professional identity such as ensuring that medical students "think, act, and feel like a physician" (Cruess et al., 2019, p. 641).

Not all graduate programs, however, have such succinct preparation parameters, leaving graduate students to grapple with merging their doctoral student identity with an anticipatory lens of what it will be like to be in academia or as a scholar-practitioner in the field. Disciplinary identity is an important facet of students' developing professional identity since it extends beyond the reach of their university (Dressen-Hammouda, 2008; Hyland, 2012) though it can also be quite multifaceted depending on the discipline and even sub-discipline(s). Students can even develop additional components of their professional identity, such as entrepreneurialism (Hayter et al., 2022; Pitt et al., 2020), which has strong potential for those serving in scholar-practitioner roles.

It is important for graduate students, such as Hector, to take stock of their various identities, nurture the facets that are the most beneficial to their career path, and explore manifestations of professional and disciplinary identities in career path options to "test out" what fits and what does not. Hector, through his T32 experience, was able to test out a scholar-practitioner identity at his internship site. Through coffee with alumni, he was also able to get glimpses of what it means to be a scholar-practitioner in the biomedical field and then compare his emergent professional identity with the alumni to see areas of overlap and areas of potential growth. For example, Hector was surprised to hear the alumni talk a lot about their role in training new employees in hardware and software. At first, he felt a pang of anxiety since he did not have any teaching roles while at his university until he reflected upon the numerous undergraduates and even early-stage PhD students he trained on the equipment in his advisor's lab. Thus, in making the transition to scholar-practitioner, it is essential to explore identity in its many forms and to begin taking on the identity of the new post-PhD program role.

Socialization

In the early 2000s, socialization theory became a major mechanism for examining the transition of graduate students into faculty careers (e.g., Antony, 2002; Austin & McDaniels, 2006; Weidman & Stein, 2003). Socialization theory, broadly defined, is the process of how an individual is enculturated into another group, including the group's norms, skills, and knowledge (Maccoby, 2007). Applied to graduate students, Weidman et al. (2001) created a framework of four overlapping circles: (a) the background and predispositions of graduate students, (b) their personal communities (e.g., family, and friends), (c) their professional communities, and (d) the commitment and identity of novice professional practitioners to the profession in which they are preparing to enter. The authors also discussed three elements of the socialization process (interaction, integration, and learning) and three core elements (knowledge acquisition, investment, and involvement), which, like pre-professoriate applications, are highly relevant to those transitioning from student to scholar-practitioner. Highlighting that slightly more than half of graduate students go on to careers outside of academia, Gardner & Doore (2020) argued the socialization process initiated in doctoral programs must go beyond the comfortable boundaries of the university and extend to the careers graduates take "in the field."

Applied to students like Hector, this socialization process should provide opportunities, such as his internship experience, to interact with potential job environments, learn about the ins and outs, and become more invested and involved over time. This exposure is critical given the academic-centered nature of most doctoral programs. Without this exposure, students cannot develop their professional identity within the aspect of the field in which they will work. Hector's meetings with alumni become crucial in his preparation, as they provide a real window into the types of positions to which he might apply, including details about the culture, norms, skills, and knowledge of companies and the larger world of scholar-practitioners in his discipline. Thus, doctoral students need to both (a) see the potential of alternative academic career paths and (b) individually, or more ideally in partnership with the department, craft meaningful engagement with scholar-practitioner careers to initiate the socialization process during graduate school and continue it as they make the important transition postgraduation.

Confidence

Confidence, better known as self-efficacy (Bandura, 1978, 1994), is one of the most important predictors of behavior and is a critical element in the transition from student to scholar-practitioner, especially considering the frequent struggle many doctoral graduates and early career professionals have with imposter syndrome (Abdelaal, 2020). Future career success is linked to graduate students' confidence in their knowledge, skills, and ability to perform at peak capacity in new, often uncharted territory. As mentioned above, graduate students are trained in self-replicating academic systems, which often places more of the burden of seeking out socializing engagement on the student. Social cognitive career theory (SCCT) provides key insight into both the importance of self-efficacy and its relationship to other key phenomena that can predict performance attainments (Lent et al., 2002). For example, Hector's internship experience, which, in SCCT, would be known as a learning experience, had a direct impact on Hector's self-efficacy in the kinds of work that scholar-practitioners engage in at the cancer institute and his outcome expectations within this career track. Per SCCT, both self-efficacy and outcome expectations then influence career interests, career choice goals, and choice actions, which then affect future performance.

Students, like Hector, need learning experiences in scholar-practitioner contexts to both advance the socialization process and increase their confidence in their ability to pursue such positions. Hector's coffee sessions with alumni provided an additional layer and a different type of learning experience that helped increase his self-efficacy. Hector came to these meetings with questions that explored the alignment of graduate program coursework with its application in the scholar-practitioner context. The alumni helped him recognize that he already had important requisite knowledge and skills and helped him identify other areas that required additional learning to prepare for that segment of the job market. Overall, self-efficacy is a vital component in the transition from student to scholar-practitioner. Whereas socialization and identity are concerned with the growing sense of fit within a work context and seeing oneself within the profession, self-efficacy is the belief that an individual can survive *and* thrive in that space.

Autonomy

As doctoral students move forward in their academic journey, they are expected to transition from dependent learners to independent experts as they advance in researcher and/or practitioner tracks. Self-determination theory is a helpful construct to help frame where autonomy fits within a larger set of psychological variables in work settings (Deci et al., 2017; Ryan & Deci, 2002). Interacting with intrinsic and extrinsic motivators, autonomy is one of three basic psychological needs that individuals require to be able to perform and be happy at work (Deci & Ryan, 2012). Competence (i.e., knowledge and skill) and connections (relatedness), the other two elements, will be discussed below. *Autonomy*, broadly defined, involves the freedom to choose the performance of work responsibilities, which has produced extensive scholarship from multiple disciplines citing its importance in employee support and productivity (Gagné & Bhave, 2010; Harris & Krueger, 2015; Slemp et al., 2015).

As graduate students enter the job market as scholar-practitioners, they experience new, increased, and different forms of autonomy than what they found in their graduate programs within a college/university environment. This change in autonomy can be overwhelming, especially if combined with a novel work environment in which they have very little knowledge and/or experience, leading to lower self-efficacy, which illustrates the interconnected nature of the seven dimensions discussed in this chapter. Hector, through his internship, experienced the type of autonomy he might expect from that career path, which he found thoroughly enjoyable though also a bit daunting as it required that he bring structure and accountability into his work at the cancer center. There were also bounds to his autonomy, given both the role of the short-duration internship and the focus of his summer position. Whereas an academic researcher might, in theory at least, have the freedom to explore any intellectual path, the scholar-practitioner must operate within limits imposed by the hiring company grounded in defined job responsibilities and primary organizational goals (e.g., profit in a for-profit entity). These limits are neither good nor bad, though are crucial in understanding the working conditions for scholar-practitioners so they can get a sense of "fit," since each company/organization may have many different manifestations of autonomous limits (for more on autonomous and self-directed learning during the doctoral journey, see Chapter 14).

Knowledge and Skills

As mentioned above, *competence* is one of the three most basic psychological needs to be successful in any work setting (Deci et al., 2017). Competence means having the necessary knowledge and skills to do something successfully. Doctoral students are exposed to extensive content in and outside of the classroom as they progress in their programs in which they gain knowledge and skills important (presumably) for various career paths. Such knowledge and skill acquisition are linked to increases in independence (Feldon et al., 2016) and socialization (Woodrow & Guest, 2017). Some authors even point to the need to develop soft skills as complementary to graduate students' "hard" research skill development (Getachew et al., 2020). The overarching point is that considerable literature has examined and advanced what knowledge and skills graduate students need to have to be successful, although a major proportion of this literature focuses on the academic career track. The result is that graduate students often need to supplement their graduate program curriculum with additional learning experiences, which increases their self-efficacy (as described previously) and adds new and important knowledge and skills for a chosen career path.

The acquisition of knowledge and skills does not and cannot conclude at the terminus of a graduate program for scholar-practitioners because of the ever-evolving nature of disciplines and fields and the importance of a lifelong learning mentality (Fischer, 2000). For example, ongoing employee knowledge acquisition is linked with advancements in innovation (Papa et al., 2020). In Hector's case, he was able to apply his current knowledge and skills, which increased his self-efficacy for pursuing that line of work. At the same time, the internship experience illustrated a few areas in which his graduate program did not provide specific knowledge and skills. Instead of lamenting this deficiency, Hector embodied a growth mindset (Dweck, 2007), embraced lifelong learning, and began to learn independently to better prepare for future positions. At coffee, alumni also hit upon the importance of staying up to date in the field and having the opportunity to learn new things to increase their toolbox of knowledge and skills. Thus, for students like Hector, it is important to examine the knowledge and skills of (a) the formal doctoral program, (b) the informal curriculum that can be pursued independently in preparation for future careers, and (c) to become a scholar-practitioner who is a lifelong learner.

Connections

The last of the three basic psychological needs, *relatedness*, can be described as having a community of peers and human interaction to prevent siloed loneliness (Deci et al., 2017). Put simply, according to self-determination theory, scholar-practitioners need to develop a work community to effectively thrive and be productive, which is congruent with social network theory and our needs as human beings to have connections with other humans in our personal and professional lives (Kadushin, 2012). We are social creatures and need other humans to find fulfillment. In addition, work contexts are becoming more and more collaborative (Mattessich & Johnson, 2018), requiring the ability to engage and connect in meaningful ways to accomplish work projects and achieve organizational and team goals. In short, it is not necessarily the number of connections that is most important, but rather the quality of those connections that is the most critical. Thus, expanding one's professional network should not be an exercise in collecting superficial connections. Instead, expanding one's network is about creating purposeful and meaningful connections.

Beyond human intrinsic value, connections can also be strategic in accomplishing individual and organizational goals by bridging the boundaries between organizations/organizational units (Burt, 2004), influencing behavior (Frank & Xu, 2020), and applying social capital to encourage certain actions and outcomes (Adler & Kwon, 2002). Put more simply, connections can be leveraged to advance and enhance an individual's professional trajectory and work to accomplish larger organizational goals. *Network connectivity* is a powerful support mechanism and a tool that can be nurtured over time to provide enriching and productive relationships. For example, as graduate students begin the job application process, those with large and deep connections will be able to tap into those individuals to identify open positions, ask questions, and obtain feedback. Students with shallow connections may reach the same number of connections but these individuals in the field may not be as inclined to help in the same way. Thus, the quality and number of connections work in unison to produce leveraged outcomes.

Applied to Hector, we already saw how he activated his doctoral program network to identify former students and then worked to build new professional connections with these individuals. Students like Hector could explore potential work environments and reach out to those with positions of interest and ask for informational interviews to learn more about the position, the company, and even the field, while at the same time expanding their professional network. Once hired, Hector could seek out individuals in his immediate department and surrounding units to get to know them, build productive working relationships, and learn more about organizational culture, processes, and procedures. Hector could make additional connections at conferences, trade shows, and other interorganizational settings to keep in touch with the larger field and facilitate exciting partnerships that benefit him professionally and his company/organization. The main point is connections are the vital connective tissue in the career development of a scholar-practitioner and should not be ignored for both personal and professional reasons.

Work-Life Balance

The last of the seven dimensions acknowledges that students and scholar-practitioners exist within larger ecosystems that contain family, friends, and other loved ones. As graduate students, there are so many hours spent in the lab, in class, and at a desk studying, filling one's mind with knowledge and development skills that will immediately and in the future be put to good use. It is easy to get wrapped up in this aspect of our identity and ignore other key dimensions of our humanity. Many speak to work-life balance as graduate students (e.g., Martinez et al., 2013; Nicklin et al., 2019) and professionals (e.g., Guest, 2002; Kalliath & Brough, 2008; Sirgy & Lee, 2018). Work-life balance can vary wildly between individuals, meaning that there is not a one-size-fits-all solution

Instead, graduate students, as they begin the transition to scholar-practitioners (which arguably could start on day one of their programs) must deeply reflect upon how work-life balance intersects with the other dimensions discussed above. For example, consider identity. Where do other facets of life fit within and around one's professional identity? How much should one's professional identity take up in comparison to other human variables? Again, there is no one right answer. The point is, graduate students need to examine and visualize what type of life they want and the desired balance between work, family, hobbies, etc.

This examination and visualization do not end upon degree conferral. They continue after the transition to a scholar-practitioner. The one constant in life is that life is always changing, professionally and personally. Thus, like a lifelong learning mentality, work-life balance is an ongoing lens in which short- and long-term adjustments will be necessary along anyone's career path. In addition, given the terminal degree and advanced experience, it is highly probable many graduate students entering the workforce as scholar-practitioners will become supervisors to other employees on their respective teams. Therefore, it is crucial to not only elevate work-life balance in one's own professional life but also in the lives of those with whom you work (see Chapter 5 for more on navigating family, academic, and work integration).

Summary

The seven dimensions (see Figure 25.1) are designed to draw out important facets of the transition from student to scholar-practitioner. As discussed above, the dimensions are interconnected with work-life balance forming a holistic box around the other variables for the overall management of a professional life. You are encouraged to work through each dimension and then view them as a combined lens that can provide insight into areas of existing strength and areas that could warrant some additional development to make the transition as productive and seamless as possible. It is also important to point out the transition period is dynamic with lots of change happening over a short period. You are encouraged to revisit this chapter a few times to celebrate your accomplishments, check for alignment between goals and actions, and identify new areas to continue to learn and grow.

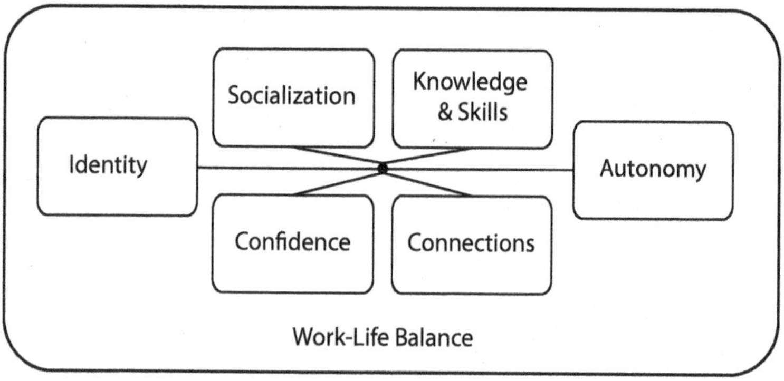

Figure 25.1 Key dimensions in the transition from student to scholar-practitioner.

In addition, regardless of being scholar-practitioner-bound, you should find the seven dimensions equally enlightening, as they provide a lens through which to examine career transitions more broadly. However, the context and content used may be different for academic researchers. Thus, the major benefit of the seven dimensions is that they allow you to examine who you are, where you are, where you want to go, and how to get there within an acceptable work-life balance.

Strategies for Success

The following six strategies are distilled from the discussion of existing literature and Hector's experiences. You are encouraged to review the strategies and create a plan to complete them in preparation for a scholar-practitioner career. In addition, you can revisit each strategy as you advance in your career preparation and even after you enter the job market.

Strategy 1:

Map out (electronically or on a large piece of paper) the facets of your professional identity. Start with your current identity to take stock of where you are now. Next, as you explore various scholar-practitioner career paths, take each one and map what you think (anticipatory) are the main elements of that professional identity. Compare your current professional identity with potential anticipatory career paths and examine areas of overlap and difference.

Strategy 2:

Request informational interviews with scholar-practitioners in your field, which could be former students of your same program and/or those who are at organizations where you might like to work. Use the dimensions discussed in this chapter to guide your questions to explore topics such as professional identity, the socialization process, and work-life balance.

Strategy 3:

Look and sign up for opportunities to intern or otherwise engage in work environments of interest. These opportunities will be vital in seeing firsthand the work environment and day-to-day operations of a scholar-practitioner.

Strategy 4:

As you learn more about the types of knowledge and skills needed for scholar-practitioner positions of interest, create a simple table. In the first column, list the concrete knowledge and skills that are needed, which will be informed by activities such as informational interviews, discussions with your advisor and other faculty, and internship experiences. In the next column, indicate your level of confidence (self-efficacy) on a 1–5 scale (1 = not at all confident; 5 = extremely confident). In the last column, draft a plan to increase your confidence in that knowledge/skill area. Revisit the table regularly.

Strategy 5:

Begin a network map of your professional connections. Include who (name, affiliation, etc.) and the nature of the connection. Periodically update and expand your network map as you advance in your career. As appropriate, add names of individuals with whom you would like to connect and then generate small and achievable plans to build and strengthen connections toward your professional goals.

Strategy 6:

Draft a statement about your desired work-life balance, especially considering the other key dimensions found in this chapter. Annually or semi-annually revisit this statement and revise as desired. In each review, take stock of your success in living up to your desired work-life balance and then devise a strategy to realign desired and lived practice accordingly.

Questions for Reflection

Ask yourself the following questions:

1. What elements constitute my *current* and *desired* professional identity as a scholar-practitioner?
2. How will I effectively socialize into a scholar-practitioner role within industry, government, or the nonprofit sectors?
3. In which areas do I need to increase my self-efficacy/confidence to make the transition to scholar-practitioner more efficacious?

4. How do I envision autonomy in my desired future work roles? What level of autonomy is ideal for me?
5. How will I continue to learn and develop new skills as I enter the workforce as a scholar-practitioner?
6. What connections will be the most important in both finding and then thriving in my role as a scholar-practitioner?
7. What is my plan to maintain work-life balance as a scholar-practitioner?

Recommended Resources

Bandura, A. (1997). *Self-efficacy: The exercise in control.* Worth Publishers.

Burke, P. J., Owens, T. J., Serpe, R., & Thoits, P. A. (eds) (2003). *Advances in identity theory and research.* Springer.

Choo, S. (2024). *Letting go of imposter syndrome: Stop overthinking, release self-doubt and anxiety, and embrace who you truly are.* Self-Published.

Edwards, A. (2010). *Being an expert professional practitioner: The relational turn in expertise.* Professional and Practice-based Learning Book 3. Springer.

Ferrazzi, K., & Raz, T (2014). *Never eat alone, expanded and updated: And other secrets to success, one relationship at a time.* Crown Currency.

Friedman, S. D., Saunders, E. G., Bregman, P., & Dowling, D. W. (2019). *HBR guide to work-life balance.* Harvard Business Review Press.

Hewlett, S. A. (2013). *Forget a mentor, find a sponsor: The new way to fast-track your career.* Harvard Business Review Press.

Ibarra, H. (2023). *Working Identity: Unconventional strategies for reinventing your career.* Harvard Business School Press.

Kramer, M. (2010). *Organizational socialization: Joining and leaving organizations.* Polity.

LinkedIn Learning, https://learning.linkedin.com

Marku, A. (2023). *Smart goals mastery: Unlocking your potential and achieving success through smart goals.* Independently Published.

Piantanida, M., McMahon, P. L., & Llewellyn, M. (2018). *On being a scholar-practitioner: Practical wisdom in action (wisdom of practice).* Learning Moments Press.

Scivicque, C. (2022). *Build your professional development plan: The ultimate career planning tool (3rd edition).* CCS Ventures, LLC.

Weidman, J. C., & DeAngelo, L. (Eds.). (2020). *Socialization in higher education and the early career: Theory, research and application* (Vol. 7). Springer Nature.

References

Abdelaal, G. (2020). Coping with imposter syndrome in academia and research. *The Biochemist, 42*(3), 62–64.
Adler, P. S., & Kwon, S. W. (2002). Social capital: Prospects for a new concept. *Academy of Management Review, 27*(1), 17–40.
Antony, J. S. (2002). Reexamining doctoral student socialization and professional development: Moving beyond the congruence and assimilation orientation. In J. C. Smart (Ed.), *Higher education: handbook of theory and research* (pp. 349–380). Springer. https://doi.org/10.1007/978-94-010-0245-5_8
Austin, A. E., & McDaniels, M. (2006). Preparing the professoriate of the future: Graduate student socialization for faculty roles. *Higher education: Handbook of theory and research, 21*, 397–456.
Bandura, A. (1978). Reflections on self-efficacy. *Advances in behaviour research and therapy, 1*(4), 237–269.
Bandura, A. (1994). Self-efficacy. In V. S. Ramachaudran (Ed.), *Encyclopedia of human behavior* (Vol. 4, pp. 71–81). Academic Press.
Burt, R. S. (2004). Structural holes and good ideas. *American Journal of Sociology, 110*(2), 349–399.
Colbeck, C. L. (2008). Professional identity development theory and doctoral education. *New Directions for Teaching and Learning, 2008*(113), 9–16.
Cruess, S. R., Cruess, R. L., & Steinert, Y. (2019). Supporting the development of a professional identity: General principles. *Medical Teacher, 41*(6), 641–649.
Deci, E. L., Olafsen, A. H., & Ryan, R. M. (2017). Self-determination theory in work organizations: The state of a science. *Annual Review of Organizational Psychology and Organizational Behavior, 4*, 19–43.
Deci, E. L., & Ryan, R. M. (2012). Self-determination theory. *Handbook of Theories of Social Psychology, 1*(20), 416–436.
Dressen-Hammouda, D. (2008). From novice to disciplinary expert: Disciplinary identity and genre mastery. *English for Specific Purposes, 27*(2), 233–252.
Dweck, C. (2007). *Mindset: The New Psychology of Success*. Random House.
Feldon, D. F., Maher, M. A., Roksa, J., & Peugh, J. (2016). Cumulative advantage in the skill development of STEM graduate students: A mixed-methods study. *American Educational Research Journal, 53*(1), 132–161.
Fischer, G. (2000). Lifelong learning—more than training. *Journal of Interactive Learning Research, 11*(3), 265–294.
Frank, K. A., & Xu, R. (2020). Causal inference for social network analysis. In R. Light & J. Moody (Eds.), *The Oxford Handbook of Social Networks* (pp. 288–310). Oxford University Press.
Gagné, M., & Bhave, D. (2010). Autonomy in the workplace: An essential ingredient to employee engagement and well-being in every culture. In V. I. Chirkov,

R. M. Ryan, & K. M. Sheldon (Eds.). *Human autonomy in cross-cultural context: Perspectives on the psychology of agency, freedom, and well-being* (pp. 163–187). Springer.

Gardner, S. K., and S. A. Doore. 2020. Doctoral Student Socialization and Professional Pathways. In J. C. Weidman, L. DeAngelo (Eds.), *Socialization in higher education and the early career: Theory, research and application* (pp. 113–127). Springer.

Getachew, A., Ayele, M., Hailu, E. M., & Tuli, F. (2020). Effectiveness of soft skill training for students' career development in higher education. *Journal of the Social Sciences, 48*(4), 1817–1832.

Gonzalez, J. A., Kim, H., & Flaster, A. (2021). Transition points: Well-being and disciplinary identity in the first years of doctoral studies. *Studies in Graduate and Postdoctoral Education, 12*(1), 26–41. https://doi.org/10.1108/SGPE-07-2020-0045

Guest, D. E. (2002). Perspectives on the study of work-life balance. *Social Science Information, 41*(2), 255–279.

Harris, S. D., & Krueger, A. B. (2015). *A proposal for modernizing labor laws for twenty-first-century work: The independent worker*. Brookings.

Hayter, C. S., Fischer, B., & Rasmussen, E. (2022). Becoming an academic entrepreneur: How scientists develop an entrepreneurial identity. *Small Business Economics, 59*, 1469–1487.

Hyland, K. (2012). *Disciplinary identities: Individuality and community in academic discourse*. Cambridge University Press.

Kadushin, C. (2012). *Understanding social networks: Theories, concepts, and findings*. Oxford University Press.

Kalliath, T., & Brough, P. (2008). Work–life balance: A review of the meaning of the balance construct. *Journal of Management & Organization, 14*(3), 323–327.

Lent, R. W., Brown, S. D., & Hackett, G. (2002). Social cognitive career theory. *Career Choice and Development, 4*(1), 255–311.

Maccoby, E. E. (2007). Historical overview of socialization research and theory. *Handbook of Socialization: Theory and Research, 1*, 13–41.

Martinez, E., Ordu, C., Della Sala, M. R., & McFarlane, A. (2013). Striving to obtain a school-work-life balance: The full-time doctoral student. *International Journal of Doctoral Studies, 8*, 39. Retrieved from http://informingscience.com/ijds/Volume8/IJDSv8p039-059Martinez0375.pdf

Mattessich, P. W., & Johnson, K. M. (2018). *Collaboration: What makes it work*. Fieldstone Alliance.

McAlister, A. M., Lilly, S., & Chiu, J. L. (2022). Exploring factors that impact physical science doctoral student role identities through a multiple case study approach. *Science Education, 106*(6), 1501–1534. https://doi.org/10.1002/sce.21754

Nicklin, J. M., Meachon, E. J., & McNall, L. A. (2019). Balancing work, school, and personal life among graduate students: A positive psychology approach. *Applied*

Research in Quality of Life, 14, 1265–1286. https://doi.org/10.1007/s11482-018-9650-z

Papa, A., Dezi, L., Gregori, G. L., Mueller, J., & Miglietta, N. (2020). Improving innovation performance through knowledge acquisition: The moderating role of employee retention and human resource management practices. *Journal of Knowledge Management, 24*(3), 589–605. https://doi.org/10.1108/JKM-09-2017-0391

Pitt, R. N., Satcher, L. A., & Drew, A. M. (2020). Optimism, innovativeness, and competitiveness: The relationship between entrepreneurial orientations and the development of science identity in scientists. *Social Currents, 7*(2), 155–172. https://doi.org/10.1177/2329496519895297

Ryan, R. M., & Deci, E. L. (2002). Overview of self-determination theory: An organismic dialectical perspective. *Handbook of Self-Determination Research, 2,* 3–33.

Sirgy, M. J., & Lee, D. J. (2018). Work-life balance: An integrative review. *Applied Research in Quality of Life, 13*, 229–254.

Slemp, G. R., Kern, M. L., & Vella-Brodrick, D. A. (2015). Workplace well-being: The role of job crafting and autonomy support. *Psychology of Well-being, 5*, 1–17. https://doi.org/10.1186/s13612-015-0034-y

Weidman, J. C., & Stein, E. L. (2003). Socialization of doctoral students to academic norms. *Research in Higher Education, 44*, 641–656.

Weidman, J. C., Twale, D. J., & Stein, E. L. (2001). Socialization of graduate and professional students in higher education: A perilous passage? *ASHE-ERIC Higher Education Report, 28*(3). *Jossey-Bass Higher and Adult Education Series*. Jossey-Bass.

Woodrow, C., & Guest, D. E. (2017). Knowledge acquisition and effective socialization: The role of the psychological contract. *Journal of Occupational and Organizational Psychology, 90*(4), 587–95.

26 Understanding the Excitement and Postdoctoral Blues Following Degree Conferment

Amanda J. Rockinson, EdD, PhD
Lucinda S. Spaulding, PhD
Elizabeth DeBolt, PhD

Introduction

Many doctoral students anticipate feelings of relief, accomplishment, and excitement after earning the title of Dr. With only 2 percent of the population holding doctoral degrees, including PhDs, EdDs, DNPs, MDs, and JDs, earning the title Dr. is a remarkable accomplishment. While there is usually a sense of joy and excitement, very few discuss that shortly after the final defense and the doctoral hooding ceremony, many graduates are blindsided when they unexpectedly experience what we have come to term *postdoctoral graduation syndrome* (also sometimes called *postdoctoral blues*). Postdoctoral graduation syndrome is the feelings of aimlessness, loss, let down, emptiness, sadness, and even, depression and anxiety after a long focused effort of achieving a life goal and reaching the perceived pinnacle of success—doctoral degree attainment. Likened to the phenomenon of post-partum depression in women after giving birth or an Olympian earning a gold medal and experiencing post-Olympic blues, recent doctoral degree recipients can experience postdoctoral graduation syndrome or postdoctoral blues as they mentally and emotionally transition into a new season of life, seeking to find new purpose and equilibrium. While there are a handful of blogs about *PhD Depression* or *PhD Blues* and a wealth of research about adverse effects on mental health during the doctoral program, there is little in the doctoral or higher education literature describing the experience *after* degree conferral. This chapter examines the postdoctoral experience, namely the postdoctoral blues, which many graduates unexpectedly experience in the aftermath of degree attainment. As research in this area is sparse, the content of this chapter is based mainly on the personal experiences of recent degree recipients from PhD and EdD programs, as shared in the following vignettes.

Vignettes

Ayanna

The doctoral process, my EdD, was a test of endurance. It is the culmination of tears cried, negotiations with family for support, and missed milestones. It was a sacrifice. My son turned one when I interviewed for the doctoral program. I started in the summer of 2020, a summer when I felt overwhelmed by the uncertainty that the pandemic brought, the uncertainty of my job, and the uncertainty of my place in a doctoral program. I was a first-generation college student. Two degrees later, I still felt lost at times, trying to navigate my first experiences with online learning and choosing my problem of practice. Everything felt so new. I had to change diapers during synchronous sessions. I rocked my son to sleep as I read an assigned article. At least three points in the program, I asked myself if it was worth it. Others asked me if it was worth it. I told myself each time that if the answer was *"yes,"* then I needed to figure out how.

The *"how"* for overcoming difficult seasons looked different every year as I navigated the pandemic, a growing child with new needs, a move, and a job change. It took me until the end of the program to recognize that I needed to lean into my community. I called on them to vent, cry, and get practical feedback. They were the only people who truly understood. From my immediate family, I asked for help to have focused time to write. I asked for patience and understanding. I requested time off from my employer to focus on my research during high-stress moments in the program. This took a level of vulnerability that I had never expressed before this process. When I successfully defended, it was not just a moment of triumph for me, but for every person who helped me along the way.

However, after I graduated it took a year for me to fully process all of what I had experienced. It took me 18 months to retrain myself to sleep through the night, as I had trained myself to wake up at 4 a.m. (and sometimes earlier) to ensure some quiet time to work on doctoral work and my dissertation. After defending, I thought I'd arrived, only to find that without publications, graduate teaching experience in my field, or a clear research agenda, I had little chance of securing a faculty position. I was so busy running the race that I almost forgot the goal I was running toward. Two years after graduation, I was still the midst of a new process, navigating the postdoctoral journey. This was a new test of endurance. Each day was a test of my will; however, I had faith that I would prevail. I meet my frustrations and challenges with the same questions that pushed me forward when I wanted to stop. Is it *still* worth it? *Yes!* I have not quite figured out the *how*, but I have the tools to navigate these new challenges.

LaShannon

My doctoral journey was a path marked by relentless discipline, sacrifice, and self-doubt. From sunup to sundown, week after week, I immersed myself in reading scholarly articles, writing, and refining my research based upon the supportive feedback I received from my dissertation chair. Guided by a structured plan developed with the assistance of my chair, I stayed on course. My chair often reminded me to walk out from reading articles and writing to focus on self-care. Yet, behind my drive for excellence was an emotional toll. I distanced myself from nearly everyone, including my beloved daughter, to stay committed. Even after completing the journey, I continue to struggle with imposter syndrome. Despite the resilience it took to earn my PhD, I often question my worthiness of the title, and I hesitate when colleagues refer to me as "Dr." My journey was not just academic—it was deeply personal, filled with silent internal battles that now continue long after my degree was earned. Obtaining a PhD was not only for me but my community, my family, and for a few Black little girls—even my own daughter.

Jessica

After having two children within two years and taking a break from my doctoral degree, I decided it was time to go back and finish. A significant motivation was job security for my current position in academia and the feeling that I was leaving something incomplete, which I knew I would regret one day. While it felt incredible to dive back into my past life of studying, researching, and writing, it was also challenging as my family walked through the numerous emotions, work transitions, and events brought on by COVID-19, while also finding out I was pregnant with my third child. Despite the grueling hours and numerous sacrifices of sleep and family time, I developed a deep passion for my research topic and, with the incredible support of my husband and committee, was driven to do my best to produce meaningful research.

As I neared the finish line, I realized I wanted more than job security in my current position. I was passionate about my research and felt a responsibility to steward my degree and "do more," developing an agenda for my research that I hoped would not only add to the body of knowledge, but live up to the transformative framework from which I conducted my research. Yet, practically, I was not really sure how to accomplish this. However, I optimistically pushed toward my final defense and commencement, only for these events to usher in a strange sense of barrenness. I immediately transitioned from pouring my time into writing and research into job hunting, feeling behind the power curve of hiring in May. I knew I was exhausted and should take time to process all that had been accomplished, but I felt a need to do more professionally, and perhaps prove to myself that all the sacrifices were actually worth it. However, my family circumstances limited me to remote work, and knowing all too well the grueling work-life balance of tenure-track academics, I was content to apply for what felt like "ideal fit" adjunct work and even private sector positions, with the hopes that doors for further research opportunities would open in the future. I had been told countless times that the PhD would open doors, but as the weeks and months went by, the silent inbox communicated that I still had not arrived. Instead of open doors, I was hitting brick walls.

The summit climb to being "PhinisheD" left me emotionally and physically drained. However, it was my faith that sustained me throughout the process, and my faith reminded me that even in this, God's purposes are far greater than I know. A year after graduating, I saw glimpses of opportunities beginning to open, but I also recognized that *my* timing is rarely a reality. While I miss the guidance of a course syllabus that lays out a clear objective and outcome, I am nonetheless committed to working toward my goals. However, with each passing day, I am learning to trust the process and look for opportunities to grow as an individual and an academic.

Megan

The doctorate was supposed to be a pinnacle, a crowning achievement. Instead, it often felt like a weight pressing down on my chest. I remember late nights at my desk and the dim light of my laptop casting shadows on papers strewn across my desk. My children's laughter echoed from downstairs—a sound I both cherished and resented. I was there, physically, but not really present. I traded bedtime stories and weekend outings for research articles and revisions. The guilt sat heavy and constant.

Imposter syndrome often clung to me like a second skin. Surrounded by peers who spoke with such certainty and ease, I questioned everything—my intelligence, my right to be in the class, and the decision to pursue the degree at all. Every milestone met was quickly overshadowed by the fear of being found out and of someone realizing I didn't belong.

Outside life? That became a myth. Birthdays and holidays passed. The world went on, and I stayed in the margins—writing, revising, questioning and rewriting. And yet, I finished.

When I walked across that stage, hood draped around my shoulders, there was no trumpet of relief and no grand celebration. It was just a quiet moment of recognition that I had survived. I had endured.

But after graduation, reality hit again. The job I landed wasn't quite what I envisioned. My degree—years of sacrifice, sleepless nights, emotional strain—often felt like an expensive trophy collecting dust in a mismatched career path. People asked, "So what are you doing with it now?" and I'd smile, dodge, and deflect. They couldn't understand the real answer.

Still, something fundamental had shifted in me. I no longer needed outside validation to know my worth. The degree didn't guarantee the future I had hoped for, but it reshaped me. It showed me who I am when everything is stripped away, when it's just me, the work, and the will to keep going. That strength, that transformation is not something any one can take away from me. It may not have ended the way I dreamed, but it gave me something far more enduring: a deeper belief in myself.

What the Research Says

The doctoral journey is a unique and often grueling educational experience, marked by a mix of emotions (Chen, 2023; Juniper et al., 2012). For some doctoral students, the experiences of dealing with microaggressions and "isms" (e.g., racism, sexism, and ableism), demanding research and teaching, tiptoeing around relational power dynamics, receiving critical feedback, experiencing isolation, and navigating toxic relationships with advisors, result in trauma leading to psychological distress, and even posttraumatic stress disorder (Bekkouche et al., 2022; Fernandez et al., 2019; Katz, 2018; Levecque et al., 2017; Satinsky et al., 2021). Even doctoral graduates who had a largely positive journey experience difficulties and challenges that evoke stress, depression, and anxiety (Beasy et al., 2021; Liu & Abliz, 2019; Park, 2005; Russell-Pinson & Harris, 2019; Schmidt & Hansson, 2018), as Ayanna described. Anxiety-provoking, stressful, and competitive are all words doctoral students have used to describe their experiences across disciplines and decades (Lovitts, 2001; Siegel & Keeler, 2020). Recently, these experiences and mental health issues in doctoral programs have been a focus of research. However, less discussed is the phenomenon of postdoctoral graduation syndrome, also known as the postdoctoral blues.

Doctoral completers expect to graduate and experience a sense of relief as well as excitement and joy regarding the significant accomplishment of earning the title of Dr. Many do experience these emotions. However, they are often surprised by the symptoms of postdoctoral graduation syndrome. This includes, as noted in the introduction, the feelings of aimlessness, loss, let down, emptiness, sadness, and even depression and anxiety after a long focused effort of achieving a life goal and reaching the perceived pinnacle of success—doctoral degree attainment. It is also inclusive of exhaustion, poor motivation, lack of purpose, sleep troubles, difficulty concentrating, loneliness, feelings of worthlessness, and identity disturbances (e.g., imposter syndrome, loss of identity).

The stress and often unrealistic demands of the doctoral program, compounded by an unstable job market, are likely factors that contribute to this phenomenon (Bekkouche et al., 2022; Fernandez et al., 2019; Siegel & Keeler, 2020). Applying for jobs and attempting to publish articles related to their dissertations, frequently experiencing rejection, can evoke self-doubt and imposter syndrome, feelings noted by Jessica and LaShannon (Kaplan-Berkley et al., 2019). Ayanna noted that even 18 months after graduation, she was still learning how to navigate the postdoctoral journey and the job market. Uncertainty about income and the source of health insurance also contributes to this (Nature, 2022). However, there are likely other factors that contribute to postdoctoral blues. As Megan, LaShannon, and Jessica noted, the postdoctoral life leads to a new test of endurance and learning to restructure a life that for years revolved around a grueling academic agenda.

Contributing Factors to Postdoctoral Blues

For a period averaging 5 to 10 years (Alvero et al., 2024; Bekkouche et al., 2022; National Center for Science and Engineering Statistics, 2023), doctoral students dedicate a significant amount of time, cognitive resources, and emotional energy to the doctoral program. Social support, emotional support, material support, and even sometimes income, come from the academic institution. As the culture of academia encourages and celebrates complete self-sacrifice for the sake of the academy, doctoral students find themselves working, studying, attending classes, and writing for around 40 to 60 hours a week (Katz, 2018; Woolston, 2019). The academic institution's emphasis on productivity for success often normalizes pushing doctoral students to work at an unrealistic and machine-level pace (Bran et al., 2023; Castelló et al., 2017; van Rooij et al., 2019; Woolston, 2019). Their entire lives become structured around the doctoral program, resulting in the abandonment of interests, social activities, hobbies, and social connections not directly associated with the academic institution. For example, LaShannon noted that she distanced herself from nearly everyone, Ayanna and Megan missed familial milestones, and Jessica had to forgo time with her young family. Many doctoral students find their purpose, identity, and worth tethered to their role as doctoral students in the academic institution (Pretorius & Macaulay, 2021; Zhang et al., 2024). Therefore, while the doctoral journey has many positive aspects, it is also marked by loss, and with its completion, another sense of loss occurs (Kaplan-Berkley et al., 2019).

There is a loss of identity, purpose, lifestyle, social relationships, and other aspects that students have come to enjoy and love during their doctoral journey. Grief ensues. For example, after giving up social activities and connections for the doctoral program, doctoral graduates may no longer know what interests or hobbies fulfil them. They may realize that they have very few friends outside of academia, leading to a lack of social support and feelings of loneliness, which can exacerbate the experience of burnout (Pyhältö et al., 2017). After expending time and cognitive and emotional resources on the doctoral journey over several years, no longer having the demanding coursework and dissertation that require these resources can also leave a void, a sense of emptiness, and aimless direction, as noted by Jessica, Megan, and Ayanna.

Additionally, cognitive, emotional, and physical exhaustion may also be by-products of the doctoral journey. These are especially consequences of the Inquiry Stage, which requires intense focus, immense time, emotional strain, and little sleep. As Ayanna explained, she would get up at 4:00 a.m., sacrificing sleep to have quiet time to work on her doctoral research. Just as sacrifices and renegotiation of priorities had to be made to make space for the arduous and momentous work of one's doctoral studies, the doctoral journey and its completion also requires aspects of one's identity to be reoriented and redefined (Empson, 2012; Thao & Trut Thuy, 2024).

Identity Issues

Impostor syndrome, which is the pervasive feeling of self-doubt, anxiety, depression, and fear of being exposed as a fraud despite evidence of success (Bravata et al., 2020), among doctoral students does not appear to resolve upon commencement easily (Chakraverty, 2020). Moreover, the identity transition from doctoral student to Dr. can be likened to a work-related identity loss (Conroy & O'Leary-Kelly, 2014). As one's identity and social role as a doctoral student come to an end, so too does the high level of commitment and research required for the degree, which can lead to feelings of confusion and grief (Li & Horta, 2024; Light & Visser, 2012). The pre-liminal experience can be further complicated when the perceived professional transition is not as smooth as expected, as noted in each vignette. These feelings are deeply personal and psychological, as one wrestles through their emotions and self-concept, contributing to the experience of postdoctoral blues. However, beyond these experiences and emotions, there is also a biological explanation for the postdoctoral *blues*.

Biological Changes

As doctoral students anticipate and work toward completing their degree, the neurotransmitter dopamine is released, which is central to motivation and the pleasure of working toward achievement (Bromberg-Martin et al., 2010). Once the goal of degree completion is achieved, dopamine levels drop, resulting in decreased motivation, feelings of pleasure, mood changes, sadness, and anxiety (Berridge & Kringelbach, 2015; Dresp-Langley, 2023; Hoffman, 2025). Additionally, dopamine serves as an important buffer against the effects of stress.

Stress in multiple domains is a frequently cited manifestation in a doctoral student's life, which contributes to a prolonged rise in cortisol levels, resulting in numerous long-term mental and physiological effects upon an individual (Bekkouche et al., 2022; Stetler & Guinn, 2020; Zunhammer et al., 2013). With the decline in dopamine levels following degree completion, the suppressed effects of stress may surface. Furthermore, chronic stress can lead to dysregulation in the dopamine system, affecting one's ability to process rewards and satisfaction. This, in turn, may result in a decreased response to the reward of completing a doctoral program, as noted by Megan and Jessica. Without a sense of relief from the experience of stressful events, such as a doctoral program, an individual may also be more prone to depression (Dong et al., 2023). Therefore, it is essential to consider the multidimensional effects of the biological, psychological, and social factors that may contribute to postdoctoral blues. Furthermore, the environmental structure of higher education and employment is yet another compounding factor that should be considered.

Changing Landscape of the Job Market

Recently minted doctoral degree recipients seeking careers in academia are entering the field as the landscape of higher education is changing dramatically. With declining birth rates, introduction of AI for personalized learning, and decreasing college student enrollment, universities are expanding their online and distance education options while streamlining their operating budgets, mainly by increasing contingent appointments (e.g., adjuncts) rather than employing full-time, tenure-track faculty positions (Anthony et al., 2020). The use of contingent appointments in US colleges and universities increased from 47% in 1987 to 68% in 2021 (Colby, 2023).

Conversely, in 1987, 39% of faculty members in US colleges and universities held full-time tenured appointments, compared with only 24% in 2021 (Colby, 2023). Private and public universities, large and small, are experiencing budget shortages and cuts in federal funding, making the higher education job market even more competitive for individuals applying for highly sought and coveted tenure-track positions (Treisman, 2025).

Furthermore, doctoral students may not be fully aware of the requirements needed to be competitive in the narrowing field of academia. Doctoral students are expected to streamline their research agenda and produce notable publications while simultaneously completing their doctoral studies, components that hold a significant weight upon their postdoctoral career, yet as evidenced in the vignettes, may be an overlooked component of the doctoral marathon (Bekkouche et al., 2022; Carciu, 2021; Kaplan-Berkley et al., 2019). Many doctoral completers face the challenging reality that despite their considerable efforts and well-deserved credentials, securing a full-time tenure-track faculty position may be elusive (American Association of University Professors, 2022; Kallio et al., 2024; McAlpine & Emmioğlu, 2013). Even within the industry, cooling labor market, hiring freezes, cautious hiring practices by companies, and increasing integration of AI into the work for purposes such as automation are making it difficult to find jobs external to academia. For example, Megan, an EdD, noted that she did not land the job in her industry that she had hoped for postgraduation.

Strategies for Success

The numerous compounding factors experienced by recent doctoral graduates point to why the transition following graduation can be challenging. It is essential to acknowledge all the emotions surrounding graduation, and the transition that accompanies it. It is also essential to develop coping mechanisms and seek the necessary support to navigate the transition and find fulfillment after graduation.

Strategy 1: Acknowledge the Full Range of Emotions

Acknowledging that the post-doctoral graduation syndrome is a real and valid response to the significant achievement of earning the title of "Dr." Sadness, anxiety, and other emotions that occur when dopamine levels drop after a long-term goal is achieved. Take time to sit with and express these emotions. Cry, vent, scream, engage in physical activity, and use other ways to process them. Repressing these emotions or forcing a false positivity will only result in a physical or mental breakdown eventually.

Strategy 2: Reframing the Goal of the Doctoral Journey

Value learning, personal growth, and development as achievements in themselves, are more important than focusing solely on graduation and degree completion as the goal. The doctoral journey is an opportunity for growth and new experiences, as is the transition. The transition can be framed from loss to gain.

Strategy 3: Celebrating the Journey and its Ending

Take time to celebrate your achievement. Recognize the effort and dedication that you put into achieving your goal of earning a doctoral degree. Acknowledge the joys, personal growth, and learning that took place during the journey.

Strategy 4: Maintain or Reestablish Connections with Friends and Family

Social support, the psychosocial resources available from a social network, provides functional support (i.e., the experience or expectancy of instrumental and emotional support), which is vital in navigating postdoctoral blues. Findings from a meta-analysis demonstrated that social support decreases the likelihood of experiencing depression (Gariépy et al., 2015). Moreover, Thoits (2011) and others (Li et al., 2023) have noted that social support from significant or similar others serves as a buffer against stress. Connection with others brings joy. The more you maintain friend and family connections outside of the academic institution during the doctoral journey, the less lonely you will feel when the journey ends.

Strategy 5: Maintain Personal and Professional Connections with Doctoral Peers

Who understand what you went through and your new identity. These connections can provide vital professional networking opportunities after graduation, as well as a community with whom you can share the isolation, loneliness, disappointments, and uncertainty you may feel postgraduation (Kaplan-Berkley et al., 2019). Sharing experiences, many of which are universal, can shed light in dark areas. Brown (2015) purported that when "we decide to share our stories and live our truth, we bring our light to the darkness" (p. 75), illuminating experiences and belonging. Technologies (e.g., video conferencing, email) are vital for staying connected, providing the ability to establish global connections and social networks (McCulloch et al., 2017) (see Chapter 6: Becoming a Digital Scholar).

Strategy 6: Mentor Others

Many students report that the postdoctoral blues are a completely unexpected experience they were not prepared for. Thus, you may seek opportunities to mentor students recently admitted to your alma mater to socialize them to the challenges they might experience on the other side of their degree attainment. The experience of helping others may allow you to find new meaning in your life while also providing you with the opportunity to further understand and express your own emotions.

Strategy 7: Develop New Routines and Find New Hobbies

After graduation, you may find that you have more time on your hands. Take this time to pursue new interests and hobbies. Engage in a creative project, join a community sports team, learn a new skill, cook, or tend to a garden. Moreover, remember to maintain a few hobbies throughout the doctoral journey. The more you give up for the doctoral journey (and you will need to back out of some commitments) and structure your life around the doctoral program, the more complex the transition out of the program will be.

Strategy 8: Develop Goals that Provide you with Renewed Excitement and Fulfillment

However, remember that these goals do not need to be more ambitious than obtaining a doctoral degree. They just need to be fulfilling.

Strategy 9: Develop a Post-Graduation Wellness Plan

Revisit the strategies in Chapter 7: Creating a Personal Wellness Plan and Chapter 8: Overcoming Stress and Burnout. Physical activity, healthy eating, adequate rest, mindfulness, and meditation can all improve overall well-being. Remember that self-sacrifice and maintaining a machine-level pace are not sustainable, normal, or healthy.

Strategy 10: Find New Purpose or Passion and Remember "the Why"

After graduation, take time to rest. Once rested, be curious about what ignites your interest and passion. Rediscover or discover a new passion and purpose. Moreover, remember why you pursued a doctoral degree. LaShannon, after the conferment of her degree reminded herself that, Obtaining a PhD is not only for me but my community, my family, and for a few Black little girls—even my own daughter.

Strategy 11: Seek Professional Help

Seeking professional help is often beneficial for navigating the complex emotions that follow graduation. Cognitive behavioral therapy (CBT) and other evidence-based therapeutic approaches can help alleviate anxiety and depression and provide a space to process the social, biological, and identity changes in the aftermath of degree-conferral.

Questions for Reflection

- What emotions am I experiencing postgraduation?
- Who is my support system?
- What new hobbies would I like to pursue?
- What routines do I need to let go of, establish, or reestablish to ensure I get sufficient rest, physical activity, and nutrition?
- Why did I pursue a doctoral degree? What was the purpose? What is my purpose now? What ignites my interest?
- Do I need to seek a counselor or professional assistance to process my emotions postdoctoral program?

Recommended Resources

Fernandez, M., Sturts, J., Duffy, L. N., Larson, L. R., Gray, J., & Powell, G. M. (2019). Surviving and thriving in graduate school. *SCHOLE: A Journal of Leisure Studies and Recreation Education*, *34*(1), 3–15. https://doi.org/10.1080/1937156X.2019.1589791

Hersey, T. (2022). *Rest is resistance: A manifesto*. Little Brown Spark.

Martha Beck's Resources on How I Find My Purpose (https://marthabeck.com/2025/02/how-do-i-find-my-life-purpose/#write)

References

Alvero, A., Peña, C., Moore, A. R., Luqueño, L., Barron, C. B., Steele, L., Eberle, S., & Botham, C. M. (2024). Time to degree, identity, and grant writing: Lessons learned from a mixed-methods longitudinal case study of biosciences PhD students. *SAGE Open*, *14*(2). https://doi.org/10.1177/21582440241253662

American Association of University Professors. (2022). *The 2022 AAUP survey of tenure practices*. https://www.aaup.org/file/2022_AAUP_Survey_of_Tenure_Practices.pdf

Anthony, W., Brown, P. L., Fynn, N., & Gadzekp, P. (2020). The plight of adjuncts in higher education. *Practitioner to Practitioner*, *10*(4), 3–10. https://files.eric.ed.gov/fulltext/EJ1246736.pdf

Beasy, K., Emery, S., & Crawford, J. (2021). Drowning in the shallows: An Australian study of the PhD experience of wellbeing. *Teaching in Higher Education*, *26*(4), 602–618. https://doi.org/10.1080/13562517.2019.1669014

Bekkouche, N. S., Schmid, R. F., & Carliner, S. (2022). "Simmering pressure": How systemic stress impacts graduate student mental health. *Performance Improvement Quarterly*, *34*(4), 547–572. https://doi.org/10.1002/piq.21365

Berridge, K. C., & Kringelbach, M. L. (2015). Pleasure systems in the brain. *Neuron*, *86*(3), 646–664. https://doi.org/10.1016/j.neuron.2015.02.018

Bran, A., Lopes, N., & Lafon, M. (2023). PhD graduates' appraisals of work demands: Challenging, hindering, and not very threatening. *Studies in Higher Education*, *49*(3), 559–575. https://doi.org/10.1080/03075079.2023.2244963

Bravata, D. M., Watts, S. A., Keefer, A. L., Madhusudhan, D. K., Taylor, K. T., Clark, D. M., Nelson, R. S., Cokley, K. O., & Hagg, H. K. (2020). Prevalence, predictors, and treatment of impostor syndrome: A systematic review. *Journal of General Internal Medicine*, *35*(4), 1252–1275.

Bromberg-Martin, E. S., Matsumoto, M., & Hikosaka, O. (2010). Dopamine in motivational control: Rewarding, aversive, and alerting. *Neuron*, *68*(5), 815–834. https://doi.org/10.1016/j.neuron.2010.11.022

Brown, B. (2015). *Rising strong*. Penguin Random House.

Carciu, O. M. (2021). Juggling early-career demands: Research publication productivity, strategies, practices. In P. Habibie & S. Burgess (Eds.), *Scholarly publication trajectories of early-career scholars*. Palgrave Macmillan. https://doi.org/10.1007/978-3-030-85784-4_2

Castelló, M., Pardo, M., Sala-Bubaré, A., & Suñe-Soler, N. (2017). Why do students consider dropping out of doctoral programs? Institutional and personal factors. *Higher Education*, *74*(6), 1053–1068. https://doi.org/10.1007/s10734-016-0106-9

Chakraverty, D. (2020). The impostor phenomenon among postdoctoral trainees in STEM: A US-based mixed-methods study. *International Journal of Doctoral Studies*, *15*, 329–352. https://doi.org/10.28945/4589

Chen, H. (2023). Anxiety or enjoyment, I feel pleasant to welcome them both: Thematic analysis of a Chinese PhD student's personal growth experiences. *Front Psychol. 14*. https://doi.org/10.3389/fpsyg.2023.1173734.

Colby, G. (2023). Data snapshot: Tenure and contingency in US higher education: Federal figures on faculty appointments and graduate student employment in US higher education. *American Association of University Professors*. https://www.aaup.org/academe/issues/spring-2025/data-snapshot-tenure-and-contingency-us-higher-education-fall-2023#:~:text=Summary%20of%20Findings&text=About%2023%20percent%20of%20faculty,47%20percent%20in%20fall%201987.

Conroy, S. A., & O'Leary-Kelly, A. M. (2014). Letting go and moving on: Work-related identity loss and recovery. *The Academy of Management Review*, *39*(1), 67–87. http://www.jstor.org/stable/43699200

Dong, Y., Liu, L., Wu, Z., Du, Y., Wang, Y., Zhao, Z., Li, Y., Zhan, Y., Wang, M., Ma, Y., & Xu, L. (2023). Stress relief as a natural resilience mechanism against depression-like behaviors. *Neuron*, *111*(20), 3312–3328.e8. https://doi.org/10.1016/j.neuron.2023.09.004

Dresp-Langley, B. (2023). From reward to anhedonia-dopamine function in the global mental health context. *Biomedicines*, *11*(9), 2469. https://doi.org/10.3390/biomedicines11092469

Empson, L. (2012). My affair with the "other": Identity journeys across the research–practice divide. *Journal of Management Inquiry*, *22*(2), 229–248. https://doi.org/10.1177/1056492612446068

Fernandez, M., Sturts, J., Duffy, L. N., Larson, L. R., Gray, J., & Powell, G. M. (2019). Surviving and thriving in graduate school. *SCHOLE: A Journal of Leisure Studies and Recreation Education*, *34*(1), 3–15.

Gariépy, G., Honkaniemi, H., & Quesnel-Vallée, A. (2015). Social support and protection from depression: Systematic review of current findings in Western countries. *British Journal of Psychiatry, 209*, 284–93. https://doi.org/10.1192/bjp.bp.115.169094

Hoffman, B. (2025). *The paradox of passion: How rewards covertly control motivation*. Bloomsbury.

Juniper, B., Walsh, E., Richardson, A., & Morley, B. (2012). A new approach to evaluating the well-being of PhD research students. *Assessment & Evaluation in Higher Education, 37*, 563–576. https://doi.org/10.1080/02602938.2011.555816

Kallio, T., Siekkinen, T., Pekkola, E., Kivistö, J., Nokkala, T., Kuoppakangas, P. (2024). Push and pull factors affecting in leaving academia. *Tertiary Education and Management 30*(1), 65–80. https://doi.org/10.1007/s11233-024-09135-4

Kaplan-Berkley, S., Strickland, C., & Dimartino, L. (2019). Post-dissertation: Surviving and thriving amidst doctoral transition. *Reflective Practice, 20*(6): 705–719. https://doi.org/10.1080/14623943.2019.1689940

Katz, R. (2018). Crises in a doctoral research project: A comparative study. *International Journal of Doctoral Studies, 13*, 211–231. https://doi.org/10.28945/4044s

Kurt, G., Tarsitani, L., Morina, N., Burchert, S., Patanè, M., Quero, S., Campos, D., Huizink, A. C., Fuhr, D. C., Spiller, T., Sijbrandij, M., & Hall, B. J. (2023). Understanding the protective effect of social support on depression symptomatology from a longitudinal network perspective. *BMJ Mental Health, 26*(1), e300802. https://doi.org/10.1136/bmjment-2023-300802.

Levecque, K., Anseel, F., Beuckelaer, A., Van der Heyden, J., & Gisle, L. (2017). Work organization and mental health problems in PhD students. *Research Policy, 46*(4), 868–879. https://doi.org/10.1016/j.respol.2017.02.008

Li, H., & Horta, H. (2024). Exploring the identity development of PhD graduates transitioning to non-researcher roles. *Higher Education Quarterly, 78*(2), 421–435. https://doi.org/10.1111/hequ.12452

Li, G., Li, Y., Lam, A. I. F., Tang, W., Seedat, S., Barbui, C., Papola, D., Panter-Brick, C., Waerden, J. van der,. Bryant, R., Mittendorfer-Rutz, E., Gémes, K., Purba, F. D., Setyowibowo, H., Pinucci, I., Palantza, C., Acarturk, C., Kurt, G., Tarsitani, L., Morina, N., … Hall, B. J. (2023). Understanding the protective effect of social support on depression symptomatology from a longitudinal network perspective. *BMJ Mental Health, 26*(1), e300802. https://doi.org/10.1136/bmjment-2023-300802

Light, A. E., & Visser, P. S. (2012). The ins and outs of the self: Contrasting role exits and role entries as predictors of self-concept clarity. *Self and Identity, 12*(3), 291–306. https://doi.org/10.1080/15298868.2012.667914

Liu, M. H., & Abliz, A. (2019). Anxiety and sources of anxiety in Chinese doctoral students. *Journal of Higher Education Science, 9*(3), 640–650. https://doi.org/10.5961/jhes.2019.361

Lovitts, B. E. (2001). *Leaving the ivory tower: The causes and consequences of departure from doctoral study*. Rowman & Littlefield.

McAlpine, L. & McKinnon, M. (2013). Supervision—the most variable of variables: Student perspectives. *Studies of Continuing Education 35*, 265–280. https://doi.org/10.1080/0158037X.2012.746227

McCulloch, S., Tusting, K., & Hamilton, M. (2017). The role of networked learning in academics' writing. *Research in Learning Technology, 25*. https://doi.org/10.25304/rlt.v25.1958

National Center for Science and Engineering Statistics (NCSES). 2023. *Doctorate recipients from U.S. Universities: 2022*. NSF 24-300. National Science Foundation. https://ncses.nsf.gov/pubs/nsf24300.b

Nature. (2022). The scandal of researchers paid less than a living wage. *Nature, 611*(8). https://doi.org/10.1038/d41586-022-03472-3

Park, C. (2005). New variant PhD: The changing nature of the doctorate in the UK. *Journal of Higher Education Policy Management, 27*(2), 189–207. https://doi.org/10.1080/13600800500120068

Pretorius, L., & Macaulay, L. (2021). Notions of human capital and academic identity in the PhD: Narratives of the disempowered. *The Journal of Higher Education, 92*(4), 623–647. https://doi.org/10.1080/00221546.2020.1854605

Pyhältö, K., McAlpine, L., Peltonen, K., & Castello, M. (2017). How does social support contribute to engaging post-PhD experience? *European Journal of Higher Education, 7*(4), 373–387. https://doi.org/10.1080/21568235.2017.1348239

Russell-Pinson, L., & Harris, M. L. (2019). Anguish and anxiety, stress and strain: Attending to writers' stress in the dissertation process. *Journal of Second Language Writing 43*, 63–71. https://doi.org/10.1016/j.jslw.2017.11.005

Satinsky, E. N., Kimura, T., Kiang, M. V., Abebe, R., Cunningham, S., Lee, H., Lin, X., Liu, C. H., Rudan, I., Sen, S., Tomlinson, M., Yaver, M. & Tsai, A. C. (2021). Systematic review and meta-analysis of depression, anxiety, and suicidal ideation among Ph.D. students. *Science Report*, 11. https://doi.org/10.1038/s41598-021-93687-7

Schmidt, M., & Hansson, E. (2018). Doctoral students' well-being: A literature review. *International Journal of Qualitative Studies on Health and Well-Being, 13*(1). https://doi.org/10.1080/17482631.2018.1508171

Siegel, J. T., & Keeler, A. (2020). Storm, stress, silence: A focus group examination of mental health culture and challenges among graduate students currently or previously experiencing depression. *Journal of College Counseling, 23*(3), 207–220. https://doi.org/10.1002/jocc.12166

Stetler, C. A., & Guinn, V. (2020). Cumulative cortisol exposure increases during the academic term: Links to performance-related and social-evaluative stressors. *Psychoneuroendocrinology, 114*, 104584. https://doi.org/10.1016/j.psyneuen.2020.104584

Thao, L. T., & Trut Thuy, P. (2024). Enhancing the doctoral experience: Factors influencing academic success and well-being of Ph.D. students in a cultural context. *Cogent Arts & Humanities, 11*(1), 2391645. https://doi.org/10.1080/23311983.2024.2391645

Thoits P. A. (2011). Mechanisms linking social ties and support to physical and mental health. *Journal of Health and Social Behavior, 52*, 145–161. https://doi.org/10.1177/0022146510395592

Treisman, R. (2025, March 12). Universities across the U.S. freeze hiring as federal funding hangs in the balance. *NPR*. https://www.npr.org/2025/03/12/nx-s1-5324496/universities-hiring-freezes-federal-funding

van Rooij, E., Fokkens-Bruinsma, M., & Jansen, E. (2019). Factors that influence PhD candidates' success: The importance of PhD project characteristics. *Studies in Continuing Education, 43*(1), 48–67. https://doi.org/10.1080/0158037X.2019.1652158

Woolston, C. (2019). PhDs: The tortuous truth. *Nature, 575*(7782), 403–406. https://doi.org/10.1038/d41586-019-03459-7

Zhang, H., Liu, L., Li, X., & Sun, Y. (2024). How doctoral students understand academic identity in China: A qualitative study based on the grounded theory. *Education Sciences, 14*(6), Article 6. https://doi.org/10.3390/educsci14060575

Zunhammer, M., Eberle, H., Eichhammer, P., & Busch, V. (2013). Somatic symptoms evoked by exam stress in university students: The role of alexithymia, neuroticism, anxiety and depression. *PLOS ONE, 8*(12), e84911. https://doi.org/10.1371/journal.pone.0084911

About the Authors

Jason D. Baker, PhD, is a professor, award-winning author, and senior technology strategist at Regent University. He holds degrees in electrical engineering, educational technology leadership, communication, and computer and information technology. He describes himself as an engineer who walked into a classroom and found a calling—using technology to help people and helping people to use technology. His current focus is harnessing artificial intelligence to promote transformational learning in an increasingly digital world.

Charles R. Cadle, EdD, is retired. He previously served as the chief executive officer of Destination Imagination. His career has involved leading strategic ventures in industry and education that result in brand development, multimillion-dollar financings, corporate-wide program enhancements and implementation of cutting-edge technologies. He has been a long-time advocate of online learning communities that enable students and subject-matter experts to share ideas and experiences. Chuck holds an EdD in curriculum and instruction, a Master of Education in educational leadership, and a Bachelor of Business Administration degree in finance and accounting. He is a licensed certified public accountant (GA), licensed school superintendent (MA), school business administrator (MA), educational leader (GA P–12), special education curriculum (GA P–12) and business education teacher (GA and MA 6–12). His professional affiliations include serving on the strategic council for the Partnership for 21st-Century Skills, and memberships in the NEA, ASCD, AASA, International MBE, Council for Exceptional Children, and Massachusetts Association of School Business Officials.

Elizabeth DeBolt, PhD, is an assistant professor of psychology at Liberty University and serves as a subject matter expert for courses on childhood development. She holds a PhD in educational leadership, an EdS in curriculum and instruction, and an MA in counseling with over 10 years of experience in higher education. She has presented at national and international conferences on women's studies, including the topics of women and mothers in academia and maternal mental health, for which she is passionate. As an educator, she continues to pursue research on supporting student self-efficacy and fostering collaborative and supportive learning relationships.

Chelsie M. Dubay, EdD, is an assistant professor and director of Instructional Design for the Department of Computing at East Tennessee State University. Her academic research centers on cultural responsiveness and broadening participation in STEM, with a particular emphasis on computing. She has over 15 years of experience in higher education across academic and technology-adjacent sectors. In addition to coordinating several continuous improvement processes supporting various accrediting bodies at the state and national levels, she facilitates the implementation of academic degree programs and initiatives.

Jennifer Fellabaum-Toston, PhD, is the senior associate dean for student success and academic affairs in the College of Education & Human Development at the University of Missouri (MU). She is also an associate teaching professor of higher education in the Department of Educational Leadership and Policy Analysis. A major focus of her role is to be an advocate for students. Jennifer's research and teaching interests include identities in higher education, postsecondary teaching and learning, student affairs, and the development of scholarly practitioners/practitioner-scholars.

Fernando Garzon, PsyD, is the associate dean for the College of Health and Behavioral Studies at Regent University. He is a member of Regent's Institutional Review Board. A licensed psychologist and professor in Regent's PsyD program in clinical psychology, Dr. Garzon's research focuses on spiritual interventions in clinical practice, multicultural issues, and lay Christian counseling approaches. His clinical experience encompasses outpatient practice, managed care, hospital, pastoral care, and church settings.

Jaclyn Gish-Lieberman, EdD, has designed instruction for adults all over the world and in every profession from law enforcement to physicians to engineers and more. Her designs are rooted in learning theory and come alive with striking visualization, captivating stories, and an authentic reflection of the learner. She believes that good instruction draws upon empathy for the learner and is evangelical about accessible and inclusive designs. She is a scholar-practitioner who currently puts her super power(point)s to work explaining the complexities of tax law for the Ohio Department of Taxation in Columbus, Ohio.

John J. S. Harrichand, PhD, LPC-S, LMHC-D, NCC, CCMHC, ACS, CCTP, is an associate professor at Montclair State University. He is a Canadian scholar of Chinese and East Indian heritage who hails from Guyana, South America. He holds an Hons. BSc. in psychology and integrative biology from the University of Toronto at Scarborough, an MA in counselling from Providence Theological Seminary, and a CACREP-accredited PhD in counselor education and supervision from Liberty University. His research focuses on culturally responsive counseling, counselor education and supervision, and leadership and advocacy, and he is committed to supporting marginalized communities and ethnic minority counseling leaders.

Jeni Hart, PhD, is the dean of the graduate school and vice provost for graduate studies at the University of Missouri (MU). She is also professor of higher education in the Department of Educational Leadership and Policy Analysis. Her primary role is to support excellence in graduate and postdoctoral education and advocate for graduate students and postdoctoral scholars at MU. Her scholarship centers on three mutually reinforcing themes: academic work, gender and feminisms, and campus climate. She is particularly interested in how higher education as an organization reinforces oppressive structures, and how faculty activism seeks to dismantle them.

Jessica Herring Watson, EdD, is an assistant professor in the College of Education and the University of Central Arkansas. With over a decade of teaching experience, Jessica focuses her work on cultivating meaningful relationships between technology-enabled learning and engaging pedagogy. Her research investigates preservice and in-service teachers' development and persistent use of technology enabled learning to cultivate more inclusive, creative, and engaging learning environments and to transform educational cultures.

Daniel Hitchcock, PhD, is an associate professor of psychology at Regent University and is chair of the Regent University Institutional Review Board. His doctoral work at Rutgers University and the University of Geneva, Switzerland, focused on developmental psychology and behavioral neuroscience. His research interests include active learning strategies for the classroom, emotion and memory, a holistic bio-psycho-social-spiritual approach to psychology, human infancy, mentoring, sexuality, the relation of cognitive schema theory to the Christian worldview, and the role of human ethics in scientific research.

Dave Holder, PhD, is an associate professor of business at Liberty University. Prior to becoming a professor, he was a K–12 teacher, IT systems administrator, small business owner, consultant, and technology director. Working with interdisciplinary colleagues he has researched in simulation and immersive learning environments, integrative technologies, and maker space technologies to foster engagement and creativity.

Michael L. Jones, PhD, is an associate professor in the Faculty of Business at the University of Wollongong, where he has taught business and management for over two decades. His research focuses on qualitative analysis and spans organizational psychology, motivation, leadership, group dynamics, organizational culture, and doctoral education. He is particularly known for his work on volunteer engagement in emergency services. From 2013 to 2017, Michael led the Australian Bushfire and Natural Hazards CRC project Improving the Retention and Engagement of Volunteers in Emergency Service Agencies. He oversaw a multidisciplinary team that developed and delivered a national leadership program for emergency service organizations. He has authored more than 100 peer-reviewed publications, with a selection available at Google Scholar Profile. Michael is senior editor-in-chief of the *International Journal of Doctoral Studies* and executive director of the Informing Science Institute.

Rebecca LaFountain, EdD, worked in the psychology program at the Pennsylvania State University (Harrisburg). She is a licensed psychologist and has a part-time private psychology practice. She has authored two books, one of which is a research text, several chapters and more than twenty-five peer-reviewed articles. Her primary interest is Alfred Adler's individual psychology. She is a diplomate in Adlerian Psychology, is on the editorial board of the *Journal of Individual Psychology*, is on the board of the North American Society of Adlerian Psychology, and is vice president of the International Association of Individual Psychology.

Lawrence M. Lesser, PhD, has taught mathematics, statistics, and mathematics education courses for almost four decades, including chairing theses and dissertations. Since 2004, he has been at The University of Texas at El Paso (UTEP), where he is a UTEP Distinguished Teaching Professor, a professor in the Department of Mathematical Sciences, and a former director of UTEP's campus-wide teaching center. His teaching innovations and 140 papers (mostly mathematics/statistics education, quantitative and qualitative research on language, ethics, teacher preparation, student success, intuition/misconceptions, mnemonics, and STEAM/edutainment) have led to state and NSF grants, textbooks, national keynotes, and international media appearances. His state and national recognitions in or beyond his discipline include elected fellow of the American Statistical Association.

Christine Mayorga, MA, LPC-Associate, is a Mexican American doctoral student and graduate research assistant at the University of Texas at San Antonio. She earned her bachelor's degree in psychology from the University of New Mexico and later completed her MS in clinical mental health counseling at Walden University. Christine's research focuses on adapting trauma theories and interventions to develop multicultural approaches.

Jessica McCleese, PsyD, is the director of Regent University's Psychological Services Center (PSC). As an associate professor, licensed clinical psychologist, and certified sex therapist, she focuses her research on improving physical and emotional intimacy for married Christians. Her clinical experience includes individual, marriage and family, and group interventions in outpatient practice. Additionally, Dr. McCleese has frequently been invited as a guest speaker, guest blogger, and podcast guest for Christian lay audiences.

Dao Nguyen, PhD, is a faculty member and applied research project coordinator for the EdD Program in Leadership and Innovation at Purdue University Global. She has extensive experience in higher education and international affairs, serving in various roles, including leader, educator, researcher, policymaker, evaluator, consultant, and advocate. Her research focuses on the intersection of leadership, policy, and practice, aiming to promote equitable access, persistence, and success for underrepresented students, teachers, and faculty. The University of Pittsburgh (Pitt) IISE, CIES, CPED, An Giang University, An Giang Department of Foreign Affairs, and the IRED Institute of Education are among the influential organizations and institutions she worked for. The P.E.O. International Peace Fellowship, the Luce Foundation Fellowship, the UNDP Young Leadership in Governance, and the Fulbright Fellowship are honors she received for and through her professional studies, research, work, and service.

Jill Alexa Perry, PhD, is the executive director of the Carnegie Project on the Educational Doctorate (CPED) and professor of practice in the Educational Foundations, Organizations and Policy at the University of Pittsburgh. Her research focuses on professional doctorate preparation in education, organizational change in higher education, and faculty leadership roles. Currently she is researching the ways EdD programs teach practitioners to utilize research evidence. She teaches and coaches how to design EdD programs and teach improvement science as a signature methodology. Her books include *Reclaiming the Education Doctorate, Challenges in (re)Designing EdD Programs, The Improvement Science Dissertation in Practice, The EdD and the Scholarly Practitioner*, and *In Their Own Words: A journey to the stewardship of the practice in education*. She has over 30 years of experience in leadership and program development in education and teaching experience at the elementary, secondary, undergraduate, and graduate levels in the United States and abroad. She is a Fulbright Scholar (Germany) and a returned Peace Corps Volunteer (Paraguay).

Michael K. Ponton, EdD, currently serves as professor of higher education in the College of Education and Human Services at East Texas A&M University. Professor Ponton has published extensively in the field of self-directed learning where his interests include human agency, personal initiative, autonomous learning, and self-efficacy. He currently serves as editor of the *International Journal of Self-Directed Learning* and *Literature Reviews in Education and Human Services* and is the 2015 recipient of the International Society for Self-Directed Learning Malcolm Knowles Award for significant lifelong contributions to the field of self-directed learning.

Sharon M. Pratt, EdD, is an associate professor of elementary and literacy education at Indiana University Northwest. Her research interests include methods for preparing preservice teachers to provide effective instructional strategies for literacy instruction, as well as how teachers support K–12 students' development as readers and writers with metacognitive strategies. She is also involved in her local literacy council to promote reading and writing from birth through adulthood. Sharon currently serves as coeditor of the *Indiana Literacy Journal* and is a member of the Notable Books for a Global Society award committee.

Mark C. Rehfuss, PhD, has been a faculty and director of the distance learning human services program in the Department of Counseling and Human Services at Old Dominion University, Norfolk, Virginia. He has worked in higher education for more than twenty years having served as an academic advisor, career counselor, professor, program director and dean of academics. He has chaired over twenty dissertations, served on numerous dissertation committees, and published over thirty peer-reviewed articles. His research interests include career counseling and guidance, narrative career interventions, online learning, qualitative research methods, and clinical mental health.

Amanda J. Rockinson, EdD, PhD, LPC, is a professor and doctoral program coordinator for a learning design and technology program at the University of Memphis. Prior to entering higher education, she served as a child and family counselor, specializing in trauma and abuse. She has over fifteen years of experience in higher education, serving both as a faculty and administrator. In her capacity as a faculty, she has chaired over 30 dissertations. As an administrator, she has held numerous positions, including chair for graduate and research programs and director for accreditation. She served as a Fulbright scholar. Rockinson worked in Timor Leste (TL), partnering with the US embassy and the National Commission for UNESCO, a semi-governmental institution under the Ministry of Higher Education Science and Culture (MHESC), to carry out a needs assessment and training initiative at five TL Universities. She provided faculty with training on the systematic design of STEM Learning. Her research has focused on developing and investigating systems (e.g., family, technological, institutional) to support the psychosocial, social, academic, and vocational success of learners, focusing primarily on: (1) doctoral education and persistence, (2) distance education and technological systems, and (3) gender and racial equity in science, technology, math, and engineering (STEM). She has secured several million dollars in grant funding to conduct research in these areas.

Alfred P. Rovai, PhD, deceased, was a native of San Jose, California, received a BA degree (mathematics) from San Jose State University, an MA degree (public administration) from the University of Northern Colorado, and an MS degree (education) and PhD degree (academic leadership) from Old Dominion University. Following his retirement from the US Army, he served as a faculty member at Old Dominion University and later at Regent University, retiring in December 2011 as associate vice president for academic affairs. During his career in academe he authored or coauthored four books and more than fifty articles in scholarly journals and served on four editorial review boards. He also created the Classroom Community Scale.

Lucinda S. Spaulding, PhD, is a professor and the director of special education programs in the School of Professional and Applied Sciences at the University of Lynchburg. After teaching elementary education, English as a second language, and special education, she transitioned into higher education where she has served as a research fellow, professor, administrative chair of research, dissertation chair, qualitative methodologist, and Fulbright specialist. Dr. Spaulding peer reviews, publishes and presents nationally and internationally on topics relating to inclusive education and factors associated with resilience and persistence in higher education.

Jacqueline S. Stephen, EdD, has more than 20 years of national and international experience in higher education. She is an assistant professor of instructional design and the director of instructional and learning design in the College of Professional Advancement at Mercer University. Her research has examined factors associated with learner persistence in online courses and high-impact practices for online teaching. She is the author of *Academic Success in Online Programs: A Resource for College Students* and an alumna of the Fulbright Program.

James A. Swezey, EdD, is a professor of education at Liberty University, where he teaches and advises doctoral candidates and helps prepare the next generation of classroom teachers. His eclectic academic research centers on a variety of topics, but especially the cross-section of faith and education. He enjoys helping his doctoral candidates complete their first publications. He served in K–12 education as a high school history teacher and a PS2-8 school administrator for 13 years and has spent the last 18 years in higher education.

Elizabeth A. Zumpe, PhD, is an assistant professor in the Department of Educational Leadership and Policy Studies at the University of Oklahoma. Dr. Zumpe conducts qualitative, action, and design-based research within research-practice partnerships to understand and co-design processes for continuous improvement in high-poverty schools and districts. Through this work, she aims to understand how to cultivate collective agency, problem solving mindsets, and teaming capacity for continuous quality improvement in contexts of complexity and adversity. A former K–12 public school teacher for over a decade with National Board Certification, Elizabeth holds a PhD in education from the University of California, Berkeley.